GRAY WORLD, GREEN HEART

THE WILEY SERIES IN SUSTAINABLE DESIGN

The Wiley Series in Sustainable Design has been created for professionals responsible for, and individuals interested in, the design and construction of the built environment. The series is dedicated to the advancement of knowledge in design and construction that serves to sustain the natural environment. Titles in the series cover innovative and emerging topics related to the design and development of the human community, within the context of preserving and enhancing the quality of the natural world. Consistent with their content, books in the series are produced with care taken in the selection of recycled and non-polluting materials.

GRAY WORLD, GREEN HEART
Technology, Nature and the Sustainable Landscape
Robert L. Thayer, University of California, Davis

REGENERATIVE DESIGN FOR SUSTAINABLE DEVELOPMENT
John T. Lyle, California State Polytechnic University, Pomona

GRAY WORLD, GREEN HEART

Technology, Nature, and the Sustainable Landscape

ROBERT L. THAYER, JR.

JOHN WILEY & SONS, INC.

New York • Chichester • Brisbane • Toronto • Singapore

This text is printed on recycled paper.

Library of Congress Cataloging in Publication Data:
Thayer, Robert L., Jr.
    Gray world, green heart : technology, nature, and the sustainable
landscape / Robert L. Thayer, Jr.
        p. cm.
    Includes bibliographical references and index.
    ISBN 0-471-57273-X (cloth : acid-free paper)
    1. Environmental degradation. 2. Human ecology. 3. Sustainable
development. 4. Technology—Social aspects. I. Title.
GE140.T48   1993
363.7—dc20   93-23134

Printed in the United States of America

10 9 8 7 6 5 4 3

To My Father,

ROBERT LYMAN THAYER

Acknowledgements

The custom upon completing a book of this length is to thank one's colleagues for comments and encouragement on portions of the manuscript; one's students for asking the most challenging questions; one's family for being understanding and allowing time and space to write; one's editors for tough but necessary surgery to the manuscript; and one's publisher for gambling that a book might finally emerge. Like other authors, I owe these people my gratitude, and duly thank them. But if strength of emotion is any indication, the individuals to whom I owe the most are the scholars and writers of the volumes I have read in the course of my own writing. Many have written such important, timeless, and towering works that it is truly exhilarating and highly rewarding, yet occasionally terrifying, to work in their shadows. I make no claim to great scholarship for myself, and will admit to moments when fear of creating insignificance was so great that running from this manuscript seemed necessary. During those times, however, I was often rescued by sheer force of delight in reading or rereading the powerful ideas of others whose works inspired me to coalesce my own. To one who is attempting to write a meaningful book, nothing is as uplifting as finding great significance and meaning in the works of his predecessors.

Some of these authors are gone; some loom heavily on the intellectual landscape; some remain little known. Still others have yet to reap the scholarly rewards they will surely harvest. Among this group of secret, silent mentors are scientists, poets, historians, geographers, landscape architects, and many who cross boundaries and do not fit one-word labels. All are worthy of formal thanks. Leo Marx has been acknowledged before, but deserves it all and more; his *Machine in the Garden* has galvanized thought on the subject for several decades, and more than any volume, must be considered the starting point for this work. Clarence Glacken's *Traces on the Rhodian Shore* is so powerful a work, so full of extraordinary scholarship, and so vital that one may never tire of reading it nor run out of fundamental ideas worthy of inclusion in crafting future works. Yi-Fu Tuan's *Topophilia* is such an elegant presentation of fundamental environmental attitudes that I sincerely hope he forgives me for borrowing and perhaps misusing his term. Gary Snyder—poet, university colleague, and inspiring bioregionalist—has through his poetry, personal comment, and example influenced my intellectual posture and gut feelings about the world more than he knows. His written words (*Axe Handles, Turtle Island, The Practice of the Wild,* and *No Nature*) and rooted presence in this region of California are a steadfast inspiration. I also thank the late O. B. Hardison, Jr., author of *Disappearing Through the Skylight,* for demonstrating in his book the possibility of packing many genuine insights per page on the subject of culture and technology. I can only hope to ever have his nimble facility with ideas and concepts.

Others have inspired me not only with their ideas, but also their courage in taking intellectual risks and facing potential ridicule from the cultural status quo; I admire Jerry Mander for taking on the steamroller of technology and being bold enough to suggest that we might not need, nor even want, the supposed benefits of many new technologies; John Lyle for awakening and redirecting the professional momentum of landscape architecture; Wes Jackson for questioning the assumptions of the agricultural establishment and envisioning a better way to provide our food; and James Lovelock for taking on the entire scientific community with his risky assertion that all life might be collectively responsible for regulating the conditions necessary for its own existence.

Perhaps more than any other, I would like to thank Kenneth Boulding, whom I openly admit to be my academic hero. I once listened, awestruck, as Boulding stood up in a Colorado Friends Meeting house in 1973 with his Benjamin Franklinesque presence and articulately discussed the spiritual likenesses between God and black holes (which astrophysicists had by then started to discover), and the importance of these equally mystical concepts to us as humans. From there I read his tiny but monumental book *The Image,* then several others, including *The World as a Total System,* which further convinced me of Boulding's true genius as a thinker and welder of spiritual, scientific, and scholarly ideas into a bold new direction for humanity.

There are many others. A glance through the references yields the extent and scope of contributions all have made to the ideas I discuss hereafter. I would like to celebrate these contributors for making the writing of this book (which colleagues had warned me would be a painful and exasperating process) both worthwhile and highly enjoyable. At the very least, I hope readers will gain a sense that very important connections are happening far beyond my ability to explain them in this book—a convergence to which some of the most illuminating thinkers are contributing, whether consciously or not. To all of those authors, living and dead, I offer my sincere gratitude.

Contents

Prologue

As I write this prologue on a microcomputer, I gaze occasionally out of the window of my second-floor home office at canopies of shade trees and patchy blue and white sky. The keys beneath my fingers click out their instructions to a plastic box full of electronics and an illuminated screen. In spite of a substantial university education, I have only the vaguest idea of how the letters actually appear before me—a fuzzy conception of electronic pulses, semiconductors, binary code, and electron beams deflected by a magnetic field onto a scintillating surface beneath a piece of glass. I have a clearer image, however, of the power that actuates my computer. Somewhere in the Sierra Nevada, streams are dammed and water impounded behind concrete barricades falls through propellor-like turbine blades, causing copper-wound armatures to turn in magnetic fields, exciting electrons along wires. Elsewhere, natural gas—the vaporous remains of long-dead plants and animals buried, crushed, and decomposed deep within the earth—is combining rapidly with oxygen, heating water and releasing steam which also turns the turbines to create electricity. Huge steel lattice towers stretch rhythmically across the central California farmland, bringing the electrical current to me—not actually transporting, of course, but only providing a seamless continuum against which electrons can bump into one another as if they were travelling.

I also know of a place in my town where wires lead into complex, tinkertoy-like lattices of steel and ceramic, gray-finned boxes, and doors posted with "Danger—High Voltage" signs. Concealing most of this electric power substation from street view is a concrete slump-block wall painted to resemble adobe brick, in front of which are planted a colorful assortment of flowering shrubs and trees. Only the erector-set tops of the lattice and an octopus of wires are visible above the landscaped wall.

Outside my window, rain has been falling. The solar home community in which I live features an "open" storm drainage system. Instead of disappearing rapidly down subsurface pipes, rain water moves along man-made "streams," soaking into the soil and overflowing to the next weir, where more water sinks

Photograph by Richard Meisinger

into the ground. Some water evaporates into the sky, rejoining the clouds en route to the Sierra to be squeezed out as droplets over the reservoirs which provide the power to run my computer. With some intellectual gymnastics and a furrowed brow, I make some connections. Somehow, the rain outside my window relates to the words on the computer screen before me, but parts of the cycle seem either vague, discontinuous, or stiffly contrived.

I remember fishing below the Bowman Lake Dam in the Sierra, which is operated by my local utility company. In the stream's rocky pools there were many trout, most of whom outsmarted me. I remember seeing the rusted sections of old irrigation flume lying about and looking up at the power lines trailing off somewhere down the hill as I stalked my prey. I could never resolve whether this was *my* dam—whether any power from the headwaters of my favorite trout stream made it into my house and my computer.

On those rides home from trout fishing, I could see the twin cooling towers of Rancho Seco nuclear power plant miles away across the low foothill cattle country. I've even paddled my canoe amongst the windsurfers in the small reservoir (affectionately nicknamed "Glow Lake" by the locals) created to provide cooling water in the event of an emergency. The cooling water will probably never be needed. The "Ranch" is shut down now—voted off-line by the utility rate payers of Sacramento. The huge, eerie towers, visible for miles around, are undergoing transformation of meaning, soon to become grand historical markers to past events and controversies. Did any of the Ranch's nuclear-generated electricity ever wind up in my word processor? I pretended not. I preferred the imagery of power wrung out of my trout stream emerging from Bowman Lake. But the word "lake" always bothered me; who was the utility company kidding? I know that Bowman Lake is actually a *reservoir,* constructed by human intention for a utilitarian purpose. What is the *real* relationship between my computer, the hydroelectric dam and its reservoir, the nuclear power station, the rock pools, the trout, the clouds, the "shrubbed-up" wall concealing the electric substation, the drainage channel with its trees in the greenbelt below me, and these words appearing on my screen? Is the relationship real or contrived? Benign or destructive? Natural or artificial? Preordained or subject to willful change?

The relation of technology to the environment is a crystal of colossal proportions and a thousand facets. Hundreds of books have been written which circumscribe this general topic. I, however, am drawn to the great American opposition of nature versus technology through the imagery of the vernacular landscape and the expectations of everyday people. This book is about ordinary Americans and their landscape images; their love of nature and land; their hopes, dreams, frustrations, actions, and reactions to technology as it molds and influences their personal, tangible worlds. It is about gardens and gadgets, parks and parking lots, cellular phones and solar homes, trees and transmission towers—about oil and soil. It is about the opposition between nature and technology in our everyday lives and surroundings, and the increasing uneasiness with which we confront this opposition.

Scarcely a day goes by in the life of most Americans without at least some form of interaction with nature, land, and technology. Often these are deliberate and pleasant interchanges, like escaping in the car for a day of fishing in the mountains. Sometimes they are inconvenient happenstances, like a broken sprinkler head in the irrigation system which floods the front lawn. Occasionally they are major news events of catastrophic proportions, such as the spilling of hundreds of thousands of gallons of oil in one of America's richest marine fisheries and most picturesque landscapes. On a day-to-day basis, however, we don't comprehend the relationship between nature, technology, and landscape in a deliberate or conscious manner, and what interactions we do experience are merely manifestations of our typical lifestyles, tastes, and desires. As contributing members of America's culture, we go about our activities for the most part unselfconsciously, accepting the essential attributes of American life and adhering to our own personal standards of

right and wrong with respect to the environment and society. In the past few years, however, world events have taken their toll on us, and we now experience a burdensome accumulation of remorse over the condition of the local, national, and global environment. Brief periods of euphoria over the end of the "Cold War" and a short-lived "victory" in the Persian Gulf are tainted with lingering images of the environmental destruction committed in Kuwait and Iraq for little apparent political advantage, and by revelations of the shocking environmental degradation wrought by uncurbed industry in the former Soviet Union. All of this is accompanied by a familiar and continuing litany of global environmental problems—loss of rainforest, mass extinctions and decline in species diversity, atmospheric pollution, ozone layer depletion, global warming, worldwide recession and no effective alternative to a technologically based "growth" economy. Countless books, news features, and magazine articles concerning these environmental issues have barraged Americans to the point that it is less and less possible to conduct one's personal life innocently—to live quietly within one's own realm without some degree of awareness and an increasing portion of shared responsibility for environmental problems. We have entered a period of deep introspection where some of the most fundamental assumptions we have long taken for granted are now being called into question. A growing number of Americans feels an oppressive sense of connection between their lifestyles, the immediate physical surroundings in which they live, play, and work, and the environmental and social problems looming in the world at large. These feelings often lead to the perception that our personal hopes and beliefs are somehow out of balance with our culturally induced, habituated behaviors and our perception of deterioration in the local and global environment.

It is possible, of course, to examine this turbulent relationship between nature, land, and technology from the perspectives of art, economics, engineering, classical sociology, ecological theory, semiotics, ethics, post-modern critical theory, planning policy, or even military strategy. This book, however, draws upon each of these perspectives, but emphasizes none in particular. Instead, it examines the land/nature/technology interface from a personal, *inside-out* framework, emphasizing the perceptions and behaviors of individuals while scrutinizing the collective evidence displayed in the everyday American landscape; not the popularized landscape notion of "cake-decoration frosting" shrubbery we place around the foundations of our homes and commercial centers, but the actual physical context of our neighborhoods, streets, freeways, churches, parks, shopping centers, gas stations, and industrial zones.

In the past few years we have finally begun to recognize that *there is* a noticeable relationship between nature, landscape, and technology—a relationship between our fossil fuel machinery, chemical and biological wizardry, and electronic gadgetry and our sensation and perception of the land and nature. However, such a relationship is not always a pleasant one. We now recognize a causal relationship between our appetite for technology and the destruction of personal value in our everyday landscape, and *we*—not some

remote *they*—are to blame. Our concern over landscape change at the hand of technology is vividly evident in oil-soaked Alaskan coastlines and Earth First! demonstrations; in "Not In My Backyard" struggles against landfill sites and in the landscaped facades in front of electric substations. It is revealed in the fake wood paneling on minivans and the redwood fences around our garbage cans. It lurks in the boutiquing of our burned-out manufacturing districts. It ranges from the rusted wheelbarrow planter in the front yard to debates about global warming and the Persian Gulf war. It is cryptically encoded in our city and county zoning ordinances, building codes, and design review guidelines, and it reverberates through popular print, motion picture, and video imagery.

The complex, paradoxical relationship between the technologies upon which our lifestyles depend and the landscapes we love is a fundamental dilemma of modern American life. It is not a new dilemma, but one whose roots trace back beyond the eighteenth-century Industrial Revolution, beyond the seventeenth-century colonization of North America by European emigrants, beyond the philosophies of Descartes, Newton, and Bacon, to the evolutionary origins of human tool use, language, and aesthetic expression. The modern world has created a landscape which is a stage for the drama of two great protagonists, Nature and Technology. The drama is especially dynamic, since Technology, like some mythic Jekyll-and-Hyde figure, has within itself two opposing faces and contrasting personalities. The drama is performed in the landscapes we cherish and those we ignore or despise; in the technologies with which we surround ourselves in hopeless addiction while bemoaning the impact of our habits. It is often a subtle, personal drama, perhaps not felt by all equally, but experienced by most in increasing intensity. Today, the dramatic tension has never been sharper, nor cries for resolution louder.

To do justice to such a complex interaction as that between nature and technology in the everyday lives and landscapes of Americans requires a rather high degree of focus and the deliberate constraining of certain boundaries. Therefore, a fundamental discussion about what this book is and isn't, what it considers and ignores, and how it defines its basic terms is critical to the success of its central argument. Of most importance is some definition of the term "landscape." I use the term landscape expansively, as if spelled with a capital "L." In my view, landscape is the broad physical and experiential arena in which human activity occurs—the land surface as physically modified (whether subtly or substantially) by humans in the course of their personal and collective existence. I do *not* constrain landscape to being just ornamental vegetation, only so-called "natural" materials, or merely the outdoor places intentionally designed for aesthetic purpose. In this book, landscape is the fundamental, physical context for human life as it is perceived and experienced. Scholars such as J. B. Jackson and Peirce Lewis have spent a lifetime trying to define what is meant by the term landscape. After some searching, I find most useful Jackson's (1984) conclusions:

> Landscape is not scenery, it is not a political unit; it is really no more than a collection, a system of man-made spaces on the surface of the earth. Whatever its shape or size, it is *never* simply a natural space, a feature of the natural environment; it is *always* artificial, always synthetic, always subject to sudden or unpredictable change. We create them and need them because every landscape is the place where we establish our own human organization of space and time. (Jackson's emphasis) (p. 156)

Geographer Peirce Lewis has skillfully articulated a broad division of American landscape into two unequal spatial categories: "areas where standards of taste are routinely invoked, and areas where they are not." (Lewis, 1990, p. 7). Lewis refers to these zones respectively as "tasteful" spaces and "taste-free" spaces. Tasteful space is the considerably smaller of the two domains, and is that area deliberately structured by design professionals according to the current but ephemeral aesthetic style. It includes parks, gardens, formal buildings, and designed urban spaces. The second, much greater area of "taste-free" space within the American landscape—where professional design matters little—is the general focus of this book. This taste-free zone roughly corresponds to Jackson's definition of *vernacular* landscape which, as I argue henceforth in the book, has generally evolved in piecemeal fashion according to practical necessity and in response to technological evolution.

I construe "technology" broadly to mean the range of practical, utilitarian endeavors undertaken by society to provide its members with those things perceived to be necessary. Such an orientation to technology admittedly leaves

a great deal open to debate with the use of the words "perceived to be necessary," since much of modern technology is justifiably under assault from many fronts as being *un*necessary to the quality of life. There is also some question as to the limitations of what is deemed "utilitarian" or "practical" in an information-saturated world. However, I take the viewpoint—which I elaborate in Chapters 1 and 2—that modern American life and culture are now primarily driven by science and technology, and that the landscape, as an object of culture, cannot help but reflect this technological determinism.

The landscape with which I am concerned, however, is shaped by another factor as well. As Jackson implies, "landscape" is never a mere feature of the natural environment, yet it can be thought of as a human modification of some baseline, "natural" condition. I use the term "nature" to imply the total realm of life forms and primordial elements composing a living earth. Although I dislike the Western, semantic history of the word "nature" for its exclusion of humans and their domain, no other would-be synonym (including the more recent terms "ecosphere" or "biosphere") is as powerful or historically comprehensible to the lay reader. Nature is a changing notion, however, and in Chapter 7 I discuss the rapid, ongoing evolution and transformation of nature as a construct. I also discuss how intentionally designed landscape, whose existence is a deliberate manifestation of an idealized nature compromised to suit human purpose, is changing accordingly.

My choice of scope and definition of these essential terms follows less what I believe they *ought* to mean from a philosophical, academic perspective and more what I believe they now broadly imply in everyday American life. There-

fore, this book is *not* intended to be a guidebook for the intentional design of landscape for *aesthetic* purpose, although it will make frequent reference to spaces which have been so designed. Instead, the book discusses aesthetics as only one of several attributes of perceived environmental quality, and argues that the essential structure and ecological function are far more critical to human well being and, in fact, should drive the surface appearance rather than vice versa. The structure and thrust of the book reflect a basic assumption that the American landscape is not only on the ground, but in the mind as well. Each person creates his or her own landscape reality, and in a transactional fashion, responds to that combined mental-physical landscape as if it were purely external. Several years ago one could start a car engine, look at a sunset, or discard an aluminum can without thinking of environmental consequences—oil wars, global warming, or overflowing landfills. No more. A fundamental shift is gradually occurring in the way in which Americans conceive of the physical environment and their relationship to it. This book is about our common landscape surroundings—national, regional, communal, and personal—our technological dependence, and our essential bond with the Earth, and with the changing meanings and values we are assigning these realms. It is also about *hope* and *action*—hope that we can develop a new vocabulary of landscape symbols, and action we can take to make our immediate landscapes not only symbolic of a solution, but part of the actual solution itself.

I

Gray World, Green Heart

1

For Love of Land and Nature

It is so small and fragile and such a precious little spot in the universe that you can block it out with your thumb, and you realize that on that small spot, that little blue and white thing is everything that means anything to you—all of history and music and poetry and art and death and birth and love, tears, joy, games, all of it on that little spot out there that you can cover with your thumb. And you realize from that perspective that you've changed, that there's something new there, that the relationship is no longer what it was.

RUSSELL SCHWEICKART

Apollo 13 astronaut Rusty Schweickart's 10-day voyage in space afforded him a unique perspective of the earth that only a few have shared first hand but all now know indirectly—an image of a black void with a blue-green and white planet small enough to be occluded by a thumb at arm's length. This image of the earth is the fitting icon of the unfolding environmental age, a picture worth not a thousand but countless millions of words. For the first time in human history, Earth's finite nature had been captured and validated in one image. Indeed, as Schweickart revealed, the relationship, although it had transcended time, would again be forever transformed.

The bond of affection joining humans with the earth has always been strong but slippery—like stream water rushing over a smooth rock; we know it exists, but by the time we put our finger on it, it has moved elsewhere. A crisp definition of our affection for nature is nearly impossible to locate and, like an elusive mountain lion, we may learn about it only by circumscription of its territory from many vantage points There is no one term which works perfectly and inclusively as a label for human emotional attachment to land and nature—only a family of related emotions: love, respect, oneness, awe, pleasure, indebtedness, dependency—and overlapping constructs for the objects of those emotions: earth, soil, place, land, "nature." But just as the individual petals of a flower meet at the center, there is a distinct oneness to both the familiar emotion and its manifold object. We all feel this bond at one time or other—some people more frequently, consciously, or intensely than others. Ancient Hawaiians, for whom such a bond was a way of life, called it *aloha 'aina,* love for the land (Dudley, 1990).

Topophilia

Perhaps the most useful description is the term "topophilia," coined by geographer Yi-Fu Tuan (1974) in a landmark book by that name. Tuan himself refers to tophophilia as "the affective bond between people and place or setting" (p. 4), or the "human love of place" (p. 92). By this definition and in much of his book, Tuan clearly includes human-altered, artifactual places as topophilic objects, but in his general description, topophilia is unmistakable skewed toward location, landscape, and natural physiography. With unique scholarship and clarity, Tuan presents a range of possible emotions under the rubric of topophilia: sudden revelation of environmental beauty in nature; physical contact and intimacy or "gentle, unselfconscious involvement" with the earth as experienced by children and older societies; interaction with the land as a material dependence common to farming peoples; pride of estate; nature as a source of health and vitality. As a general statement, Tuan defines the term topophilia as coupling "sentiment with place" (p. 113). With a bow

The sign for this alfalfa and cattle ranch near Fort Jones, California, is evidence of topophilia—a strong emotional attachment to the land.

Affection for the earth is often most acutely felt through aesthetic experience in natural landscapes. Grand Canyon National Park, Arizona.

(and perhaps an apology) to Professor Tuan, I will borrow his term and employ it to designate *the range of positive human emotions relating to affection for land, earth, and nature.* I could have borrowed other descriptive terms, such as E. O. Wilson's (1984) *biophilia,* which he describes as "the innate tendency to focus on life and life-like processes" (p. 1). Other terms might have been invented: perhaps "Gaiaphilia" will emerge in response to James Lovelock's controversial but gripping theory of the Earth as a singular, living, self-regulating organism. However, Wilson's use of biophilia seems exclusive to living plants and animals, while Lovelocks' Gaia hypothesis requires, at present, too significant a leap of faith. Tuan's topophilia, when skewed slightly away from the geographers' term "place" toward the less implicitly artifactual realms of earth, land, and nature, is the clearest yet most comprehensive term for the bonds I wish to describe.

Topophilia has individual as well as cultural significance, and may only occasionally break through to the level of consciousness where a person is keenly aware of experiencing such a bond at any particular moment. Such a moment for me came on an early summer retreat with three friends to the Canyonlands National Park of Utah. It had been a stressful year, and both the pressures of academia and the local noon heat overwhelmed me. Finding a narrow crevasse with a moist, sandy bottom and steep, brilliant red rock walls, I lay down in the damp sand, marveling at the luxuriant vegetation which, in contrast to the harsh scrub above, survived in the deep shade of the canyon walls. The canyon bottom felt cool and comforting. Soon I found myself weeping with a combination of joy, love, and release. I felt as if I were a child, and Earth were truly embracing me. I could feel my worries literally draining into the sand. Afterword, somewhat bewildered, I analyzed the experience perhaps too much, but in the years that have passed since, I have realized that this was the moment when I felt most nurtured by the land, and the moment I loved the Earth most in return. Surely this was topophilia in its most acute manifestation.

Aesthetic Experience

The most publically recognizable side of topophilia is likely to be the aesthetic experience in natural surroundings. My profession of landscape architecture has examined this aspect heavily from the standpoint of which attributes of the landscape are most likely to result in aesthetic appreciation, a rather reductionist, "supply-side" approach to aesthetic experience. At the extreme, two U.S. Forest Service researchers succeeded in 1969 to develop a mathematical regression equation which, when "plugged" with variables measured from photographs of natural scenes, would fairly accurately gauge the relative level of favorable human response to those scenes (Brush and Shafer, 1975).[1] A flurry of empirical research has followed in the two decades since, with every conceivable scientific and empirical technique applied, most aimed at studying the landscape rather than the human participant. The result is that topophilia (at least in terms of human appreciation for natural scenery as depicted in photographs) has been upheld: people respond positively to so-called "natural" landscapes and prefer them to those landscapes with signs of human influence (Zube et al., 1982).

Scant attention has been paid, however, to understanding *why* this is so— how the actual, human *experience* of pleasurable response to the land operates. Ironically, the factors that emerged from the Forest Service equations contributed little to the theory of human behavior. In 1989 two investigators, Richard Chenoweth and Paul Gobster, gave their landscape architecture students diaries with structured and open-ended questions, and told them to record all of their aesthetic experiences during the spring semester and answer questions about them in their diaries (Chenoweth and Gobster, 1990). Chenoweth and Gobster found that the students' aesthetic experiences were less frequent, more sudden, and fleeting than expected, and that the experiences were unevenly distributed in space and time. Many different themes emerged which characterized the experiences: feelings of insignificance of the individual in a vast landscape, intensive absorption in the event, new-found awareness and appreciation of familiar environments, rebirth, and changing seasons. Most reported that their experiences took place outside during daylight, dawn, or dusk hours, involved "nature" or natural features, and that

Scenic Quality Inventory/Evaluation
Rating Criteria and Score

Landform	Vegetation	Water	Color	Adjacent Scenery	Scarcity	Cultural Modifications
High vertical relief such as prominent cliffs, spires or massive rock outcrops; or severe surface variation or highly eroded formations including major badlands or dune systems; or detail features dominant and exceptionally striking and intriguing such as glaciers. **5**	A variety of vegetative types in interesting forms, textures, and patterns. **5**	Clear and clean appearing, still, or cascading white water, any of which are a dominant factor in the landscape. **5**	Rich color combinations, variety or vivid color; or pleasing contrasts in the soil, rock, vegetation, water or snow fields. **5**	Adjacent scenery greatly enhances visual quality. **5**	One of a kind; or unusually memorable, or very rare within region. Consistent chance for exceptional wildlife or wildflower viewing. **6**	Free from aesthetically undesirable or discordant sights and influences; or modifications add favorably to visual variety. **2**
Steep canyons, mesas, buttes, cinder cones and drumlins; or interesting erosional patterns or variation in size and shape of landforms; or detail features present and interesting though not dominant or exceptional. **3**	Some variety of vegetation, but only one or two types. **3**	Flowing or still, but not dominant in the landscape. **3**	Some intensity or variety in colors and contrast of the soil, rock and vegetation, but not a dominant scenic element. **3**	Adjacent scenery moderately enhances overall visual quality. **3**	Distinctive, though somewhat similar to others within the region. **2**	Scenic quality is somewhat depreciated by inharmonious intrusions, but not so extensively that they are entirely negated; or modifications add little or no visual variety to the area. **0**
Low, rolling hills, foothills or flat valley bottoms. Interesting, detailed landscape features few or lacking. **1**	Little or no variety or contrast in vegetation. **1**	Absent, or not noticeable. **0**	Subtle color variations, contrast or interest; generally muted tones. **1**	Adjacent scenery has little or no influence on overall visual quality. **0**	Interesting within its setting, but fairly common within the region. **1**	Modifications are so extensive that scenic qualities are mostly nullified or substantially reduced. **-4**

The U.S. Bureau of Land Management's scenic quality rating classifications. Federal agencies such as BLM and the U.S. Forest Service quantify scenic beauty to facilitate multiple-use management decisions. Courtesy of Land Management.

their moods improved after the event. A great many felt that the aesthetic experience was as good or better than any other positive experience they had during the week. In summary, the authors wrote:

> Our results showed that aesthetic experiences tended to occur unexpectedly rather than being sought out by a person, occurred most often as a result of interactions with natural objects, and tended to occur in familiar places. Together, these findings suggest that opportunities should be provided for people to experience nature in their home environments as part of their everyday activities. (p. 8)

Tuan himself defends the importance of surface or aesthetic response to landscapes to everyday human well being:

> So much of life occurs at the surface that, as students of the human scene we [geographers] are obliged to pay far more attention to its character (subtlety, variety, and density) than we have done. The scholar's neglect and suspicion of surface phenomena is a consequence of a dichotomy in Western thought between surface and depth, sensory appreciation and intellectual understanding, with bias against the first two terms.

Tuan, 1989, p. 233

Aiming his argument at fellow geographers, Tuan makes four major points. First, we live mostly in response to surface appearance, both of the landscape and of life's events. Second, although attractive, appearances may hide even greater realities. Third, plain or ugly surfaces are deceptive, for they may hide "pearls of great prize," and fourth, beautiful surfaces are not always trustworthy for they may hide ugliness or other, deep flaws. He concludes that since aesthetic experiences and impulses are so universal to human life, we should study them carefully and not venture too far from the surface reality lest we lose sight of the venue "where nearly all human joys and sorrows unfold."

In the case of appreciation or response to land and landscape, surface values have great importance, and our bond with the earth is clearly dependent upon them. Landscape painters and, later, photographers of postcards and travel posters, played a significant role in shaping our aesthetic experience of the land's surface (Stilgoe, 1984). The National Park Service locates signs with camera icons near commonly photographed scenic spots in national parks. A vast majority of the visitors to Great Smoky Mountains National Park never leave their automobiles, but presumably enjoy a topophilic, aesthetic experience entirely through their car windows. This level of aesthetic bond with the land appears satisfactory for many people. Aesthetic experiences, it seems, are like sex in that they are short, pleasurable episodes which occur infrequently (compared to the time spent in other daily activities). Yet, just as with sex, much of the aesthetic pleasure of life revolves around *anticipating the possibility* that an aesthetic experience might occur, and enjoying the knowledge that the sources or stimuli for such occurrences exist somewhere in perpetuity. A house with a view of distant mountains sells for thousands more than one whose view is of the neighbor's fence, but if the actual frequency of conscious aesthetic appreciation of the distant view were measured, one might conclude that little time was actually spent in such activity. Hence, the aesthetic dimension of the bond to land and nature is more important than just the actual time spent enjoying a view in the present. It includes the pleasure of knowing that aesthetic experiences might occur again in the future.

Beyond Aesthetics

Even when anticipation is considered, aesthetic experience falls far short of defining the totality of topophilia. A farmer plowing his field is unlikely to experience continual aesthetic euphoria, and a gardener weeding her vegetable garden is unlikely to classify the event as an aesthetic experience, yet both achieve a strong sense of attachment to the very earth they work. The satisfaction each derives is a critical part of the topophilic bond. It has been frequently claimed in recent literature that modern American society has, in both the literal and figurative sense, lost "touch" with the soil, and we are the poorer for it. For better or worse, occupations such as farming, forestry, fisheries, and even mining require an emotional bond with the land by virtue of their requisite physical contact with it. As Tuan indicates, the strength and emotional direction of that bond may depend on the relative economic return from work with the land and the resultant social stature of the person working on it. Recent and heated conflict between environmentalists and the northwestern timber industry over federal protection of old growth forests from cutting as a means to preserve the Spotted Owl and other endangered species has pitted two manifestations of topophilia against one another. Environmentalists see the typical clearcut harvest practices of the timber companies as a violation of inherent ecological value and a symbol of human callousness toward the rest of nature. Loggers fear their livelihoods will be eliminated and their utilitarian bond with the forest broken. Both positions grow from topophilia, and it is likely that in some subconscious recess of the mind, forest advocates hold some respect for the loggers who gain their living from the forest, and loggers hold some reverence for the earthly context upon which they depend. But layer upon layer of social symbol and economic construct have divided the two inextricably from one another, and observers can only hope for some future solution which satisfies both.

In response to the loss of physical contact with the land by modern society and the concurrent, impersonal abuse of the land by vast, highly technological corporate farming enterprises, there has been a quiet resurgence of interest in alternative social structures which offer a new human utilitarian relationship to the land. In spite of its maligned treatment by history and its popularized image of poor peasants slaving to bring in their crops on small patches of land, medieval feudalism is being reexamined and proposals for a "neo feudalism" are being advanced (Daly and Cobb, 1989; Naess and Rothenberg, 1989; Thompson, 1989). Being neither capitalistic nor socialistic, neo feudalism combines emphasis on both communality and individual enterprise, and if modified to meet the challenges of a more ecological economic structure, implies a modest return to a smaller scale of activity involving greater exposure of humans to the surfaces of the land and the physical ecosystems that provide their sustenance.

The emotional attachment to the land has other dimensions as well. Land embodies such feelings as patriotism at the largest scale ("amber waves of grain" and "purple mountain majesties"), regional identity at the intermediate level (e.g., Cajuns in bayou country), and civic pride or spiritual gratitude at the smallest scales. The turf grass is mowed almost too often in local parks; to allow it to grow too long is to broadcast a symbolic sense of neglect of the community by people living in it. Lawsuits have been brought against individual homeowners who stop mowing their lawns altogether, allowing prairie grasses and native plants to establish according to an emerging ecological ethic, by those who see in unmowed yards the loss of real estate and other neighborhood values. Both sides of this controversy are merely different symbolic representations of the "self" as projected through the front yard. Various aspects of affection for the earth are evident in the personal and social symbols people employ to define who they are in relationship to the greater community. The symbols chosen to reinforce a particular group's bond with the land are often technological or artifactual in nature, and often in conflict. Cross-country skiers resent snowmobilers, and hikers object to off-road motorcyclists. In an enlightened study in the Boundary Waters Canoe Area bordering Minnesota and Ontario, groups of canoeists and motorboaters were each asked to draw on a map the boundaries of what they felt was true "wilderness." Motorboat users drew a wider domain and included the presence of canoeists as part of the wilderness experience, whereas canoeists, resenting the presence of motorboats as antithetical to their notions of wilderness, drew much smaller domains. Canoes symbolized wilderness for the motorboaters, but the reverse did not hold (Lucas, 1970).

Evolutionary Theories

What are the origins of human attachment to land and nature? Certainly our dependence upon the earth to sustain both our bodies and our spirits has acted upon us through transmission of both cultural as well as genetic information. Unlike our earliest homonid ancestors, most of us no longer need to hunt our prey, gather or grow our food, or protect ourselves from predatory animals or competing bands of our own species. These atavistic predispositions are now likely to surface as hunting, fishing, gardening, and organized sports—transformed by layer upon layer of cultural evolution and symbolic ritual. What binds these modern activities to their primitive antecedents is a basic perceptual, spatial, and emotive response to landscape itself. We may no longer rely on cues from the landscape for our survival, but we respond to and appreciate landscape as if we still did.

Reviewing the research on this topic, David Pitt (1982) summarizes four genetically based hypotheses which, while not constituting an integrated theory, partially explain human response to land in evolutionary terms. These hypotheses can be referred to as "Human Naturalness," "Habitat Theory," "Prospect-Refuge Theory," and "Making Sense and Involvement."

The "Human Naturalness" hypothesis presumes that humans possess an innate desire to return to the natural environment of their evolutionary past. Pitt summarizes:

> The evolution of primate vision, human cognition, social bonds and cultural systems in this primeval natural environment thus gives man an innate aesthetic preference for landscapes characterized by natural elements as opposed to the architectonic environments that have developed since the advent of modern civilization. (p. 11)

Countless studies have reinforced this hypothesis (Zube et al., 1982), and most readers will be able to recall personal experiences which further validate this assumption. A simple look at the amount of energy and money invested in placing plants within everyday landscapes should confirm that we simply seem to need to have objects representative of nature around us as much as possible. When reduced to its lowest common denominator, the profession of landscape architecture is often ridiculed as the mere "shrubbing up" of the built environment. The fact that one of landscape architecture's major activities is the design and placement of trees, shrubs, groundcovers, and vines, although not considered as essential or socially important as provision of shelter and roads, nevertheless seems an indispensable human need. Landscape plants are associated with nature and are therefore highly desired.

The other basic validation of this tendency is the great value humans place on the perceived naturalness of landscapes. Witness the American appetite for camping in "natural" surroundings and the widespread appreciation of paintings, films, and photographs of nature. While evidence of our love of these natural activities, objects and environments has been abundant, it has been harder to distinguish whether such fondness stems from cultural familiarity or genetic predisposition. As will be discussed later in this chapter, recent evidence from human physiology reveals that positive response to nature may be one of our most basic, ingrained behaviors.

The late evolutionary biologist Rene Dubos (1980) suggested that humans prefer landscapes that most resemble those habitats in which their ancestors were best able to satisfy all of their biological needs. Specifically, Dubos was referring to the savanna environments of Africa with their scattered trees and grasslands, where the contemporary human species is presumed to have evolved from earlier, tree-dwelling primates. Dubos noted that the primordial, ideal human habitat also included areas of water (an obvious necessity) and patches of dense woods offering protection. Pitt even suggests that part of the American cowboy mystique and American fondness for viewing open landscapes where sheep and cattle graze could be related to the presumption that humans first evolved consciousness in African savanna environments where hoofed, grazing animals were abundant. In many formal research studies and common cultural manifestations, landscapes that include water, open clearings, or meadows with grazing animals and distant vistas are considered among the most beautiful and desirable.

In 1982, Balling and Falk reported finding support for their hypothesis that humans had an innate preference for savanna-like environments. They argued that any "innate predisposition" would show up more strongly in children than adults, since adults are likely to have had more experience living in biomes other than savannas. The authors showed photographs of five different biomes (tropical forest, deciduous forest, coniferous forest, east African savanna, and desert) to 548 people from six different age groups (8, 11, 15, 18, 35, and 70 or over). None of the photos included water or animals. Subjects were asked to rate their preferences for each biome. Eight-year-olds preferred the savanna environments over all others, while from age 15 on, savanna, deciduous forest, and coniferous forest were equally well liked. The desert was least preferred for all groups. The Balling and Falk study may help to explain why the common suburban park, consisting of scattered trees and expanses of green grass, seems such an ubiquitously accepted and sought-after model for urban open space.

Perhaps the most provocative theory among genetic explanations for human response to landscape has been Jay Appleton's articulation of prospect-refuge theory. Appleton's fundamental assumption is that like both predators and prey, humans prefer environments where they can "see without being seen." According to this theory, environments can be examined in terms of prospects—the unimpeded ability to see potential food sources or approaching predators, refuges—opportunities to hide from predators, and hazards—threats, both animate and physiographic, toward the particular creature's survival. When landscapes successfully present opportunities for seeing without being seen, hazards can be avoided and survival assured (i.e., predators will catch prey, or from the opposite point of view, prey may escape).

There are many instances in the typical human appreciation of nature where prospect refuge theory seems to apply. Selection of picnic or camp sites nestled among trees (a refuge) at the edge of a clearing, body of water, or meadow (prospects) is something most campers have experienced. Individuals often choose seating locations in public outdoor places where their backs are protected by walls and their views are outward toward passersby. The siting of a cabin or house at the intersecting edge of forest and field is a common manifestation of prospect-refuge theory. Even the commonplace, residential, open front yard and enclosed backyard can be linked to this theory as well.

Based upon perceptual psychologist J. J. Gibson's theory of *affordances*,

A turf-and-tree park landscape in Sacramento which could be anywhere in the United States; its savanna-like character may harken back to the most universal and primitive of human preferences for landscape.

Stephen and Rachel Kaplan (1982a) propose a theory of human preference for landscapes which allow a high degree of ability to become involved with and make sense of the environment. For Gibson, an affordance is a fixed property of an environment that affords the organism (i.e., a perceiving animal or human) an opportunity to gain something it needs: shelter, water, food, fire, tools, or escape. The Kaplans expand upon this theory and articulate four properties of landscapes—coherence, complexity, legibility, and mystery— which are fundamental to the way in which human environmental perception has evolved and the manner in which our minds continue to register environmental stimuli. The four concepts can be considered as a two-by-two matrix. Coherence is the property that allows a landscape to "hang together" as a perceptual whole, or to be identifiable, familiar, and redundant, allowing us to make sense of it in a static, present sense through perceptual means. Complexity, on the other hand, is a measure of perceived diversity or richness from a single viewpoint. Legibility is a more dynamic relative of coherence—a property of environments that affords humans the ability to move through and explore without getting lost. Mystery, according to the Kaplans, is another dynamic environmental property representing the ability of humans to acquire new knowledge as if traveling deeper into the scene. In this manner, the so-called "natural" environments most closely resembling the primordial conditions in which the human mind evolved offer us an ability to satisfy both our

Prospect-refuge theory is demonstrated in the configuration of this 800-year-old Anasazi cliff dwelling in Mesa Verde National Park, Colorado. Cliff dwellings such as this offered great protection with a commanding view outward.

need to comprehend existing conditions and our need to explore new territories.

   In essence, the human appetite for environmental stimulation is much like the appetite for food. The mind quickly bores of perceiving the exact same surroundings and conditions, and begins to "hunger" for stimulation and new spatial and perceptual experience. But just as the stomach naturally digests recently eaten food, there is a corresponding tendency by which humans process or "digest" new perceptual information into knowledge useful for survival. This evolutionarily based model of human perceptual "ingestion" and cognitive "digestion" is often satisfied through experiences in natural environments, and it is often through such experiences that we most strongly feel our bond with the earth. Rachel and Stephen Kaplan, in their book *The Experience of Nature* (1989), state that "preference [i.e., for particular landscapes] seems to be intimately related to effective functioning" (p. 68). However, effective functioning, in the authors' sense, is a subconscious response rather than a rational, analytical decision. "Without realizing it, humans interpret the environment in terms of their needs and prefer settings in which they are likely to function more effectively" (p. 68). But the needs which the Kaplans speak of are those perceptual appetites which evolved thousands of years ago in conditions that no longer commonly exist in our technologically based world, but can still be found in natural settings—wilderness hikes, nearby

	Exploration: Seeking Involvement with the Environment	Understanding: Making Sense of the Environment
Present, Immediate, or Static	**Complexity:** - richness, diversity of the environment	**Coherence:** - environment "hangs together" -- is familiar, redundant
Future, Promised, or Dynamic	**Mystery:** - ability to acquire new knowledge by moving *into* the environment	**Legibility:** - ability to explore the environment without getting lost

Four characteristics which affect preference for particular landscapes, adapted from Kaplan and Kaplan (1982). Humans simultaneously need to explore the environment and to make sense of it, and prefer environments that allow these primitive preferences.

parks, and gardens. In underscoring the perpetual human bond with nature, the Kaplan's conclude:

> Viewed as an amenity, nature may be replaced by some greater technological achievement. Viewed as an essential bond between humans and other living things, the natural environment has no substitutes. (p. 204)

Psychophysiology and Response to Nature

Although it is generally agreed that humans prefer natural landscapes to those primarily consisting of human constructions, it is less clear to what extent such a response is culturally transmitted as opposed to innate. In the past several years, research evidence has begun to accumulate which explains our positive response to nature and landscape in terms of human physiology and biology. This research builds an increasingly convincing argument in favor of a genetic predisposition toward natural environments and objects representing nature. In studying patients recovering from hospital stays for gall bladder operations, Roger Ulrich (1984) found that patients with window views of trees and vegetation recovered faster and required less pain medication than those whose windows looked out upon a bare wall. Pursuing this line of research further, Ulrich found that exposure to scenes of natural landscapes produced a profound, "quick-onset" reaction in the parasympathetic nervous system among subjects in heart rate deceleration, a physiographic indicator of stress reduction. Apparently, natural scenes can have an immediate calming effect which can be automatically triggered without any lengthy cognitive processing. Ulrich does not discount that natural scenery also appears to affect human response positively through fascinated attention, such as that which might occur when a person gazes for a length of time at a scenic, natural vista. Likewise, he acknowledges that cultural transmission plays a great role in communicating the concept of "nature." However, the studies by Ulrich and others point to a dimension of the topophilic (or biophilic) bond which operates at the most basic level of human biology, and which is simply not capable of explanation by cultural argument. It is becoming increasingly apparent that human fondness for nature and landscapes which we perceive as natural is "hard-wired" into our basic biological essence.

With respect to technology, however, the line of investigation pioneered by Ulrich and others has led to some extremely disturbing consequences. Researchers have found that electronically backlighted, photographic *displays* of natural scenery which vary sky color and intensity to resemble the daily tonal and light conditions found in natural cycles produce similar healing effects for hospital patients. Even Ulrich's 1991 study (Ulrich et al., 1991) used videotapes of natural scenery which themselves represented an intervening technological layer between the perceiver and the natural stimulus. Marketing specialists eagerly sought Dr. Ulrich's approval to develop product technologies for hospitals which, based upon his research, would achieve healing effects through simulations of natural environments. The replacement of natural environments by high-technology imitations which can achieve the same physiological effects on humans is a frightening turn of events with tremendous ethical implications for our future. It is a topic central to the theme of this book and will be discussed thoroughly in later chapters. However, technology's ability to produce surrogate natural stimuli (after all, the photographs of beautiful scenery in Sierra Club calendars can be construed as technologically based simulations) does not contradict the fact that our response to such stimuli appear to be ingrained in our genetic structure; it only implies that such a genetic predisposition might fall victim to unethical use, or misuse, by technology.

Cultural Manifestations

In examining the human bond with earth, land, and nature, the role of culture cannot be ignored. So much of the cultural heritage of the United States pivots around nature, land, and wilderness values that it would be impossible to do justice to any kind of summary here. Scholars such as Leo Marx (1963), Aldo Leopold (1949), Clarence Glacken (1967), and Roderick Nash (1967) have already produced seminal and authoritative volumes on our cultural attachment to the land. Instead, I would like to focus on one aspect of our national heritage—the persistence of the pastoral ideal—as the most fundamental example of the American cultural bond with nature.

The myth of a simple, peaceful, natural life in a rural, "middle" landscape

where humans and nature meet without conflict is perhaps the most fundamental cultural determinant of landscape aesthetic tastes still operant in
American culture. Consider the archetypal, scenic landscape with large,
middle-ground expanses of open, green land with cattle or sheep grazing and
few buildings, roads, or technological structures. Such an agrarian ideal
adorns countless postcards, television commercials, calendars, book covers,
and, ironically, even billboards. Although possibly related to genetic preference for savanna landscapes, the pastoral ideal is best understood if traced
back through America's early ties to the British Isles. Shepherding has been a
dominant landscape force in Great Britain for centuries, and sheep still out-
number humans. The pastoral ideal begins with a shepherd watching a flock
of sheep—protecting them from the predators of the wilderness, while enjoying a simple, healthful life in a rural setting far from the sins of the city. The
pastoral grew to encompass a host of constructs involving art, literature,
poetry, and landscape tastes, all of which drew upon the central idea of a
peaceful, harmonious existence in a rural setting where nature and man could
meet and influence one another on equal terms. The pastoral evolved to
become a symbol for nature itself. However, this was not a "wild" nature, nor
was it the earlier, medieval definition of nature as universal context, but a
tame and romanticized nature exemplified by country values and mild agrarian influences. During the eighteenth century, the pastoral ideal was exalted by
the English literati to a near-religious status. From its inception, the Industrial Revolution became an immediate threat to the foundations of agrarian
life by pulling people away from the countryside to work under the squalid
conditions of cities and factories. Self-sufficient yeomanry in rural surroundings gave way to demeaning labor at the hand of the machine. The reaction
among artists, poets, writers, and the makers of gardens was a deification of
the pastoral life in word, paint, verse, and landscape. The English word "landscape" was first used in the sixteenth century to describe the backgrounds of
Dutch paintings which depicted rural life, and by the eighteenth century, the
aesthetic or painterly characteristics of the landscape were an essential characteristic of the English pastoral (Schenker, 1988).

The pastoral ideal exerted tremendous influence over the aesthetic norms
of landscape painting and garden design. Schenker (1988) writes that during
the enclosure process at the end of the eighteenth century, English land-
holders and farmers applied aesthetic standards derived from the arts, virtually redesigning the English countryside.

> When William Gilpin developed a specific aesthetic for landscape appreciation, called
> the "picturesque," and began to survey the English countryside for illustrative exam-
> ples, the act of viewing the land itself was choreographed. Rural scenery became
> subject to analysis according to specific aesthetic qualities derived from the arts.
> (p. 6)

Yet, in an accelerating, cyclical fashion, the aesthetic principles that were now
applied to landscape had sprung from the romanticization of rural existence

on the land itself. Pastoral qualities had been extracted from early agrarian life, mythologized, and formulaically reapplied to the land. At its paramount, the English affection for the pastoral landscape was a kind of hyperreality—a supreme fondness for a heightened and glorified interpretation of simple agrarian values. The more the development of technological and industrial machinery threatened basic rural lifestyles, the more the English embraced the pastoral ideal.

The English affection for a pastoral, romanticized, and humanized form of nature and landscape aesthetics spread to the new American colonies as part of a greater cultural migration from Great Britain. The manner in which this predisposition should translate to the uniqueness of the American landscape and fledgling culture was the subject of great debate among early American intellectuals and artists, and even today scholars are unsure of the details of the transition. There was no greater contemporaneous influence, however, than Thomas Jefferson, who believed strongly that America ought to be a country of independent, yeoman farmers living in dignity, harmony, and self-sufficiency in a rural landscape, leaving the nasty business of industrial production and its accompanying urban ills to the mother country of England. For Jefferson, Thoreau, Emerson, and artists like Thomas Cole, the unique, wild nature of the American land was, in philosophical terms, a source of near-divine transcendence and the symbol of the emergent American character. Cole, an American who had studied painting in England, defended the American landscape against its more Anglophile critics, who felt it was raw and lacking both picturesqueness and sublimity:

> . . . though American scenery is destitute of many of those circumstances that give value to the European, it still has features, and glorious ones, unknown to Europe . . . the most distinctive, and perhaps the most impressive, characteristic of American scenery is its wildness.

Cole, 1836

Early American affection for land and nature, therefore, was a unique combination of affection for both the pastoral and the wild. America was influenced not only by the dominant pastoral theme imported from England, but also by the presence and immensity of so much raw wilderness at its back door. Pioneer American landscape architect Frederick Law Olmsted, perhaps more than any other individual, embodied this duality in the origin of American landscape taste and affection for nature. Olmsted, the son of a merchant, at one time or other in his career became a yeoman farmer, civil engineer, social critic, administrator, and ultimately founded the profession of landscape architecture. His designs for Central Park and countless other urban open space systems in the late nineteenth century reflected strongly the pastoral aesthetic he had studied in England at Birkenhead Park, Stourhead, and other classic romantic English gardens and parks. Olmsted was known less for his innovative landscape *design* form (his aesthetic can be definitively linked to England) than his unique and widespread application of it to the American social condition. However, Olmsted's truly unique formal contribution to American landscape preferences was his advocacy of saving magnificent examples of wild scenery, such as Yosemite Valley, and recommending the establishment of a system of national parks, believing that "the experience of viewing magnificent landscape scenery was invaluable for building American character (Schenker, 1988)."

Although not solely responsible for landscape taste in nineteenth century America, Olmsted served as both a catalyst for establishment of the earliest urban parks as well as a litmus test of their significance. With his work on Central Park, Yosemite, and numerous parks in between, Olmsted firmly established the notion that pleasant and beautiful landscape, whether derived by man, nature or both; whether conceived through design, preservation, or both; as interpreted through aesthetic experience, was a central feature of American culture. Through Olmsted, we can trace American landscape affection to its dual roots in the English pastoral tradition of Central Park and in the raw wilderness of Yosemite Valley.

Today, this cultural dualism survives in American landscape taste, as both pastoral, "middle" landscape ideals (involving agricultural themes, grazing land, large expanses of turfgrass, rural referent objects and buildings) and wilderness themes (picturesque mountains, vast forests, undisturbed lakes

Wilderness, pastoralism, and technological nostalgia blend in this rural scene near Smithers, British Columbia, Canada.

and streams) combine to form a mythic frame of American passion for nature. Pastoral images of nature persist today, influencing such pragmatic activities as land use zoning and real estate development, and have played significant roles in the evolution of suburban values. Wilderness imagery permeates American cinema, literature, advertising, and all aspects of popular material culture. Countless scientific studies have shown that Americans prefer scenes with little or no evidence of man-made materials (Zube et al., 1982), and if human activity is to be present, the bias is toward agricultural and wildland recreation themes.

What of urbanism and technology in American topophilia? Early in the nineteenth century when industrial activity became inevitable for the growth of the fledgling United States, even Jefferson revealed his inability to adhere to his own dream of America as a pastoral refuge, and succumbed to the mounting pressure of what Leo Marx calls the "machine in the garden." (Marx, 1963)

> Looking to America's future, Jefferson anticipates the tragic ambivalence [e.g., love-hatred of the emergence of technology as a formative role on American society] that is the hallmark of our most resonant pastoral fables. 'Our enemy [Britain during the War of 1812] . . . has indeed the consolation of Satan on removing our first parents from Paradise: from a peaceable and agricultural nation, he makes us a military and manufacturing one.'"
>
> *Marx, 1963, quoting Jefferson, 1814*

Leo Marx establishes the railroad as the dominant metaphor for the emergence of technology as a competing, yet highly ambivalent, affection of the American psyche. Marx writes skillfully of the futility of American attempts to include technology as an acceptable element in an American pastoral:

> The railroad is the chosen vehicle for bringing America into its own as a pastoral utopia. That it also means planting Kansas City where the garden was supposed to be does not often occur to the popular rhetoricians. (p. 225)

Citing the stark, industrial themes of American landscape painter Charles Sheeler as evidence of lingering attempts to integrate technology to America's pastoral dreams, Marx concludes:

> This . . . [Sheeler's painting 'American Landscape'] is the industrial landscape pastoralized. By superimposing order, peace, and harmony upon our modern chaos, Sheeler represents the anomalous *blend of illusion and reality in the American consciousness* [my emphasis]. (p. 356)

The previous quote from Marx is useful as a foundation for my current thesis: America has failed to include an adequate symbology of technology in its definitions of what is natural, ethical, and emotionally desirable. This, in turn, has spawned a debilitating, yet apparently seamless gulf between reality and fantasy in the American landscape. American affection for nature, land, and

The American pastoral ideal ironically persists in this billboard amid urban communication relays in Oklahoma City.

earth still centers on both wilderness ideals and pastoral dreams, yet technology has so vastly distorted these constructs that what we consider true wilderness and genuine pastoral beauty are disappearing from the real landscape. The functional necessity of pastoralism has long since waned, but we have yet to allow technology a similarly favored place in our hearts. The land is our true love, but technology is merely a concubine—a surrogate imposter, and a two-faced, untrustworthy one at that. So the pastoral myth refuses to die. Just as the round pit-house dwellings of the ancient southwestern basketmaker people were abandoned for everyday life but eventually evolved into the ceremonial, religious *kivas* of their Anasazi successors, so the American pastoral ideal is a quasi-religious relic rapidly disappearing into the electronic mythology of the American Dream.

The Future of Topophilia

Gary Snyder, poet and wilderness advocate, maintains that we must "practice" the wild (Snyder, 1990). Snyder distinguishes between *nature, wild,* and *wilderness.* He regards the word *nature* as meaning the "physical universe and all its properties," but acknowledges that other meanings of nature, such as "outdoors" and "other-than-human" cannot be avoided. In contrast, *wild,* he maintains, is a word which, when traced back through its Norse, Teutonic,

Latin, and Indo-European roots, seems to have maintained its primal meaning over generations.

> It comes to an understanding of the subtle but critical difference of meaning between the terms *nature* and *wild*. Nature is the subject, they say, of science. Nature can be deeply probed, as in microbiology. The wild is not to be made subject or object in this manner; to be approached it must be admitted from within as a quality intrinsic to who we are. Nature is ultimately in no way endangered; wilderness is. The wild is indestructible, but we might not *see* the wild.
>
> *Snyder, 1990, p. 181*

In this fashion, modern technology may be natural, but it is not wild, and it is wildness that Gary Snyder implores us to preserve; not a reckless, irresponsible wildness, but a thoughtful, loving connection to actual wild places on earth as well as the wild places inside each of us. As an avid spokesperson for bioregionalism, Snyder asks his students and listeners to learn where they are as they travel or live on the earth not by artifactual, politically determined boundaries such as states, counties, or towns, but by reference to physiographic features such as river watersheds, geological and topographic formations, plant/animal ecosystems, and relative elevations above sea level. The bond of topophilia starts with an awareness of where one is with respect to essential attributes of the earth, and upon this firm foundation, it can grow and flourish.

Siskiyou Wilderness scene in the Klamath Mountains of northern California. Photograph by Dave Van De Mark.

Perpetuating the bond with wildness requires wild places, and Gary Snyder has become a larger-than-life voice in the wilderness movement. His enthusiasm, however, is not limited to the obvious, large, and spectacular roadless areas being formally proposed for wilderness classification, but extends to the subtle, fragmentary, wild pieces including the remnants of former logging operations and old mine tailings. It is this type of environment—Snyder's locally loved pockets of wildness—which is most rapidly disappearing from the American landscape. The "nearby wild nature" of riparian fragments, remnant forests, and undisturbed open land is being eroded by encroaching housing developments, bisected by roads and powerlines, punctured by electronic communications devices, and replaced by close-cropped turfgrass parks, birch trees, and automatic irrigation. Perhaps more importantly, though, is the loss of the ecological functions of these disappearing wild places as habitats for animals and plants, as receptacles and buffers for storm water, and as producers of oxygen and gene-pool variety. Wildness ceases to function in the human mind as it loses function in the ambient ecosystem.

The love relationship between humans and nature is changing, just as the relationship between two human partners must change when each or both are evolving. As the land increasingly reflects our technological preoccupations, the character of topophilia must respond accordingly. With each debit in the real landscape at the hand of technology comes an increased credit in the amount of idealized, wild landscape we must create in our minds. In this fashion we witness the mythological transgenesis of wilderness from a real place on earth to an electronic venue of the mind. Concurrent with the encroachment of technological impacts on actual landscapes is an increasing human use of technology as a means of expressing topophilia and acting out our deepening wilderness myths.

A ponderous question we now face is just how far our love of land and nature can be sustained without real referent objects in our landscape to sustain them. Gross extrapolation from present trends paints a picture of a real landscape totally saturated by technological intrusion and a topophilic bond with nature that feeds entirely on myth. Nature writer David Rains Wallace, weaving together myth and science of the Klamath Mountains in *The Klamath Knot* (Wallace, 1983), speaks eloquently of the giant creatures (colloquially referred to as "Sasquatch" or "Bigfoot") who have inhabited the mythic (and some would argue, real) spaces of the northwestern mountains as the presumed evolutionary relatives of humans. In Wallace's view, these giants deserve more consideration than that engendered by their familiar cartoon caricatures:

> We begin to see in them the possibility of a consciousness quite different from our own, of a being that may be very close to us in homonid origins, but that may have evolved in mysterious ways. We imagine an animal that somehow has understood the world more deeply than we have, and that thus inhabits it more comfortably and freely, while eluding our self-involved attempts to capture it.

> Giants can have a new function in an evolutionary myth. They link us to lakes, rivers, forests, and meadows that are our home as well as theirs. They lure us into the wilderness, as they lured me, not to devour us but to remind us where we are, on a living planet.

Wallace, p. 138

Wallace's Klamath Mountain giants are manifestations of a perhaps impossible yet idealized state of human grace with respect to the earth. Unlike humans, they have found a way to live in the forest and the rest of the natural world without destroying it, while relating peacefully and undestructively to each other and to other species. The fact that few traces of the giants have ever been discovered and that they seem to need absolutely no discernable technology to survive or to mark their presence only enlarges their mythic power. The giants are pure, anthropomorphic personifications of earth-love itself, standing completely naked of technological trappings. Wallace concludes the book:

> If giants do not exist, to paraphrase Voltaire, it is necessary to invent them.

Wallace, p. 138

The mythical giants of the Klamath stand for topophilia in the truest sense, and anchor a corner of the triangle of forces forming the contemporary American landscape.

NOTES

1. Brush and Shafer's method involved overlaying photographs of natural landscapes with a transparent grid of squares, determining immediate, intermediate and distant zones, and measuring the perimeter of immediate vegetation (X_1), perimeter of intermediate nonvegetation (X_2), perimeter of distant vegetation (X_3), area of intermediate vegetation (X_4), area of any kind of water (X_5), and area of distant nonvegetation (X_6). A statistical regression procedure resulted in an equation which predicted scenic preference (Y):

$$Y = 184.8 - 0.5436X_1 - 0.09298X_2 + 0.002069\,(X_1 \times X_3) + 0.0005538\,(X_1 \times X_4) - 0.002596\,(X_3 \times X_5) + 0.001634\,(X_2 \times X_6) - 0.0008441\,(X_4 \times X_6) - 0.0004131\,(X_4 \times X_5) + 0.0006666X_2^2 + 0.0001327X_5^2$$

No theoretical presumptions could be made from the equation, which predicted scenic preference among photographs of natural landscapes with reasonable accuracy.

2

Technophilia and Landscape

The most mysterious and wonderful thing about the hand axe is that it is unnecessarily beautiful. The delicacy and symmetry in its design, the quality of the workmanship involved, and the time devoted to its manufacture, all go far beyond functional demand. Why did they go to all this trouble? Why did they bother, when a cruder instrument, much more simply made, would have been just as effective?

There is no obvious solution to the presence of this same lovely artifact across so wide an area, nor to its persistence over so long a period of time. But there is no question about its importance or its significance; it was our first, specialized, unarguable tool. It ushered in the Stone Age and it laid the foundations for both technology and art. It was our first essay in style, the first real evidence of creativity.

LYALL WATSON, 1982

By definition, humans are tool-using animals. Accompanying some of the earliest hominid archaeological sites are remains of pebbles, bone, or wood fragments that could only have been used to aid the process of killing and consuming prey for food. About one million years ago, the classic oval or teardrop-shaped hand axes to which Lyall Watson refers above began to appear in conjunction with *Homo* caves and campsites. First found in the Somme Valley of France near St. Acheul, these Acheulean hand axes, as they are now known, appeared in virtually every region where early humans occurred, ranging over what is now Europe, the Middle East, and Africa (Watson, p. 23). They are closely associated with the emergence of a newer, more intelligent species of hominid, *Homo erectus* (Schick and Toth, 1993).

For many years, tool use has been the predominant paradigm set forth by anthropologists marking the evolutionary departure of humans from other primates mammals. The currently favored paleoanthropological lineage, *Australopithicus afarensis, Homo habilis, Homo erectus, Homo sapiens,* implies that tool use preceded rapid mental development. *Homo habilis,* or "handy

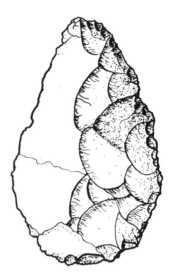

An Acheulean stone hand axe. Was this the simultaneous origin of both art and technology? Drawing by Douglas Thayer.

man" is named after them, and *habilis* was the first species to be commonly found in association with crude stone tools. But rapid development of the powers of long-term memory, symbolic thinking, and language were only thought to emerge in the transition from *erectus* to *sapiens*—"sapienization" as it is known to human evolution (Lumsden and Wilson, 1983).

Origins of Art and Technology

Watson's image of early humans creating both primitive beauty and necessary function directly from pieces of the elemental earth has a mysterious potency to it, especially for those of us looking for clues to the connection between the human affection for the earth and human preoccupation with technology. Watson's information came from discussions with Raymond Dart, a preeminent paleontologist who first discovered *Australopithicus afarensis.* It is understandable how anthropologists before Dart could classify early hominids according to their use of tools; relics of tools can be readily found at archaeological sites, whereas clues to language and memory development are much more speculative and difficult to discover. It is also understandable that many paleontologists considered tool use as the definitive boundary between humans and other primates. But Raymond Dart began a long line of divergent opinion—he speculated that tool use must have been accompanied by the development of other mental faculties. If his line of thinking is accepted, the Acheulean hand axes marked a striking and momentary congruence between art, technology, and earthly landscape context. Imagine for a moment a hypothetical scene one million years ago—a diminutive *Homo erectus* female sits cross-legged on a stony ledge in the middle of the Olduvai Gorge of Africa. Picking up a boulder of quartzite lying on the rock ledge nearby, she lifts it overhead and heaves it on to another boulder, splitting off a large core. She then begins skillfully chipping away at the quartzite core in her left hand with a cobble hammer stone held in her right. As the sun drops below the ridge to the west, shadows creep across the rock ledge and sunlight sparkles on the stone flakes beside her. She pauses for a moment, gazing at the last fragment of sun as it disappears, then holds the rough hand axe at arms length, checking for symmetry in its outline against the fading sunlight. From deep within

The world of *Homo erectus*, the species of man intermediate between habline and modern man, a speculative reconstruction.

Homo erectus, *the humanlike ancestor closely associated with Acheulean handaxe culture. Drawing by Whitney Powell from* Promethian Fire, *1983, C. Lumsden and E. Wilson, Harvard University Press.*

her, a flush of warmth emanates to her fingertips, and for a fleeting moment, she becomes aware of this pleasant congruence of feelings.

From this brief flight of fantasy, we can imagine a human-like creature who, although capable of making stone tools deftly and unselfconsciously, taxes her limited mental acuity to understand the feelings she is experiencing from watching the sun burn and fade across the landscape and seeing the teardrop shape of her hand axe emerge from a raw piece of that same landscape. At this theoretical moment, human, tool, landscape, and experience are indeed one. This scenario, however far fetched, cries out with urgent questions: How did art evolve to lose function, and tools (and eventually, machines) come to lose beauty? How did art and technology become so ideologically severed from each other and from the land? Did tool use precede the development of human self-consciousness, creative problem solving, and feelings of aesthetic experience, or was the opposite true? If the development of tools was a necessary prerequisite for the evolution of human mental capacity, then we may indeed be the natural victims of our own technological determinism. If, however, tool use was coincidental, or perhaps even secondary to the development of our mental powers, creativity, and the evolution of human aesthetic experience, then an entirely different relationship between humanity and technology is implied.

Lewis Mumford, in his book *The Myth of the Machine,* Volume 1, *Technics and Human Development* (1967) reexamined and rejected the widely held assumption that tool use separated humans from other species. Instead, Mumford believed that the evolution of human symbolic language and abstract thought must have preceded tools, making the emergence of the bone and stone fragments which had so consumed the anthropologists less of a major event. Mumford claimed that technics never "disassociated itself from the larger cultural whole in which man . . . has always functioned" until the modern age.

> At its point of origin, technics was related to the whole nature of man, and that nature played a part in every aspect of industry: thus technics, at the beginning, was broadly life-centered, not work centered or power centered.
>
> *Mumford, as quoted in Miller, 1986, p. 310*

Other animals use tools. Sea otters break open abalone with rocks; chimpanzees dig termites from their mounds with sticks; crows drop walnuts from great heights onto asphalt roads (a learned behavior) to break out the meat from the shell. Mumford observed that a human five year old who can read, write, and reason shows less proclivity for tool use and tool making than gorillas or chimpanzees. The evolution of tool use and ultimately, technology, thought Mumford, was facilitated by a brain capable of linguistic symbols, aesthetic designs, and social transmission of knowledge, not the other way around. In his view, a brain capable of inventing technology was also capable of inventing a cure for it.

In spite of Mumford's very plausible point of view, I subscribe to the alternate theory that tool use, symbolic language, and the evolution of true human thought probably coevolved together in a mutually causative, epigenetic fashion: mental power facilitated tool use and tool use led to greater mental power (Lumsden and Wilson, 1983; Thompson, 1989; Schick and Toth, 1993). Mumford himself posited that the first *real* tools that human ancestors developed were their own bodies—hands, eyes, and brains which, when accompanied by the first primitive bone and stone implements, allowed the mouth to be freed for the rapid evolution of speech and language. Linguistic pioneer Noam Chomsky advanced the theory that the principles of human language are innate and genetically patterned in the human brain, a theory now being born out by research (Horning, 1991).

Separate Constructs

While it is arguable whether tool use or mental development preceded the other in evolution, the eventual separation of technology and earthly landscape context into distinct and now combative constructs is not. In the modern era, a quick look around tells us that contemporary humans have somehow evolved strong, if not fickle, bonds to their technologies and the lifestyles these technologies have made possible.

One way of looking at technology is as a natural survival mechanism—an extension of the human proclivity to solve problems in the physical world. The evolution of bipedalism, the use of the hands to make tools, long-term memory, the invention of symbolic language, and the ability to imagine and create eventually allowed humans to invent and construct whole new worlds. Addressing the birth of technology, Langdon Winner points out that we may speak of tools in terms of their *making* and of their *use* (Winner, 1986, p. 5). It seems that the making of tools was (and still is) something for which we are certainly genetically well equipped and mentally predisposed to do. Creative problem-solving comes as easily to humans as sniffing tree trunks is to a dog. However, only once the making and use of tools—the establishment of both the *hardware* (tools and ultimately, machines) *and* the social structures governing their creation and use—became the speciality of the few rather than the necessity of the many, was technology truly born. From that point of birth technology drifted apart from the creation of beauty (art) and the relation to earthly context (landscape). Lewis Mumford went so far as to suggest that true technology—the "combination of resistant parts, each specialized in function, operating under human control, to transmit motion and to perform work" (Miller, 1986, p. 316) was first evident in "human machines"—the centralized social structures of the earliest "god-king" societies ranging from Mesopotamia, Egypt, China, Cambodia, the Yucatan, and Peru. These wondrous landscapes—the Pyramid at Giza, the Mayan, Axtecan, and Inca temples, the

Ruins of the ancient Inca city of Machu Picchu in the Peruvian Andes. Lewis Mumford believed the rigid social hierarchies necessary to construct places like Machu Picchu were the true precursors of technological society. Photograph by Kerry Dawson.

Great Wall of China—were all a result not of complex "hardware" machines (most used only human labor aided by primitive "classical" machines, such as the inclined plane), but by rigidly controlled armies of compliant human workers who, with ant-like regimentation, were able to produce what are considered among the most stunning artifactual landscapes on the face of the earth. Mumford's point was that this organized, machine-like, human social system was the true technological breakthrough which allowed a rapid explosion of technical hardware.

The Context, Means, and Reasons for Living

If the Acheulean hand axe represented an intersection of beauty, technique, and earthly context, it was not long before these realms of human existence evolved away from one another. Consider for a moment a triangular, framework of life "essentials" with which most people could identify. At one corner is the *means* for living and survival, first encompassing utilitarian tool use and ultimately, all of technology. At a second corner is the *context* for life, encompassing our relationship to the earth, atmosphere, artifactual environment, and other living things and beings (ecology in the broadest sense).

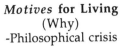

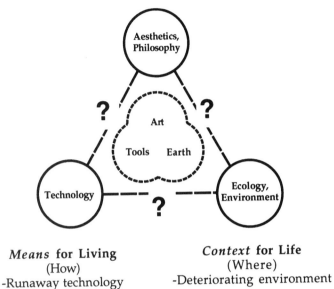

A human "Life Essentials" triangle. A presumed primitive integration (shown in dashed lines) has been exploded by modern technological existence. In some ways, technology has become the "motive" and the "context" as well as the means.

Finally, at the triangle's uppermost apex are the *reasons, or motivations* for living, including aesthetic experience, art, and other affective states relating to the *quality* of our existence. Surely at the dawn of human evolution this triangular relationship did not exist; means, reasons, and context for life were bound up in one unselfconscious state of being. In modern American life, however, the triangle has emerged and expanded to the point where relationships between the reasons, means, and context for life are so tenuously stretched and incongruous that the three realms often seem compartmentalized and no longer truly connected. Whether Mumford is correct and we have a way out of technological determinism or whether we are evolutionarily locked into technology as a way of life, the landscape we now inhabit betrays the migration of technology and nature away from each other, and away from the center of our collective being.

Evidence from the landscape would suggest that America today is preoccupied by the utilitarian means for living at the expense of both the reasons and the context. In fact, one might conclude that an addictive preoccupation with means has become the "reason." Technology is a substantial subculture and, arguably, the dominant theme in American culture as a whole (see

Chapter 3). But at the root of technology may lie a hard-wired human predisposition to invent tools and use them creatively to solve problems. The earliest adaptive strategies of creating tools once assured early *Homo sapiens* of survival as a species, and by any external observation, modern technology has certainly not only allowed us to survive, but to thrive overwhelmingly at the expense of other species.

However, there may be no such similarly innate human mechanism for living in a world of our own creation. Authors Ornstein and Erlich argue that *"human judgement and humanity's ability to deal with the consequences of its creations lags behind its ability to create"* (original emphasis; Ornstein and Erlich, 1989, p. 9). In this argument lies an essential message of this book: *The American landscape simultaneously reflects our deep reverence for our natural context, our ingrained tendency to solve problems creatively to survive, as well as our discomfort with and apparent inability to tolerate living in a physical world comprised largely of the products of our own creation.* The ambivalence of the third topic will be dealt with in Chapter 4. In this chapter we examine human affection for technology and how this affection is expressed and revealed in the landscape.

Technophilia: In Love with Mr. Wizard

It cannot be denied that cultural evolution has changed the way we approach utilitarian demands for survival since our days of chipping stones to make tools. Utilitarian concerns, starting with agriculture and continuing through the industrial revolution, the emergence of the steam engine, automobile, telephone, airplane, and television, have virtually dictated the form of the American landscape we occupy today. In spite of these drastic changes, America remains faithful to the god of technological invention. Thomas Edison and Alexander Graham Bell are true national heroes. In spite of the fact that America has lost its edge in manufacturing the material culture we so readily consume, we have never lost the myth that technological innovation and invention is America's rightful spiritual territory, and that we have merely grown too lazy to manufacture the creations we so brilliantly think up. Clearly Americans place greater social value upon those people whose occupations involve scientific discovery and technological development than on those who deal with social issues or problems. Starting salaries for engineers are roughly twice those of social workers or teachers. Our national fears of losing economic advantage to the Japanese are not based upon comparisons of art, music, health, sports, or the quality of our environment, but on math and science test scores and high-technology production. In spite of having already lost this battle, America still holds breakthrough scientific discovery, individual invention, and maverick technological entrepreneurship as its reigning social ideal; iconoclastic computer wizards Steve Jobs, founder of Apple Computer, and

A functioning oil well near the Oklahoma State Capitol.

Bill Gates of Microsoft, occupy the pinnacle of the American technological spirit. The personal computer is a fitting icon of this quasi-religious movement. Even as the silicon idol takes its place on the altar, however, the engineered carbon-based molecule jockeys to take its place. At the time of this writing, scientists have recently succeeded in building a computing device entirely from organic molecules. While Eric Drexler (1986) and Stewart Brand (1987) speak eloquently and cautiously about the pros and cons of such a technological future, their basic enthusiasm shows through their writing. According to Brand, when the steamroller of technology rolls over you, you either become part of the steamroller or part of the road. On the other hand, social critic Jeremy Rifkin (1989), environmental writer Bill McKibben (1989), and political scientist Lester Milbrath (1989) argue vigorously against the unchecked steamroller of genetic and molecular engineering. So far, none of these authors' arguments have been proven or disproven, and the technological steamroller rumbles forward with a brick on the accelerator.

Technology as Dictator of the Vernacular Landscape

As Geographer Peirce Lewis (1990) explains, most of the built landscape is "taste-free," or not designed by professionals with symbolic or aesthetic agendas, but has evolved through the peculiar and unselfconscious needs of everyday people. The modern American vernacular landscape is a tribute to the formative technologies which drove American culture in the decades of the twentieth century. Although the original fabric of our landscape dates back to more elementary causes such as the location of frontier settlements, river ports, wagon roads, early surveyors' grids, and the railroad, the modern landscape in which we live now owes its form primarily to the automobile. Residential landscapes are dominated by the driveway and garage, and auto access drives the shape of residential lots and entire communities. Automobile sizes, speeds, turning radii, and parking requirements combine with the least expensive durable paving technology (i.e,. asphalt) to dictate the character and form of urban and suburban streets. Cul de sacs are "designed" by the turning requirements of fire engines and garbage trucks. Feeder and collectors streets define our neighborhoods, while universal traffic standards dictate whether intersections have stoplights or stop signs. Freeways tie our cities together or tear them apart, depending on one's point of view. Since automobiles have no regional design differences, neither do our auto-dictated neighborhoods; a subdivision layout in Milwaukee looks like one in Miami, Monterey, or Montpelier. Of course, we have an entire automobile "culture," and some would argue that to presume the landscape is dictated only by technology is naive. But the automobile dictates the physical manifestations of that culture. Strip highway shopping evolved because of the automobile, not the reverse.

Landscape architects and other professionals involved with site planning soon realize the power of the car to dictate design. As a young landscape architect and park planner working for the State of Colorado, I discovered that I could develop preliminary recreation area site plans entirely by magic marker. In 1 in. = 100 ft scale, a single lane of asphalt park road was one marker tip wide in the narrow dimensions; two lanes were two marker tips wide, while each 90 degree, off-street parking space could be quickly delineated by placing the marker tip down once perpendicular to the road in question. At 40 ft scale, the other common working scale in our office, I merely had to rotate the marker 90 degrees and run the broad tip sideways to delineate a lane of traffic. Since automobile access and parking dictated much of the park master planning work we did, this simple time-saving device allowed freehand exploration of many a proposed circulation and parking layout. Those readers who are landscape architects or site planners may have arrived at similar revelations independently.

To my fellow landscape architects, the following statement will be heresy, but most of the American landscape is designed by civil engineers or engineering technicians—most often by a formulaic approach based on technical specifications and performance standards, with few "degrees of freedom" left for aesthetically expressive, socially reflective, or ecologically appropriate variation. Although landscape architectural design is gradually becoming computerized, civil engineering is highly so for the simple reason that design by technical standards is much more easily facilitated by the computer than design for aesthetic, social, or ecological factors. Add the gravity of protecting

SUBDIVISION LAYOUT PROCEDURES

Residential subdivision of a tract of land requires considerable attention to design options and principles. Some of these are illustrated and described below.

REDUCE TRAFFIC HAZARD POTENTIAL BY USE OF RIGHT ANGLE INTERSECTIONS

ANGLE OF INTERSECTION

AVOID SMALL IRREGULAR BLOCKS THAT MAY BE DIFFICULT TO SERVICE AND NOT COST EFFECTIVE

BLOCK SHAPE AND SIZE

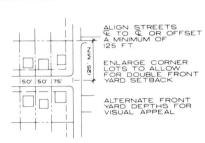

ALIGN STREETS ₵ TO ₵ OR OFFSET A MINIMUM OF 125 FT.

ENLARGE CORNER LOTS TO ALLOW FOR DOUBLE FRONT YARD SETBACK

ALTERNATE FRONT YARD DEPTHS FOR VISUAL APPEAL

INTERSECTION OFFSET, FRONT YARD SETBACK, AND CORNER LOTS

DEEPEN PERIMETER LOTS THAT ABUT UNKNOWN OR DIFFERENT LAND USES

ENLARGE CUL-DE-SAC LOTS FOR BUILDABLE AREA

ADJACENT LAND USE CONDITION / CUL-DE-SACS

AVOID DOUBLE FRONTAGE OF RESIDENTIAL LOTS

DOUBLE FRONTED LOTS

ALIGN LOT LINE WITH CENTERLINE OF STREET TO MINIMIZE NIGHTTIME GLARE OF AUTO LAMPS INTO HOUSE

LOT LINE STREET OFFSET

ADJUST STREET RIGHT OF WAY TO ACCOMMODATE EXISTING TREES OR OTHER SIGNIFICANT NATURAL FEATURES

AMENITY CONSIDERATIONS

Housing subdivision design standards reveal the extent to which American communities are shaped by the automobile in spite of regional differences in climate, topography, vegetation, or economic base. Reprinted from Architectural Graphic Standards, *8th ed., Wiley, New York, 1988.*

the "public health, safety, and welfare" from instrinsic environmental failure and the hair-trigger lawsuits being filed for every so-called professional "error and omission," and the result is even more emphasis on design by proven technical standards.

The American vernacular landscape still depends on engineering in spite of its lack of attention to high-style aesthetic or social purpose. The bottom line for thousands of city and county governments is not whether a particular part of the built landscape satisfies a social or aesthetic need, but whether it will prevent the city or county from being sued. When taken to its logical conclusion, the tendency for unidimensional, technical, standard-based, engineer-designed landscapes will result in even the engineer being removed and replaced by a computer. One can easily envision the replacement of countless civil engineers, building and public works department officials with a cybernetic computer system that "cranks out" designs for roads, subdivisions, sewer and water lines, and lighting systems with less and less human input. In the future, it is only partially humorous to consider that outcomes of lawsuits could merely be fed back directly into the computer system to make minor adjustments to the technical specifications which spit out the street, lot, water, sewer, electrical, and structural layouts that form our neighborhoods.

Technophilia and the Deliberate Landscape

In addition to the vernacular, even the professionally designed, intentional landscape is a tribute to technophilia as well. An entire "Green Industry" of landscape equipment suppliers, contractors, and designers has exerted subtle but considerable influence over the direction of landscape design for decades. Central to every American Society of Landscape Architect's annual convention is an enormous exhibit hall, with vendor booths displaying the wide range of technological products which now define the state-of-the-art of deliberate landscapes: computer-controlled irrigation, complex drainage pipe systems, erosion control fabrics, plant staking and tying systems, self-irrigating specimen plant containers, modular retaining wall systems, prefabricated bridges, benches, and picnic tables, synthetic rock work, modular paving systems, computer-controlled and movement-activated outdoor lighting, prefabricated play structures, synthetic plants and plastic turf, pelletized fertilizers, and injection devices. Two relative newcomers to recent ASLA convention exhibit halls are the purveyors of fog or misting systems for simulating rainforest conditions in indoor gardens and one solitary company who manufactures play structure components from recycled plastic milk cartons. The exhibit hall at any ASLA national convention is a surrogate landscape itself, captured under a roof, with each display booth a garden of technological gadgetry.

The same companies who display their products in the exhibit halls at the annual meetings also purchase advertising space in the professional magazine *Landscape Architecture*. Examination of this publication reveals two often separate directions for landscape architectural design—one implied by the critical articles reviewing actual places and trends in professional practice and theory, the other a *de facto* norm which emerges from the beautiful glossy photographs of landscape hardware and technology. The implicit message to the practicing professionals cruising the ASLA exhibit halls or browsing *Landscape Architecture* magazine is that unless one specifies these technological products, one is not keeping abreast of one's profession. Close examination of the collective impact of these advertising ventures reveals a *de facto* philosophy of landscape design: "clean, green, and hooked on the machine." One supplier, who manufactures synthetic waterfalls, plastic porpoises, and fake coral reefs recently advertised itself directly in a full-page ad in *Landscape Architecture Magazine* as the "nature and fantasy specialists," while on the opposite page an article by a prominent architect espoused the exact opposite—a search for fresh landscape meaning based on environmental activism apart from formulaic approaches (Thayer, 1992). The juxtaposition of articles advocating environmental, social, or aesthetic considerations with advertisements suggesting technological fixes is a telling indication of the ongoing battle between technophilia and topophilia for the hearts, minds, and checkbooks of landscape architects. The battle is evident in the urban landscape. Hidden behind the architectonic, yet "green" facade of most urban landscape design is a matrix of technological support devices and systems needed to perpetuate an idealized, mechanistic, and now highly automated image of nature.

Unlike architects, whose building designs are created nearly entirely out of technological systems of manufactured or assembled man-made parts, landscape architects work in a medium consisting of both "softscape" and "hardscape," to use the profession's own jargon. "Softscape" consists of the organic, so-called "natural" materials (plants and earth), whereas "hardscape" refers to the paving, structural elements, and technological paraphernalia such as irrigation systems, lighting, erosion control devices, and drainage inlets. In recent years there has been an explosion of "hardscape" suppliers, and there are new products appearing every month. Most of these "hardscape" products have some legitimate value or application in making enduring urban landscapes. However, manufactured components and technological hardware have their own embodied costs, both economic and environmental; irrigation pipe is made from polyethylene and PVC, both petroleum byproducts, and the aluminum in outdoor furniture requires immense amounts of energy (often from hydroelectric dams on environmentally sensitive rivers) to manufacture. Teak for landscape furniture is often cut from old-growth rainforests. Furthermore, like many other fields of human endeavor in America, much of the new landscape technology seems to be driving the demand and creating its own markets. Manufactured items in the landscape are increasingly predesigned; where landscape architects once specified materials, now they are specifying whole assemblies. The creation of intentional landscapes today is moving away from the traditional detail design skills of the landscape architect and the craftsmanship of the landscape contractor toward selecting predesigned, premanufactured components from catalogs and having supplier representatives install them in the landscape to minimize liability insurance risk. In this fashion, urban landscape architecture is becoming industrial design.

Although most landscape architects are fully aware of when and where technological solutions are appropriate and necessary and when a more organic approach is called for, the producers of landscape technology products have their own momentum going, and it is driving the nature of urban landscape design more than most landscape architects care to admit. ASLA budget analyses divide revenue and expenses for the annual conventions between the "exhibit" (of technological products) portion and the "meeting" (lectures and educational sessions for members) portion. Exhibitors pay ASLA a fee to display their products in the exhibit hall, which is perused by ASLA members during the convention, while the meeting portion earns money from attendee registration fees. In 1986 the ASLA convention netted more money from the meeting attendees than from the exhibitors. Since 1986, the annual convention revenues from the educational meeting have declined each year, and in 1991 there was a net loss of revenue from the meeting, while the exhibit maintained the same high level of profit. It is easy to see that as this trend continues, technological gadgetry will play an increasingly influential role in the affairs of the landscape architecture profession and the state of the *art* of landscape architecture.[1]

Amidst the growing dependence on manufactured components in landscape construction, it is easy to forget that landscapes can actually *exist* without the technological paraphernalia that product vendors would like us to believe is necessary to our livelihood and to society in general. A competing school of thoughts is emerging in the profession which looks at the landscape primarily from an ecological point of view. Technological products allow a more antiseptic, durable, low maintenance landscape; however, the result is less apt to be truly "alive," since the generation, deterioration, recycling, and regeneration of natural materials in the landscape is what enables life to exist. The hard urban landscapes of today, while more durable and maintenance-free than ever before, and often animated by high technology, are also more sterile and "lifeless." An emerging trend seeks to reanimate urban landscapes through more concern for ecological and biological values and less technological determinism.

Technology as a Symbol of Nature

The evolution of a technological industry supporting, if not driving, the direction of intentionally designed landscapes is a manifestation of technophilia wherein *the array of material byproducts begins to serve as a symbol for the landscape itself.* Here topophilia is reinforced by technophilia to the point that the latter attitude replaces the former. Just as modern doctors often care more about the disease than the patient, landscape architecture often reveals a fascination with the support technology as a substitute for a meaningful relationship to the land. To a great extent, the purveyors of landscape equipment, together with their advertising departments and agencies, deliberately create and foster the public association of natural landscape values with their technological products. For years I have clipped advertisements out of the many landscape professional and industry magazines that arrive in my mailbox in an ongoing and informal research effort to determine the role of such advertising on landscape perceptions and expectations. Several of these advertisements are worthy of mention.

One ongoing landscape debate in the western United States is over landscape water use and conservation, and subsequently, the amount of turfgrass necessary in designed landscapes. Manufacturers of irrigation equipment technology and suppliers of turf, as might be expected, are greatly interested in the direction of such deliberations. A full-page advertisement by one irrigation supplier showed a close-up view of lush green turf extending from individual blades of grass in the foreground to a cluster of romantically out-of-focus turf irrigation spray plumes in the distant background. The caption read "Look at it this way." The hardly disguised intention of the advertisement is to influence the expected aesthetic commonly held by the landscape design readers of the magazine. By creating an aesthetic ideal of lush green landscape imagery (which cannot exist without irrigation technology in the western United States), the industry and their advertisers hope to ensure the ongoing purchase of irrigation equipment.

A more recent advertisement by another irrigation supplier features two photographic images. The top image is a stunning landscape of snow melting in a mountain stream—a beautiful example of "nature" photography by any standard. Under this photograph is the caption "Source." Below is a lush green turf landscape, again featuring turf irrigation spray heads in action. The caption under this photo reads "Resource." Here one sees a deliberate attempt to merge the natural with the technologically based imagery so that the line between them is blurred and that any positive associations with the top photograph (natural) are projected onto the bottom photo (technological product).

In 1990 there began a series of advertisements for automobiles where technophilic and topophilic values were indistinguishably blended. Prior to the gender revolution, car makers often advertised their products to the potential buying public (which was mostly male) with scantily clad female models. Subsequently society has come to recognize such advertising as sexually manipulative and degrading to women. Furthermore, women are now buying cars in increasing numbers. Looking about for substitute imagery with equally high public appeal, automakers and their ad agencies have discovered landscapes and nature. Most automobile makers show their cars traveling through rural countrysides, scenic highways, or in front of high-style architecture. Recently, however, the urge to associate the car with nature was pushed to the limit. For the first time ever, Nissan ran a TV commercial for their Infiniti car which featured a remote rural landscape *and no car image whatsoever.* Mazda followed suit by producing marketing brochures for its MPV minivan and its Navajo Sport Utility vehicle. The Mazda brochures are the first I have ever seen to *not* include an image of the car on either front or back cover. On the front of the MPV brochure is a close-up of deeply shadowed vine maple leaves with a touch of moss-covered granite in the background. Similarly, the Navajo brochure cover is a close-up photograph of a deep red sandstone rock cliff. Here are the feminine (moist, lush green foliage with dark moss) and masculine (hard, red rock) landscape equivalents of sexy human models. The advertising agency, of course, knew that women tend to dictate the sales of minivans, in which they drive their children to school, little league, and so on, and mostly men buy four-wheel-drive sport vehicles, which they often purchase for their "macho" image rather than for utilitarian purposes.

An even more recent television ad featured a TV set on the rim of the Grand

Canyon, with an image of the canyon on the TV screen. A child exclaims exuberantly to his father about seeing the Grand Canyon, while looking at the screen image, not the real canyon beyond. In a strange, ironic convolution, the substitution of nature/landscape imagery for technological imagery implies its opposite; if nature equals technology, then technology can equal nature. If we can't go to Canyon de Chelly to see the real rock cliffs, we can at least watch TV or drive our sport truck.

Another venue for this substitution of technophilia for topophilic affection is the garden catalog. Smith and Hawken, the up-scale supplier of gardening tools and equipment, must have realized long ago that America's infatuation with tools and technology allowed not only the tools to represent the garden, but the tool *catalog* to do so as well. Looking at garden catalogs stimulates both our technophilic and topophilic urges, and in the absence of adequate time and/or venue for real gardening, becomes a symbolic act in lieu of gardening itself.

The most salient example of technophilic displacement of tophophilia is the evolution of the now-immense outdoor recreational product market. Concurrent with the development of appreciation for wilderness has been an explosion of technologies to support "wildland" recreation. Boats for bass fisherman now frequently feature small electric trolling motors, 150-hp outboard engines for streaking between bass holes at 40 mph, and three-dimensional, computer graphic fish-finding sonar which beeps when fish are located. Like the ASLA exhibits, hunting and fishing shows turn urban exhibit halls into surrogate wild landscapes, complete with trout in tanks, hunting dog trials, all-terrain vehicle demonstrations, and so forth. In the tradition of L. L. Bean, the catalogs of outdoor equipment suppliers feature enticing scenes of hunting, fishing, backpacking, mountain climbing, or canoeing in magnificent natural landscapes punctuated by people (usually solitary or numbering only a few) enjoying the outdoors, while inside the catalog, page after page of products are arrayed. The names of the companies and product lines speak of their intended relationship to the human bond with natural landscapes: Sierra Designs, Trek, North Face, Mountain Safety Research, Wilderness Trails, Mad River Canoe Company, and so on. The names of a few companies (e.g., Perception kayaks) allude to the heightened sense of awareness that using their products in wild landscapes will surely bring.

Paramount among examples of vicarious love of nature personified in high-tech equipment is the retail chain Recreational Equipment, Inc. (REI) which was started in Seattle by mountaineering enthusiasts. The REI retail stores are also surrogate natural landscapes, where the products of recreational technology conjure up images of the types of places and experiences in which the equipment is to be used. There are displays of tents, sleeping bags, canoes, kayaks, mountain bicycles, outdoor stoves, freeze-dried food, rainwear, and books on nature, wilderness travel, camping, survival, and environmental stewardship. The REI retail store walls are graced with color posters by the best outdoor photographers. Most retail stores have an indoor rock climbing

REI showrooms like this one in Salt Lake City are surrogate wildland recreation landscapes, where displays of outdoor recreation products symbolize or "stand in for" the places where they are typically used. Photograph by Steve Tregeale.

wall (the rock is synthetic, of course). Only "muscle-powered" outdoor recreational gear is carried by the Co-op—products and clothing for climbing, camping, backpacking, bicycling, paddle sports, skiing, walking, and hiking. Buyers seeking hunting rifles, power boats, or off-road motorcycles must look elsewhere. At REI stores the spirit of environmental stewardship abounds. REI's environmental centers (located in every retail store) offer educational resources on how people may get involved in local conservation activities. Owned by its members (I am one), REI's board of directors frequently lends financial and material support to outdoor explorations and conservation causes. If one is an outdoor enthusiast, walking into an REI showroom is a profoundly positive experience wherein the products themselves conjure up both the reminiscence of past outdoor adventures as well as anticipation of landscape experiences to come.

There appears to be no end to the creative manipulation of technology to facilitate appreciation of the environment. Real "wilderness" experience once consisted of cooking over a fire and drinking out of the stream. Curiously, if backpackers want to drink water in the wilderness, they must first use one of several, high-tech filters now available for removing the debilitating Giardia microbe from wilderness waters. It is a sad commentary that the free-flowing waters of back-country streams and lakes are now too dangerous to drink, and the firewood too scarce or air already too laden with CO_2 to build a fire, but these drawbacks are quickly made up for by a plethora of technological products available to the backpacker. The ownership and use of the small, fuel-efficient gas stove for backpacking in the wilderness now signifies the utmost level of respect for the land, where fuel wood is scarce and open fires are considered a major breach of environmental etiquette. In the replacement of the campfire by the high-tech stove, the symbolic substitution of technophilia for topophilia is complete.

The Silicon Landscape

As America's technophilic preoccupations turn from mechanical movement and conversion of material toward electronic manipulation of information, the notion of landscape is being profoundly affected. Landscape, as the mitigating construct between nature and human presence, ultimately must bridge the gap between a rapidly evolving technology and a changing definition of nature. In addition to the computer-aided technical design done by engineers, computer technology is now routinely applied in the development of geographic information systems (GIS), where a land area is divided into cells and data concerning slope, wildlife habitat, soil character, sun angles, hydrological features, visibility from distant points, and so forth, may be stored, retrieved, and manipulated relative to each cell. Data analysis performed using this computer layering system adds a significant new, invisible dimension to the land itself, allowing the breakdown of any landscape into its component parts and the evaluation of the land area in question for many prospective conditions from preservation through intense development. Landscapes can now be represented entirely by digital data and mathematical algorithms, and one may now employ computer animation programs to "fly" in three dimensions through these silicon landscape surrogates in order to learn about the real landscapes they purport to represent. The model of the Los Angeles region produced by Jet Propulsion Laboratory is a tour de force of the power of the computer to simulate the real landscape in real time. When seen on television by people familiar with the Los Angeles area, it is actually difficult to discern whether one is seeing the real thing or a facsimile.

The ability to represent any land area by numerical data and mathematical algorithms has both profound positive and negative implications. As widespread social adoption of technology increasingly impacts the actual landscape, the ability to measure, monitor, and hopefully, predict the consequences of human action to the land becomes both inevitable and essential. Underlying the evolution of computer-based land analysis and simulation are two implications. The first implication is that technology's actual, negative consequences to real landscapes can best be controlled by employing technology's own information and decision-making capabilities to counteract it. Proponents of the inevitability and necessity of technological development point optimistically to the rapid advances in GIS processing as a means for staying

This photo is a "frozen" video screen image from L.A.: the Movie, *an animated, computer-simulated flight around the Los Angeles area created at the Jet Propulsion Laboratory. The movie was synthesized from one LANDSAT aerial photograph taken from an altitude of 580 miles and combined with topographic data. The scene above is of Santa Anita Racetrack, Arcadia, and the San Gabriel Mountains in the background. The original movie is in color.*

on top of actual impacts on the land wrought largely by the negative impacts of technology. Models of particular landscapes can be "constructed" graphically and mathematically, subjected to various hypothetical scenarios of human intervention and change, and evaluated to determine the best possible outcome. Unfortunately, there is a second, less-recognized implication. These same capabilities for safeguarding actual landscapes can be used to simulate imaginary ones, and a potentially dangerous and inevitable consequence emerges in the blurring of the line between the simulation and the reality, or the substitution of one for the other. Like most technologies, the new computer simulation cuts both ways, as I elaborate in Chapter 8.

War, Land, and Technophilia

The Persian Gulf War of 1991 revealed the extent to which America is preoccupied with technology and the degree to which information technology can both literally and figuratively impact landscape. Images of television-guided "smart bombs" homing in on Iraqi targets are now emblazoned on the American mind. Cruise missiles literally followed digitally stored road maps, turning corners at major street intersections to destroy targets in Baghdad. Regardless of one's opinion of the war and its causes, two of its effects cannot be denied. First, the production of weapons and quasi-"intelligent" guidance systems is now an area of technology in which the United States can still claim supremacy. As with the atomic bomb and the moon landing, American technophilia was effectively demonstrated to the world by the Persian Gulf War, and our so-called preeminence as a world technological power was once again assured. Second, a great blow was struck to the earth itself, which, for months afterward, lay polluted and burning; a political war was won, while an environmental war was lost; American technophilia had thoroughly overwhelmed the simple human bonds to the desert landscapes of Kuwait and Iraq.

Amid the almost incessant TV coverage of the war I recall a public television broadcast of research findings by Jane Goodall as she observed chimpanzees in Africa. A small, young male chimpanzee discovered one of Goodall's empty metal fuel cans and by rolling it around among his fellow troupe members and making an impressive racket in his rainforest landscape, he was able to intimidate the larger, previously dominant male and assume the position of "alpha" male for himself. Like humans, chimpanzees engage in highly theatrical male dominance displays, and this incident constituted the discovery and intentional use of a "tool" as an object of personal power and status. I was reminded of the great parades of missiles in Baghdad, the prewar cover stories in *Newsweek* and *Time* showing off America's smart weapons, the full-color spreads on high-tech American jet fighters and bombers, and the media sparring between Saddam Hussein and George Bush. As has been the case since the dawn of human consciousness, the *making* of the tools seems to come naturally—technophilia presents itself almost without effort, yet the consequences of the *use* of our technological tools we can rarely anticipate, and seem to proceed with few restraints. It is almost as if, once created, the products of our technology assume an animate form of their own and go about their evolution oblivious to our concerns or their effects. No one had to file an environmental impact statement for the Persian Gulf War. After the war, Kurdistan lay in shambles, hundreds of thousands of people died, the region was destabilized, vast tracts of land were devastated, water and air were polluted, and for some time, one tenth of the world's daily supply of oil burned uselessly into the atmosphere over Kuwait. To the more obvious overt and covert reasons for the Persian Gulf war—curbing an arrogant dictator, "liberating" Kuwait, ensuring American hegemony in an oil-rich region, ridding the nation of Vietnam War "losers" guilt—must be added another obvious reason: *we were infatuated with our military technology and wanted to see how it worked.* It worked extraordinarily well, and the environment became the Persian Gulf war's most obvious loser.

We are a culture so shaped by technology that any attempt to outwardly distinguish between our affection for nature and the earth and our dependent fascination with technology is likely to be impossible. The landscape we inhabit daily is a field of perceptual stimuli made up substantially of our own technical creations and our own alterations to the natural context. Increas-

An abandoned car sits in a pool of oil in Kuwait after the Persian Gulf War. In the background, oil burns uselessly, polluting the air. Photograph by Steve McCurry, Magnum.

ingly, our infatuation with technology and our use of its consumer products seems to be a necessary, intervening step enabling us to act out our affection for land and landscape. The blurring of the line between technology and nature and the incorporation of the two concepts into one might be beneficial if the construct of technology to which we subscribed was truly benign and supportive of the values we admire in nature. But this is not usually the case. Technology has another persona, a dark side, a fatal flaw which prevents us from accepting it fully into our hearts. We have allowed technology to move beyond a *means* for living; it is now becoming the principal *reason*. If there is any true relationship between today's technology and nature, it is that technology, like nature, now has a life of its own. We have become, as Leo Marx (1963) wrote in paraphrase of Thoreau, the "tools of our tools."

NOTES

1. In 1992, I served on a national ASLA committee to make recommendations on future annual convention sites. In spite of my minority view, the committee recommended that all locations for future annual conventions continue to be located only at hotel or convention center facilities which could house the immense exhibit of commercial and technical product suppliers.

3

Technophobia and Landscape Guilt

It is possible that ugliness in the works of man, whether architectural or landscape, did not arise until there came a conflict between the use of the surface of the earth and the use of what lay beneath.

SIR GEOFFREY JELLICOE

On July 14, 1991 a Southern Pacific freight train derailed on the Cantara Loop just south of Mount Shasta near Dunsmuir, California, and a tank car filled with the weed killer metam sodium dumped most of its poisonous contents directly into the upper Sacramento River, one of California's blue-ribbon trout streams. Within hours, 45 miles of river were completely sterilized. The dead fish floated belly up and lodged in the rocks from Dunsmuir to Shasta Reservoir. Noxious fumes caused the evacuation of most of the towns-people of Dunsmuir, and virtually all of the people residing along the down-stream river corridor; many would later report long periods of illness, nausea, weakness, and skin lesions. Leaves and branches from dead trees by the river-side crackled underfoot, and a state Fish and Game biologist who conducted a dive in the river shortly after the spill reported that the "whole aquatic ecosystem—every last living thing—was gone. It was all dead."

In a special editorial to the *Sacramento Bee* on October 13, 1991, attorney William L. Berry, Jr. described his own complex range of feelings in reaction to the accident. Berry had grown up around trains, and while in college took a summer job as a Southern Pacific brakeman. He had also learned to fly fish with his father in the Sacramento River south of Dunsmuir, staying in the old motels overlooking the river within sight and sound of both river and railway. In Berry's words, "those sounds seemed a perfect blend of two dearly held themes in my life's experience."

After buying a vacation cabin on the river later in life, Berry watched as the railroad grew more careless with cargo, roadbed conditions, and freight train configurations. Then, in 1976, he felt the consequences of a foreboding event; the spill of detergent from derailed tank cars on the Cantara Loop. This early

The 1991 Sacramento River chemical spill. Photograph by Jay Mather.

spill had killed trout for several miles downriver, and could have been prevented were it not for cost-cutting measures, such as the failure to include a
"pusher" engine in the train as it snaked down the Cantara Loop from Mount
Shasta. Berry began writing letters and testifying at hearings in a futile attempt to reverse the railroad's lax safety precautions. When the recent, inevitably major spill occurred, he was angry and devastated, and ended his
editorial:

> But it will be very hard for me to listen to the sound of trains. I heard them on that
> first visit to Dunsmuir after the spill, and they were near obscene as they growled up
> the canyon and snuffed out the voice of the river.

I, too, have fly fished for trout in the Upper Sacramento near Dunsmuir, and
like Berry, passed through the horrible stench of noxious gasses from the spill
while en route to Alaska on Interstate 5 through the canyon. The Dunsmuir
spill struck me as an Exxon Valdez debacle in miniature—happening in my
own bioregion to places of personal importance. Most of us have a story like
Berry's tucked away somewhere—a tale of affection for a place of nature
violated by a technology somehow gone wrong. Berry's affection for the river
(topophilia) and for the railroad in general (technophilia) were both victims of
technophobia—the sinking, pit-of-the stomach feeling that technology upon
which we depend has gotten the best of us, and is now beginning to destroy
our favorite places. Arguably, the fault lay less with the technology of railroads

than with penny-pinching management errors and a lack of concern for the river as anything other than a transportation corridor and occasional dumping ground for the railroad. But humans will always make mistakes. Technologies, unfortunately, magnify them.

For Leo Marx (1963), the railroad is the formative symbol of technology in American culture:

> There is nothing in the visible landscape—no tradition, no standard, no institution—capable of standing up to the forces of which the railroad is the symbol. (pp. 352–353)

Yet the railroad today is also a beacon of nostalgic affection for Americans—a symbol often capable of wrapping technophilia and topophilia together in one blanket. William Berry's lamentation of the freight train chemical spill in the Sacramento River Canyon is symbolic of an American loss of innocence—no longer does it seem possible for topophilia and technophilia to be so innocently bonded. A combination of bureaucratic bungling, mechanical sloppiness, and chemical potency resulted in an ecological disaster capable of wholesale reversal of the meaning of a river landscape from the harmonious marriage of the machine and nature to a hideous rape. For Berry and all of us like him, perhaps the most tragic consequence is the realization that all of us, by unselfconscious participation in modern life where some of our consumer goods are toxic and arrive by rail, participate in such tragedies. We share a perceived burden of guilt over technological assaults on nature, and when fed back into the process of landscape development itself, this "landscape" guilt achieves visible and spatial form. The triangle is now complete; our reverence for earth and nature is tied both to a fascinated addiction to technology and to technology's negative impacts to our earthly context. Like some tensile form, this three-pointed star represents the true dilemma of the modern landscape.

The Empire of Technology

There are 184 million registered motor vehicles in the United States which consume 128 billion gallons of fuel per year. There are 4 million linear miles of paved roads and streets, 202 million television sets, and 55 million microwave ovens. Forty-five million personal computers are used in households, and 14 million are used for business. The United States has 103 million housing units, 61 million of which are single-family detached homes. Sixty-five million homes are air conditioned. Ninety-seven percent of all United States citizens live in cities whose average residential densities are five houses per acre or greater (U.S. Bureau of the Census, 1990). American companies produce over 86 million tons of synthetic organic chemicals, apply 19 million tons of chemical fertilizer to the soil, emit 48 million tons of nitrous oxide, sulfur

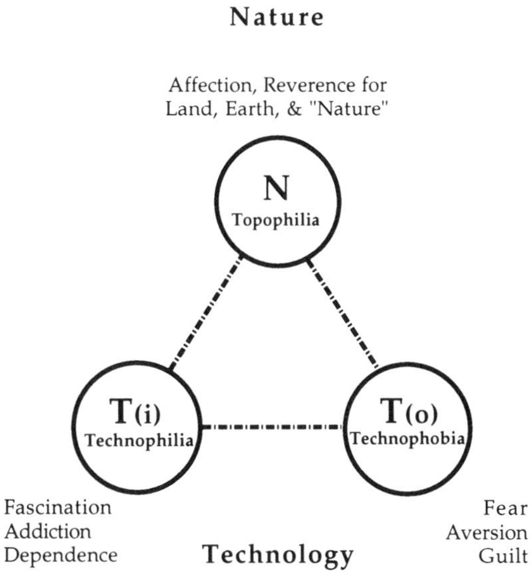

Nature

Affection, Reverence for
Land, Earth, & "Nature"

N
Topophilia

T(i)
Technophilia

T(o)
Technophobia

Fascination
Addiction
Dependence

Technology

Fear
Aversion
Guilt

The essential triangle of conflict in the American landscape; affection for land and nature collide with a love–hate ambivalence toward technology.

dioxide, and particulates into the atmosphere, and release 250 thousand tons of toxic chemicals into the water each year. Two hundred ten million tons of solid waste are buried in American landfills each year. To sustain the population of American towns and cities for one year, 11 trillion gallons of captured water are required. To feed its people, American agriculture uses 140 trillion gallons of water *per day*, or 511×10^{11} gallons per year (Worldwatch Institute, 1990). From these staggering numbers, we are able to construct a vivid mental image of the extent to which technology has altered our landscape. Today we live in a physical world dominated by the products of our own invention. A high percentage of the actual field of vision throughout which we work, play, reside, and travel each day has been constructed or conspicuously altered by human hands and machines. Our basic functional interactions with the landscape—the air we breath, the water we drink and in which we bathe, the food we eat, the waste we pass on—are altered or defined by technology. We are tied to the land by a complex system of intervening technologies without which most of us would not survive.

In spite of arguments that American cultural heritage set about early on to "conquer" and subdue nature, such a vast degree of impact on the land was not the intent of technology; technological development merely proceeded in relative ignorance of environmental consequences. America followed a pattern of social and technological development set in motion several hundred years ago and only refined in the modern era. The result has been a decidedly ambivalent attitude. Americans alive today grew up with accelerated technological change and are fascinated with technology, eager to consume its material goods, dependent upon it as a means of economic livelihood, yet appalled at its impact on local landscapes, communities, natural resources and ecosystems. *Technophobia*—the suspicion, fear, and aversion to certain technologies and their physical manifestations—is now as inherent in the everyday landscape as technophilia. To understand how this ambivalence emerged requires a discussion of the philosophical and social underpinnings of technology in America.

It is tempting to look at our apparent subservience to the technologies in our daily lives as the product of a monolithic technological determinism, where scientific discoveries emerging from pure research lead to technological applications and thence to marketable products which are sold widely to a compliant, if not eager, consuming public, with the result that our social structures are irrevocably and uncontrollably altered and transformed. Although there are elements of truth in this scenario, this model of technological determinism ignores the social and political consequences in which technology evolves and the limited yet significant social choices we can and have made regarding the direction technology takes. Philosopher Langdon Winner (1986) prefers the model of "technological somnambulism," likening our unguided development of technology to "sleepwalking"—ambling unconsciously through the process of reconstructing our worlds by technological means with little conscious concern for where we are going. In Winner's view, technological development yields new "forms of life," arguing that telephony, automobility, electric lighting, and computing change human behavior and social patterns in very powerful ways, making life without them scarcely thinkable. For Winner, technological systems carry implicit social systems, altering the balance of *power* and *authority* in ways which we either do not understand or choose to ignore. Although he states that blaming the hardware is sometimes worse than blaming the victim, Winner argues that technological systems carry political significance in their own right, and "appear to require or to be strongly compatible with particular kinds of political relationships" (p. 22). Clearly, the need to control the proliferation of nuclear fuels, for example, leads to a nuclear technology that is accompanied by large scale, highly centralized, authoritarian social structures, while the use of certain renewable resource technologies, such as solar energy, allows social structures which are more decentralized and flexible. That many of our current technologies lead to centralized, authoritarian hierarchies should be news to no one. A study I conducted with Heather Hansen, for example, found that although people wish to have more of a say in the choice of fuel sources and technologies which produce their electrical energy, they are content to let the local public utility company make most of the decisions about their energy supply (Thayer and Hansen, 1989). The energy distribution system, for example, is a technology which few people really understand, yet most accept with blind faith as a given until the relatively cheap price of their energy is raised or their supply interrupted.

Concurrent with the evolution of machine power was an evolution away from personal control of the machines by those doing the work toward centralized control by remote administrative bureaucracies. Farm animals, horse-drawn carriages, and woodlots gave way not only to hydroelectric dams, fossil fuel power plants, and gasoline, but to utility companies and oil conglomerates. By the mid-nineteenth century, the old social hierarchies based on religion and tradition had come under attack, only to be replaced by the centralized hierarchies of modern technology. The tyranny by social institutions in the seventeenth and eighteenth centuries which led to the migration of Europeans to America was ultimately replaced by the tyranny of large-scale technological systems.

Accompanying this shift to the centralized, authoritarian, hierarchical structure for most technological necessities was the growth in the presumption that in America, material abundance and personal freedom were synonymous. Winner (1986) writes:

> Material abundance would make it possible for everybody to have enough to be perfectly happy. Eventually Americans took this notion to be a generally applicable theory: economic enterprise driven by the engine of technical improvement was the very essence of human freedom. (p. 45)

A corollary to this theory emerged that technology would build a good society *automatically*, and that any improvement in the human condition could be correlated with the efficiency of its technological systems. By the twentieth century, Americans had become so addicted to material gains from modern technology that "the prevailing consensus seems to be that people love a life of high consumption, tremble at the thought that it might end, and are displeased about having to clean up the messes that modern technologies sometimes bring" (Winner, 1986, p. 51).

The irony in the replacement of socially based tyranny by technologically derived tyranny is that we are no more "free" than we ever were. The social institutions of the seventeenth century Europe and early eighteenth century America were specific targets for which individuals or groups could be singled out as responsible for whatever ills society blamed on them (e.g., the King of England's role in the Boston Tea Party). In contrast, modern technological tyranny is harder to pin on any one group, since it largely feeds on our own appetite for the material fruits of technological production and the ubiquitous, slippery nature of the technological systems themselves. It is hard to blame Lee Iacocca or "Ma Bell" for the deleterious social or environmental impacts of automobiles or telephones when we are driving down the freeway talking into our cellular phones.

Conscious and deliberate development of technology leads to widespread adoption of its material products and a concurrent revolution in the social structures associated with these technologies. Human *use* of the technologies requires conformance to the evolving social norms resulting from the technology, even though for many of the technologies, consumption still centers

Americans have been led to believe their lives will automatically be made better by technology. Technology does not necessarily fulfill this implicit expectation.

on the individual. At first glance, the automobile could be considered a highly decentralized, theoretically "democratic" technology. Individuals have control over the purchase and use of automobiles according to their own tastes and needs. Closer inspection, however, reveals that automobilia is merely a centralized authoritarian technology "atomized" to consumers in discreet bundles; the production of roads, gasoline, and autos themselves is concentrated in a few hierarchical institutions with a virtual stranglehold on government policy.

Technophobia: The Dilemma of Power and Powerlessness

It seems to be an American tradition to resist social change from political forces while blindly accepting the social transformations inherent in technological advances without question. Further examination of this apparent inconsistency reveals that while we reject heavy-handed government by politicians *consciously,* we react to the tyrannical and deleterious effects of technology on a *subconscious* level. Politicians speak to us through rhetoric captured by the news media before the fact, yet *technology talks to us through its manifestations on the landscape after the fact.* As the twentieth century comes to a close and we see clearly the vastness of the physical impact of our technological creature comforts on the landscape, we are somehow uncomfortable. Technologies such as the automobile, which are marketed to us as highly symbolic devices aimed at increasing our sense of personal power, freedom, and status, may actually result in curtailment of our power and freedom. A 200 hp prestige car begins to look and feel ridiculous when trapped in a traffic jam by thousands of other people's prestige automobiles, and we are suddenly unable to make it home for dinner. Automobiles are designed and marketed as if they were individual elements in the landscape. Advertisements for cars usually feature only one vehicle by itself in a background of natural scenery, pastoral romanticism, or urban sophistication—rarely are any other vehicles shown in the picture. However, it is the multiplication of the effect of personal car ownership by 150 million that tends to render the individual powerless. The automobile is acceptable and even highly desirable in the landscape as a private social symbol, but when lost in an anonymous sea of parking or stalled in freeway gridlock, any individualism in the design or ownership of the automobile is overwhelmed by sheer numbers. Yet the landscape, with the exception of our homes and private gardens, reflects the influences of the masses. Individual design considerations dissolve with larger scale as the widespread adoption of technologies drives the form of the land. No technology—not even the railroad—has had more of an effect on the form of the landscape we see every day than the automobile. It has shaped our houses, streets, neighborhoods, cities, regions and our national landscape. One can hardly imagine a political, social, or ecological crisis powerful enough to wrench American hands from the steering wheel. Each successive lesson not learned—the latest being a costly Persian Gulf War—only gives us white knuckles as we clutch the wheel ever harder.

It is quite possible that nothing in our genetic constitution has prepared us to live in a world where much of the visual field we see day to day consists of man-made elements, and much of our basic relationship to landscape is filtered through technology. We receive some of the information about our physical world partly by direct feedback—we *experience* first hand the snarled traffic and choked air. Other technological impacts we are only told about by the news media and cannot see, such as the hole in the ozone layer or the increase in global temperatures. Although the relationship of what we can *see* in the landscape and what we *know* is at the root of our problem, we form opinions about the quality of our world through both direct experience and indirect communication. When unable to anchor our increasing environmental awareness to actual visible elements in our immediate landscape, our creative imagination takes over, filling in the blanks with negative imagery. Much of what we conclude about the condition of the environment these days is negative. We feel a deep sense of guilt and shame over what our technological habits have done to the land, to our ecosystems, and to "nature" and the planet as a whole

Countless news stories, public television shows, advertisements, books, and

The traffic jam is an ironic symbol of technological power and personal powerlessness.

magazine articles acknowledge this environmental guilt. Many corporations now exploit it for corporate benefit. "Green" marketing guides have become fashionable. The catalog from one modern women's clothing manufacturer deftly juxtaposes the various environmental dilemmas and challenges we face in the form of brief questions (e.g., "wildlife habitats or an Astroturf world?") next to shots of stylishly-clothed young women in landscape settings of glistening water, solid rock, or beige sand. The catalog is printed on recycled paper, of course, and a general concern for the environment is both implied by the pictures and directly claimed by the manufacturer, *but the questions are not answered.* Taking a stand on any of the environmental issues used in the advertising copy would potentially exclude 50% of the possible market. Instead, the association of the product with the environmental *issue* itself is used as the teaser to sell the clothing. The *awareness of the problem* and the guilt we feel over the environmental condition is presumed, yet the solutions are not.

Environmental Guilt

Dictionaries define "guilt" as the *fact* or state of having committed an offense, crime, or violation against some moral or ethical code, or the *feeling* of responsibility or remorse for such an offense or crime, whether the offense is real or imaginary. An individual is only capable of feeling guilt if he or she adheres to some moral or ethical code against which any transgression is measured. I won't feel guilty if I consider my crime trivial in the first place. All societies, in their own ways, establish moral or ethical codes of behavior which individuals are presumed to respect. An individual may feel no guilt if the transgression of one code is justified under some presumably higher standard. For example, one might not feel guilty for exceeding the speed limit while driving a laboring mother-to-be to the obstetrics ward. On the other hand, feelings of guilt may emerge in certain members of society in relation to a social code previously broken by others—European Americans may feel guilty about their forefather's near extermination of Native Americans or their enslavement of African Americans, for example—even though the individuals feeling guilty were not the actual transgressors of the code, but only representatives or associates of those doing the transgression (hence guilt by "association"). Guilt can be experienced by both individuals and whole cultures, as with the case of the Germans in relationship to the holocaust in World War II.

A central premise of this book is that *Americans, in increasing numbers and intensities, feel guilty about what technological development has done to the landscape, to "nature," and to the earth.* Implicit in this definition of "environmental guilt" is the assumption of a code of ethics or morals with respect to the land that somehow, when transgressed, causes feelings of unease on the part of society, either individually or collectively. If no such code of morals or ethics existed, there would be no environmental guilt. But environmental guilt is both common and increasing, and its very existence implies that some sort of environmental ethic, however latent or suppressed, is operative in today's culture.

In the literature of environmental ethics, discussions about environment and guilt often lead back to assumptions or claims about religious foundations. In religious terms, environmental guilt is nothing new. The Judeo-Christian creation myth is only one of many religious creation myths to presume a fallen position for humans in relation to the earth. Like Adam and Eve of Judaism and Christianity, the original mythical humans of many religious traditions were somehow expelled from the garden-like purity of a primeval world and destined perpetually to atone for their sins against the environment. Even the unique creation story of the Hopi assumed the evolution of "imperfect" humans through four different "worlds." Each time the ancestral people selfishly failed to maintain respect for one another and for the plans of the Creator, Taiowa, their world was destroyed and a chosen few were selectively allowed entrance into the next world. In the Hopi legends, mankind was born perfect, yet fell from grace by neglecting to respect the earth and fellow humans (Waters, 1963). In the Judeo-Christian myth, mankind, having originally violated the laws of the garden, is a guilty party destined to search in vain for reentrance to it.

Two different forms of the ancient Hopi Emergence or "Mother Earth" symbol, representing the spiritual rebirth of the Hopi people from one world to the next. Drawings by Oswald White Bear Fredericks from the Book of the Hopi, *by Frank Waters (1963).*

The Controversy Over Christianity and the Environment

The presumption of a theological origin of the modern ecological crisis has been intensely and inconclusively debated since Lynn White's provocative 1966 address to the American Association for Advancement of Science. White initiated a lasting controversy when he placed responsibility for the environmental crisis on Judeo-Christian religious traditions which he claimed anthropocentrically defined man as being made in the image of God, thereby excluding from moral or ethical consideration all other living entities (White, 1967). White's arguments were subsequently echoed by landscape architect Ian McHarg in his book *Design With Nature* (1969), which outlined a practical means of planning land areas by overlay mapping of presumably objective, scientific data. By tapping a contemporaneous dissatisfaction with Judeo-Christian dogma in the late 1960s and 1970s, this view provided an early rallying point for the loose coalescence of established and nascent philosophies behind the early environmental movement (Chase, 1987).

The controversy stemming from White's paper opens a critical and unavoidable point of discussion regarding the relationship, if any, between Christianity and environmental guilt. Arguably, the Bible itself offers little in the way of elaboration of the notions of nature, dominion and stewardship beyond the first book of Genesis. Most of the modern debate has centered around the exegetical literary interpretation of Christian theology and the historical analysis of the words and actions of peoples over the course of two thousand years. This topic could consume many additional volumes; I will limit my discussion to several scholars whose views circumscribe the issue, often from opposing positions: Roderick Nash (1967), Clarence Glacken (1967), Jaques Ellul (1964), Arne Naess (1989), Thomas Berry (1988), and Rene Dubos (1980).

Wilderness historian Roderick Nash was among the first to pick up White's standard. Nash's focus is on wilderness as a correlate of nature and, historically, as both a foreboding, accursed land and a disciplinary venue or force leading to the purification of faith. In his interpretation, early Christian theology placed man in a middle position closer to God than nature, and because of this, nature was essentially secularized. Preoccupation with nature was thought to detract from man's true mission of salvation and proper relationship to God. Nash also describes the Puritan position that wilderness was something evil to be overcome, and something wild from which a garden was to be carved. Nash alludes to the New England colonists seeing themselves as "Christ's Army" in a war against wilderness, and he concurs with de Toqueville's assumption that living amidst the wilderness produced a bias against it among the early colonists.[1]

Clarence Glacken's *Traces on the Rhodian Shore* (1967) is considered by many to be the definitive analysis of nature and culture in early Western thought and philosophy. Glacken forged an analysis of Christian theology based upon the notion of *creation*. "Christianity and the ideas which lay behind it is a religion and a philosophy of creation. It is preoccupied with the Creator, with the things he created and their relationships to him and among themselves" (p. 168). In a thoughtfully balanced display of scholarship, Glacken identifies in Christianity both a *contemptus mundi*, "a rejection literally of the earth as the dwelling place of man, a distaste for, and disinterest in, nature" as well as an opposing *"theologica naturalis*, the belief that one can find in the creation the handiwork of a reasonable, loving, and beneficent creator" (p. 161). Humans were placed in a middle position between God and the rest of his creation, and were given dominion over them as well as responsibility for them. But since salvation was to be gained by worshipping the Creator directly, not the creature, this fundamental position had the effect of secularizing the nonhuman earth. God was "transcendent, the creation is by him, but not of him, and it is only a partial teacher" (p. 161). Hence, Glacken echoes other scholars and theologians (or more likely, they echo him) who find in Christian tradition a basis for ignoring the possibility of a sacred earth.

On the other hand, Glacken also finds in the biblical wisdom literature "evidence of a love for and delight in nature and of a belief that it is a manifestation of God's handiwork" (p. 161). In Saint Francis of Assisi's *Canticle of Brother Sun*, written in the last two years of the saint's life, Glacken finds strong support for the notion of a *theologica naturalis*, as St. Francis offers praise for the Lord and all his creatures, including Sister Moon, Brother Wind, Brother Fire, Sister Mother Earth, and manifold other living entities. In St. Thomas's *Summa Theologiae*, Glacken sees "the idea of order, planning, and design . . . joined with thoughts on the beauty of the creation, described in the Scriptures to produce a rigorous natural theology" (p. 231). Glacken's conclusion is that "Man's power as a vice-regent of God on earth is part of the design of the creation and there is in this fully elaborated conception far less room for arrogance and pride than the bare reading of the words would suggest" (p. 166). In the Christian idea of creation is found Glacken's "design hypothesis"—a unique bond between God, humans, and the earth, and an explanation for the dilemma of dominion and stewardship with respect to nature. God both establishes humanity's position as unique and superior among his creations, but by providing the natural world for continuation of his handiwork through human action, God gives humans the difficult responsibility of stewardship—a creative stewardship implying both alteration of and care for nature.

Christianity and Technology

Although many have attempted to sort out Christianity's attitude toward the natural world, few scholars have addressed its implications to the genesis of technology. French sociologist and historian Jaques Ellul (1964) adds vital clarity to this issue by challenging the supposed Christian foundations of the Western conquest of nature. Ellul, who as a Catholic layman was active in the ecumenical movement, prefers to examine the sociological and historical evidence of religious influence rather than the dogma itself. Looking not so much at the construction of the idea of nature as at the genesis of industry and technology, Ellul notes that the early Christian era, from the fourth to the fourteenth century, is identified with the "breakdown of the established Roman technique in every area—on the level of organization as well as in the construction of cities, in industry, and in transport" (p. 33). Early Christians placed far greater importance on theological pursuits than practical technique, and far from being considered proponents of invention, science, and technology (and hence environmental exploitation), Christianity could be considered an historic hindrance to the evolution of technological advances in agriculture and industry. This is a far cry from being the root cause of environmental guilt.

While also admitting that Christianity may have secularized nature by placing humans in a middle position superior to the rest of creation, Ellul finds in early Christian traditions and practices no support, either moral or evidential, for a predisposition toward technology or its exploitation of the earth. By contrast, he finds evidence of great Christian resistance to science, objective technique, and industry well into the seventeenth century, when the transformation to the secular, scientific world view identified with Galileo, Bacon, and Descartes was well established. In the secularized and mechanized social systems that followed this transition, Ellul finds the true industrial revolution (and hence the origins of technologically based desecration of the environment). Previous to this time, Christian ideology and its hardened moral positions actually constituted a set of taboos: "the natural order must not be tampered with and anything new must be submitted to moral judgment" (p. 37).

By the time of the Puritan colonization of New England, however, these prevailing religious taboos against practical and utilitarian endeavors had all but dissolved. The Puritan Calvinists of New England (whose antipathy toward the wilderness is ascribed by Nash as a root cause of environmental desecration in early American history) believed strongly in predestination, an austere and religious life where affairs of church and state were separate, and in the piety of hard work, enterprise, and utilitarian pursuits. After politically failing to topple the Church of England, the English Puritans brought a "practical and utilitarian mentality" to America "that emphasized the use and even the exploitation of the good things of this world given by God to men." Ellul concludes that "The relationship of this trend to the development of capitalism is well known" (p. 56).

It is clear from Ellul's point of view that the systematic ascendency and increasing dominion of science and technology over humanity, however, not its incorporation into Puritan philosophy, is the predominant influence in the modern world. Ellul debunks the idea of a golden age of science and technology, likening it more to a dictatorship: "In comparison, Hitler's was a trifling affair. That it is to be a dictatorship of test tubes rather than of hobnailed boots will not make it any less of a dictatorship" (p. 434). Nearly 30 years after Ellul wrote those words, the idea of a dictatorship of test tubes is ironically implicit in the projections of biotechnologists, and is vigorously protested by many environmentalists, some of whom are motivated by strong religious beliefs.

Compassion From a Deep Ecologist; Critique by a Christian Monk

The ironies of the "Christianity/environmental crisis" debate do not stop there. Arne Naess, a Norwegian philosopher, is credited with the term "Deep Ecology," and is the *de facto* founder of the movement now known by that name—a movement which has been highly critical of the theological position toward the environment ascribed to Christianity (Devall and Sessions, 1985). Yet upon examination, the reader finds in Naess' recent views on Christian theology (Naess and Rothenberg, 1989) surprisingly strong and optimistic support for an ecological consciousness based on Christian foundations. While also echoing Glacken's notion of a Christian *contemptus mundi,* emphasizing the direct and transcendent worship of God as opposed to preoccupation with nature, Naess emphasizes that in biblical tradition God gives humanity "rights of use, not property rights" (p. 184). Humans are to go forth and multiply to fill the earth, but not by squeezing other creatures out. Naess notes that throughout history, the Bible has been used to support vastly different and mutually inconsistent positions. He finds in the ideas behind Christian humility and stewardship the possibility of a

> strengthening of awareness in ecological responsibility. *The religious background for such an awareness is an irreplaceable plus* (italics original). . . . A person's opinion about the ecological movement cannot be derived from the fact that he or she

Anglican chapel near the Alaska Highway, Hudson Hope, British Columbia, Canada.

"believes in the Bible" . . . Christian theologians who have studied mankind's critical ecological situation tend to embrace the ecological movement, and they find full support in the Bible. (pp. 186–187)

Naess concludes that Christian theology is neither universal nor homogeneous, and should not be treated as such.

As a solitary Catholic monk, Father Thomas Berry (1988) examines the Christian link to the environmental question from within, in a cautious, gently critical, yet highly constructive and optimistic manner. An environmentalist and widely educated scholar, Berry has devoted a lifetime to the study of Christian, East Indian, American Indian, Japanese, and Chinese philosophies, as well as the underlying revelations of modern science, the analysis of modern corporate and economic institutions, technological processes, and legal institutions in an attempt to uncover a universal explanation for the human/natural condition. Berry focuses on public spirituality, which he describes as

the functional values and their means or attainment in an identifiable human community. This public spirituality is . . . much more significant than the cultivated spirituality of marginal groups or individuals engaged in intensive prayer and mediation apart from the dynamics of the larger human community. . . the ultimate spiritual issues are those dealt with in the cruel and compassionate world of active human existence . . . (p. 111)

Berry puts forth the discovery in the twentieth century of a new origin story, "the story of the universe as emergent evolutionary process over some fifteen billion years," as a significant new challenge which must be addressed by the religious community, presumably not just Christians either. "The real tragedy . . . is that religious and spiritual persons themselves remain unaware of their need to provide for themselves and for the society a more significant evaluation of this large context of our lives. On both sides, the scientific and the religious, there is a naivete that is ruinous to the human community, to the essential functioning of the biosphere, and eventually disastrous to the earth itself" (pp. 112–113).

Berry also cites the Christian ideas of a human–divine covenant which secularizes nature, of a human destiny beyond and apart from that of other living creatures, and of a millennial vision of a blessed future, as strongly influential to America. When the millennium predicted by the scriptures did not appear by God's will, American people felt the need to bring it about by human effort. This interpretation, plus the influences of Cartesian thought, allowed devoutly religious Americans to substitute educational, scientific, technological, political, and commercial means for millennial transformation of the earth.

Yet Berry's surprisingly critical view of post-Reformation Christian practice in America is tempered by his understanding of religious tradition as a fluid "process: "There is no definitive Christianity or Hinduism or Buddhism, but only an identifiable Christian process, Hindu process, or Buddhist process" (p. 117). In light of the monumental realities now facing humanity, Berry clearly prefers to look not backward, but forward to those aspects of religion which account for and incorporate a new, more universal and spiritual regard for the environment.

A Human Biologist Looks at the Evidence

In *The Wooing of Earth* (Dubos, 1980) human biologist Rene Dubos takes issue with the position of blaming the environmental crisis on Judeo-Christian theology by enumerating several points. First, considerable extensive and lasting environmental degradation took place long ago in many regions far removed from Judeo-Christian influences. In spite of the reverence of Chinese poets and scholars for nature, deforestation and soil erosion was widespread in China long before the age of Christ. Most of the early ruination of the land, according to Dubos, was the consequence of intense population pressure, exploitative agriculture, and ignorance of long-term implications of primitive farming techniques. Dubos argues that people destroyed nature not out of an original absence or eventual loss of respect for it, but because intervention by technological means had become much more powerful. The Indians of the American plains lived in "harmony with Nature" so long as their environmental impact was limited to what they could do with bows and arrows. Once given firearms and horses, however, they began to decimate the vast herds of bison. White hunters with special Buffalo rifles, often riding the railroads out to the great herds, slaughtered the rest. As long as Caucasians had only stone or metal axes, forests lasted for centuries or even millennia, but now entire forest can be clearcut by heavy equipment in a matter of days. For Dubos, technology, not religion, was the cause of the crisis:

> The historical origin of the present ecological crisis is therefore not in Genesis 1:28, but in the failure of people to anticipate the long-range consequences of their activities—consequences that have recently been aggravated by the power and misuse of modern technology.

> *Dubos, 1980. p. 72*

Other scholars as well as Dubos have argued that the environmental degradation of the modern world has occurred in spite of and against the grain of Judeo-Christian and Moslem teachings (Denig, 1985). Virtually all modern industrialized societies manifest great environmental degradation, regardless of their primary religious contexts. Shinto and Buddist Japan, the Islamic Middle East, Protestant Western Europe, and Catholic Italy, Spain, and South America are as affected as the United States. Dubos believed that the degree of development of technology, rather than the religious predisposition of a region, accurately determined environmental degradation. In the former Soviet Union, where the practice of religion was restricted for 75 years, pollution and environmental destruction have evolved to unprecedented levels. Some estimates of the environmental degradation in certain Soviet oil fields, for example, place the level of destruction equivalent to that of 400 Exxon Valdez oil spills (Yergin, 1992). Japan, the center of an "eastern" religious tradition popularly identified by Westerners with environmentalism, has the second most consumptive economy on earth, with concurrent problems of nuclear and toxic waste disposal, air pollution, and transportation gridlock. China, another country identified with eastern religious traditions, burns coal as a primary energy source, and as the world's third largest carbon emitting nation, has tremendous air pollution problems causing widespread deforestation and health risks (Worldwatch Institute, 1991, 1992).

In the final analysis, Berry, the Catholic monk critiquing Christian views, Naess, the deep ecologist/philosopher defending the Christian biblical potential for stewardship, Dubos, the human biologist searching for universal human purpose, and a great many other contemporary scholars and scientists—Herman Daly and John Cobb (1989), Kenneth Boulding (Wright, 1988), and James Lovelock (Joseph, 1990), to name but a few—all arrive at the same implicit conclusion: there is a need for a new spiritualism which can inclusively build upon diverse religious traditions, including Christianity, toward a more universal, ecological sensitivity. This view is echoed vigorously by Vice President Albert Gore, whose recent book builds a strong and similar case for a multireligious "environmentalism of the spirit" (Gore, 1992).

My interpretation of this controversy is that *no single, historical religious tradition can be considered either the root cause or the fundamental solution to the crisis of technology and nature.* Neither the strict interpretation of original scriptures, nor the examination of contemporary evidence point to any major world religious practice as the genesis of environmental degradation. If one accepts Thomas Berry's assumption that "public" spirituality can be determined from "active human existence," then the only conclusion one could reach after examination of the modern world is that *technologically driven economic development has become the surrogate god and consumerism the de facto code of behavior.*

All of this brings us back to the discussion of environmental or landscape guilt—the obvious sense of remorse we feel toward our technological impact on the land. Were it not for some residual sense of having violated a moral or ethical code, we would not feel any guilt over technology's earthly impacts, and we would not find it necessary to cover them up, or to camouflage, transform, or remove technological features on the landscape to places out of sight and mind. In some sense, *the presence of landscape guilt*—a phenomenon of the late modern period—*assures us that some faint code of environmental ethics is still operative,* in spite of (and perhaps in opposition to those who would blame) religious tradition. What could possibly be the cause of this hint of a residual environmental ethic in an age of scientific/technological determinism? To the sources of technophobia I have already mentioned must be added another highly plausible cause; perhaps Americans feel guilty that technology has so thoroughly displaced religion as the primary force guiding behavior in today's world. Bryan Appleyard, British author and columnist on matters of philosophy and science, suggests that technology "transports the entire issue of life on earth from the realm of the moral or the transcendent to the realm of the possible" (Appleyard, 1992). It is possible to argue that it is a *lack* of faith in or adherence to *any* religious notion of stewardship or reverence for the environment, either novel or traditional, which is responsible for allowing the continuous technological assault on nature. The modern "technological credo" not only clashes with past and present religious and cultural tenets, but also with our innate, topophilic predispositions and affections.

New Demons in an Urban Wilderness

Although environmental degradation is found around the world as a consequence of western-style, developed technologies, the environmental guilt manifest by the landscape is perhaps most acute in North America. Poor countries are too preoccupied to reflect upon the possible meanings of technology beyond immediate survival. To understand American landscape guilt, we must come full circle back to Roderick Nash's domain—back to the ambivalence with which Americans viewed their most significant landscape heritage—the wilderness. From the onset, early Americans viewed the wild land lying before them as both a home for demons and a protective realm for ascetic encounter with God, "showing the same ambivalence toward the waste lands that we can find in the Old and New Testaments" (Tuan, p. 110). From this early, bipolar attitude, wilderness gradually gained public respect through the words of a succession of writers from de Tocqueville, Thoreau, Greely, Marsh, Olmsted, and Muir to Aldo Leopold. It is no coincidence that the increasing stature of wilderness at the expense of reverence for the city parallels the growth and diffusion of American technological expertise and the emergence of guilt for the "sins" of technology as well. As our national capacity to reconfigure the entire landscape according to the steamboat, railroad, automobile, and airplane grew, the perceived value of wilderness grew also, and with it the visual evidence of the ill effects of technology on our cities and towns. The officially designated "natural" wilderness that is preserved today in remote corners of our country is not the wilderness faced by the earliest settlers stepping off boats from Europe. As Tuan (1974) ironically implies, wilderness has now become "a symbol of the orderly processes of nature. As a state of the mind, true wilderness exists only in the great sprawling cities" (p. 112). The demonic beings once thought to inhabit the early American wilderness have been replaced by the new demons of an urban culture driven toward disintegration by runaway technological development, godless or not. This reversal of symbolic roles has given a new dimension to the guilt presumed to have been experienced by Adam and Eve; the apple can now be reinterpreted as a bionic product of technology, and we have lost the garden because of it.

"Natural" is Better than "Human-Made"

How does environmental guilt reveal itself in our landscapes? In 1978 Ronald Hodgson and I undertook a study of three different populations of people in California. Each group of subjects (university students, suburban Sacramento residents, and recreational vehicle visitors to a state park) was divided into two subgroups, and each subgroup was shown an identical set of color photographs of rural landscapes taken to be deliberately ambiguous as to their respective evidence of influence by humans. In one subgroup, 4 of the 15 photographs had labels implying "natural" conditions: *lake, pond, stream bank,* and *forest growth*. In the other subgroup, the exact same four photos had labels implying human influence or utility: *reservoir, irrigation, road cut,* and *tree farm*. The remaining 11 photos in each subgroup were identically labeled with a mixture of natural and human-influenced connotations. Subjects were asked to rank the 15 photos from most to least beautiful. Photographs with "natural" labels were ranked consistently higher than those with labels implying human influence. Although the study was not designed to

In a scientific experiment, the photograph labelled "lake" above was found to be significantly more beautiful than the identical photograph labelled "reservoir" below (from Hodgson and Thayer, 1980).

determine *why* or *how* this effect came to be, it was clear that we had uncovered the bias against landscapes people *presumed* were influenced by humans (Hodgson and Thayer, 1980). Somehow, the subjects had evaluated the photographs in relation to their valuations of categories conjured up by the labels, and had found the human-influence condition less desirable. Later, an editor termed this phenomenon "Landscape Guilt."

Scrutiny of our designed and vernacular landscapes reveals several levels of additional evidence of technophobia and landscape guilt. In the immediate, human-scale landscape, electrical power stations, trash dumpsters, and air conditioners are concealed behind fences or walls and "decorated" with landscape plants and shrubbery. Local suburban utility lines are buried. Landscape sprinklers are colored green to blend in with the lawns they irrigate or flat black to recede into the visual background. All across America, the hard edges, utilitarian forms, and shiny surfaces of human technological development are "softened" by landscape trees, shrubs, and groundcovers—symbols of "nature"—according to the plans of my fellow landscape architects, and, I admit, occasionally by my own design work.

Such manipulation, disguise, and displacement of conspicuous technological elements with nature symbols can, of course, be attributed to an entire cultural evolution of landscape taste which has increasingly emphasized the natural and suppressed the human-made, even if it makes a replica of the former by means of the latter. On the other hand, the phenomenon of preference for presumably natural landscapes can be seen as evidence of a deeper, more fundamental human predisposition. That humans prefer the "natural" over the human-made is well-established fact. The question is why.

Types of Landscape Guilt

"Landscape guilt" is a useful neologism for the physical manifestations of technophobia—the actual changes made to the landscape when affection for nature clashes dissonantly with negative evaluations of technology's impact on land, ecosystems, or "nature." Landscape guilt manifests itself in many different ways and at many different scales and degrees of specificity, but all permutations of landscape guilt imply a condition of *cognitive dissonance* (Festinger, 1963). When an individual's feelings, beliefs, and/or actions are not congruent (i.e., when a person acts in a fashion that contradicts one's belief structure or feels strong emotions that seem to contradict one's actions), that person is said to experience cognitive dissonance. Implicit within cognitive dissonance is a motivation to bring the dissonant belief, feeling, or action into consonance with the other two. For example, if one believes smoking is wrong, while still craving and smoking cigarettes, one must either stop smoking or start believing that smoking is acceptable in order to resolve his internal state of cognitive dissonance. In a similar fashion, if I believe air conditioning is a wrongful waste of energy and generally bad for the environment, yet I can't tolerate my overheated house, I am also feeling cognitive dissonance, and I may manifest this feeling by building a redwood screen around the air conditioner. In other words, I have landscape guilt.

For my purposes, cognitive dissonance, technophobia, environmental guilt, and landscape guilt are a family of nested but related constructs. Cognitive dissonance is a disjunction between thought, feeling, and action; technophobia is cognitive dissonance over technology, or an adverse reaction to technology because of its impact on ecological and social order; environmental guilt is technophobia due to the environmental impact of technology; landscape guilt is the manifestation of environmental guilt in actual, physical landscape.

The landscape manifestations of technophobia encompass: (a) zoning and other forms of locational regulation to keep technologies at a distance from residential and recreational areas; (b) NIMBY (not in my backyard!), or *de facto* locational constraints which accomplish the same end result through ad hoc, grass-roots initiative; (c) concealment, or direct hiding of technological features behind architectural or landscape architectural screens; (d) camouflage of technological features by manipulation of color, form, or texture; (e) symbolic transformation of technological features into more favorable "meanings" other than that of technology; (f) simulations of nature which appear on the surface as "natural" yet are facilitated and actuated by technological means, and (g) denial or avoidance of technology altogether by means of cognitive "tuning out" of technological features from the internalized cognitive maps of individuals.

Zoning and Locational Regulation

Landscape guilt is clearly evident in the regulation of technological or utilitarian landscape features to out-of-the-way locations or specific zones away from "idealized" spaces such as homes, communities, and recreational and scenic areas. In planning terminology, "zoning" is the regulation of land uses by establishment of zones in which only certain development activities and building types are permitted. As a form of land use regulation, zoning typically divides cities or counties into residential, commercial, industrial, agricultural, recreational, and other use areas, and sets conditions and procedures by which development can occur in each zone. Although zoning is a complex phenomenon which embodies and reflects numerous social and political issues, it can be examined in relationship to the evolution of technological development and expanding industrialism in the United States.

Legally, zoning has been upheld by the courts as a valid use of police power to prohibit public nuisance which would presumably occur if development were allowed to occur without it. In the 1926 U.S. Supreme Court Case,

Village of Euclid v. Ambler Realty Company, the constitutionality of zoning was upheld, and since then nearly every local jurisdiction in the United States has adopted a zoning ordinance as a means of regulating land use. However, *Euclid v. Ambler* is worth examining more closely, for *it contains evidence of technophilia, technophobia, and the first "official" manifestations of landscape guilt.*

The case involved several large property owners who jointly owned 68 acres in what was at the time an incorporated village of Euclid, a residential suburb abutting Cleveland, Ohio to the northeast on the shore of Lake Erie. Following the City of New York's lead in establishing a zoning ordinance, the state of Ohio had passed legislation enabling cities to establish zoning ordinances. As a wealthy suburb of Cleveland, Euclid was the third community in Ohio to adopt comprehensive zoning. Euclid's ordinance separated all village land uses into six districts, regulating building height, lot area, and use zones in the pyramid fashion, where only single family residence zones were exclusive of all others (i.e., a single family residence could be built in any zone, but no other building types could be built within single-family residence zones).

The Ambler Realty company owned, among other large properties, a 68-acre parcel of land in Euclid near Cleveland's eastern boundary between Euclid Avenue, a major east–west thoroughfare, and the Nickel Plate Railroad tracks to the north. Cleveland was at the time a rapidly developing industrial center, and Ambler Realty fully expected heavy industry to occur along both Euclid Avenue and the railroad lines. However, the 1922 Euclid zoning ordinance limited industrial zoning to a narrow band between the two major railroads bisecting the village, and half of Ambler 68-acre parcel was zoned for residential, including the portion fronting on Euclid Avenue. Ambler Realty believed that this zoning designation constituted a "taking" of land without compensation, and since no court case had ever established the legality of the new zoning concept, Ambler challenged the ordinance in district court, hiring Newton Baker, a prominent local attorney and former mayor of Cleveland, to argue the case. Arguing on behalf of the Village of Euclid was another prominent Cleveland attorney, James Meztenbaum, who was chairman of the Euclid Planning and Zoning Commission.

As with any case heard and ruled upon by the Supreme Court, the complexity of legal interpretations and the resulting historic significance of *Euclid v. Ambler* have both been immense, for this case enabled widespread zoning to occur in the United States. From a legal and land use standpoint, the case essentially argued the rights of a local community to regulate land use for public health, safety, and welfare versus the rights of private property owners to freely develop their properties according to the ebb and flow of local economic and social factors. Closer inspection of the circumstances surrounding the case reveals a different interpretation: Baker argued that the zoning constituted an unconstitutional flight from reality by the Village of Euclid, which he considered a yet to be developed portion of the Cleveland metropolitan area—"a highly organized industrial community of more than one million

Regulating
Satellite
Dish Antennas

Harry B. Roth

American Planning Association

Planning Advisory Service
Report Number 394

Zoning and other legal mechanisms are commonly used to restrict the location and siting of utilitarian land uses or technological features such as airports, factories, and even satellite antennae (the subject of this American Planning Association monograph). Cover illustration by Dennis McClendon.

people." Baker felt that the restrictions on the Ambler parcel suggested "an aesthetic or exclusionary purpose not connected to the public health and safety" (Brooks, 1989). Metzenbaum, on the other hand, felt he was defending the American home and the right of local residents to avoid the "smoke-filled condition of the city" in favor of "fresh air and sunlight and a yard for children." Further on in his brief, Metzenbaum argued that "zoning prevents huddling and indiscriminate throwing together of homes and factories . . ." [Affirmative brief of the defendant, *Ambler v. Euclid,* Equity #898 at 16., 56].

Legalizing Landscape Guilt

Here within this landmark case is distinctive evidence of the divergence of technophilia and technophobia—perhaps the seed of a legalized response to landscape guilt. During the first half of the twentieth century, American industrial development was peaking, and the United States was becoming a world technological power. Railroads had connected the country, heavy industry had spread throughout the north-central and northeastern United States, and the automobile industry and its supporting industries were expanding rapidly in Detroit, Michigan, Gary, Indiana, and Cleveland, Ohio as well. Urban Americans were beginning to witness first hand not only the economic, political, and social rewards but the regional environmental devastation attributable to heavy industrial technology and the expansion of railroads and highways. The real significance of *Euclid v. Ambler* is that it involved *zoning to avoid heavy industry in favor of large lot rural residential land use.* By doing so, it *legitimized the division of the domains of American life and culture into a real-world zone of technologically based heavy industry and business on the one hand and the idealized, pastoral vision of home life on the other.*

By withstanding the scrutiny of the U.S. Supreme Court, zoning allowed the cognitive as well as spatial compartmentalization of certain domains of American life; Americans would develop industrial technologies which consumptively exploited land and nonrenewable resources to make a living, and then withdraw to what Baker rightly called a "rural, exclusive, and aesthetic" vision of home. A critical severance occurred in *Euclid v. Ambler*—one that enabled the consumptive means upon which America built its economic survival to be officially separated from the idealized, suburban remnants of Jefferson's agrarian pastoralist dream. Before zoning, the heavy industry resulting from rapid technological development could (and often did) abut the homes of those whose lives depended upon it, and visible feedback of the negative environmental consequences of industrial technologies was often inescapable and acutely felt. After *Euclid v. Ambler,* it became both legal and, it would seem, socially necessary to isolate housing from the negative effects of heavy industrial technology. In this manner, the pastoral illusion could be preserved and people (especially those with larger lots and bigger houses who presumably not only benefited most financially from industrial development but held positions of power on zoning boards and government bodies) would not have to experience the environmental downside of industrial technology on a daily basis—out of sight, out of mind. *Euclid v. Ambler* also seemed to legitimize a community's right to become what economists refer to as a "free-rider"—to reap the benefits of industrial technologies while not sharing in the local impacts.

There are, of course, very legitimate reasons for zoning and significant public benefits to be gained in the protection of the public's health and safety. Furthermore, no person nor community is an island; all provide some service to the economy and reap certain economic benefits in return. Total decentralized, self-sufficiency is a romantic notion impossible in modern developed economies. However, zoning gave Americans the official permission to act upon their natural mistrust of technology—their technophobia—and to relegate heavy industry to zones where residents (at least those of moderate or greater income) would neither see it nor have to face up to its devastating effects upon the land.

Today there are countless examples of zoning which aim to exclude land uses that are technologically distasteful yet economically necessary. Many bedroom communities provide no zones for land uses relating to industrial technology at all, yet their residents live by means of the same technological products as all other communities. Davis, California, where I live, is a university campus town and as such, has a rather minimal industrial base. One industry that has been located in Davis for several decades is tomato processing; a tomato cannery is located in the northeast sector of town on land long zoned for industrial use. Until recently, the surrounding land to the north and east of the plant was not within city limits, and the county had zoned it industrial as well. As Davis' population exploded in the last decade, a 1987 general plan for the city unwisely redesignated the surrounding county land for single-family housing north and east. Because prevailing summer breezes blow from the southwest, odors of cooking tomatoes and industrial noise will affect land to the northeast. Night lighting during summer harvest operations will also affect adjacent land. The developer of a proposed housing project adjacent to the tomato plant wants the tomato cannery to severely curtail the light, noise, and odor. The plant maintains correctly that it was "there first" and that it can't curtail such outputs and stay in business. The City of Davis' failure to designate the adjacent land industrial or to otherwise provide buffering land uses has resulted in a three-way stalemate between the city, the developer, and the industry.

Airports are another technological feature which Americans use frequently but do not want next door. At the time of construction, metropolitan airports are usually far enough away from the center city to alleviate conflict between airplane noise and residential housing. Zoning supposedly protects land around airports from incompatible (i.e., residential) uses; often airports form the nucleus of industrial development. However, because they cause growth, airports often act as magnets for urban expansion. In Sacramento, new housing has extended northeast toward Sacramento Metro Airport, and land use which once was zoned in compatible uses has been rezoned to residential. Denver, whose airport once was far out of town, is now moving its airport further east to stay ahead of the development that will inevitably follow. Once established in their new homes, residents begin to complain about airplane noise and flight paths. Because land use classifications can be changed readily, zoning often provides a thin and penetrable way of "protecting" the public from the negative impacts of technology. The flip side of this argument, however, is that zoning does have the ability to respond to changing social, economic, and technological realities. However, the irony inherent in the relatively short shelf-life of a particular zoning designation was anticipated by attorney Baker in a brief he wrote for *Euclid v. Ambler* in 1926:

> In Detroit, for instance, any plan for the growth of Detroit before the advent of the motor car industry there would have been entirely useless and probably worse. . . In every instance with which I am acquainted a zoning ordinance has become out of date within two or three years after its passage. . . .

This irony is borne out today. The 68-acre parcel in Euclid, Ohio which became the battlefield where zoning—to prevent feared industrial technology from overwhelming an upperclass residential neighborhood—was officially interpreted as constitutional is now completely covered by the giant Inland Plant of the General Motors Corporation (Brooks, 1989) and produces automobile bodies. Retrospectively, one senses that even the creation of zoning was only a temporary delay enabling us to preserve the myth a bit longer that we were still a rural nation—that we still had some time before necessarily and inevitably confronting the impacts of our industrial technology on the land.

There have been numerous other governmentally sanctioned exclusions of unfavored technologies from local landscapes. Many cities including Davis have officially declared themselves "nuclear-free" zones by passing ordinances prohibiting the shipment of nuclear fuels or wastes across city thoroughfares or boundaries. The city of Warren, Massachusetts amended its bylaws to allow only the interment of toxic wastes within the boundaries of the city that had been generated by city residents themselves. Few such actions have been tested in higher courts, but all represent honest attempts by local governmental officials to establish more control over the types of land use that respond to the desires of their constituents. In many cases, public officials are increasingly pressured to exclude such uses as airport expansions, gravel extractions, power plants, solid or toxic waste repositories, freeways, or other "dirty" technological industries.

NIMBY

If zoning and general plan designation are the officially sanctioned means by which communities exclude certain technologies from their borders, NIMBY is the unofficial, *ad hoc* exclusion by an angry public after local government fails to respond. NIMBY refers to the vigorous resistance of individuals and groups to the proposed location of technological, utilitarian features (or otherwise objectionable land uses or landscapes) near one's home. In the American, high-tech industrial economy, generation and distribution of goods and services is largely centralized, while consumption is, of course, highly decentralized. Many public "goods" have both local and widespread benefits as well as local and widespread environmental "costs." Because of centralization, the positive benefits of many "public goods" (e.g., electricity) are widely distributed, while the environmental costs (e.g., exhaust from fossil fuel power plants) may be felt only in the local downwind region surrounding the plant. Ironically, NIMBYs (as the term is used referring to individual citizens) presumably participate in a lifestyle that achieves some benefit or implicitly sanctions the use of certain technological products while refusing to accept the localized environmental consequences of the manufacturing and disposal of those same products. For example, homeowners may use ant spray, motor oil, or barbecue lighter fluid but object to the nearby establishment of a facility intended to reprocess wastes from such household chemicals for resale.

NIMBY is essentially a *de facto* siting or zoning regulation for all technological landscapes and land uses. Local groups who are faced with the prospect of an unwanted technological facility locating next door take political steps to prevent that from happening and, by doing so, inadvertently (or sometimes consciously) imply that it should be placed in someone else's backyard. The NIMBY phenomenon, therefore, often results in the inability to site anywhere technological facilities presumed necessary for the proper functioning of society. When such facilities are sited, they are often in locations with either few residents or residents with little political or economic power. In Massachusetts, the state legislature passed the Hazardous Waste Facility Siting Act, which established a procedure for facility developers, two state agencies, and local governments to work together in siting private facilities intended to recover, reprocess, and sell hazardous chemicals originally manufactured in Massachusetts. However, the act failed to provide an adequate means for local residents to participate in the process. As a result of subsequent, localized, grass-roots action, all six Massachusetts proposals for toxic waste recovery plants during the period from 1981 to 1990 were effectively blocked (Brion, 1991).

As expected, the NIMBY phenomenon can be interpreted from several points of view. From the point of view of corporate officials, NIMBYs are naive in their lack of "real knowledge" of the technological processes, and are selfish and short-sighted in their objections to the proposed facility. From an economist's standpoint, NIMBY's are "free-riders," persons who share all of the benefits but not the costs of a proposed facility. Unfortunately, however, the costs of many technologies to the consumer do not include "externalities" such as the potential damage to an ecosystem by toxic waste. If the true environmental costs were represented in the price charged for the products of a technology and were borne equally by all users, many technologies would necessarily price themselves out of the market. In essence, this is what has happened to the nuclear industry. Because of local opposition to siting of nuclear power plants and because of widespread public outcry for stronger safety regulations and techniques (and, some would include, because of ineptness and callousness on the part of the industry itself), the price for nuclear-generated electricity has risen to a point where nuclear power plants are no longer economical. In the case of nuclear energy, NIMBY reactions have been a means by which "external" costs have been internalized. If the costs of toxic waste recovery and treatment were to be borne by the producers of household chemicals and added to the price of the chemical products themselves, homeowners would use far fewer chemicals; the price "signals" would more accurately resolve the problem of overconsumption.

NIMBY reactants themselves, however, are not nearly as naive nor Machiavellian in their motives as their corporate critics would like to believe (Kraft and Clary, 1991). Not only are many local opposers of certain facilities very well informed and outspoken, but many have formed networks to help other communities oppose similar facilities proposed for *their* backyards. As happened in the nuclear industry, NIMBY tends to become NIABY—"not in *anyone's* backyard" (Heiman, 1990). When localized opposition forms networks and becomes widespread opposition, it must be reinterpreted as feedback to the technology itself. Langdon Winner pointed out in 1991 that fully 75% of Americans polled preferred renewable energy development to nuclear, yet the Bush administration energy policy heavily favored the nuclear industry. Winner suggested that the government begin listening to the will of the people (Winner, 1991).

My own research, however, has shown that people react strongly to *any* locally sited technological facility even if it is relatively benign or renewable, as was the case with several California windfarm proposals (Thayer and Hansen, 1991). Because the general public seems increasingly distrustful of all technological facility siting, one way of looking at the NIMBY phenomenon is as a public check on runaway technological "progress" imposed by the people themselves in lieu of adequate evaluations and checks by government.

Concealment, Camouflage, and Symbolic Transformation

The guilt people feel over the predominance of technology in their lives is most easily revealed by the concealment of technological features by trees, shrubs, fences, walls, earthforms, or less threatening architectural facades or features. Virtually every student of landscape architecture learns at an early age that the clients want to hide the utility meters, screen the parking lots, build walls around the trash dumpster, or bury the "ugly" power lines. In communities all across the country, electrical substations are surrounded by fences or walls and "shrubbed up" with plants. Unfortunately, landscape archi-

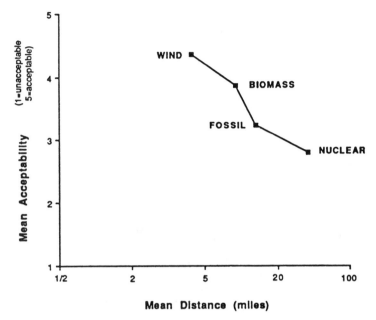

Energy in your backyard? A graph of the average distance away from their homes residents of Solano County, California would accept various power plant types plotted against their overall willingness to accept the particular plant type anywhere in the county. Residents found wind farms most acceptable, but still wanted them an average of 3–4 miles from their homes. In contrast, nuclear plants were less acceptable, and at an average of 35 miles from home. From Thayer and Hansen (1989).

tecture is the profession by which the public attempts to create an idealized version of nature and reality, and modern American culture applies strict but unwritten codes to what technological features it considers appropriate in residential gardens and townscapes. As will be discussed in the next section, most active technologies necessary to support life in America are considered unworthy of visual expression, whereas nostalgic or futuristic ones are sometimes acceptable. One common technological feature considered generally unworthy of public view is the building air conditioner. After a multimillion dollar, high-status, postmodern addition to the Davis university campus library was recently completed, the administration noticed that the air-conditioning apparatus on the roof was left unscreened by the architect and remained visible from the surrounding campus area. A $160,000 facade was designed and installed to cover it up. Air conditioning is now widespread throughout America, yet we seem to be unable to accept the visual evidence of our desire to stay cool. Concealment of such features as air conditioners and powerlines is perhaps the most direct and telling example of landscape guilt in America.

Often it is impossible to completely cover up a technological feature, and

Landscape guilt revealed from the air. This oil terminal island off the coast of Long Beach, California is disguised as a tropical condominium resort. Photograph by Baron Wollman.

prevailing "aesthetic" taste combined with budgetary constraints often default to the next best thing—camouflage. Camouflage is the manipulation of the surface pattern, texture, color, or form of the technological feature to blend in with "natural" landscape context or to appear as a less threatening architectural feature. To pass the rather rigorous aesthetic controls in the Colorado ski area of Vail, a microwave transmission tower was designed as an abstract piece of modern architecture in a manner so successful that few passersby can decipher its true function; it won an award from the American Institute of Architects. Off the coast of Long Beach harbor, architectural tower facades which look like resort condominiums but enclose no space and house no people surround an oil terminal to disguise the hidden technological nature of the facility. To the north off the Santa Barbara coast, tall palm trees disguise an offshore cluster of oil wells built on fill, appealing to our long-held positive association of palms with tropical islands and notions of paradise.

In the national forests, considerable controversy has been generated by systems of visual resource management (VRM) which aim to manipulate the form, color, and texture to create clear cuts that look more "natural" and blend in with the surrounding landscape context. Although a genuine step forward in "scenic resource management," such techniques have come under fire for potentially misleading the public into thinking that such clear cuts are not even happening (Wood, 1989). The technique of clear-cut harvesting is widespread throughout the western United States, and has been increasingly criticized as a threat to many species of animals dependent upon old-growth, climax forests (Robinson, 1988). To these critics, the attempt to make irregularly bounded clear cuts out of sight behind ridges represents environmentally unethical cosmetology, and raises fundamental questions about the relationship between "surface" (i.e., visible) and "core" ecological values.

There are many more examples of camouflage of technical landscape features; electrical transmission towers painted the color of the background landscape; grass-green colored lawn sprinklers which, in the words of one company's advertisement, "do their job and drop out of sight." Often when it is impossible to either hide a technology or camouflage it to look like the natural background, a process of symbolic transformation is then attempted. Symbolic transformation is the alteration of the surface symbolism of technological features such that a symbol of nature or romanticized culture counteracts, contradicts, or replaces the essential symbolism of the technology. One of the more interesting examples of symbolic transformation is a satellite dish antenna in Point Arena, on the northern coast of California. Located in a landscape composition together with an old-fashioned fishing boat in the middle of a motel parking lot, the antenna is painted to resemble a large abalone shell. No one is fooled, of course, but the symbolic transformation is serious in its intent. I have also seen similar satellite dishes painted with scenic

Technologies placed in this motel landscape in Point Arena, California achieve acceptability by symbolic transformation (the abalone shell antenna) or nostalgia (the historic fishing boat).

landscapes as if they were canvases hung on the wall. The city of Mount Vernon, Washington has painted a large tulip flower on an old industrial smokestack. Both of these cases are attempts to redefine the symbolic meaning of the technology and to place it in topophilic context.

Technological Nature Surrogates

The deliberate substitution of realistic, technological surrogates for "natural" features or landscapes is another example of landscape guilt. These surrogate landscapes may be one of three types: (a) hyperreal "hardware" replicas, (b) virtual-reality "software" facsimiles, or (in the near future) (c) combinations of both. In recent years, electronic, simulated golf has become popular, and players play on "courses" that combine video images of actual landscapes controlled by computerized feedback measured from an actual golf ball hit off a tee or synthetic turf "fairway" strip toward the interactive video screen—an example of a "software-based" facsimile of an outdoor landscape.

There has been a recent explosion of hardware facsimiles of nature made possible by innovations in manufacturing technology. Synthetic rocks and water features are now commonplace in high-style resort gardens, hotel plazas, and urban parks. Highly realistic, imitation plants are often mixed in with real landscape plant material, and stamped, poured-in-place concrete successfully copies granite, slate, or brick pavers. Throughout the intentionally designed landscape, the visible expression of material honesty has yielded to material illusion and deception.

Both "soft" and "hard" imitations of natural landscapes represent a unique type of landscape guilt—a denial that the technological processes which enable their existence is worthy of expression in their own right. I once suggested to a manufacturer of popular, imitation paving materials that he experiment with new forms and patterns that would express and celebrate the advantages of concrete rather than mimic presumably higher "status" materials such as marble or brick. This admittedly modernist suggestion fell on deaf ears—no such patterns have been released by the company.

Denial and Avoidance

Americans seem so ashamed of the impacts of their technology-dependent lifestyles that when technological facilities are absolutely necessary, they are often "tuned out" or simply erased from a person's mental map. Ask a few people in your community where their water or electricity comes from, or where their waste goes. Few will have any idea of the whereabouts of their sewage treatment plant, power plant, or which fuel resources provide their electrical power. Furthermore, it has been to the advantage of utility companies and public works departments *not* to bring these utilitarian land uses into public focus; the less the public is informed, the easier it is to make profitable, uncomplicated decisions. When it comes to the essential umbilicals that connect us to the physical world, we are largely ignorant, and worse yet, we don't even seem to want to know, for to do so is to confront the basic conflict of our technological existence on earth.

Technophobia is a source of environmental guilt, and environmental guilt is commonly observable in the landscape. But none of these three nested manifestations of the same construct can be thought of as simply positive or negative. Landscape guilt itself is an ambivalent phenomenon; it is both a collective cry for help as well as a faint indicator that we have not totally succumbed to the tyranny of technology. In terms of mental health, guilt is a useful emotion only when it leads to positive change; prolonged, unresolved guilt may lead to destruction of the "self." Like its individual human counterpart, widespread landscape guilt is only constructive as an agent of transformation in the environmental status quo. If unchecked, it too will ultimately contribute to social disintegration.

NOTES

1. I challenge this point of view, however, and ascribe it to the fact that Europeans arrived in North American laden with an environmental/cultural predisposition forged in Europe. Had the early Euro-American settlers been established on the North American continent several thousand years earlier, as were American Indians, their cultural evolution "among the wilds" of America might have produced something more akin to reverence.

4

Gray World, Green Heart

The contrast between the machine and the pastoral ideal dramatizes the great issue of our culture. It is the germ . . . of the most final of all generalizations about America.

LEO MARX

The pastoral ideal of a middle landscape of humanized nature pleasantly suspended between extreme wilderness and crowded cities has driven much of American landscape development for 200 years. In spite of changing definitions of what is "wild" or "natural," landscapes dominated by the machine have had little success in *bona fide* acceptance as part of the mythical natural order of things, managing at best to coexist with symbols of nature as a parallel but separate realm, and at worst, serving as the root cause of environmental guilt. The railroad in the nineteenth century and the automobile in the twentieth led an assault by technology on the pastoral ideal of harmonious integration of humans and nature that has never been adequately resolved. The railroad has come closer to a resolution than the automobile. When the multitude of privately owned rail passenger lines at midcentury fell to only a few, and interstate trucks and passenger airplanes began to out-compete the trains, rail nostalgia began to blossom, and the railroad seemed rapidly on its way toward a mythical reconciliation with nature in a nostalgic American past. Railroad museums appeared everywhere. But how could we continue to hold a grudge against a dying old gentlemen, who, in his youth had so thoroughly violated nature yet, in his old age, seemed so romantically wise, yet physically impotent? But "Old Man Railroad" has fooled us; just when we thought the train was breathing its last breath, we now find it struggling to reemerge like some transformed phoenix in the new guise of "light rail" or "mass transit." Having passed into nostalgic status prematurely, the train refused to die and has resurfaced as a pragmatic solution to the unsustainable transportation quandary presented by the automobile.

The car, on the other hand, is a different, nearly opposite story. In spite of

Scene near Ridgeway, Colorado.

early inclusion of the car into idealized views of American landscape, and despite billions of dollars spent by the auto industry to design and produce cars which made us feel like they were alive and natural, with names like Stingray, Falcon, Barracuda, or Bronco, and marketing strategies to convince us to "see the USA in our Chevrolet," our society has never fully allowed this mechanized, gasoline-guzzling demon a permanent place of status in the idealized order of nature. The automobile wreaked havoc upon the middle landscape, continually pushing the edge of the pastoral image farther out beyond the city. Nowadays the names of cars are changing and losing their natural referents, to be replaced by vague, onomatopoetic "culture, mood, and status" names like Festiva, Eurovan, Altima, Expo, or Achieva.

"Good" Technology and "Bad"

The habit of associating cars and other technological entities with animals or landscapes is but one of many futile attempts to deal with the cognitive dissonance between technology and nature. Society's principal means of coping with this dissonance has been to split the persona of technology into two domains. One part, the personal domain, serves as a vital extender and facilitator of our modern lifestyle. It is this sense of technophilia that emerges when we use technologies to conduct the everyday utilitarian tasks of our lives. Life

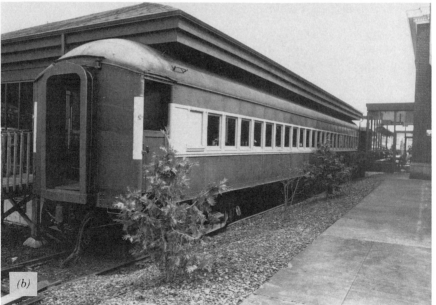

Railroad-theme restaurants have popped up across the United States, featuring rail memorabilia and dining in railroad cars and cabooses. This one is in Eugene, Oregon.

without the gas water heater, telephone, computer, automobile, or refrigerator is now unthinkable. Once adopted, technologies influence the direction our lives take, most often irreversibly. But beyond direct, utilitarian influence on our everyday lives, the consumer products of technology symbolically define *who we are*. In this sense, *we become what we own*. We are *our* car, *our* leaf blower, *our* personal computer. Although these are human-made creations, they collectively and symbolically *create* and define us. With efficient systems of marketing to create demand and distribution to meet it, America continues to serve as the world's most exemplary inventor and consumer of new technologies. To a large extent, the Iron Curtain fell for want of more TV's, automobiles, computers, and blue jeans. With such an efficient engine of technological development, production, marketing, and consumption, it is no wonder that Americans have come to construct their own personal identities, social institutions, and often their landscapes around specific consumer products, and that these products are incorporated into the idealized view an individual holds about the world.

The other part of the technological persona, however, is the impersonal, omnipresent "system" of technologies that has violated the environment, polluted the air and water, stolen jobs, and wiped out some species while threatening to wipe out others even, in some cases, our own. By mentally constructing technology as if it were two separate entities (our *personal* technological necessities vs. the ubiquitous technological systems of the world), we continue to delude ourselves into thinking the problem either doesn't really exist or isn't that critical, and that it is a problem "out there" rather than "here" at home. To be sure, many of us feel trapped by the lifestyle implicit in a world dependent upon the consumer products of technology. If most of our peers own two or more cars, commute 30 miles from the suburbs to jobs on the urban fringe, watch six hours of television per day, spend most of their paychecks on consumer entertainment and related paraphernalia, and manage their home economies via electronic credit, teller machines, and humanless, touch-tone voice decision trees, why shouldn't we? Aren't we merely conforming to the normative expectations of American lifestyles?

This is a false logic, however. We act as if such a lifestyle were imposed upon us by others, when, in fact, we actively construct and maintain it. By participating in the technologically determined lifestyle, we reinforce it. Americans stubbornly resist being told how to act or what to believe by other humans or political systems, but find no difficulty in sheepishly conforming to the behavioral changes implicit in a rapidly changing technology. How many readers of this book felt foolish when first talking into a telephone recording machine? No longer. We have grown rapidly comfortable conversing with machines and listening to anonymous, taped voices telling us which button to push on our touch-tone phones, yet we often have difficulty entering into face-to-face conversations with real human beings. The mediating factor of information technology takes away some of the effort, but also much of the reward inherent in face-to-face human communication.

While rapidly adjusting our outward behaviors to the sweeping social changes implicit in technological development, we are increasingly aware that all is not well with our environment (social as well biophysical), and that flagrant technological determinism and mass consumerism has not fulfilled its promise of a better world. At the most fundamental, core levels, we sense a *dis-ease,* and at the same time, we have intensified the debate about the condition of the environment and what we could or should do about it. We have divided the realm of technology into the "I's" and the "Theys," while largely ignoring the "We's."

These two conflicting realms of the technological persona emerge from different parts of the human mind. On the one hand, we are naturally opportunistic, intuitive animals; if given a short cut to individual survival, we will certainly take it. Psychologist Robert Ornstein and biologist Paul Erlich (1989) remind us that humans still operate in the modern world with an "old" brain genetically adapted to a largely natural physical context in which we evolved but no longer live. Thus, a time-saving or effort-saving technology is an intuitive choice. In this real sense, it is very *natural* to want to drive one's car to the supermarket if it represents both an individual savings of caloric effort in getting there, and an increased likelihood of assuring adequate food supplies when one arrives. Likewise, NIMBY behavior, commonly considered irrational by representatives of industry or government, is actually very logical; why shouldn't someone want the localized benefits but not the costs of a technology if given a choice? Taking advantage of technology's personal benefits while avoiding its personal costs is an understandable reaction rooted in the most basic evolutionary patterns of human response to the environment.

To respond any other way to technology requires higher levels of thought: observations of external phenomena; extraction, evaluation and generalization of results; abstraction of essential lessons about causes and effects; conscious extrapolation and prediction of future actions; and—most importantly—the ability to monitor small, incremental changes over long periods of time. Walking to the grocery store to reduce fossil fuel combustion which might otherwise pollute the air, warm the global atmosphere, lower soil productivity, or provide less food at greater real cost is certainly counterintuitive and requires a kind of extraordinary social foresight unavailable to most individuals. It is much more likely that a reduction of automobile driving will come about from intuitive, rather than rational feedback, such as not finding a parking place, paying too much money for gas, or when walking assumes a higher social status than driving and yields more affirmation by one's peers and gratification of one's ego. All of these motives are closer to the core of human existence.

By separating the personal, intuitive (i.e., "good") realms of technology upon which we individually depend from the intellectualized field of "bad" technologies "out there" which cause social and environmental problems, we dissociate personal technological benefits from real costs. By pretending that the two realms are not connected, we momentarily free ourselves from the oppression of environmental guilt. Such a dissociation, however, becomes harder and harder to maintain in the face of daily barrages of news stories which have the effect of constructing *connections* between our personal, intuitively operated lifestyles and our collective social responsibility for environmental degradation.

The Natural Feeling of Technology

The most striking thing about technophilia is how *natural* it seems to the individual. Our personally owned products of technology often make us feel good, and rapidly ascend to a high level of affection and status. I admit to having a strong emotional bond with my recently acquired whitewater canoe—the product of a sophisticated technology whereby layers of fossil-fuel byproducts (plastics) are laminated and vacuum formed into a hull shape which was ingeniously created by a human designer and rigorously tested on America's streams and rivers. My canoe has even acquired an animal nickname: "Sockeye" (our other two canoes are "Chinook" and "Coho"). Upon arriving or leaving our carport I often pause to look longingly and affectionately at the canoe hanging upside down, wishing I could be guiding it through the rapids in some western whitewater stream. For me, there is a fusion of the technological product, its intended landscape venues, and the pleasant experiences, both anticipated and remembered, in which I, the canoe, and the landscape were or will be joined. In this semiotic transformation, the technological product *becomes* the pleasurable place or experience. I do, however, recognize the danger of this substitution, especially when it is taken to extremes. If somehow I perceived that the widespread manufacture and use of whitewater canoes had begun to cause the deterioration of the very river environments for which my canoe was intended, I would no doubt change my perception and sell the canoe. Yet I also know that I might never realize when or if that point had occurred.

Not all of my technological possessions garner such personal status or contribute so significantly to my self image. But the personal utilization of technology often leads to the type and intensity of mythical bond usually reserved for attributes of nature, and even the more mundane, utilitarian technologies of everyday life become a necessary part of an idealized construction of reality. If asked to envision a personal, idealized world in which all environmental and social problems were solved, most of us would still include our favorite technological toys, labor-saving gadgets, and entertainment devices. It is through these technologies that we intuitively act out our personal realities. For many people, the line between personal technophilia and topophilia is fuzzy. Our particular affection for land and landscape is very often actualized through the use of technological products, from the high-resolution, imported binoculars of the most avid Sierra Club environmentalist to the mammoth fat-tire pick-ups of macho off-road enthusiasts. Oddly enough, both tophophilia and personal technophilia seem inherently connected in the natural, self-centered manner by which we express our unique brand of affection for the land and our place upon it. Our intuitive response to the earth—a gut-level combination of primal affection for nature and intuitive dependency on certain technologies—allows us to feed both our bodies and our souls on the earth's bounty.

Tool use, once incidental to human experience of nature, has evolved into *technology*, which is now central to that experience, and in the near future, threatens to completely *replace* it. At what point will the "experience" of nature be so removed from the tangible landscape and so mediated by electronically simulated, biologically engineered, or mechanically articulated means that it will cease to be genuine? Will we know when that point has occurred? Does it matter? Sometimes we are unaware that our experience of nature is so highly modified by our technologies, and our technophilic and topophilic tendencies seem like one unified emotional response. Sometimes, like the hypothetical *Homo erectus* female of Chapter 2, or like a speeding sailboarder catching an evening wind, we may experience the heightened aesthetic fusion of tool and context. At other times, we become keenly aware of our technologies and the fact that were it not for them, we would stand facing nature, helpless, naked, and frightened. At such times, we become aware that topophilia and technophilia are separate emotions. Subconsciously, we may long for the integration of topophilia and technophilia—for the total fusion of landscape and tool. Consciously, however, it may be necessary for us to maintain our awareness of the emotional differences between feeling connected directly to nature and merely being seduced by technology.

It is only when we are forced to confront the collective effects of our intuitive postures toward nature and technology that we manifest the ambivalence inherent in our emotional response to technology. This ambivalence can be traced to the evolution and ultimate dominance of science—the process of careful and systematic examination of natural phenomena. With the emergence of science as the operative religion and guiding philosophy for American life, we began to lose trust in our intuition. The scientific method implored us to accept counterintuitive "null" hypotheses until they could be exhaustively tested and finally rejected. The birth of the scientific method was a two-edged sword. It allowed us access to a level of natural phenomena beyond the surface of human sensation and intuition, unlocking many secrets which could be transformed into technologies, allowing us to more efficiently exploit the resources around us to our collective advantage as a species. At the same time, however, science also gave us tools by which we could examine the widespread effects of this new level of resource exploitation. Had we never evolved a scientific, analytical approach to nature, we would no doubt be a far less populous species. Our intuitive survival strategies would have frequently "failed" (or by some viewpoints, "succeeded") and held our population in check and our impact on the earth to proportions more in tune with those of other species. Environmental planner Ian McHarg often includes in his lectures an only half-joking scenario of two primordial slimes sitting together on a seaside rock in the year 10,000 AD after the presumed demise of *Homo sapiens*. One of the slimes says to the other: "Next time, no brains!."

If on the other hand we are to believe Robert Ornstein and Paul Erlich, brains are needed now more than ever. We have evolved as far as we can go by intuition and genetic selection. Any evolution from now on must be deliberately conscious, employing careful, long-term analysis of the incremental, deleterious effects of our actions, as opposed to the knee-jerk, quick responses to sudden environmental changes we have inherited from our hunter–gatherer days. Ornstein and Erlich believe that reliance on statistical analysis is essential for us to distinguish the slowly deteriorating and often imperceptible environmental conditions that are truly dangerous from those that are quick, perceivable, and conspicuous, yet imply no long-term threat. Earthquakes, forest fires, and floods result in much faster political action and more government emergency aid and financial support than ozone holes, global warming, acid rain, or groundwater pollution, yet the latter are far more critical to species survival than the former.

Although the human faculties responsible for developing technologies are the same as those necessary to analyze their impacts, the creative work of technological development has always been more "fun" for humans (and, of course, far more economically rewarding) than the drudgery of technological "police" work. Because of this, our ability to analyze the impacts of technology lags significantly behind our ability to create new technologies. This, then, is the dilemma of a scientific and technological world; the same scientific process that keeps on churning out new technologies which radically alter ecosystems and social fabric is also expected to evaluate and police those same technologies. Our struggle over the effects of technology implores us not to trust our intuition when managing our affairs with nature. Yet at the same time we are often presented with conflicting scientific views of reality and the likely effects of our actions. In the recent Exxon Valdez oil spill in Alaska, scientists' views polarized across political boundaries like iron filings on a magnet, with the fishing industry's scientists arriving at one set of conclusions as to the extent of the damage done, and Exxon's scientists concluding the opposite. The political and financial implications of the results of these research investigations were staggering; scientific findings on both sides were held in secret by top-down gag orders, making a mockery of the so-called objectivity of the scientific method.

It is in the fuzzy, cognitive domain that we place the other dissociated half of the technological persona; the technological impacts of the universal "they." This strategy allows us to beg the question of environmental impacts of technology, since even the experts don't agree, and by dividing technology in two, we can listen to the intuitive voice inside our head that says: "Go ahead, drive three blocks to the grocery store" or "run the air-conditioner; it won't really matter!" In spite of these attempts to quell the dissonance, conflicting messages from an ambivalent mind keep bombarding us, and in the face of this assault, we are increasingly uncomfortable.

Fantasy, Creativity, and Survival

It is possible, then, to examine the triangle of topophilia, technophilia, and technophobia in light of how we structure our personal world views—how we imagine idealized worlds, and how we adjust to the knowledge that the "real" world falls short of our ideal expectations. Most of us hold vivid mental images of the way the world *ought* to be. It is likely that all species possess some sort of innate optimism about surviving in the world, ranging from the autonomic responses of the simplest life forms to the complex, cultural, symbol-laden manifestations of humans. Imagination and creativity are essential to human existence, and it is through the very act of *creativity* that humans manifest this sense of optimism necessary for survival. Scholars of creativity insist that the creation of imaginary worlds is essential to human problem solving, and hence, to survival itself. Silvano Arieti (1976) maintains that creativity often requires a kind of "paleologic"—a necessarily prerational association of meanings, events, and environments which are common to both creative artists as well as schizophrenic patients. Both employ a kind of false logic ("A is *like* B, B is *like* C, therefore A *is* C"), but unlike the schizophrenic person, the creative artist presumably can move back and forth across the boundary between paleologic and Aristotelian logic in a conscious, deliberate fashion, making use of the paleologic as a vehicle for creative breakthroughs. Most of the major advances in science (relativity, quantum mechanics, and plate tectonics, to name a few) assumed a type of paleological relationship requiring great stretches of the imagination in order to explain heretofore unexplainable physical phenomena.

Likewise, in artistic and environmental design fields, imagination is absolutely essential in order to provide glimpses of possible future sensory realities or to create new physical ones (Sommer, 1978). Planners and designers must hold complex spatial and visual images of what their proposed projects will be prior to the production of the actual drawings and documents which will result in the construction of those projects in reality. Although now there are many sophisticated techniques to simulate physical changes a priori, design images must originate in the mind of the designer, and must gestate in a set of imaginary conditions favorable to their development. Creating anything "new" in the world, then, requires the assumption of certain idealized conditions. Architects, designers, musicians, poets, artists, scientists, and engineers must at least temporarily or momentarily assume an idealized posture with respect to the world, or risk becoming mired in the "analysis paralysis" of real-world limitations.

Landscape architecture has long been associated with the creation of discrete spaces on the land which embody an idealized relationship between

The Olmstedian pastoral ideal still dominates the American residential land-scape, as in this Sacramento condominium complex.

humans and nature. Central Park, Frederick Law Olmsted's revolutionary archetype of urban landscape design, articulated a new form of pastoral nature in the midst of the city. Where before there had been an obvious separation between rural and urban values, Olmsted advocated a deliberate change in the expected context such that rural, pastoral values could be represented in the middle of the city to provide humans with the best of both worlds. From Olmsted's launching of the profession, landscape architecture has attempted to mediate between human affection for earth and nature and the more pragmatic domains of human survival. Grappling with the problems of New York in the mid-nineteenth century, a city which had begun to be shaped by the machine and its influence on commerce and societal patterns, Olmsted drew upon park prototypes in England and his own aesthetic affection for rural values. The Olmstedian manifestation of idealized worlds comprising the "best" of pastoral and urban values remains, for better or worse, the dominant form of the designed American landscape to this day.

Ideal and Real Images

Each of us lives simultaneously in two often competing worlds: the *ideal* and the *real*. Our inherent optimism, rooted at the most basic level in evolutionary response to our surroundings, yet strongly developed and modified by thou-

The Ideal Image: The world as we wish it could be. From "Waterfall Valley," an original painting by Charles Wysocki from the 1975 Americana™ Calendar. Copyright 1974 AMCAL, Inc.

sands of years of cultural adaptation, seems to result in the cognitive construction of an ideal image of the world. This ideal image is influenced by fantasy and aesthetic values; emphasizes quality over quantity; and embraces the heart, soul, and spirit. It is the image of philosophy and personal meaning, remaining relatively constant under assault from a rapidly changing "real" image. As an individually centered world, the ideal image is under our personal control. It emphasizes our best notions of "peace," "home," and recreation. And in today's conditions, it is a world which must incorporate both ideal nature and ideal technology. Ideal nature incorporates our personal affections for the earthly context of our lives, while ideal technology includes those pragmatic, artifactual devices that we have found personally essential, either out of habit of use (without which life would be radically different) or out of personal symbolism of the technology as representative of the self.

A simple example—my father's riding lawn mower—represents a technology which, were it not available, would make the two acres of pastoral Pennsylvania on which he lives in his retirement inconceivable to him. Beyond utilitarian necessity, mowing his immense lawn is a symbolic act of identification for my father, and one of the ways he constructs his sense of self. Most of us can name numerous products of technology by which we shape and declare who we are—I have mentioned some of mine already: canoes, bicycles, and (I will add) my beloved acoustic guitar. Western philosophy draws a line of demarcation between human (i.e., artifactual) and nonhuman (i.e., natural) realms. Although we long for an idealized existence closer to nature, the trip to such a place would no doubt require us to pack a number of technological gadgets. In a very personal sense, our own ideal "nature" includes both idealized places and idealized objects. In our personal worlds, there is little operational distinction remaining between ideal nature and ideal technology. They might be placed in different descriptive categories; however, both are subsumed under our intuitive response to the world.

In contrast, our *real* image of the world is an image we construct based upon pieces of information and events originating beyond our control. It is an image of functional and pragmatic considerations, politics, economics, and science. It changes rapidly whether we like it or not, and what little order it possesses seems to be imposed on us. In contrast to the ideal image, we as

The Real Image: The world as we know it actually is—a freeway interchange and development seen from an airplane over Tennessee.

individuals are not at the center of the real image, but peripheral to it, and we are swept up by its forces. While the ideal image is subject to our personal control, we experience the real image as a world out of control, at least *our* control. As individuals, we perceive we had nothing to do with the invention and proliferation of the microcomputer, the deterioration of the ozone layer, the collapse of the Soviet Union, the bloodshed in Bosnia, the latest economic recession, or the Tuesday rush-hour traffic jam. The real image is the world of political compromise and economic necessity (as opposed to philosophical or ethical steadfastness), objective cost (as opposed to personal value and meaning), function (as opposed to aesthetics), and quantity (as opposed to quality). Most importantly, the real image is the progenitor of technophobia. Under the continual media barrage and mounting physical evidence of the environmental impact of rapid technological change, the relationship between the real image and the ideal image becomes increasingly strained.

In everyday landscapes, the ideal image and the real image play out differently. Ideal images weigh heavily on our choice of homes and venues for recreation, vacation, and entertainment, whereas real image concerns guide our choice of jobs and economic matters. The intentionally designed landscape follows the ideal image, while the vernacular landscape represents and is defined by the real. NIMBY is the classic battle between the two; the ideal image of our personal domain under attack by the real world beyond our control. Even though we fly in airplanes, cook, heat, and illuminate with electricity, and discard trash, we don't want the airport, power plant, or landfill next to our neighborhood because the landscapes implied by these real image necessities are a threat to the idealized notion of Home. By conservatively resisting change, the ideal image is a mitigating device we employ to reinforce our personally constructed world. The ideal image only changes under the most continual and vigorous assault by the real image, and this resistance to change is both psychologically and sociologically essential. Were it not for a resilient, idealized image of the world, individuals would literally go insane and cultures would disintegrate under the immense pressure of rapid change. Fantasy, imagination, and the ability to construct ideal images of the world, therefore, are essential to human survival.

But how much fantasy is too much? Inherent in the relationship between ideal and real images is a kind of tension in equilibrium, where the cognitive dissonance or "distance" between the ideal and real remains within certain limits. What we know in the real world and what we wish in the ideal are distinct and different, yet we adjust to the difference and learn to use the ideal image as a kind of yardstick by which to measure and evaluate reality, and vice versa. Both new landscapes and new, unfamiliar technologies are measured and assessed according to known, tested standards, but actual landscapes and emerging technologies evolve and change much faster than our idealizations of them. Because of this, there is always a gap between ideal and real notions of the world.

It is unlikely that the ideal and real images possessed by any individual are

A variety store in Koloa, Kaui, Hawaii. Playful imagination, fantasy, and creativity are necessary to human survival and essential to the way we structure our physical world.

ever concentric. Most of us perceive the real world as considerably less than ideal, with ample room for improvement. In a Gallup poll published in *Newsweek* (March 2, 1992), nearly 90% of Americans expressed satisfaction with their personal life (the ideal image), but only 32% were satisfied with "the way things are in the United States" (the real image). In some sense, the cognitive dissonance between ideal and real images is like the gap size on a spark plug necessary to fire the cylinders of change. If the spark gap narrows to nothing and the electrodes touch, no spark occurs. In a world where ideal and real images coincide, there is little human motivation to change; culture becomes content and stable, and no "progress" occurs, in the Western sense of the word. Although certain primitive cultures and ascetic eastern philosophies espouse acceptance of the limitations of reality and freedom from desire, human existence is characterized in the United States and other "developed" nations by the struggle to "improve" upon existing conditions. Desires are created never to be satisfied. Yet, as the 1992 Gallup poll reveals, there are times when existing real-world conditions have changed so radically that the gap between the ideal image and the real image is experienced as a chasm. These are times of high "potential energy" in the social system: either the ideal image must change, or major revolutions must occur in the means by which society structures itself.

The Renaissance, the Industrial Revolution, and the current transformation of society by information technology all reveal similar patterns of gross readjustments of the ideal image to positions more in conformity with the changing real image. During the Renaissance, the idealized state of human existence was transformed from that of stark adherence to religious codes of purity and piety to the celebration of human potential, scientific discovery, and artistic sensitivity. The Industrial Revolution brought radical changes in ideal world views which replaced an organically perceived universe with one of machine-like precision and efficiency. In each case, the structure of ideal images dramatically adjusted to a changing reality. Now, in the midst of the "Information Revolution," the ideal image has again become the target of intense pressure to change. Through media technology and manipulation, our real image— they way we presumably know the world *actually* is—and its increasingly intractable problems can be dismissed as just another social construction. We have begun to lose the distinct boundaries by which we can tell ideal from real. Instead, the new ideal image is a synthesized, heterogeneous collage of sound and video bites, emphasizing entertainment over problem-solving, electronic myth over physical "fact," surface image over substantive depth, yesterday and tomorrow over today. Our new, postmodern ideal image of the world is in an acute state of *denial,* struggling hard to cut its umbilical to reality, as if it could exist by itself. "Reality" isn't what it used to be; although each of us still possesses a real image, we are less sure of it than ever before (Anderson, 1990). Our world view is increasingly based upon vicarious, technologically mediated "experience" instead of real, tangible experience and physical interaction. Today's information-saturated world threatens nothing less than the complete blurring of reality and fantasy, and we must ask ourselves whether that condition is ultimately inevitable or desirable.

Technology Divided

Today we find ourselves in a deeply fragmented situation where we love nature, but depend on technology. Ironically, as we recognize the harm technology has done to the land, we also depend on an illusion of *not* being dependent on technology. In essence, we divide technology into that which *feels natural* to us (even though we may know of it operationally and intellectually as "technology" distinct from "nature") and that which doesn't. Our own, personal, self-defining technological products and the intuitive dependencies of our

Idealized technologies (futuristic, high-tech rail cars and nostalgic teak launches) move people about in the luxurious Hyatt Waikoloa resort on Hawaii's Big Island. Cars are immediately driven off to a hidden parking lot by valets dressed in tan shorts and pith helmets.

technological lifestyles join our affection for place, land, and nature in the domain of the ideal image. This is the remnant of our primordial, hunter–gatherer outlook on the world, where our feelings, beliefs, and actions were more integrated. The omnipresent world of technology—those dominating technological systems "out there" which we now know to have caused the earth considerable environmental trauma—are the result of a mind unable to prevent the evolution of simple tool use into a complex spiral of technological dependence. It is a real world in which we must survive and with which we must somehow cope. By shutting out from our minds and severing the obvious connections between "their" technologies "out there" and "our" technologies "in here" as a matter of course, we maintain the illusion that we as individuals are neither part of nor responsible for the enveloping technological fabric that makes up our contemporary world.

Lewis Mumford and the Megamachine

In his career of contemplation of the role of technology in human life, Lewis Mumford, as mentioned in Chapter 2, concluded that the true machine age started not with the steam engine or fossil fuel, but several thousand years ago when the first centralized, authoritarian social structures allowed power to be concentrated in the hands of god-kings who presided over both enormous stores of slave labor as well as secret priesthoods of scientific and technological knowledge. To Mumford, Ancient Egyptian, Mayan, Chinese, and Incan civilizations were "megamachines"—machine-like authoritarian social hierarchies capable of producing great pyramids, walls, temples, and road systems: in short, the first large-scale system of control over both human society and wild nature whereby humans were able to construct artifactual landscapes on a scope never before seen. By means of power vested in central authority, by a corps of technological elite to whom alone were entrusted the scientific secrets of the universe, and by literally using the common human laborer as "fuel," the megamachine anticipated the bureaucratic, military–industrial economies of the United States and the former Soviet Union by hundreds or thousands of years.

Mumford's notion of the megamachine—the combination of both physical technique and the mass societal structure to apply it—fits aptly into the split persona of technology we face today. The ghost of Mumford's megamachine now haunts us—the bureaucratic, self-perpetuating, perceptually externalized *system* of technological determinism which, in its momentous march into the future, cuts a swath through our primitive environmental sensibilities. Mumford maintained that the "myth of the machine" was false; humanity only had to come to its senses and realize the absurdity of the seemingly automatic promise of a better life for the individual implicit in the autonomous machine. To share in Mumford's conception of technology, however, seems to require of individuals psychological power of heroic proportions. Authors David Bohm and Mark Edwards (1991) maintain that the steady growth of technology was paralleled by an equally persistent psychological degeneration. The most primitive and genuinely "human" existence was in the highly cooperative, social bands of primal humans. But as tool use and its accompanying social structure evolved into more complex technology, the nature of thought itself changed, causing the individual consciousness to fragment into two: one part consisting of the "self" as a subjective observer and experiencer of reality, and the other part being the general representation of society including all "externalities:" the "environment," friends, relatives, even the "self-as-object" rather than "self-as-subject." For many scholars, the division of modern human consciousness into distinct *observer* and *observed* components—the "I" or "we" and the "they" or "it"—and the Western notion of a "self" independent of "environment" lies at the crux of the current environmental/technological dilemma.

The debilitating severance of *self* from *context* represents the point of intellectual convergence between ecophilosophers (Berry, 1988; Ralston, 1988; and Naess and Rothenberg, 1989), advocates of sustainable development (Rees, 1988), scientists (Bateson, 1979), psychologists (Ornstein and Erlich, 1989), poets (Snyder, 1989), and social critics like Lewis Mumford himself. The evolution of human consciousness to the dangerous point of considering itself separate from context is now considered by many to be a serious human deception, and the gross cause of accelerating social and environmental violence; "*I* am distinct from the local and global *environment. We* aren't burning down the Amazonian rainforest; *they* are." Separation of self from context is an easy escape from responsibility.

Mumford felt the anguish of this human severance personally and intensely. By splitting the persona of technology in two and locating the phobic portion beyond our control, we desperately hope to avoid the anguish Mumford felt throughout his life as an increasingly pessimistic observer of the evolution of technology and its effects on human existence. William Rees even suggests that we abandon the word "environment" because it furthers this destructive split:

> By definition, humankind cannot be part of the "environment." The very word separates "us" from "it." But the global reality belies the myth. The truth is that human beings are now the dominant species in all the world's ecosystems and the most powerful geological force on earth. From this perspective, we do not have environmental problems, the biosphere has a people problem. There can be no solution to our present dilemma unless we are prepared to accept this reality.
>
> There is only a singularity, the biosphere, and we are in the thick of it. Like it or not there is no "away." It is ironic, that to resolve the environmental crisis we must first give up the environment." (original emphasis).
>
> *Rees, 1988, p. 17*

Lewis Mumford was an organicist who, according to Marx (1990), clung to the holistic hope of a "massive transformation of human consciousness" which

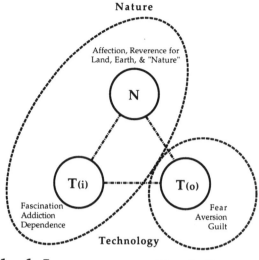

Ideal Image   Real Image

Our personally owned technologies and our affection for nature and land join in our idealized view of the world, while the "real" image we have of the world is dominated by the problems caused by technology in general (i.e., everyone else's technologies).

would ultimately deliver humanity from the jaws of the technological monster. Because Mumford believed that imagination, symbolic thought, advanced mental faculty, and abstract language preceded tool use in the evolution of true humanness, Mumford could place his faith in an escape route out of the dilemma of technology by reestablishing an organic vitalism to replace a mechanistic order, and by explosion of the myth of the machine as an automatic savior. Only time will tell whether Mumford's hopeful but risky hypothesis is correct. In the meantime, we struggle with a collective Green Heart in an ambivalent, technological Gray World of our own making.

Suspended in the Triangle

I have tried to show in these first four chapters that Americans live their lives in landscapes forged from the tension between three forces: topophilia, technophilia, and technophobia. As part of an ideal image of the world, topophilia and technophilia seem natural enough to us, but technophobia is the unpleasant byproduct of a technologically determined reality. Our inherent affection for the earth, land and nature propels us into conflict with our ambivalence toward technologies we have invented, ostensibly to make our lives better. We are collectively responsible for this condition, even though it is a condition we react to as if it were imposed on us by some external power. It is a nagging, three-way stalemate—a dissonant phenomenon which begs for resolution. Embedded in our human character are our love of land and nature, our propensity to imagine and invent idealized worlds, and our ability to creatively solve the problems of our own survival through tangible techniques, while an ambivalent mind struggles to reconcile the deteriorating technological world we perceive around us which our seemingly natural tendencies appear to have caused.

Sustainable Technologies and Landscapes

In the midst of this crisis, we have arrived at the new and increasingly popular notion of **sustainability**. As we try to reconcile a self divorced from the environment—*what* we experience around us, *where* we are, and *who we have become*—we have begun to ask questions about our technologies, our landscapes, and our selves. Are there technologies which can be considered "natural"? Are there possible human landscapes which do not result in the destruction of local and global ecosystems? Must we continue to exist as divided persons in this tyranny of technology which also separates us from our companion life forms? Is there a way out of the technology–nature conflict? I am convinced that the notion of sustainability has vaulted to the forefront of American thought and policy debate largely because it promises to respond to the dilemma of technology and nature.

Sustainability, sustainable development, sustainable technologies, sustainable communities, and *sustainable landscapes* are overlapping terms which have entered the popular, global lexicon so quickly and thoroughly that our natural distrust of buzzwords has been put on alert. I will discuss the etymological history of sustainability and related terms at greater length in Chapter 9. However, there is ample reason for the rapid, popular ascension of sustainability as a concept. "Sustainability" implies a *limitation on the degree and rate of human impact such that the natural carrying capacity of the earth's ecosystems can be perpetually maintained.* Central to the notion of sustainability is the idea of *time,* and the necessity of not expending resources or disturbing ecosystems at *rates* faster than that which can be compensated by the *regeneration* of those resources or ecosystems under natural conditions. If landscapes or ecosystems are disturbed or resources consumed beyond those rates, the future of all life forms dependent upon them becomes unsustainable, including humankind itself.

For the purposes of this book I will adopt the following definitions first put forth in *Caring for the Land: A Strategy for Sustainable Living* (IUCN/UNEP/WWF, 1991), a publication jointly released by the United Nations and a family of related international organizations:

Sustainability: A characteristic of a process or state that can be maintained indefinitely.

Sustainable development: Improving the quality of human life while living within the carrying capacity of supporting ecosystems.

Sustainable use: Use of an organism, ecosystem, or other renewable resource at a rate within its capacity for renewal.

Carrying capacity: Capacity of an ecosystem to support healthy organisms while maintaining its productivity, adaptability, and capability of renewal. (pp. 210–211)

Building on these definitions, I add my own: A *sustainable landscape is a place where human communities, resource uses, and the carrying capacities of surrounding ecosystems can all be perpetually maintained.*

A *sustainable technology is a technology which, when employed productively by humans, results in no loss of ecosystem carrying capacity, resource availability, or cultural integrity.*

Quite simply, the urgency of the nature/technology conflict has made the movement toward sustainability both inevitable and necessary. The idea of sustainability in landscape and community planning, technological and economic development, and environmental management springs directly from the sense of tension between topophilia, technophilia, and technophobia. In the following chapters I argue that *sustainable* landscape planning, design, and development is a major means of easing this tension. By transforming our currently blind and unchecked technological addictions through careful normative evaluation, by development of only those technologies that reveal themselves to be truly sustainable, and by applying those technologies to the land in manner guided by an overriding environmental ethic, we may move toward a resolution.

However, approaching sustainability will require us to alter radically the various entrenched meanings implicit in our lives, technologies, and landscapes. Just as the need for fundamental change is being felt ever more acutely, an exponential increase is occurring in the ability of information technologies to gloss over real environmental problems and create a landscape fantasy so vivid it threatens to replace reality altogether. Sustainability, I believe, springs not only from the guilt associated with technology's *physical* impact on nature, but also from the growing tendency of technology to replace nature in our minds as well.

II

Technology
in the Landscape:
Dimensions,
Dynamics,
and Dilemmas

*I*n the first section, three basic forces shaping the modern American landscape were presented: affection for earth, land, and nature; addictive fascination and dependence upon technology; and dissonance, fear, and guilt over technology's negative consequences to the environment. As domains of attitude affecting the landscape, however, these three forces have evolved slowly over time and have asserted themselves in varying proportions and by diverse means, only recently combining to necessitate a response toward something now called "sustainability."

In the next three chapters, I examine the landscape in terms of the dynamic interaction of these three social forces, and discuss the field of landscape meanings that arise from this three-way tension. In Chapter 5 I offer a three-dimensional, theoretical framework of relationships between the perceptual, functional, and symbolic

A fossil-fuel power plant across the Sacramento River as seen from the cemetery in Collinsville, California.

characteristics of utilitarian landscapes and their resultant social implications and interactions. The various interpretations I present are not intended as sharply focused presumptions of absolute truth. Instead, I offer a set of rather indeterminately bounded social meanings for various landscapes—meanings that have struck me as salient and somewhat generalizable across modern American culture. In Chapter 6 I review several case studies of specific American landscapes which demonstrate how the modern dilemma of nature and technology has evolved over time, revealed itself in contemporary culture, and presented alternative directions for the future. Chapter 7 elaborates the rapidly evolving changes to the meaning of "nature" and "technology" and relates these changes to the changing sensible form and social role of the landscape. Chapter 8 chronicles the emergence of a growing condition of hyperreality in which the boundary between reality and simulation, the differences between technology and nature, and the clarity of the relationship between surface and core properties of the landscape all seem to dissolve.

Section 2 articulates and illustrates the dimensions, dynamics, and essential dilemma of technology, nature, and landscape as they have evolved through time, operated in the present, and begun to construct the future.

5

Dimensions of Technology in the Landscape

Humans have the tendency to assign subjective meanings to environmental stimuli, then react to these meanings as if they were part of the environment.

RENE DUBOS

Landscapes influenced by technology form the context for everyday life in America. Over the course of several hundred years, an American landscape consisting primarily of "natural" elements was transformed into one where human artifice extends ubiquitously across our common view. Today most of the American population lives in cities and suburbs, where the human hand on the land is most obvious, and the greatest proportion of our experimential backdrop has been visibly altered by humans. Much of this highly visible alteration is vernacular in origin, pragmatic and economic considerations have taken precedence over intentional design for stylistic or aesthetic purposes. The most common visual backdrop for contemporary Americans, therefore, is a landscape forged of practical necessity by the operative technologies of modern life.

As this transformation from "natural" to "human influenced" landscape conditions took place, and as American life gradually evolved into the highly complex interaction with technologies that it is today, the vernacular landscapes influenced by those technologies took on an expanding complexity of meaning. Many volumes have been written about the accrual of landscape "meaning," and conflicting theories abound. I chose the opening quotation for this chapter from Rene Dubos (it was later paraphrased by Amos Rapoport, 1977) because I believe it summarizes in quite simple terms a highly plausible theory of the role of meaning in the interactions of humans with landscapes, particularly with those landscapes highly influenced by technology. Meaning, of course, is a devilishly tricky concept. Is meaning part of the environment, or is it in the mind of the observer? Is a solid waste landfill *inherently* ugly because of some intrinsic pattern or characteristic independent of human experience, or does it trigger a complex set of culturally generated feelings and beliefs about human-generated waste? My conclusions from 20 years of research in landscape perception is that *"environmental" meaning ultimately resides in the observer, but the observer acts as though the meaning resides in the environment.*

Planners and designers, of course, have preferred to believe that meaning resides in the environment because it enables them to make more sweeping generalizations about the role the environment plays in human well-being. If landscape meaning were in the mind of the individual participant only and no generalizations *across* social groups about the visual meaning or aesthetic quality of the landscape were possible, there would be no profession of landscape architecture, no architectural critiques, no "styles" of design, no design review commissions, no billboard restrictions, and no visual resource management programs in the federal landholding agencies. Obviously, to at least some degree, there are sufficient, commonly held meanings presumed to be at least partially attachable to the landscape to warrant great effort and economic activity on the part of thousands of Americans in the design and visual occupations. The real estate profession would no doubt put forth a vigorous argument against the idea that common environmental meanings do not exist.

The fact that we are able to presume that certain meanings can be thought to attach to the environment itself can be explained by the idea of *culture.* Culture is nothing more than a system of commonly held beliefs, symbols, and behaviors. Culture itself presumes certain commonality among individuals, and material culture assumes that some of that commonality can be ascribed to elements in the environment. In addressing "material culture," anthropologists look for common meaning in objects and environments by which they can make inferences about social groups. Yet there is, of course, much variation across different groups and even between individuals in groups. A landfill may mean something quite different to me than to my brother or colleague. Furthermore, each *individual* (as well as each social group) may perceive many different levels of meaning in the *same landscape* at different times. One day a landfill may mean an "eyesore," while on another day, it may mean an "untapped resource." Inevitably, different meanings of a single landscape may be experienced simultaneously by the same person or group. Generalizations about landscape meanings, therefore, are always only "general" and are subject to much situational and individual variation. However, this does not mean that generalizations are not applicable or useful, because they literally hold culture together.

Although cultural experience molds a great deal of the meaning we presume to see in the landscape, strong arguments exist that at least part of the meaning comes from more primal sources—our most basic genetic predisposition as human animals. In the familiar and oversimplified "nature versus nurture" debate, I take an inclusive, middle position that landscapes reflect a "dual inheritance model" of evolution, where both genetically and culturally adaptive strategies have come into play. Technology, however, is a relatively modern phenomenon, and the extent of technologically influenced landscapes in the everyday human context has only occurred recently. Our widespread discomfort with our technologically manipulated surroundings may stem from a conflict between a kind of biologically grounded affection we feel for nature and a "runaway" or "drift-away" cultural evolution favoring the symbolic prestige and indirect "advantages" we have assigned to technology as a shortcut to our survival (Boyd and Richerson, 1985). It is not necessary to choose between genotypical or phenotypical explanations for the conflict between technology and nature; both are at work in the landscape. Only questions of the levels and types of interaction remain. In this chapter I attempt to weave a general theory of how technologies have acquired meaning in the landscape, for the landscape meanings of technology form the heart of the conflict and potential for resolution central to this book.

A Cross-Cultural Landscape Scenario

Imagine for a moment that a 5-year-old boy from an aboriginal people deep within the Amazon basin—who has never before set eyes upon a Western, "developed" landscape nor any human being other than members of his own tribe—is magically transported and set down in the middle of an oil refinery near Philadelphia. Given his basic, human perceptual faculties and his unique experience in his own environment, how would the Amazonian boy decipher this new landscape? Most certainly, he would perceive himself to be standing upright, as usual, on the ground, with the sky above him and the earth below. His senses could tell him a great deal about light and dark, near and far, enclosed and open spaces. He might perceive the refinery towers as vertical elements a certain distance from him, much as he might sense the canopy of trees a certain distance from a clearing in his home forest. Moving his head from side to side, he could perhaps see that objects in the foreground, although unfamiliar, occluded other, equally unfamiliar objects in the background. Although he would find a refinery tower with its spaghetti-like plumbing or a spherical natural gas tank with a spiral ladder completely unorthodox, he could perhaps sense that these items were perceptual "wholes" unto themselves, with properties making them "hang together" as complete spatial and physical units. By moving about in the environment, he might also determine how far away he was from the nearest object, and how large it was with respect to him.

At this point, however, his perceptual experience might begin to fail him. Instead of recognizing anything green (the predominant color in his native environment), he would be presented with a palette of grays and browns. The intricacy of the plumbing, while of a texture similar to that of certain tree branches, would be of a unique pattern comprised almost entirely of straight

An oil refinery near Rodeo, California.

lines running parallel and at right angles, with few gentle curves and little of the random, fractal variation characteristic of his Amazonian home. As such, he might conclude that this was a place made by sorcerers. He might stamp or rub his bare feet in amazement at the strange, dark, hard, rock-like (asphalt) surface beneath him. Walking carefully closer to touch one of the shiny metal pipes, he might be shocked at how such a highly reflective surface could feel so smooth, hard, and cold to the touch. Breathing in, he would find the smell completely other-worldy, and might conclude that the place was evil and unfit for humans.

The particular referential significance which most Americans would associate with the oil refinery would be completely lost on the Amazonian boy. He would share no concept of the function of an oil refinery with our culture—no association of the refinery with keeping warm, getting from one place to another, cooking food, or making clothing. He would, of course, know nothing of the relative social and economic value of the refinery as a "heavy industrial" zone within the land use planning context of greater Philadelphia. Finally, although his own symbolic construction of his world would be as elaborate and detailed as that of any American boy his age, the Amazonian boy could not be expected to understand our symbolic "meanings" of the refinery as a source of employment, a tax base for Philadelphia, a cause of pollution and source of global warming, or a patriotic icon of American energy independence. Even an American five-year old would not yet comprehend this level of meaning.

In trying to understand how landscapes acquire meaning, a pivotal concern has to do with how much of human perception is based upon innate characteristics presumably common to all humans and how much is dependent upon specific culture and experience. One can find considerable research evidence supporting both polar assumptions; and increasingly, researchers are converging on coevolutionary explanations which acknowledge certain deeply ingrained human perceptual faculties as well as tremendous variation among perceptual response depending on learning, culture, mood, predisposition, personality, concurrent activity, and other variables.

Semantically, "technology" has only existed since the term was coined by a Harvard professor in 1844 (Marx, 1963). As an operational construct, the notion of technology has no doubt been in effect considerably longer, but certainly not long enough to have had much effect on genetic or inherited human characteristics, which require thousands of years before influencing human genetic predisposition. Many others (Ornstein and Erlich, 1989; Kaplan and Kaplan, 1982b; Boyd and Richerson, 1985) have cogently argued that we are trying to live in a technologically engineered environment with an out-of-date perceptual apparatus which evolved thousands of years ago and which has not had time biologically to process and incorporate the new technological reality. Two major implications spring from this condition; first, that we must therefore rely heavily upon cultural transmission, or *learning* to cope with and survive in this technological world, and second, that such learned coping strategies are bound to drift away and ultimately clash (often violently) with the more innate, biological way we might have responded if we had lived thousands of years ago in a more "natural" environment. Out of necessity, we have manufactured a complex set of *meanings* for the technological surroundings we occupy. In the *deliberately designed* environment (wherein the form of buildings and landscape elements were generated by professional architects or landscape architects partly to induce certain aesthetic responses and appeal to or create symbolic values independent of extrinsic or intrinsic function), form and meaning beyond utilitarian dimensions is of primary importance. However, the farther away one moves in terms of perspective, the more the built environment can be viewed as a collective indicator of the technological meaning of American culture. From 40,000 feet up in an airplane, aesthetic and symbolic dimensions blur, and the American landscape reveals the great degree to which it has evolved in response to utilitarian influences and technological developments. From this perspective Pierce Lewis' taste-free landscape (or the vernacular landscape concerns of J. B. Jackson) takes precedence.

The concept of *meaning* is central to the remaining discussion in this chapter. Architectural psychologist Jon Lang offers a framework useful to describe the rather slippery concept of "meaning" in the landscape which attempts to weld together the best of genetic, gestalt, or "sensation-based" theory, and "information-based" theories of environmental perception (Lang, 1987). As an experiencing participant in a landscape, a person must first be able to perceive light and dark and form and pattern, and to distinguish figure from ground—tasks most easily explained through sensation-based perceptual theory. Then, with increasing experience, a person may begin to recognize utilitarian functions in the landscape. Ultimately, the person must decipher and comprehend symbolic meanings which may have no intrinsic relationship to the more fundamental perceptual or functional properties of a landscape.[1]

The first task—that of recognizing elementary pattern and form—is less dependent upon "higher," abstract meaning levels, and is likely to be more consistent across human subcultures. For example, both the Amazonian boy and a five-year old from the Philadelphia suburbs could be expected to be able perceptually to navigate their way in and around the oil refinery towers, perhaps with nearly equal levels of amazement. At this most primitive and immediate level of perceptual interpretation, it is safe to assume certain common, genetically based perceptual faculties shared by all human beings regardless of cultural milieu.

On the other hand, "use meaning" or functional significance involves recognition that a landscape has a fundamental, utilitarian purpose psychologically inseparable from the form. For the American five-year old, for example, a "farm" has fields and a barn. Such an association between a landscape and its function necessarily depends on cultural transmission of information, and it is likely that members of the culture who use a particular landscape feature in a certain way are unable to "sever" the perception of the use from that of the raw stimulus. The American boy might recognize the refinery as a place where oil is made. For the Amazonian boy, however, there would be presumably no recognizable function for the oil refinery, and he would be left with other meaning dimensions by which to understand the strange, unfamiliar environment.

Symbolic meanings of the landscape are more easily *detachable* from the landscape itself, and may be perceived and understood only through significant participation of the individual within a culture and its system of commonly held symbols. While there may be only a few specific use meanings associated with a utilitarian landscape, there are many possible symbolic meanings, each of which can coexist simultaneously as part of an individual's construction of reality. People add new symbolic meanings gradually to existing symbol vocabularies, incorporating new elements in such a fashion that the whole symbol system remains comprehensible and easy to remember (Boyd and Richerson, 1985). A nuclear power plant in the landscape may represent danger, jobs, energy independence, or political folly. However, none of these alternative symbolic constructs is expressed automatically in the form of the visible landscape without prior experience or social convention. The Amazonian boy witnessing the oil refinery for the first time would struggle to incorporate the forms into his own unique cultural and personal symbol structure, just as a naive American boy would struggle to make sense out of the unfamiliar and highly symbolic environment of the Amazonian rain forest.

I have created the hypothetical scenario of the Amazonian boy to suggest that in some small, recessive corner of the human psyche, we Americans may find we have more in common with the Amazonian boy in terms of our response to the oil refinery than we might think. Landscape meaning is a phenomenon of interacting levels of meaning, some of which appear to be quite basic to human existence and others which require high degrees of exposure to the complexities of a particular culture. It is highly probable that in the interaction of levels of landscape meaning, particularly those associated with modern technology, dissonance may occur between levels, and this dissonance may relate fundamentally to the conflict between nature and technology.

Three Dimensions

Starting from the discussion in the previous section, it is possible to construct a three-dimensional framework for examining the meanings of landscape—particularly that which has been influenced by technology and utilitarian necessity—and its impact on human affect or emotional response. We respond to landscapes as forms and patterns of light and dark distinguishable from background; as the result of or context for human functions and actions; and as symbols of particular social or personal value. Let us assume a three-dimensional model where each dimension can be displayed as perpendicular to the other two dimensions. The first row will be called the *perceptual* dimension, where technological manifestations in the landscape are categorized according to their degree of *perceivability* and *conspicuousness* in the landscape as differentiated from the so-called "natural" background. The second dimension consists of the major, familiar *functional* associations or groups of technologies the typical American might recognize in the landscape. Finally, the third dimension organizes technologies in terms of their *symbolic* implications with respect to the land.

   A simple experience in the author's life may help to illustrate the three basic meaning dimensions of any technological landscape feature. While on a backpack trip 20 years ago across a section of the Continental Divide in the Colorado Rockies, my friend and I paused for a breather part way up the trail. About one mile away we could see the saddle of land between two peaks—a pass across the divide which would take us down to our lakeside destination for that evening. There in the distance, but in plain site, were several patches of a very shiny material against the rocky background. We immediately entered into a debate, my friend insisting that these surfaces were of natural origins—perhaps a patch of ice or snow, and I asserting they were manmade. The debate spawned a bet for a bottle of wine. Travelling another 200 yards, we both concluded that I had won the bet. Although we were not yet near enough to make out many details, the shiny patches were definitely metallic in origin, and did not seem to be arranged in a pattern we recognized as part of the normal mountain context. (At this point, we had experienced the *perceptual* level of this technological landscape intrusion). Only when we had approached within several hundred feet of the metallic surfaces did we recognize them as the wreckage of a light airplane (we had then experienced the *functional* level). Upon arriving at the scene, we were relieved to discover that the wreckage was at least several weeks old, and the pilot and any similarly unlucky passengers or their bodies had long since been evacuated. We lingered at the wreckage site for some time, excited but saddened, pondering the unfortunate accident. Picking up the pilot's headphones, my companion examined them, put them on his head, and after a serious and introspective pause, speculated about the possibility of living humans communicating with the dead. At this point, the radio earphones had become *symbolic* of that hypothesis. Hence my companion and I had successively experienced three basic significant levels of human intrusion on the landscape. Attracted initially to a visual stimulus set off from its context, we first perceived the stimulus as "technological" and human-made without knowing its function. Later, we recognized the function, and finally, made some symbolic connections.

My purpose in developing this framework is to suggest that each dimension contributes, both individually and perhaps synergistically, to a participant's *affective response* to a particular utilitarian or technological landscape, and that by examining each dimension separately and more closely, we can learn much about how we react to the technologically influenced landscapes that form the context of our daily American existence. In the case of our encounter with the airplane wreckage in the Rockies, my companion and I had approached in a linear fashion, and our experience of each dimension was therefore sequential. Had we stumbled upon the wreckage suddenly, however, we might have experienced all levels simultaneously. Whether the experience of complex levels of landscape meaning is linear (i.e., information processing) or simultaneous (e.g., Gestalt) and whether the perceptual, functional, and symbolic levels act independently of one another or in an interactive, interdependent manner, is unclear. However, I am convinced that humans evaluate the three meaning dimensions according to inner "positive–negative" scales or operative procedures. In short, each meaning dimension or significance level contributes something to overall affective or emotional response, be it negative or positive. Our response to utilitarian, technologically influenced landscapes is partly dependent on characteristics of each dimension, and each dimension can be broken down into more discrete categories which further influence affective response.

In the following discussion I suggest three presumably orthogonal dimensions of the meaning of technological/utilitarian landscapes, each successively more dependent upon cultural learning. Within each dimension, I suggest a set of particular characteristics which can be *generally* ordered as to their likely influence on human emotional response (I admit that considerable variation between and among groups and individuals will exist). Finally, I attempt to illustrate these dimensions and characteristics by reference to specific landscape examples.

The Perceptual Dimension

At its most basic level, a technologically influenced landscape is recognizable as a set of patterns resulting from changes in the wavelength and intensity of light emanating from the landscape—the basic stimuli upon which all visual perception is based. Upon first seeing the oil refinery, the Amazonian boy would compare the new visual patterns with his own perceptual storehouse of environmental images, and would undoubtedly find the new landscape strikingly different at several very basic levels. Searching his own environmental reality for something comparable to what he was seeing, he would find nothing similar, and would be forced to assign totally new meaning to this unfamiliar landscape. For any human viewing a totally unfamiliar environment, the basic perceptual stimuli are quickly organized into forms and patterns. It is safe to assume that *initial recognition of a technology (i.e., a human, utilitarian alteration to "natural" surroundings) is through form, color, reflectivity, texture, and pattern* (Wohlwill, 1983).

Although humankind is presumed to have evolved consciousness thousands of years ago in a largely contoured, vegetated world, Americans now live in a context dominated by straight lines, reflective flat planes, shiny surfaces, man-made materials, Euclidian patterns, greater movement, and more noise. At the most fundamental level of perceptual meaning, technology is certainly recognized and "read" through a vocabulary of concrete stimuli as if set against a more random, background context of "nature" unaltered by humans. There is growing evidence of genotypical or evolutionary explanations for the human preference for so-called "natural" surroundings over those that are man-made (Ulrich et al., 1991; Balling and Falk, 1982; Pitt, 1982). Although we "depend" on this technological landscape for our modern existence, our perception has not had time in a few short hundred years of living amid technological development to evolve to a point where we *prefer* the technological over the so-called natural context. Consequently, we may at a rather elementary level perceive man-made or technological features as radical and sometimes threatening changes in the "natural" visual backdrop even if we do not consciously know how they function or what they really mean. Hence, there is some of the Amazonian boy in all of us.

At the simplest level, we might presume that humans are biologically predisposed to respond positively to so-called natural contexts and negatively to so-called technological intrusions which, at the most basic level, are perceived as radical deviations to the form, color, reflectivity, pattern, or activity level of the natural background context. At the most fundamental level, we may not often know the *function* or *abstract meaning* of a technological intrusion, but at least we can often tell a man-made intrusion when we see one. There are certainly many fine gradations of the degree to which technological or utilitarian alterations to landscape are visible and distinctly perceivable. To illustrate this graded spectrum, I define four basic categories of technological intrusion at the perceptual level: *invisible, implicit, explicit, and iconic.* Based on the well-supported evidence that humans prefer "natural" landscapes over those that are "man-made," the four basic categories can be arranged in a general order from most to least acceptable in the public eye.

Invisible technology, in landscape terms, is that wherein the principle technological change has minimal or no *visible* effect on landscape structure, form, or materials—at least for the untrained eye. At this level of perception, it is impossible to detect the influence of a technology against the "natural" background. Many modern information or biological technologies are primarily "landscape"-invisible, such as engineered DNA, microwave signals, and nuclear radiation. If the effect of a technology is not immediately visible or perceivable in the landscape we experience, we rely solely on second-hand cognitive processing or our own imaginations to understand and assign relative value to it. This can lead to rather wild fluctuations in assigned value. The nuclear industry is a case in point. Because nuclear radiation is basically invisible and its tangible landscape effects lie latent for years, public willingness to live near nuclear power plants has been severely polarized; those who comprehend and believe the likelihood and extent of potential radiation damage find nuclear power plants abhorrent and would not live near a nuclear power plant, even if it were out of sight (Thayer and Hansen, 1989). On the other hand, others ignore or dismiss as erroneous the associated risks, and seeing no tangible evidence of radiation extending outward from a nuclear power plant, form positive opinions about nuclear energy. Those who live in close proximity to nuclear plants tend to favor nuclear energy more strongly than those living farther away (Otway et al., 1978). The relative invisibility of nuclear energy's impact has been fundamental to its recent curtailment by public protest, and at the same time, has been a key marketing point by the industry itself, which claims nuclear energy is beneficial to air quality. Similar questions about the invisibility of attributes of technology and nature weigh heavily on the future of American culture and landscape.

Implicit technology is the form or pattern left on the land when technological machinery or other essential hardware has "come and gone." Implicit technology may dramatically alter or rearrange the "natural" landscape of soil, rock, vegetation, and water, but leave little in the way of obvious manufactured materials such as asphalt, concrete, plastic, or steel. Agricultural patterns—ploughing, cultivating, land shaping, crop planting, creation of orchards and vineyards, and man-made bodies of water—are examples of implicit technology. So are the historic earthen revetments of Revolutionary and Civil War battlegrounds that once concealed artillery, and the remnant gravel mounds found along old California gold-dredging sites. Implicit technology in the landscape, then, consists of obviously human patterns made of "natural" materials. Because of the manipulation of materials commonly perceived as "natural," implicit technology is often reacted to as part of the "natural" world, although the altered landscape may hardly resemble the original character present before alteration by humans.

A social value hierarchy exists for materials as parts of landscape composition; earth, rock, water, plants, and wood are generally perceived to have higher status as components of the vernacular landscape than materials involving more complex human processes like concrete, metal, asphalt, or plastic. The latter group seems not to be capable of expressing our idealized relationship to nature. However, there are actually no "unnatural" materials in the landscape—only those that may *look* unnatural and take more energy and human ingenuity to transform; plastic is made from petroleum, which in turn came from plants long crushed beneath the earth's surface. Metals are concentrated and refined from naturally existing rock ores. However, in neither case does the final form, texture, color, pattern, or reflectivity of the final material resemble that of the original, natural condition. Hence, for implicit technologies, a mechanical or technological *trace* or *pattern* left in a natural material context or background seems more palatable than landscape technologies leaving visibly different *materials* in addition to obvious man-made patterns.

I define *explicit* technology as that which is part of the overall utilitarian landscape matrix or context, and is obviously comprised of man-made materials and forms or "hardscape." Explicit technology is quite visible and so widespread as to be perceived as integral and essential to the total landscape. Explicit technology has an ubiquitous presence; most "development" is explicit—streets, highways, power poles, railroad tracks, industrial zones, vernacular buildings and auto strip developments, for example. In the explicit technological landscape, what little architectural and landscape aesthetic meaning was intended is overwhelmed by the vernacular communication of utilitarian purposes. Because of its saturation in the visible landscape, the most predominating forms in terms of visible area, such as asphalt streets, concrete sidewalks, stucco buildings, and telephone poles are frequently "tuned out" and not noticed. In a direct way, explicit landscape technology is the *contextual fabric of our modern experience*—the human-altered backdrop against which most of our daily life occurs.

Iconic technology includes visible technological features which, either as a result of large scale, unique form or function or controversial nature, are highly *conspicuous*. An iconic technological landscape feature can be a negative space, such as a strip mine site, or a positive element, such as a nuclear power plant. Iconic technology can be differentiated from explicit technology by standing out from the background, attracting attention, and taking on "larger than life" proportions. The referential characteristics of iconic technologies are often direct and powerful; a reactor cooling tower "stands for" nuclear energy in general and all its associated meanings, which vary according to public attitudes toward the referent technology itself.

Implicit technology in the landscape. The shape and form of this plowed orchard near Winters, California, expresses the processes but not the materials of agricultural machinery.

On a simple, one-dimensional value scale, a very coarse generalization can be made that the more conspicuous and visually dominant a technology is, the less it is likely to be valued in the American landscape regardless of its functional or symbolic overtones. Americans still cherish the pastoral illusion and, at the most fundamental level, conspicuous utilitarian intrusions contrasting to rural or wild backgrounds are simply less appreciated by the public. Were it possible, Americans would probably like to have their cake and eat it, too—or, in terms of the landscape, to make personal use of the *benefits* of a technology without seeing what everyone's use of that technology does to impair one's personal landscape. As a result, power lines are buried, parking lots are screened, and power plants are placed as far from residential areas as possible. Americans don't like landscape *change,* and so they are forced to make compromises between their own use of technological innovations and the resulting impacts of widespread use of technologies by society. Ideally, we would prefer each highway to be a scenic one, and ours to be the only car upon it. We want the surrounding landscape as viewed *from our car* to be beautiful, but the view *of* the road and of everyone else's car to be nonexistent. While some technological intrusions into the natural landscape achieve a certain curiosity value, all things considered, the more conspicuous the utilitarian "disturbance," the less valued the landscape.

Rancho Seco, an iconic technology in the landscape, was the first nuclear power plant in the United States to be shut down by vote of the local utility rate payers.

The Functional Dimension

The Amazonian boy, when looking at a fish spear made by his father, would recognize its function if it were lying on the ground, held in his father's hand, or suspended from a tree. To an American five-year old, the basic utilitarian meaning of a park bench would remain "attached" to the bench even if it were ripped from its foundation and mounted vertically on end as a piece of pop sculpture. It is a fair assumption that for a human environment or object of utilitarian purpose, a major portion of its visual meaning or significance results from the association between its form and its particular utility in human life. This, of course, implies a learned relationship between the environment or object and the human using it. The nature of this associative meaning stemming from direct use might be positive, such as a gardener's feeling of affinity for a particular plot of soil, or a carpenter's sense of appreciation for his hammer. On the other hand, an association between place or object and its inherent function might be valued negatively, as between a convict and the prison yard, or an underpaid farm worker to an orchard of overripe fruit. Regardless of whether the value is positive or negative, the association between an environment or object and the specific use for which it is intended is a perceptual bond of considerable strength and magnitude. Gestalt psychologists proposed the disputed assumption that there were certain inherent qualities of objects in the perceptual field which demanded certain behaviors: "Each thing says what it is . . ." (Koffka, 1935). Arguments have continued since about how objects acquire such properties, or whether those functional attributes are actually in the mind of the perceiver. Whether they are or not, humans tend to respond to the use meanings of environments or objects *as if they were* properties of those environments or objects themselves.

Few individuals can be said to actually and directly "use" a complex facility such as an oil refinery or dairy farm; however, our education and experience have enabled us to associate certain forms with certain essential human purposes. The concept of human "use" is slippery. We all use energy, water, food, and clothing, but in an age of specialization, few of us have firsthand experience with a hydroelectric power plant, cattle feedlot, or textile mill. However, most of us would be able to recognize enough visible attributes of those environments to place them within an elementary framework of relative value to modern life.

The functional dimension of the framework presumes an association on the part of the viewer (or landscape participant) between the perceived technological landscape manifestation and its utilitarian purpose. This is an admittedly tenuous assumption as the technological function becomes more specific and more complex. Some landscapes merely "look technological" (a *perceptual* differentiation) and a lay person may have no idea what goes on behind the buildings, structures, and landforms. However, the American public is not as naive as is commonly claimed; the recognizability of function plays a significant role in the formation of attitudes toward a particular category of technology as a component of the landscape. Recall that in the scientific experiment described in Chapter 3, an identical photo of a "reservoir" (a utilitarian association) was gauged significantly less beautiful than the exact same photo with the label "lake."

Assuming, therefore, that functional meanings of technological landscapes are both recognizable and *generally* ranked in a value hierarchy, five *major* categories of technological function in the American landscape are easily identifiable. I call them: *transformative, transportive, energetic, agricultural, and informative.* There are many minor categories and many bifurcations, but these five categories constitute the major technological categories which shape American landscapes.

Transformative technology, such as mining, manufacturing, and construction, involves the *conversion of raw materials from the earth's surface and subsurface into other materials, goods, or structures.* The form these outputs take may be either transitory or permanent. This category of technology is most significant in its impact upon the landscape, for its major function is that of transforming portions of earthly materials for human utility. The places where this transformation occurs strongly influence our attitudes and overall landscape character. The effects of material transformation on the environment have spawned the notion of "environmental impact" and have resulted in the American planning tradition of zoning, which aims to locate transformative uses away from primary residential areas, ostensibly to protect the public health, safety and welfare. Such zoning, however commonplace, creates a dual value hierarchy. While valued by some as critical to economic development, transformative technologies are low on the ideological value scales of most citizens. No one seems to want to live near a strip mine, factory, or solid waste dump, yet our collective economic behavior as consumers not only justifies but demands the existence of such facilities.

Energetic technology transforms energy resources into useful work, and therefore provides the means by which other utilitarian technologies operate. This may occur by either *renewable* or *nonrenewable* means. Much energy technology is environmentally conspicuous, like power plants and refineries, electrical transmission towers, and gasoline stations. The electric utility grid itself—the spatial network that delivers electrical power—is a good example of a system which is visually conspicuous, but spatially and functionally incomprehensible. From looking at power lines, one has difficulty determining origin and destination. Power lines stretch between horizons, and wires lead into various technologically looking contraptions. Nowadays, the single power line actuating one's home environment is often buried underground and only emerges at the electric meter. Partly because of this state of confusion, individuals lack the visual, spatial, and economic feedback necessary to make informed decisions about energy supply, and leave the entire task to the government and utility decision-makers. As a result, energetic technologies in the landscape are often misunderstood and mistakenly construed as site specific locations or events (*the* Exxon oil spill, *the* nuclear power plant, etc.) rather than the true, intricate networks that they are.

Transportive technology is that which *moves people, material, or goods* °from one location to another. Together with transformative and energetic technology, transportive technology has drastically impacted and largely *defined* the landscape we inhabit today. The railroads and ultimately, the automobile, have assumed dominant roles in forming the modern American landscape. In spite of the increasing gridlock in American cities and atmospheric effects of exhaust, Americans love to move. From the nineteenth century reporting of de Tocqueville to the present, the theme of motion asserts itself over and over throughout American landscape history and culture. The relationship between technophilic automotive addiction and topophilic appreciation for experience in nature is a salient and undeniable fact of American culture, (e.g., *"See the USA in your Chevrolet"*) one that is certainly not lost to advertising agencies charged with selling cars. Therefore, although transportive technologies admittedly contribute to some of our worst environmental problems, they are generally more highly valued than transformative or energetic technologies. Often the *energetic* landscape (gas stations, refineries, etc.) is the necessarily evil prerequisite for the transportive landscape; Americans would like nothing more than to be able to move rapidly between two points without consuming energy or damaging the environment, but they won't give up the former to achieve the latter.

Interstate Highway 5 crossing the Sacramento River floodway in California—a "transportive" landscape. Prior to construction of causeways like this, auto transportation across the wide Sacramento River floodplain was often impossible during the winter rainy season.

First trains and then later automobiles filled the mythical role of physical and spiritual transcendence in American culture. Witness the recurrent story: restless American leaves his oppressive city job, gasses up his car, and heads for the hills to confront the challenges and rewards of nature. Fixated on reenacting this national scenario, Americans have yet to fully grasp the extent of global or local landscape devastation owed to their automotive excesses. Our addiction to the car is guided by a romantic myth of transcendence (the car is the modern equivalent to the cowboy's horse), fueled by the automotive industry, and necessitated by the fact that we live in a world which is simply inoperative without the motor vehicle. The automobile provides three characteristics which virtually guarantee its perpetual use in our culture, barring significant cultural revolution: (1) it is a *human multiplier* which gives its operator a feeling of exaggerated power—a small movement of the accelerator pedal results in tremendous motion; (2) it is a *random access* vehicle which presumably goes almost everywhere its operator wishes; (3) it is a portable *personal space* from which the operator and passengers may exclude others and prevent unwanted social contact in an increasingly fearful world. Ironically, the psychosocially attractive properties of the automobile do not carry over into the *landscape* which the automobile must occupy. Automobiles are both a transcendent cultural symbol and a utilitarian necessity in the current American lifestyle. The landscape of streets, roads, and superhighways can be both a prison and/or a means of escape. This ironic contradiction places the transportive landscape somewhere in the middle of a general hierarchy of functional meanings.

Agricultural technology is the manipulation of the surface of the earth and water for the production of food and fiber. Globally significant in terms of its impact on the earth's surface, agriculture somehow garners a higher visual status, due in part to the essential necessity of food and fiber, the age-old nostalgia for rural life, or some evolutionary affinity we feel for the soil itself. Allen Carlson (1985) argues that in spite of the coarse scale, visually monotonous, monocultural nature of the modern agricultural landscape, we will eventually forgive it of its presumed ugliness because of its direct connection to human survival. We don't *have* to drive our cars or watch television; we *must* eat. America was culturally forged from the rural dreams and agrarian ideals of people like Thomas Jefferson, who claimed the transcendent nature of the agricultural landscape and lifestyle as the prime source of American values (Marx, 1963). This deep-seated bias in favor of rural landscapes runs deeply in American culture; "amber waves of grain" assume a status equivalent to "purple mountain majesties." In spite of public alarm concerning pesticide use and irrigation waste, and in spite of how much modern farms seem to resemble machines in their own right, such as the mammoth, center pivot irrigation systems now dotting the plains (Sutton, 1977), agricultural landscapes still rank high in the American hierarchy of visual and spatial values (Carlson, 1985).

Informative technology differs from other functional categories in that it involves the *generation, transmission, dispersal, and digestion of information* rather than physical materials or hard goods. Informative technologies have far fewer visible manifestations since their main product—information—is an "invisible" concept. Even though information technology results in specific hardware, its physical characteristics are of secondary importance to its role in the manipulation of information. Although the "Information Age" will undoubtedly make an immense impact on the form of the American landscape, it will be significantly different in character from the changes caused by transformative or transportive technologies whose effects remain visibly prominent on the surface of the land itself. Depending upon how inclusive or exclusive one defines information, it is largely *invisible* in landscape terms. While one radical physicist, Edward Fredkin, speculates that information is actually the basic building block of the universe, most concur that information is the invisible companion to matter and energy which has allowed ordered life to evolve into its manifold complexities. Scientists like Fredkin argue that only by a greatly accelerated level of information flow can the increasingly complex technological world be made to function properly (Wright, 1988); others argue that "information" is a misnomer—more and more *data* is translating into less and less *information,* much less *knowledge,* and hardly any *wisdom* (Jackson, 1987).

In the future, the manifestations of information will likely be less and less

Center-pivot irrigation rigs like this one in western Nevada produce the now-familiar circular agricultural landscapes frequently seen from airplanes.

directly obvious to the landscape. Although it could be argued that the railroad, the automobile, and the inexpensive, stud-wall house have virtually defined the modern American landscape, it is less easy to predict the specific landscape effects of genetically engineered crops, buried fiber-optic communication cables, microcomputers, and artificial intelligence. Early attempts to predict the impact of information technology on the American landscape were rosy; "electronic cottages" linked invisibly to "teleports" were to replace ugly suburbs linked to industrial and office complexes by crowded freeways. There was, of course, an early reaction of landscape guilt over the rapid explosion in the presence of TV antennae, but the onset of satellites and buried TV cable to most urban and suburban houses has replaced that problem out of sight. For now, the relative landscape-invisibility of information itself and the unknown secondary and tertiary effects of a society structured around the transmission of information rather than the consumption of goods places information technology in a relatively high position of landscape value—certainly higher than transformative or energetic landscapes. Compared to the functional attributes of other, more landscape-intensive technologies, there is little *inherent* unpleasantness in the few visible landscape manifestations of the transfer of information.

The Symbolic Dimension

The third dimension is the most abstract of all the dimensions proposed in this chapter. It is based upon symbolic associations, or what the technology "stands for" beyond its straightforward use in the landscape. It is also the most fluid in terms of associated values. The reader could very well ask *which* among a myriad of possible symbolic attributes to technological or utilitarian landscapes should be discussed. The word "technology" itself conjures up many possible associated constructs: jobs, power, utility, dominance, ingenuity, environmental destruction, social anonymity, economic survival, efficiency, and so forth. However, for the purposes of this book, I am most interested in the symbolic meanings that bear upon and reflect the meaning of the technology not in static isolation, but in a dynamic, *time*-dependent dialog with a landscape setting. As we look upon our relationship to technology as it is manifest in common American landscapes, we are increasingly aware of the element of time. How much longer can we continue the current consumptive relationship?

The symbolic dimension I describe is highly time dependent, and the categories I offer are *consumptive, sustainable, utopian,* and *nostalgic.* In the simplest of descriptions, *nostalgic* technological landscapes represent only the *past* and its related associations. *Consumptive* technologies dominate the present world *today,* but are incapable of sustained interaction with land systems in the future. *Sustainable* technologies, on the other hand, have

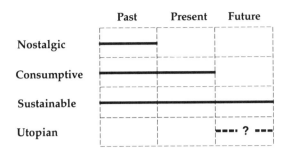

Nostalgic, consumptive, sustainable, and utopian technologies: the symbolism of time in the landscape. We hold futuristic and nostalgic technology in high esteem, while the consumptive technologies of today are often associated with environmental degradation. We have yet to fully comprehend sustainable technologies as lasting influences on our landscape.

sometimes existed in the past, are here (to an unfortunately limited extent) now, and *are* capable of continuous use into the future. Finally, *utopian* technologies belong almost entirely to the *future;* they are as yet a promise unfulfilled.

Consumptive technology is the predominant technology of the *present* and recent past, and includes most transformative technologies operative today, such as mining, manufacturing, and construction. Consumptive technology can be characterized as a one-way equation—a one-time conversion of raw materials—*a taking from the earth for a short-term gain.* By quickly taking and not returning, its message is one of *"conspicuous consumption."* Consumptive technology dominates the world economy and has virtually created the landscape in which we live today, contributing greatly to the origins of technophobia. By actually *ripping open and consuming* parts of the earth, consumptive technology symbolizes a wounding and consumption of the earth's "flesh." This symbolic wounding results in a kind of negative "synesthesia" (a sensation received through one sense yet felt through another) among people. British landscape architect Sir Geoffrey Jellicoe (whose quotation introduced Chapter 3) suggests that true landscape ugliness did not evolve until we began noticeably extracting resources from below the earth's surface. This explains why we react less strongly to agriculture as a landscape intrusion (a surface use) than to manufacturing, mining, or waste disposal (subsurface uses). Like observers at an open-heart surgery, we find the cutting and disgorging of the earth which normally accompanies heavy construction, mining, and manufacturing physically abhorrent. Consumptive technology colors our evaluation of all technology as antithetical to landscape values such as nature, beauty, and transcendence; we sense in consumptive technology a certain violation of the body of nature, and this negative reaction spills over into all other technologies through guilt by association.

Explicit, consumptive technology is so widespread (e.g., paved roads) that

At this modern gold mine in Napa County, California, each ton of ore excavated nets 0.125 ounces of gold. Although the mine meets and exceeds state-of-the-art environmental standards, the landscape effect is one of consumption by technology.

many technological landscapes, regardless of what type of technology they incorporate, gain a bad image. We hold consumptive technology responsible for the pollution of atmosphere, water, soil, and the waste of land itself. Therefore, although presumably essential to our current lifestyle, consumptive technology is most often considered ugly and is frequently concealed, camouflaged, disguised, placed far away from population centers, or deliberately ignored and erased from society's mental map (Do *you* know where your toxic waste ends up?). Surface manipulation of the landscape can only conceal so much of this type of radical surgery. Given the currently growing level of public technophobia, we will not long be able to sustain the level of consumptive interference with the body of the earth.

Utopian technology represents the technology of the *future.* Utopian technology is that which has not yet come fully "on line," and is not yet so broadly diffused throughout society as to garner much negative reaction. Most technology evolves through some sort of utopian stage. Many Americans still remember when nuclear power was promoted as a benevolent genie emerging from a bottle. The utopian technologies boldly praised today include genetic engineering, "cold" nuclear fusion, and artificial intelligence, all of which seem to shimmer on the developmental horizon as cures for the ills mostly caused by preceding technologies. The public naturally assigns higher visual status to those emergent technologies that show the *potential* to solve some of our current problems. When the subsequent problems with the technology are revealed, the visual status slips. American society reserves more affection for the promise of tomorrow's technology than for the operative technologies of the present, which in their inevitable failings have generated new problems as they have solved old ones. Utopian technology, because of its relatively untested nature and unsaturated landscape presence, offers only *promise*, without the onus of current impact. For this reason, artists' renderings often show utopian technologies in idyllic landscape settings. The newest technologies previously mentioned are "landscape invisible," and therefore fit easily into the utopian category. In spite of the increasing invisibility of the newest technologies, society seems impelled to translate utopian visions into physically and spatially perceivable symbols, and so utopian landscapes continue to emerge (Hough, 1990). "World's Fairs" of avante garde technophilia recur every few years, and Disney's Epcot Center still illuminates a vision (currently being updated) of the future world as if to tame the monster of the technological unknown into a benign and subservient being. It remains to be seen how successfully, or even *if*, the emerging, largely invisible technologies can translate into utopian landscape symbols.

I define *nostalgic technology* as that which is associated with the *past*, is no longer viable, and has become part of history—abandoned mining districts, old farming or logging equipment, covered bridges, wagon wheels, and, at a

Radio telescopes in the Owens Valley of California. By being rare and referring only to the promise of the future, utopian landscape symbols avoid being saddled with the environmental and social "sins" of today's consumptive technologies.

grand scale, the National Park Service's repackaging of defunct industrial zones as "national heritage" districts (Krohe, 1990). Being part of the past, nostalgic technology gains visual status and is proudly and conspicuously displayed in the landscape. This type of technology is clear manifestation of technophilia, providing assurance of a continuum of culture anchoring us to our heritage and hearkening back to the so-called "good old days" when things were supposedly better, or at least less complicated. Nostalgic technologies ease the unpleasant taste of landscape guilt by connecting us with a familiar past. Because they have been "neutered" by the passage of time, nostalgic technologies seem somehow harmless, and their original sins easy to forgive. In California, Malakoff Diggings, the site of severe environmental damage from nineteenth century hydraulic mining which nearly ruined California's agriculture by man-made erosion and siltation, has been classified as a State Historic Park. Historic park status places a frame of temporal distance around the site, "sanctifying" it and conferring upon it a degree of visual meaning which is somehow eerily aesthetic. Even the color of rust seems to connect the old, scattered fragments of mining machinery effectively to the surrounding landscape. Readers will no doubt recall a myriad of front yard landscapes across urban, suburban, and rural America which have been decorated with old mining carts, wagons, ploughs, rusting tractors, miniature windmills, bucksaws, or old-fashioned, steel wheel barrows. At best, such symbols glorify a former utilitarian bond between human, machine, and the land, and speak of personal and familial roots to past cultures; at worst, they become kitschy landscape tokens of middle class affiliation. Of all the symbolic dimensions, nostalgic technology seems to garner the highest visual landscape status. In the spirit of technophilia as it is revealed in the landscape, it may be said that the only good technology is a "dead" one.

Sustainable technology, as indicated in Chapter 4, is capable of sustained operation over an indefinite period of time without reducing the carrying capacity of the local or global ecosystems. Sustainable technology creates useful energy or goods but does so by relying on renewable resources and respecting culture, human scale, existing land integrity, and ecosystem stability. Although few technologies are absolutely benign or purely sustainable, the degree to which there are significant differences in the impact of different technologies on landscapes and ecosystems is becoming perfectly clear. Examples of sustainable technologies include wind power plants, solar energy systems, material recycling facilities, minimum tillage and organic farming practices, drip irrigation systems, bicycle transportation networks, small-scale on-site stormwater retention systems, and multipurpose wastewater treatment wetlands which double as wildlife reserves or recreation areas.

Sustainable technology offers a means of reducing the cognitive dissonance of landscape guilt by acquiring positive symbolic value through a gradual diffusion into common use in a phenomenon which I have previously labelled "*conspicuous non-consumption*" (Thayer, 1980). The example of California's wind energy plants is a case in point. Once considered utopian symbols of the

Designation as a California State Historic Park places a more positive, nostalgic frame of reference around Malakoff Diggings, once the site of environmentally destructive hydraulic gold mining. Photograph by Tim Woodward.

future, windfarms soon evolved through a period of negative landscape status as symbolic "tax dodges" and "ugly, technological intrusions." Gradually in the last few years, the public has begun to recognize that the benefits of such a relatively benign and renewable energy source far outweigh the impacts, most of which are visual and not geophysical or ecological in nature (Thayer and Freeman, 1987). In the future, it is likely that the public will find wind plants to be sustainable energy sources and emergent environmental symbols vastly preferable to Persian Gulf wars, oil spills, or smog. Thus, although many technologies evolve through a utopian phase, some will ultimately be judged positively in accordance with their relatively mild environmental impact and will come to symbolize a more respectful attitude toward the earth. The transition to a world supported by sustainable technology rather than dominated by consumptive technology is an emerging social goal shared by numerous scholars, cultures, and international governments.

Why the Theoretical Framework?

Why articulate such a framework for considering the various levels of meaning of technological or utilitarian landscapes? Clearly, technology is not only a

A contemporary wind power plant near Altamont Pass, California. As a sustainable and relatively benign source of energy, wind plants have the potential to express past, present, and future.

major determinant of physical form and essential landscape structure, but the landscapes resulting from the influence of technology read as an index of our past, present, and possible future environmental attitudes—our social "posture" with respect to the earth. The three major dimensions (perceptual, functional, symbolic) and their various categories change with time and interact with each other to determine the degree to which a particular utilitarian or technologically influenced landscape is deemed undesirable or intolerable by the public. Ultimately, by examining the perceptual, functional, and symbolic attributes of a technological landscape, one can gain a clearer understanding of the multiplicity of its effects on human perceptions, attitudes, and behaviors.

In the figure below I have provided a generalized, hypothetical rank ordering of the various categories previously discussed for each of the three dimensions. At the perceptual level, the less conspicuous the technological landscape, the more it is likely to be valued by the general public. At the functional level, agricultural and information land uses are likely to be more highly valued by the general public than those that transform land or physical resources (mining, manufacturing, construction) or those requiring the consumption of energy.

The symbolic level is admittedly the hardest to pin down, but here value is time dependent, with the reality of the present valued less than the memory of the past or the promise of the future. Nostalgic technologies have achieved high visual status because they are no longer operationally threatening; utopian technologies are nearly as unthreatening, representing promise and hope without operational impacts. It is the consumptive technologies in widespread use today that seem to have caused all the problems, and they garner little symbolic status among the general population. However, people are too unfamiliar with sustainable alternatives to grant them much visual status yet either.

By representing this three-dimensional rank ordering in terms of shades of gray on this rectangular graphic framework, with darker tones being less desirable, an overall sense of the relative general desirability or status of technological landscapes can be compared. The lighter tones at the apex of the framework reveal that barely visible or implicit, nostalgic, agricultural, or information landscapes are likely to be most preferred, for example, the faint trail of the old Pony Express or an old fashioned split-rail pasture fence. Rotating the framework 180 degrees, however, would yield the most undesirable technological landscapes with the darkest tones nearest the foreground corner: conspicuous icons of today's consumptive, transformative technology,

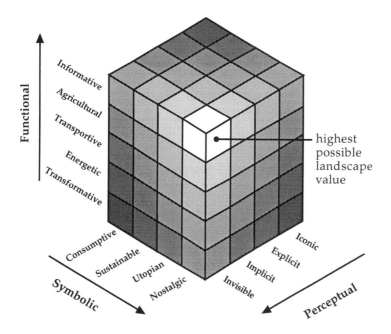

Theoretical "meaning" dimensions of technological/utilitarian landscapes. Each landscape may be considered in terms of perpetual, functional, and symbolic dimensions which interact to yield an overall relative evaluation of the landscape. In this diagram, arrows point towards higher public value; landscapes represented by the darker cells are less acceptable, whereas those represented by lighter cells are more acceptable.

such as a coal-fired power plant, strip mine, or hazardous waste dump. Between these extremes lie numerous landscape/technology interactions which fall in the grayer areas of perceptual, functional, and symbolic value. In these areas one would expect to find the most fluidity and change among landscape meanings over time. For example, as today's consumptive technology gradually becomes uneconomical and inoperative, it will evolve into the nostalgic category and will become more acceptable as a visual landscape intrusion; defunct "Rust Belt" factories are gaining landmark status even as I write. One would hope, however, that society can also learn to assign a higher value to the more sustainable technologies, even though some degree of resistance to any technological intrusion or landscape change, whether sustainable or consumptive, is inevitable, natural, and probably necessary.

Topophilia, Technophilia, and Technophobia

Most landscapes, examined at any scale, embody elements of all three social attitudes of topophilia, technophilia, and technophobia. At the Marine World/Africa USA theme park in Vallejo, California, stylized versions of natural animal habitats coexist with water-skiing demonstration lagoons. Here, topophilia is represented in the landscape plantings and animal displays, technophilia in the lighting effects and water-ski boats, and technophobia in the concealment of the irrigation system, water pumps and filters, and air conditioning units, and the visual screening of the parking lots. Characterizing the proportional mixture of these three attitudes or forces for any landscape can be facilitated by the use of a triangle, with topophilia at the top, technophilia at the lower left corner, and technophobia at the lower right corner. Any landscape in question can be "located" on a triangle based upon the proportion of each of the three generalized attitudes embodied in the landscape.

This model is hypothetical and not meant to be mathematically precise, for in any given landscape, the symbolic meaning is often arguable and the causative forces hard to determine. However, the triangular framework allows some comparisons between landscapes and facilitates the "framing" of the main body of landscape meaning by extreme examples near the corners of the triangle. For instance, a toxic waste repository can be considered an almost entirely technophobic landscape, while a wilderness trail is nearly completely topophilic. An automobile drag strip exemplifies an near-complete technophilic landscape. A housing subdivision is a blend of all three. Subdivisions are frequently given topophilic names of the natural or pastoral features in the landscape (e.g., "Quail Ridge," "Green Meadows," "Arlington Farms") they have replaced. Although subdivisions are structured for easy automobile access, automotive themes are visually downplayed, and technological features like TV aerials, utility meters, and power lines are often screened, disguised, or buried.

Topophilia

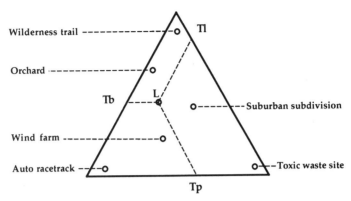

For any landscape L, L(Tp) = % Topophilia,
L(Tl) = % Technophilia, and L (Tb) = % Technophobia

Landscapes can be "located" on a triangular field of attitudes according to the relative degree to which each embodies topophilia, technophilia, or technophobia. For any landscape L, L(Tp) = % topophilia, L(Tl) = % technophilia, and L(Tb) = % technophobia. Although some landscapes seem to embody only one attitude, most embody some combination of all three.

A wind energy power plant, on the other hand, is a highly technophilic landscape. Telephoto views of modern wind turbines have been used in marketing as positive symbols of quiet power to sell automobiles (British Honda Motor Company) and Christian music compact discs (Petra). However, some people find modern wind farms to be an objectionable visual (i.e., technophobic) assault on romantic pastoral conditions.

A fruit orchard such as any found in the Central Valley of California represents a similar combination of topophilia and technophilia. Its material manifestations (i.e., trees) are less threatening to many people than the mechanical appearance of modern wind turbines. However, orchards are nearly as mechanized as wind farms; the strict geometric grid patterns of the fruiting trees is an unmistakable sign of human manipulation, and planting, irrigating, spraying, and harvesting of orchards are increasingly done using machines and chemicals. In spite of this, most people would attribute a sense of "natural" order, harmony, bounty, and beauty in an orchard landscape that combines both topophilia and technophilia.

There are, no doubt, other variables on other dimensions which could have been included in this framework. A major point of this book, however, is that *some proportion of the three attitudes or social forces of topophilia, techno-*

philia, and technophobia are embodied in simultaneous, tensile relationship to one another in nearly every landscape.

The triangular nature/technology framework bears resemblance to other triangular frameworks relating to social systems and dynamics. Economist Kenneth Boulding describes all human social constructs and institutions in terms of a similar triangular combination, with the components *threat, exchange,* and *integration* at the apexes. For example, in Boulding's framework, banks and stock markets have a high proportion of *exchange,* police and armed forces have high *threat,* and churches, families, and schools have high *integration,* while local governments attempt to combine and reconcile all three. (Boulding, 1985, p. 86).

A similar triangular framework can be offered which might be labelled a "Necessities of Life" triangle: the *reasons* or *motives* for living, the *means* to live, and the *context* for life. Chapter 2 presented a hypothetical glimpse of a possible simultaneous evolution of both art and technology springing directly out of an earthly context; it is with considerable remorse that we moderns look back upon a time when we presume that the means, motives, and context for life were part of a single, integrated construct. Today, the means for living relates strongly to technology, while the reasons and motivations relate strongly to the aesthetic and topophilic dimensions. The context for life is clearly the earthly ecosystem as modified by humans—largely through tech-

Integration   Motives for Living
                                                    (Why)

Church   Art,
Family   Ethics,
                                               Philosophy
Law
Police   Stock   Technology   Ecology,
            Market   Environment

Threat   Exchange   Means for Living   Context for Life
                                            (How)   (Where)

Boulding's "Social Triangle"   A "Necessities of Life" Triangle

Boulding theorized that all social   The personal necessities of human
institutions and organizations could   life characterized by a field bounded
be classified with respect to the   by the technological and practical
proportions of *threat, exchange,* and   *means,* the reasons, or *motives,*
integration.   and the environmental *context* .

A) Boulding's "Social Triangle": Boulding (1985) theorized that social institutions could be classified with respect to the proportions of threat, exchange *and* integration. *B) The "Life Essentials" triangle from Chapter Two: human life characterized as a field bounded by the technological and practical* means, *the reasons or* motives, *and the environmental* context.

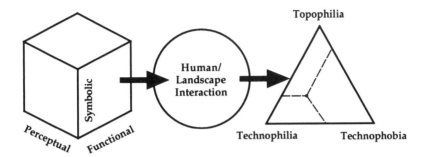

"Meaning" Dimensions of Technological Landscapes	Emotions/Attitudes Toward a Specific Landscape
Through repeated experience with many landscapes, participant mentally constructs a cognitive framework of subjective meanings based on perceptual, functional, and symbolic dimensions.	Participant responds to a specific landscape as if it were an "objective" stimuli, placing it in a relative attitude or emotional response "field" of various proportions of topophilia, technophilia, and technophobia.

A transactional model of human response to technological/utilitarian landscapes. Through repeated experience, a participant categorizes a landscape according to a framework of subjective meanings based on perceptual, functional, and symbolic dimensions, then responds to that specific landscape as if it were an "objective" stimulus, "placing" it in a relative attitude "field" framed by topophilia, technophilia, and technophobia.

nological means. From our current perspective, we sense that a considerable tension has arisen between technology at the one corner, ecology and environmental quality at another corner, and aesthetic, spiritual, and philosophical motives for living at the third, as if somehow the original integration has stretched like a rubber band in three different directions and is now about to break.

Thus the familiar nature/technology framework which has been the focus of this book relates strongly to a family of other triangular frameworks. Just as a triangle is the simplest polygon which defines an interior space, the triangular framework with three directional apexes allows a simple elegance in circumscribing and defining an area of sociocultural meaning.

In conclusion, the figure below suggests a generalized model of human response to utilitarian technological landscapes. Through repeated exposure to the perceptual, functional, and symbolic dimensions of many utilitarian landscapes over time, people construct a hierarchical framework of subjective meanings. This hierarchical framework results from both social norms and individual preferences. When interacting with a specific technological landscape, this mental framework of meanings allows the individual to respond to a specific landscape as if it were an objective stimulus, "placing" it within the familiar, triangular field of attitudes and emotions (topophilia, technophilia, and technophobia).

To review the main points of this chapter, let us examine the previously illustrated wind farm landscape on page 128. The technology is highly conspicuous because of differences in pattern, reflectivity, and rhythmic order of the turbines in comparison to the "natural" (i.e., pastoral grazing land) background. At this fundamental level, a substantial man-made intrusion to a baseline "natural" landscape condition has occurred. (Regardless of "higher" meanings, any landscape intrusion recognized as technological in character is likely to influence public acceptance and response—see Thayer and Hansen, 1989.) At the functional level, the wind farm is understood in terms of its utilitarian meaning: wind blows, turbines spin, and electricity is generated. Recognition of this utilitarian purpose may also influence the way in which the public evaluates the windfarm; the public may or may not care whether electrical energy is produced. Finally, at the symbolic level, a number of more abstract meanings may be inferred which further affect public response to the wind farm. Since there are cattle in the landscape and they seem to be successfully coexisting with the turbines as they spin, the entire landscape composition may be read as a symbol of efficient, benign, multiple use of rural land. Furthermore, viewing the wind farm landscape shown in the photograph might provoke a high degree of *technophilia* (the turbines are new and technically fascinating), and a moderate degree of *topophilia* (the scene is rural and animated by livestock, the essential pastoral ingredient), and only very mild *technophobia*, depending, of course, on who is doing the viewing.

The model illustrated and example described are admittedly speculative; I have offered only one suggested ordering of the various categories along the three model dimensions. In reality, an engineer might value certain categories by different means and in different rank order than would a psychologist, salesman, or farmer, and all would come up with at least slightly different interpretations of the wind farm. Undoubtedly, like all models of psychological phenomena, this one loses flexibility as it attempts to simplify.

However reduced, the model illustrates a useful relationship by which to consider technological landscapes. By responding to familiar dimensions of landscape meaning, we form a range of attitudes toward those landscapes. Technological or utilitarian landscapes take on multidimensional meanings which result in different human responses, and both society and the individual ultimately classify and respond to technological landscapes according to some unique mix of topophilia, technophilia, and technophobia.

Although this chapter aims at both deliberate and "unselfconscious" landscapes, the focus has been on the latter—those landscapes that have evolved directly from utilitarian or technological imperatives and that would be included in J. B. Jackson's (1984) lexicon of the vernacular, or geographer Pierce Lewis' categorization of "taste-free" space (Lewis, 1990). These unselfconscious landscapes constitute *most of the landscape we experience daily,* and embody much of the reason we feel uncomfortable about the current, conflicted relationship between land, technology, and nature. The theory offered, although simplified, allows the reader a possible explanation of how the current dilemma is experienced. In the next chapter I discuss several specific American landscapes which illuminate how we arrived at this dilemma and how the American landscape has already begun to respond.

NOTES

1. For a more detailed discussion of plausible alternative models of environmental perception and cognition, see Amos Rapoport's *Human Aspects of Environmental Form*, 1977; Howard Gardner's *The Mind's New Science*, 1985; and Roger Ulrich's "Aesthetic and Affective Response to Natural Environment," in *Behavior and the Natural Environment*, edited by Altman and Wohlwill, 1983).

6

Dynamics and Philosophical Dilemmas

> *The peculiar thing about a scientific society is that it takes the world apart, and it doesn't put it back together.*
>
> GARRETT ECKBO

Somewhere in the evolution of Western thought, *technology* emerged out of human nature to become something unique and separate from either humans or nature. This current feeling of *dis*integration, although widespread, is by no means universal, static, or monolithic. Concepts of "nature," "technology," and "landscape" evolve and change, and mean different things to different people at different times. It is possible to find American landscapes existing today which mark different phases in the evolution of nature and technology as concepts; the growth of an independent notion of technology apart from nature, the bifurcation of human response to technology into opposing realms of affinity and aversion, and the possibility of some form of reunification.

We cannot be sure of the origins of the concepts we now know as nature and technology. Clarence Glacken's comprehensive examination of nature and culture (1967) begins with the origins of "western" culture in ancient Greek and Sumerian theology, while Leo Marx's *The Machine in the Garden* (1963) looks back only secondarily to the Greeks, beginning his principle discussion with Shakespeare and occasionally referring back as far as Virgil. But what of *primal* humans? Did a separate mental construct like "technology" exist for them, or was there an original state of integration where tools, environment, and human consciousness were experienced as a unified whole? The best evidence that such a state might have ever really existed is that people seem to want to return to it with such passion.

By the time they had begun burying their dead, ancestral humans had most certainly begun to see themselves differently from other animals. Equipped with a body of archaeological, historic, and literary evidence, and spurred by

View from a cliff dwelling, Bandolier National Monument, New Mexico.

the environmental guilt we feel today, we aim our analysis backward toward a hypothetical point of origin and integration. Recently several archaeological sites were unearthed by modern excavation equipment during construction of a housing development near my home town in California. The burials contained over 270 bodies dating from about 3000 to 1300 years old. One man's body was found buried with the entire intact skeleton of a Tule elk. Women had been interred holding stone mortars and *metates;* men with atlatl stones, stone knives, or other hunting tools. Many bodies were found with hands clasped around crystals. In nearly all burials, the heads were oriented to the west, and in one burial, the skull was found resting in an abalone shell as if it were a modern-day pillow. After discussing these burials at length with the archaeologist in charge of the exhumation, I could only conclude that these were a people who seemed to display an undifferentiated reverence for earth, animals, tools, and human life.

A "Water Droplet" Model of Nature and Technology

We prefer to imagine our ancestral origins in a state of wholeness, like that of a perfect water droplet, where the antecedents of what would become "nature" and "technology" are indistinguishably bound together with humanity in a single, original unity. The droplet analogy can be expanded to represent the evolution of nature and technology; the water droplet begins to "fall" through time—the gravitational pull of history. At some identifiable stage, humans have become keenly knowledgeable of their surroundings and increasingly aware of their own uniqueness from other life forms. They begin to make more sophisticated tools, ceremonial structures, and the beginnings of a fine art. In this "primal" stage, the falling water droplet begins to form two joined droplets: "self" and "nonself," or for our purposes, human technology and nonhuman nature. Yet even at this moment in the model, separation is inconceivable; although unique, humans and their tools are still part of an overarching natural order. For this primal stage at least, the emerging water droplets cannot be pulled from each other, but the distinctive human/environment bipolarity has become noticeable.

Farther along, the "gravitational pull" of Western history finds human self-consciousness and exploitation of technique to have grown in the European context of a divinely created heaven and earth. Humanity and nature are still bound together by the Judeo-Christian concept of Creation and the notion of teleological purpose in the universe. Humanity is placed on earth to finish God's creative work; humans are to occupy a position of dominion and stewardship over the rest of nature, which has been made available for the continued benefit of humanity, as livestock is given to the shepherd or clay to the potter. There are two opposing subthemes in this religious philosophy: one, that a divine and wonderful world has been expressly made by God for a near-divine humanity, and two, an opposing theme that sinful humans deserve an imperfect world wherein they must toil to survive. Both are wefts woven into the warp of Western culture. In spite of this duality, human-created artifice is both distinct from nature and inspired by the artisanship of the one true God as the original Creator. Here, in what might be considered a medieval stage, the metaphoric water droplets strain to become distinct, but are still connected by the thread of creative artifice: that of God on the one side, that of humans on the other (Glacken, 1967).

In what might be termed a "naive" modern era, the droplets have fallen farther and split apart. Something called "technology" now exists as distinct and separate from something else called "nature," and the separation has more to do with science and less with God. Copernicus, Galileo, and Kepler (all deeply religious men), have illuminated a new conception of the physical universe. Bacon has legitimized the scientific method; Descartes has declared the human mind independent from the body. Newton has devised a mathematical explanation of the movement of the heavens. Watt's steam engine has ushered in an age of nonanimal, fossil fuel power. Western industrialists have

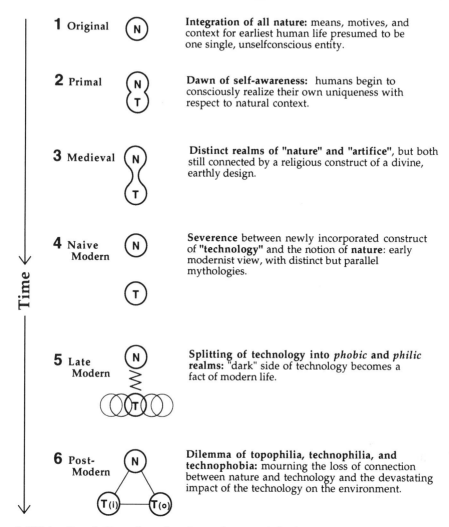

1 Original (N) — Integration of all nature: means, motives, and context for earliest human life presumed to be one single, unselfconscious entity.

2 Primal (N)(T) — Dawn of self-awareness: humans begin to consciously realize their own uniqueness with respect to natural context.

3 Medieval (N)(T) — Distinct realms of "nature" and "artifice", but both still connected by a religious construct of a divine, earthly design.

4 Naive Modern (N) (T) — Severence between newly incorporated construct of "technology" and the notion of nature: early modernist view, with distinct but parallel mythologies.

5 Late Modern (N) (T) — Splitting of technology into *phobic* and *philic* realms: "dark" side of technology becomes a fact of modern life.

6 Post-Modern (N) T(i)—T(o) — Dilemma of topophilia, technophilia, and technophobia: mourning the loss of connection between nature and technology and the devastating impact of the technology on the environment.

Time

A "Water-Droplet" analogy for the evolution of the human constructs of nature and technology. "Falling" through historical time, separate aspects of nature and technology appear, grow farther apart, disconnect, and ultimately create dissonance in the human mind.

turned archaic craft guilds into efficient, new social machines of production. At this point, there is the world of humans and their technology, and there is also nature's world. They are now identifiable as separate constructs, coexisting in parallel as the modern era progresses and the water droplet continues to fall through time.

With the rapid increase in the scale of technological impact during what could be called a late modern period, the "technology" droplet begins to divide in two, one part characterized by fear or remorse and the other by affinity;

technology has become the tool of human evolutionary success as well as the cause of much environmental damage and social distress. Certain government officials and scientists warn of the predicament of Earth in the balance, while other government officials, scientists, and industrialists search for new technologies around which to build a continually growing economy. Cars are both loved and hated. Pollution worsens, computers become more lifelike, and people retreat further into fantasy landscapes.

In present-day, postmodern America there are now three distinct water droplets; we have arrived at the familiar, triangular, nature–technology diagram described in previous chapters. Keenly aware and often ashamed of the apparent disintegration inherent in this world view, Americans search for a response to the dilemma.

Surface and Core

To a great extent, the evolution of the relationship between nature and technology can be measured in the widening dislocation between *surface* and *core* values of the landscapes in which we live. *Surface* values are those that one can readily see and sense—the interaction by which one engages the landscape at its most immediate level (Tuan, 1989). *Core* values are the functional, technological, and ecological properties of the landscape, or the way in which the landscape *operatively* connects with the larger ecological context, including that of humans.

Landscapes can be said to be *transparent* if their core properties are visible or otherwise accessible; one is able to *see into them*. *Opaque* landscapes are those whose ecological connections and technological function remains obscure and inaccessible. If the surface and core values are compatible, the landscape can be said to be *congruent;* what one sees does not contradict what one gets. If, however, surface and core properties are incompatible and contradictory, landscapes can be said to be *incongruent*.

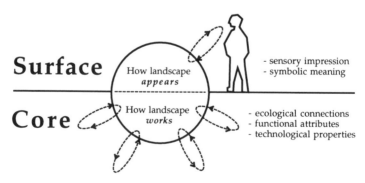

"Surface" and "core" properties of landscapes.

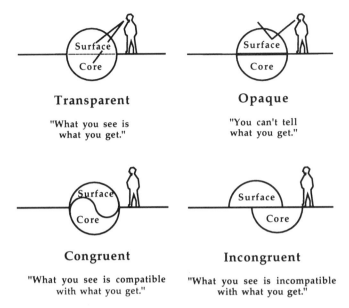

Transparent

"What you see is
what you get."

Opaque

"You can't tell
what you get."

Congruent

"What you see is compatible
with what you get."

Incongruent

"What you see is incompatible
with what you get."

Transparency vs. opaqueness; congruity vs. incongruity in the landscape—the relationship between surface and core, or between "what you see" and "what you get."

The water droplet metaphor described above chronicles the historic increase in the complexity of the core, accompanied by a corresponding increase in the opacity and incongruity between the core and the surface. We have arrived today at a juncture of great crisis; what we *see* around us seems ever more incompatible with what we *know.* Surface and core properties have grown more divergent and disjunctive. At the center of this postmodern dilemma is the gradual replacement of concern for the core by surface concerns, to the point of rendering core properties relatively invisible (Hardison, 1989). People know less about how their increasingly technological world really works, and seem to care more about surface impressions and images. But the ecological and technological implications of landscapes are the essence of the core; they are what literally keeps us alive. In spite of significant public alarm over environmental quality, ecological crises, and runaway technological determinism, the momentum of postmodern culture carries us deeper into preoccupation with surfaces and farther away from core concerns.

A Choice of Paths

Society has three possible responses to the postmodern dilemma of technology and nature. To borrow from the literature of drug dependency and recovery,

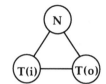

Post-modern Dilemma:

Dilemma of nature and technology
leads to **three alternative responses:**

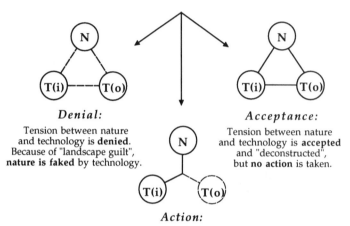

Denial:

Tension between nature
and technology is **denied.**
Because of "landscape guilt",
nature is faked by technology.

Acceptance:

Tension between nature
and technology is **accepted**
and "deconstructed",
but **no action** is taken.

Action:

Sustainable landscapes
attempt to **resolve** nature/technology
tension by incorporating regenerative
technologies in a transparent fashion.

Three possible responses to the current state of dissonance between nature and technology in the landscape.

one choice is *denial* of the problem altogether, which is usually accompanied by a cover-up. Landscapes, of course, offer an easy means of falsification of the relationship between surface and core, either through disguise, concealment, or even total simulation. Another choice is *acceptance*. Like the drug addict who admits having a problem, our culture may fully realize and come to decipher or "deconstruct" the mythology of technology in relation to nature. However, admission does not always imply action. The third choice, *action,* is the key ingredient behind the movement toward a "sustainable" landscape. Sustainable landscapes seek to ease the evolutionary tension between nature and technology by reconfiguring the *core properties* of the technologies upon which we depend for our lifestyles and livelihoods and by *redefining* the surface of the landscape and making it more congruent with the core. In structuring landscapes which are transparent, sustainable, and congruent, society takes a significant step toward resolving the conflict between nature and technology.

Four Case Studies

While preparing this book I visited and studied four landscapes which mark the course of evolution of the nature/technology conflict from its origin to the suggestion of a possible resolution. The Anasazi ruins of Chaco Canyon, the resource-extractive landscapes of Alaska, the simulated nature of Las Vegas' Mirage Hotel and Casino, and the Arcata wastewater treatment wetlands and wildlife refuge all represent unique points in the relationship between nature and technology. Each differs in the relative transparency and congruency of its core processes, the intensity and type of energy flowing through the landscape, the relative presence or absence of landscape guilt, and the entropy and sustainability inherent in the landscape over time. All of these landscapes— easily observable by a person in the same year—reveal a span of a thousand years in the evolution of nature and technology.

Primal Technology—Chaco Canyon

In the San Juan River drainage of New Mexico lie the ruins of the great Anasazi dwellings of the Chaco Culture which reached its apogee in 1130 A.D. Much has been written about the impressive pueblos, cliff dwellings, and kivas, and of the artifacts unearthed in them. Taken together, they have painted a picture of a society popularly interpreted as deeply in tune with the surrounding natural environment, yet technically and architecturally skilled. Pueblo Bonito, an elegant, semicircular megastructure sited at the base of a cliff in Chaco Canyon, has been shown to have tempered the extremes of the desert climate for its original inhabitants through careful manipulation of solar access, thermal mass, and self shading (Baxter, 1982). The ruins of Pueblo Bonito became the *de facto* spiritual center for the "solar age" of the 1970s, appearing in numerous books and journals on solar energy and serving as inspiration for a hoped-for return to a sustainable society. The architecture of Chaco Canyon and the Anasazi in general have inspired contemporary architects with the sublime relationship between building and site through use of indigenous materials and superbly sensitive site planning and building techniques.

The artifacts found in the ruins of Chaco Canyon all reveal a fundamental yet elegant dependence upon local resources available in or near the San Juan basin. Metates and mortars made from local stone still mark the floors of the pueblo plazas. Contemporaneous energy use was apparently low and energy sources renewable in origin (sun, wood); entropy seemed low as well—the culture maintained a high population in an arid environment for centuries with only the simplest of technologies forged from the immediate, surrounding landscape. As we look back romantically upon the remnant landscapes of

The Great Kiva at Pueblo Bonito, the ceremonial center of Chacoan culture, San Juan Basin, New Mexico.

Chacoan culture, little distinction between "technology" and "nature" is evident. We imagine their lives to have been in pleasant, rhythmic integration with their natural surroundings for several hundred years.

But if their conception of nature and human artifice was unified and their living methods truly sustainable, why did they disappear? Did their "appropriate" architectural and agricultural technologies fail them? Recent anthropological, archaeological, and architectural research sources have established certain facts which temper our romanticized image of a people totally integrated with nature. First, environmental consequences may have contributed to the Chacoans' decline. A mild but persistent, 50-year drought reduced the average summer rainfall from its long-term average of 3.1 inches to an average of 2.7 inches from 1130 to 1180 A.D. Second, far fewer human burial remains were found in the areas of Chaco Canyon than would be expected of a region with so many living quarters (Gillespie, 1984). Third, up to 10 times as much broken pottery was found, much of it in association with the kivas, as could be explained by the estimated living capacity of the pueblos. Finally, aerial satellite imagery revealed remnants of extensive, straight roads up to 30 feet wide leading radially to Chaco Canyon from surrounding regions (Powers, 1984). From the evidence it has been proposed that Chaco Canyon was a large, ceremonial center where surrounding peoples made pilgrimages to gather in the hundreds of kivas, sleep temporarily in the rectangular rooms, and engage in their mysterious ceremonies, some of which must have involved breaking pottery. The purpose of such wide, straight roadways for a people with no means of transportation other than walking remains a mystery. One theory holds that the civilization had made contact through trade with the sophisticated Aztec civilizations to the south, and had begun to emulate Aztecan ceremonial architecture and site planning.

The Chaco phenomenon has long captured the scholarly and public interest with its seemingly exemplary blend of contextually generated "sustainable" technologies (irrigated agriculture, indigenous architectural techniques, building thermal response, solar access siting, locally produced tools) and a mysteriously inspiring material culture. On the surface, technology and nature at Chaco Canyon seem to have been integrated and congruent. There is little evidence of social dissonance over the impact of technology—certainly nothing that could be considered landscape guilt. At first glance, there is a delightful transparency in the landscape surface, and an apparent congruency

Pre-columbian architectural technology within future U.S. borders reached its peak at Chaco Canyon. These doorway details suggest a possible connection to the indigenous Mexican cultures flourishing to the south.

between our surface impressions of the Chacoan landscape and the core ecological systems upon which the civilization depended. However, there is in the ceremonial dimensions of the Chaco region the hint of a certain opacity; did the Chacoan's later-period indulgence in ceremonies which wasted resources overextend their culture beyond some point of sustainability?

Chaco Canyon is viewed today as an inspiring, primal landscape wherein many of the retrospective qualities we admire in archaic cultures are present—an architecture highly sensitive to local climate; ingenious use of local resources as tools; a sophisticated, yet low-energy agricultural system; an obvious spiritual reverence for the earth. Yet deeper analysis reveals that an imminent separation of nature and technology into distinct constructs had begun at the time the culture vanished. While the Chaco culture achieved impressive levels of sustainability in a harsh environment for hundreds of years, in the end, something failed. Archaeologists now see in the Chaco culture evidence of much higher complexity than was first thought. With the expansion of its role as a ceremonial site, Chaco Canyon civilization was becoming highly self-conscious, and was unable to adjust to a significant fluctuation in natural conditions. At the height of Chacoan culture, a nascent separation may have begun between a preoccupation with human affairs and an adaptability to conditions in the surrounding natural environment. The abandonment of the once-sustainable Chacoan landscape marks a beginning of the theme of this book; the subsequent divergence of technology from nature and the search for a reunification between the two.

Alaskan Landscapes—Naive Juxtapositions

860 years later and 3000 miles northwest near Delta Junction Alaska, a 4-ft diameter stainless steel pipeline snakes across the permafrost landscapes of tundra and taiga on concrete stilts and vaults across the silt-laden water of the Tanana River slung by a cabled suspension bridge. Chain link and barbed wire fence and electric spotlights give the Alaska Pipeline a paramilitary appearance. Every 25 feet, pipe segments are joined by ultra hightech, heated couplings which keep the oil warm and flowing in winter, while refrigerants in the coupling support structures keep the permafrost from melting under the warmth and weight of the oil. As a result, the pipeline itself is a major consumer of energy year round. Looking at the pipeline, it is difficult for one to imagine it stretching 850 miles across stark wilderness. It is even more difficult to imagine that 25% of all the U.S. production of oil flows through the pipe at any given time. If the Alaska Pipeline does not represent the belly of the American technological beast, it is certainly the umbilical cord.

Like the pipeline, most Alaskan landscapes are studies in simultaneous topophilia and technophilia. The immense natural scale, beauty, and ecological abundance of the surrounding wild land is matched only by the degree to

The Alaska Pipeline crossing the Tanana River.

which Alaskans depend on transportation technologies to move about in it and extractive, consumptive industrial technologies to make a living from it. In Ketchikan, a utilitarian fishing and lumber town in Southeastern Alaska, the airport is reached by ferry boat across the Tongass narrows, in the midst of which ply drift net boats, State ferries, cruise ships, seaplanes, outboard skiffs, and helicopters. Fish canneries share center stage with motels, bowling alleys, and dry docks. The odor of steamed fish hangs in the air until five miles north of town, where it changes to the sulfurous smell of wood pulp. It can be said assuredly of Alaskan landscapes that the essential technologies fundamental to survival are interspersed unselfconsciously and without guilt in the developed landscape. In the small city of Haines, for example, the diesel-powered generator which produces municipal electric power chugs away right next to City Hall.

Technophilia dominates not just the essential utilitarian industries of Alaska, but its recreational landscape as well. In suburban Anchorage there is a subdivision of sprawling ranch houses whose garden lawns sweep down to a lake ringed with "boat" docks. Tied up to each one is a sea plane, and take-offs or landings occur constantly throughout the day. A clause in the restrictive covenants for the subdivision indicate that float planes have the right of way over swimmers, canoeists, boaters, or fisherman.

Golden Heart Park Plaza lies along the Chena River in Fairbanks, directly adjacent to the Visitor Center. It is an obvious piece of professionally designed landscape, with paving, retaining walls, planters, and a central fountain and sculpture reminiscent of those found in many urban centers in the lower forty-eight states. Above the fountain is a bronze statue of three Athabascan natives in traditional garb, whose bronzed, hooded parkas reflect the shape and southern-facing spatial orientation of the satellite dish antennae on the tops of most surrounding buildings. Dominating and surrounding the plaza on low retaining walls are two dozen bronzed "Vignettes of History" plaques with inscriptions glorifying the role of various industries and technologies in Alaska's development: Arco Oil Company; Standard Oil Company; Alyeska Pipeline Company; Usibelli Coal Mine, Inc.; Alaska International Construction Company; Nerco Minerals Company; AlasCom (the satellite communications network); and the U.S. military. Lost amid more than a dozen such tributes to Alaska's technophilic past (and, according to the plaques, its future) is one panel paying tribute to the native Athabascan people whose land and lifestyle have been taken over by the extractive industries. It is an intentional landscape composition of formalized technophilia offered to the visiting public with much pride and no guilt.

In the rural parts of Alaska's interior, log architecture, moose antlers, satellite dish antennae, and 55-gallon oil drums prevail. Front yards are places for storage and collection, and not infrequently, garbage dumping. There is the occasional log game cache, a small log structure on tall log stilts. The log meat cache is a nostalgic technology of an earlier era when Alaskans stored their frozen game kills in these natural freezers well beyond the grasp of grizzly bears. For the most part, the Alaskan landscape is a double-portrait of topophilia and technophilia in the same frame. In spite of the recent Exxon oil spill, there is little visual evidence of technophobia or landscape guilt. Consumptive, fossil fuel technology is essential to Alaska's current recreational and economic landscape. Even though a 1991 *Wall Street Journal* poll revealed that 8 out of 10 Americans consider themselves "environmentalists," an *Anchorage Times* poll the same year indicated that 9 out of 10 Alaskans favored opening the Arctic National Wildlife Refuge for oil exploration. Environmentalism, although struggling to attach itself, has not caught on with the Alaskan public to any degree. To many Alaskans, environmentalists are associated with "outsiders," conspirators, or the federal government (McBeath and Morehouse, 1987).

The immense scale of the Alaskan landscape and the relative youth of its extractive industries leads to its naivete. The richness of Alaska's mineral deposits, the scenic grandeur of its viewsheds, the vast distances between its human settlements, and the abundance of its fishery and timber resources

Golden Heart Plaza in downtown Fairbanks, Alaska. A satellite dish mimics the southward gaze of embronzed figures of an Athabascan native family, surrounded by bronze plaques glorifying the role of American corporations in extracting resources and creating modern Alaska.

A rural Alaskan "front yard" landscape: 55-gallon oil drums, a bush plane, and the requisite moose antlers over the garage.

combine to not only allow but to make necessary the appearance of the most violently consumptive industrial and transportation technologies and the most spectacular natural scenery in the same visual frame. Alaska is the classic, adolescent version of American landscape heritage—the naive frontier before the fall of technology. Like the new lover in a teenage relationship, Alaskans are blind to the ultimate finiteness of their landscape and the eventual incompatibility of pristine ecosystems and consuming technologies.

In Alaskan landscapes, the separation between nature and technology has fully evolved; technology and nature are now two very distinct constructs. Both are evident and abundant in the landscape. After the discovery of vast oil deposits in 1969, Alaskan legislators met at a conference with the Brookings Institute to chart an economic policy for the state. Session participants called for "preserving the unique Alaskan life-style, defining it as one which 'affords the conveniences of technological innovation combined with the opportunity and values of living as close to nature as possible'" (Naske and Slotnick, 1987, p. 180). This quote captures the quintessential naivete of the Alaskan landscape; although the technologies used in Alaskan landscapes are conspicuous and obvious, there is little indication of widespread public awareness of natural limits or constraints on technology in relation to the land.

In conclusion, Alaska is naively modern. Its transparent landscapes reveal technology and nature as two separate but equal forces. Although a sense of landscape guilt in Alaska has yet to develop, an ultimate incongruity exists between the surface image of endless natural and scenic resources and the core realities of nonrenewable resource extraction and consumption. It is a highly entropic landscape which is most certainly unsustainable in its present form. The Alaskan landscape is one where, in adolescent fashion, people believe they may have their cake and eat it too.

The Mirage Hotel Casino—Hyperreality

Nevada shares some kinship with Alaska. As western frontiers, both share vast, seemingly empty spaces punctuated by small towns and an occasional, modestly sized city. Yet even more than Alaska, Nevada is the land of Emptiness. The principal city, Las Vegas, can perhaps be explained as a Jungian collective unconscious overreaction to the stark realities of the Nevada landscape. Las Vegas is a spaceship for hedonists—a voluntary pleasure entrapment—a space colony floating in a vast desert sea connected by an invisible, technological lifeline to the heavily impounded Colorado River and to the region's natural gas, coal, and hydroelectric power networks.

The Mirage Casino Hotel is at least aptly named. Although it competes with other gaudy pleasure palaces on the Las Vegas strip, the Mirage semantically acknowledges the sensory deprivation of the desert and the inherent overreaction of the human mind in imagining places of fantasy and relief. The name "Mirage" beats would-be critics to the punch. There is no need for apologies by a casino created to appeal to the natural tendency of the human mind to fantasize an earthly paradise in a harsh region.

The landscape outside the Mirage is less a place and more of an event. The Volcano, now known all over the world (and advertised only in partial jest by the casino as "Nevada's only actively erupting volcano") spews forth every 15 minutes each evening after dark until 1 A.M. People gather in front of the hotel on cue above five minutes prior to eruption. The beginning of eruption is signaled by small vents of steam coming from the top of the "mountain," which, when the volcano is "inactive," doubles as a colossal fountain and centerpiece of a system of fountains pumping about 20,000 cubic feet per second, 24 hours per day, 365 days per year. The spray plume enlarges with each pulse, and soon is accompanied by brilliant flares of natural gas, small at first, but eventually engulfing the entire "mountain" top. Then, gas flames spread to the nearby waterfall and cascade down the stair-step fountains, climaxing in stabbing ridges of flame which emerge from the shallow water pond as if fissures or shafts of molten rock. Red lights illuminate the water cascade in a mockery of glowing lava, while huge speakers mounted near the railings create the deep, throaty sounds of eruption and the high hiss of steam. It is all over in two minutes or so, and the fountains return to their watery configuration. People "ooh" and "aah" and then drift away. Five minutes later, few remain, and what has almost achieved a sense of place again seems empty and unnoticed.

The analogy between the volcano's eruption and sexual encounter is not

The Mirage Casino "Volcano:" significant consumption of natural gas, electricity, and water create a simulation of nature.

lost on the visitors (and certainly not on the volcano's creators, either), as men and women preen, photograph each other, and generally parade conspicuously until the eruption begins. Afterward, they move on their way with haste to other experiences elsewhere on the Strip.

Behind the massive entrance volcano and fountain is a staggering techno-logical complexity—recessed between every tree or shrub or concealed below or behind the surface is some article of technical support: lights, sprinkler valves and anemometers, wind vanes, loudspeakers, electrical utility junction boxes, vacuum breakers, gas lines, electronic ignition units, and so forth. Were one to X ray the fountain/volcano complex, stripping away the water, fake rock, and plants, one would gaze upon a labyrinth of pipes, wires, pumps, jets, and gadgets. A permanent, full-time maintenance staff of four people works on outdoor lighting for the casino only—six full time personnel are dedicated to the plantings. There is an entire technical support arm, complete with in-house expertise to attend to every aspect of the volcano's eruption. The "Mirage Engineering Department" label on the trucks speaks ironically to the high level of technical infrastructure, personnel, and resources needed to keep the fantasy alive and well. My persistent attempts to delve further into the technological specifications and quantities of water and energy consumed were met with deliberate, endless telephone tag; I was told that the Public Relations Department handled such information, but none was forthcoming from them or from any other possible source.

The Mirage theme is one borrowed directly from the Big Island of Hawaii, where real volcanic eruptions and the well-established mythology of the ancient Hawaiian goddess Pele capture the imagination of visitors from the mainland. The Mirage borrows Hawaii's "hot-humid" symbolic associations and, using hidden technology, transports them to the "hot-arid" landscape of southern Nevada. With irrigation, palms will grow in any hot climate, and the extraneous vegetational themes of the Mirage capture tropical imagination: bird-of-paradise plant motifs in the casino carpets; a color scheme capturing the corals, magentas, pinks, and turquoise of hot-humid latitudes. Two white tigers (animals from the tropics) live in a "habitat" consisting of all-white, postmodern, fabricated fantasy trees and classic columns dominated by a colorful, Rousseau-like mural-caricature of a jungle. The tigers are used each night in a stagehall magic show. An entire wall of glass allows throngs of visitors to gaze upon the well-lit display at all hours of the day or night. Across from this rather cruel surrogate for a zoo habitat, souvenir shops sell stuffed, toy white tigers and tee shirts.

Beyond the immense pool complex, with more synthetic rock waterfalls, grottoes, and thatched-roof bar and snack pavilions borrowed intact from those of Hawaiian luxury hotels, is the Dolphin lagoon, a thematic offspring of the Hyatt Regency Waikoloa on Hawaii. One and one-half million gallons of sea water synthesized from imported sea salt and fresh water are home to four Atlantic dolphins, who swim in an exhibit consisting of fake coral reefs (claimed as safe and "nontoxic" to the dolphins by hotel docents). As with the Hyatt Waikoloa, dolphins are the antidote for guests overwhelmed by the fantastic extravagance of the hotel—a touch of nature in the marine mammal flesh to assuage any environmental guilt and convince the public of management's concern for nature.

Central to the vast casino floor is an atrium rain forest, facilitated by the latest misting devices one encounters at zoos and landscape industry exhibits. Orchids, tree ferns, and a variety of tropical flowering plants surround a synthetic rock steam and pool. Close examination of the atrium landscape reveals a combination of plastic plants intermingled with real ones. The eye strains to decipher the difference, and many guests passing by notice the fake vines on the railings and soon enter into debate, pointing upward in an attempt to distinguish fake plant from real. Like the entire Mirage environment, the line between organic and inorganic, plastic and chlorophyll, real and fantasy, is indeterminate—no pretense at making such a distinction is given. At the Mirage fantasy is the normative state of being. Technology makes the fakery of nature happen, yet this enabling technology is hidden from view. Reality is unreality.

Nothing on the strip or in the entire City of Las Vegas can compete with the Mirage for attention. One is hard pressed to imagine what fantastic landscapes competing casino hotels will develop to win back a share of a consuming public increasingly saturated by ever-greater degrees of technology-induced nature fakery—perhaps a holographic earthquake fault or a synthetic glacier

THE VOLCANO
ERUPTS
AFTER DARK
EVERY 15 MINUTES
UNTIL 1:00 AM
EXCEPT DAYS WHEN THE
RED LIGHT IS BLINKING

By day, the "volcano" sleeps as a fountain centerpiece. At any given time, the amount of water pumped through the immense Mirage fountain system exceeds the flood stage flow rates of most western rivers.

and iceberg break-off with a Titanic that sinks every 15 minutes. Perhaps the casinos will wait until ultrarealistic computer technology allows visitors to link up with an entire portfolio of synthesized landscape experiences without ever leaving the casino floor. Whatever possible stretch of human imagination for thematic environmental fantasy is no doubt already being contemplated for Las Vegas, engineers are probably conducting technical feasibility studies for ways of realizing such fantasies. A proposal for a Venetian canal through downtown Las Vegas is being taken seriously and has already been supported by engineering reports. One such report shows that the proposed one-third mile canal will evaporate 6.5 million gallons of water each year into the desert air while local city residents are being asked to voluntarily conserve water.

If Alaskans want to have their cake and eat it too, the Mirage Hotel, in seasoned, postmodern fashion, devours the cake and replaces it with a cardboard facsimile. At the Mirage guests never "visit" the desert. The desert context is ignored or overwhelmed by an immersion into tropical fantasy made possible by applications of highly sophisticated, nearly invisible technology and conspicuous consumption of water, electricity, and fossil fuel.

Some have argued that it is fitting for Las Vegas to be a quasi-official domain of the subconscious—part physical, part mythological place where human imagination, technological wizardry, and resource exploitation know no limits in the production of hyperreal landscapes. Perhaps, as the argument goes, only by probing the limits of fantasy will we really come to know reality. On the other hand, there lurks a danger in places like the Mirage, where reality, like matter and energy near a black hole, cannot exist, but gets sucked into the void of fantasy, never to emerge. Fantasy is only as constructive as the reality it can inform and enrich. At some point, an environmental and perceptual price is paid for technological fantasy, and both individuals and societies must be able to afford that price. Extension of the superficial philosophy embodied in the Mirage and its volcano yields a world where landscape experience takes place only in fantasy, because reality, with its accompanying burden of landscape guilt over the impact of technology on nature, is no longer tolerable. Like a hundred-dollar-a-day drug habit, the Mirage is an expensive escape from reality. The Mirage assaults nature, kills it, and refabricates a technological surrogate for mass consumption. It is an opaque and incongruous landscape; what one sees is *not* what one gets. As such, the Mirage represents the landscape of denial; its solution to environmental and resource problems is to pretend there are none, but in the pretending, the problems are exacerbated.

Arcata Marsh—An Emerging Sustainable Landscape

The sewage treatment plant at Arcata on California's foggy northern coast is about as far removed from the Mirage volcano as a person can get in terms of ecosystems, ideology, and appearance. Being somewhat iconoclastic in its environmental predisposition in a region dominated by the timber industry, Arcata is a progressive, environmentally oriented community. It is home of the campus of Humboldt State University, renowned for its natural resource departments. In the 1970s, population growth and increasingly strict environmental standards rendered Arcata's wastewater treatment facility, which once dumped sewage into Humboldt Bay, obsolete. A proposed regional wastewater facility serving Eureka, Arcata, and other bay communities was rejected by Stan Harris, Arcata's former public works director, who believed the cost would be prohibitive and the environmental implications undesirable. For several years, Professor George Allen of Humboldt State University had been experimenting with raising salmon and coastal cutthroat trout in water mixed with treated sewage effluent. The public works director and the aquaculture professor were joined by Robert Gearheart, an environmental engineering professor, in proposing an expansion of Arcata's wastewater treatment facility which would incorporate ponds and marshes as the secondary and tertiary treatment components and use the highly treated wastewater in an expanded aquaculture facility. After a lengthy political process, the project was imple-

*At the Arcata Marsh, aquatic vegetation (foreground) purifies wastewater efflu-
ent while riparian shrubs provide habitat for nesting egrets (background right).
Photograph by Ellen Land-Weber.*

mented. Since the late 1980s, the Arcata Marsh—a collective term for the
wastewater treatment wetlands, wildlife ponds, and aquaculture facility—have
set a new standard for ecological engineering.

Waste from the town population of 14,000 enters the facility, where solids
are eliminated and the wastewater is clarified by conventional primary technology. Then the water is chlorinated, dechlorinated, and fed through a succession of bullrush ponds into the secondary oxidizing lagoons, after which it
passes into an additional set of ponds and wildlife enhancement marshes
which fix much of the nitrogen in the food chains of typical bay marsh
ecosystems. The enhancement ponds form part of the local seashore park,
after which the highly cleansed effluent, now much cleaner than the bay water
itself, is released into the estuary of Jolly Giant Creek. Some of the tertiary
water passes through an additional set of ponds and is mixed with sea water, in
which silver salmon, cutthroat trout, and sturgeon are raised. The survival
rate of these hatchery-grown fish is a healthy 90% (Stewart, 1990).

The Arcata Marsh is well used and revered by local residents and frequently
visited by travelers—bird as well as human. One gets the sense that, for a

change, humans and wildlife have struck a symbiotic relationship. The symbolic meaning of human sewage and its places of treatment, perhaps the most unmentionable and subconsciously buried of all possible sources of pollution, has been turned around completely by the Arcata Marsh, whose humorous logo shows a salmon leaping from a toilet bowl upon which a blue heron is proudly perched. The caption reads: "Flush With Pride!"

The Arcata Marsh offers a starkly contrasting alternative to places like the Mirage "Volcano." The Marsh is a manifestation of technology where a symbiotic process, carefully developed out of concern for the larger natural community of birds, fish, microorganisms, and humans sets a conspicuous and sustainable example for community development. It brings the essential human/nature/technology interaction to the visible surface, manipulating it in such a way that waste becomes natural resource. Salmon, trout, and waterfowl thrive in a wetland environment where residents jog, watch birds, or picnic. There is a reassuring feeling of congruency, where one's aesthetic views fit cleanly within a cognitive understanding of the processes by which the ecological synergy of wildlife and wastewater is working. In total opposition to the Mirage "Volcano," the Arcata Marsh landscape is transparent, congruent, responsible, and sustainable. In Arcata's wastewater lagoons, a resolution of

Bird-watching at Arcata Marsh. The marsh has become a well-loved place for residents and visitors, human and animal alike. Photograph by Ellen Land-Weber.

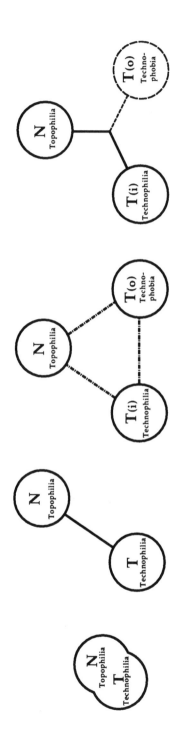

Chaco Canyon

- Technology & nature appear to be unified.

- Transparent: technological processes expressed.

- Congruent: no contradiction between surface and core.

- No technophobia or landscape guilt.

- Low, renewable energy use.

- Low entropy.

- Sustainability unknown, but assumed

Alaska

- Technology and nature separate constructs.

- Transparent: technological processes conspicuously expressed.

- Incongruity between surface (endless natural/scenic resource) and core reality (non-renewable resource extraction).

- Naivety: no guilt yet. Technology proudly displayed, nothing hidden or disguised.

- High, non-renewable energy.

- High entropy.

- Unsustainable over time.

Mirage Hotel Casino

- Technology creates superficial simulation of nature.

- Opaque: technological processes hidden from view.

- Incongruity between surface (volcano, dolphins, rainforest) and core reality (desert context, fossil fuel and water consumption).

- Technophobia and denial of technology as part of desired "natural" simulation.

- High, non-renewable energy.

- High entropy.

- Unsustainable over time.

Arcata Wastewater Wetlands

- Technology reintegrated into nature. Symbiotic relationship.

- Transparent technological processes revealed and expressed.

- Congruent: what you see is what you get. Minor legibility problems (piping to/from treatment ponds is hidden, confusing).

- Landscape guilt reduced: technophobic attitude toward human waste treatment nearly eliminated. Motto: "Flush with Pride!"

- Moderate energy use, part renewable.

- Lower entropy.

- Sustainable.

The four case study landscapes represent different stages in the evolution of the relationship between nature and technology.

guilt and tension between technology, humanity, and nature is indeed happening.

Denial, Acceptance, and/or Action?

We have arrived, then, at the very fulcrum of the book. In response to the post-modern dilemma of technology and nature, society has a choice of three cards it can play, either alone or in some combination. It may deny that a problem exists; it may accept that there is a problem, and finally, it may act toward resolving the problem. The landscape is an experimental grounds for a people desperate to rediscover the integration of human artifice and earthly "natural" context.

Unfortunately, the easiest societal response is to deny that there is a problem at all and to live in a world of surfaces, facades, and mirrors. From the paralysis of the NIMBY response in the siting of technical facilities, to the concealment and camouflage of technological "necessities," to the overt production of replicas of nature by technological means, American's first line of defense against environmental guilt is to employ the potential for opaqueness in the landscape. This can be easily done—by living in a private, gated, fenced subdivision located on the exurban fringe and named after a vanished "natural" feature; by owning three cars and commuting alone 50 miles to work; by opposing the widening of the freeway and the expansion of the county landfill; by building a redwood screen around the air conditioner and the swimming pool pump and filter; by vacationing at an exclusive resort where the social and environmental realities are cleanly displaced to the next state or country, and the thunder, fire, and rain are made by machines designed by engineers, controlled by computers, hidden behind synthesized rock walls "shrubbed up" by professional landscape architects, and maintained by armies of underpaid workers and a few highly paid "experts."

But the emotional burden of such self-deceit has become unbearable. Those who grapple each day with intentional landscape significance and environmental meaning—the artists, designers, and landscape architects probing the edges of the technology–nature conflict—have at least entered the "acceptance" stage. In the rarified atmosphere of "landscape as art and social comment," technological referents abound, from the intriguing spectral effects of Robert Behrens' solar-optical sculptures to Nancy Holt's glorification of the stormwater catch basin, to the deconstructionist, machine-like images of architect Bernard Tschumi. In George Hargreaves' Byxbee Park, reclaimed from a bay-edge landfill near San Francisco, a ceremonial methane flame flares from the decomposing garbage below, while columns reminiscent of abandoned dock pilings mimic the runway flight path angle at the adjacent Palo Alto airport (Hess, 1992). With a few exceptions, most such artful environments fall short of substantial corrective or "healing" action, but they succeed in their implicit, primary purpose in changing our awareness. They provide a necessary, first step—that of retrieving the technology/nature dialectic from beneath the surface and transparently exposing its obvious inconsistencies and incongruities with the popular pastoral illusion.

Some sculptors and designers seek both awareness *and* change. San Diegan artists Helen Mayer Harrison and Newton Harrison have offered their unique visions of the environmental rehabilitation of large-scale technologically degraded landscapes—sometimes whole river watersheds—as a high-art form successfully for several decades (Harrison and Harrison, 1990). Kansas environmental sculptor Richard Hansen constructs small, microcosmic "process" pieces which probe the nature of landscape healing. Most creative artists and designers working the nature–technology edge are content to reveal and expose the cognitive dissonance and to use it to define a new aesthetic, leaving the actual act of healing and resolution of surface/core connections to others.

The vernacular landscape reveals that society does its share of acceptance as well. The facade of denial can only be stretched so thin, and the incongruent relationship of the dual gods Technology and Nature must be tolerated, if not celebrated in the vast fabric of American urban/suburban development. Leo Marx, Lewis Mumford, and others have made that much crystal clear. Most Americans must subconsciously *practice acceptance* of the nature–technology inconsistency every day of their lives lest they be driven crazy by an overwhelmingly ambivalent landscape. Indeed, some are.

Sustainability, Action, and the Struggle for Reintegration

The arrival, acceptance, and rapid diffusion of the notion of sustainability in the past few years marks the third alternative response: *action*. Having long denied the problem only to finally recognize, accept, and try to cope with environmental guilt, a significant number of Americans have had enough, and are eager and ready to *act*. For these people, even the simple possibility of tangible, constructive environmental action in the future offers a twang of release in the solar plexus, like snipping a rubber band which has been squeezing one's soul. Resolution of the technology–nature conflict seems to call from somewhere deep within us. Although there is great danger in any rapidly evolved catchword, the notion of *sustainability*—the ability to provide for the needs of today without depriving future generations of people *and* other life forms of the ability to meet their needs—carries with it the seeds of resolution through action. Arcata's humble, homespun wastewater wetlands and other similarly sustainable landscapes appeal to our need for a resolution, and offer a kind of gut-level satis*faction* akin to throwing away the syringe, crushing the box of cigarettes, or pouring the whiskey down the kitchen sink.

It is likely that the American landscape will continue to reflect a mixture of denial, acceptance, and responsible action with respect to the technology–

nature dilemma for a very long time. Sustainable landscapes offer the most promise. But in moderation, fantasy and denial are essential human responses, and adaptive acceptance has been a natural human coping mechanism for survival for thousands, if not millions of years. Furthermore, as sustainable landscapes show potential to resolve the tension between technology and nature, the very *nature* of both "nature" and "technology" is evolving extremely rapidly. Human adaptation to the changing constructs of nature and technology poses its own set of problems, which have begun to be recognized by numerous post-modern theorists. A convoluted, superficial version of a reconciliation between artifice and earthly context may beat sustainable development to the punch. Denial, detachment, and the simulated replacement of nature are all racing sustainability for supremacy over American hearts and minds. It is this fundamental upheaval that I address in Chapters 7 and 8.

7

The Changing Nature of Nature

If science is a human creation, we have caught the mind in the very act of swallowing up the world, which is another way of saying that we have witnessed nature in the process of disappearing.

O. B. HARDISON, JR.

Nature and technology are not what they used to be, and we can only imagine what they are becoming. Consider, for instance, the conclusions of a sample of nine contemporary scholars. Historian Carolyn Merchant (1980) writes of the sixteenth and seventeenth century loss of an organic cosmology to a mechanistic, scientific world view as the *death* of nature. Philosopher O. B. Hardison (1989), chronicling twentieth-century changes in culture and technology, describes the transformation of nature from a set of visible objects in the middle distance to an illusive set of mathematical principles and scientific discoveries beyond the visible limits of human perception—a process he refers to as the *disappearance* of nature. In *The End of Nature* Bill McKibben (1989) declares and laments the contemporary loss of that domain of nature which has been "eternal and separate" from that of humans. Social critic William Irwin Thompson (1991) observes that the information/media/consumer society, with its out-of-control preoccupation with entertainment and its rapid attenuation toward mediocrity and homogeneity, is *replacing* nature with technology.

There is an equivalent and similarly astonishing flux in the notion of technology itself. Langdon Winner (1977) examines the increasingly desperate and commonly shared conclusion that technology has broken the bounds of social control and become *autonomous*. Neil Postman (1992) describes the

Streamer chamber image of an experiment searching for elementary particles resulting from proton-to-proton interactions. Courtesy of Richard Lander, Department of Physics, University of California, Davis.

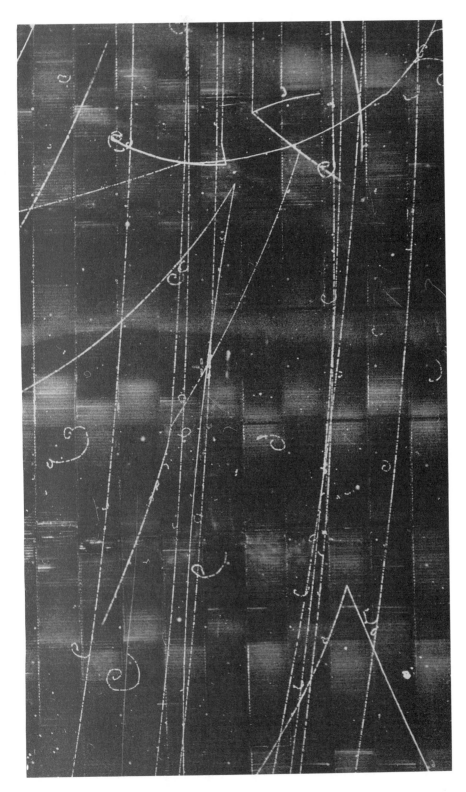

unchecked expansion of technology as *technopoly,* or the totalitarian dominance of technology and its apparent ability to exterminate alternatives to itself. As if to anticipate and illustrate Postman's technopoly in action, K. Eric Drexler offers a deterministic scenario of *nanotechnology,* a radically new technology of a self-replicating, artificially intelligent series of molecular-scale tools capable of handling "individual atoms and molecules with control and precision," and which will "change our world in more ways than we can imagine." Drexler's bold presumptions are not the stuff of science fiction, but extrapolate from an advanced working research group at MIT. Stewart Brand (1987) and Howard Rheingold (1991) consider advances in computer-graphic generation of artificial perception (i.e., "virtual reality") and cognition (i.e., "artificial intelligence") as foregone conclusions waiting to rock the very foundations of our culture.

If we are to believe these authors, nature has "ended," "died," "disappeared," or been "replaced;" technology has become autonomous, totalitarian, lifelike, and molecular in scale; we may no longer be assured that what we perceive or know is real. In this bold transformation of nature and technology, something is certainly happening which is of immense importance to landscape. As the traditional locus of mediation between technology and nature, landscape is struggling to maintain relevance. Whether intentionally designed or unconsciously developed, landscape is a physical embodiment of the metaphoric compromise between nature and human artifice. In spite of their tangible manifestations, technology and nature are social constructs; landscape mediates the space between the two in a language of symbols derived from patterns of earthly materials, but when technology and nature are so radically transformed, the ability of landscape to serve its traditional mediating role is strained to the breaking point, and it remains to be seen whether "landscape," in either its vernacular or intentional form, can even remain a relevant construct in the future.

From the changes in nature and the changes in technology we can extrapolate some potential changes in the landscape.

Nature and Artifice Through the Same Historical Lense

The first conclusion one draws when attempting to examine both the history of nature and the history of technology is that they are, in essence, the same history. Technology has revolutionized both nature and culture by overt as well as covert means. Advances in tool making allowed advances in scientific discovery, which served to constantly expand the cultural boundaries of "nature" beyond the familiar. The struggles of Galileo, Newton, and Darwin to account for their new scientific theories within the old framework of religious doctrine are but milestones along the highway of social transformation. Scientific instruments like the telescope, microscope, compass, and clock allowed even greater expansion in the horizons of nature, and with these expansions came increasing questions about the presumption of reality and cosmic order.

Technology also, of course, provided more advances in the *techniques* of living, changing the economic basis for culture and the sociological nature of individual work and employment. Neil Postman (1992) articulates three stages in the history of technology. He describes the first stage as that of tool-using cultures. These cultures were both "ingenious and productive in solving problems of the physical environment," but in such societies, the tools were not "intruders" and were integrated into the culture in ways that did not pose significant contradictions to the predominant world view. Postman (1992) cites Europe in the Middle Ages as an example of a tool-using culture with a high correlation between tool use and world view:

> Medieval theologians developed an elaborate and systematic description of the relationship of man to God, man to nature, man to man, and man to his tools. Their theology took as a first and last principle that all knowledge and goodness come from God, and that therefore all human enterprise must be directed toward the service of God. Theology, not technology, provided people with authorization for what to do or think. (p. 26)

Grain milling stones, nearly 2000 years old, found at a Roman archaeological site in Gloucestershire, England.

Such a view is a corroboration of historian Clarence Glacken's "design" hypothesis, where the view of "human as artisan" shaping the immediate environment in the everyday world was reflected in the view of a benign God who had, in a similar artisan-like fashion, shaped nature for human benefit. In this first stage, tool use by humans was entirely consistent with views of Nature as the handiwork of God as Artisan. This consistency between theocracy and tool use was emphasized by Postman:

> We may say . . . that all tool-using cultures—from the technologically most primitive to the most sophisticated—are theocratic or, if not that, unified by some metaphysical theory. Such a theology or metaphysics provides order and meaning to existence, making it almost impossible for technics to subordinate people to its own needs. (p. 26)

Slowly and steadily, however, tool-using culture gave rise to western "technocracies," as Postman labels them. In a technocracy, "tools are not integrated into the culture; they attack the culture and seek to *become* the culture" (p. 28). Like many other tools, the telescope became a radical, iconoclastic device. After Copernicus, Kepler, and Galileo, the assumption that the Earth was the center of the universe began to crumble, taking with it much of the underlying structure of Judeo-Christian philosophy: ". . . the Earth had become a lonely wanderer in an obscure galaxy in some hidden corner of the universe, and this left the Western world to wonder if God had any interest in us at all." (Postman, 1992, p. 29). But none of the three eminent astronomers had any intention of destroying the religious world views to which they each subscribed until their deaths. It was perhaps not until Francis Bacon that deliberate connection was made between the scientific process and the betterment of the human condition. For his articulate advocacy of a scientific method which bypassed religious philosophy and went directly to the business of "improving" secular human life, Bacon gained the posthumous reputation as the "founding father" of scientific-technological determinism (Postman's second stage) where tools were no longer subservient to culture, but instead, became their own separate and parallel realm.

Bacon's rather patriarchal views were targeted by historian Carolyn Merchant (1980) in her now-famous feminist critique of the history of science. Merchant pointed out that in both Western and non-Western cultures, nature was a traditionally feminine concept, and that the new scientific determinism signaled by Bacon represented a "death" of nature and a substitution of a patriarchal and mechanistic science:

> Between the 16th and 17th centuries the image of an organic cosmos with a living female earth at its center gave way to a mechanistic world view in which nature was reconstructed as dead and passive, to be dominated and controlled by humans. (p. xvi.)

Merchant comments on the effects of this increasingly mechanistic view:

> Mechanistic assumptions about nature push us increasingly in the direction of
> artificial environments, mechanized control over more and more aspects of human
> life, and a loss of the quality of life itself. (p. 291).

By changing and mechanizing the practical world of daily toil and by revolu-
tionizing the cosmic, inner world view of nature and the place of an individual
in a larger philosophical framework, technology assaulted the philosophical
status quo from both within and without. Postman's second-stage of cultural
relationship to technology, which he calls *technocracy*, is an appropriate description of the evolution of the modern nature–technology dilemma. By
1850 the transition from artisanship to mechanization was in full swing.
Single-copy, artisan-made necessities of life were being replaced by mass-
produced, machine-made items. Money replaced land as the essential element
of wealth, and an economic system emerged which can still be considered a
"social" machine or supreme organizing "mechanism" unto itself. Technology
had begun to show potential for a life of its own, as machines were now made
which could make other machines. But the greatest contribution of the Industrial Revolution was *invention* itself (Whitehead, 1929). Even today, for better
or worse and whether accurately or inaccurately, inventiveness is considered a
particularly American virtue. In a technocracy, tools come to dominate both
everyday economic activities and the practical realms of life. While having
become a separate branch of cultural evolution from that of the moral, religious authority of the former tool-using culture, the new technology had not
yet become strong enough to prune off the old stem of traditional values.

Technocracy gave both scale and supremacy to the notions of "progress,"
"speed," "efficiency," and "economy." But in spite of these radical new measures of human existence, Postman's second-stage notion of technocracy
stopped short of annihilating traditional values altogether. "The citizens of a
technocracy knew that science and technology did not provide philosophies by
which to live, and they clung to the philosophies of their fathers. . . they
continued to believe that for all their dependence upon machinery, tools ought
still to be their servants, not their masters." (pp. 48–49) But by this time,
technological evolution had developed too much momentum; any hope of
continued subservience of technology to humanity was to fade away into its
opposite.

Familiar Notions of Nature and Technology

"In the nineteenth century," writes O. B. Hardison, Jr., (1989) "science presented nature as a group of objects set comfortably and solidly in the middle
distance before the eyes of the beholder." This is an apt description of the

traditional role landscape has played in symbolizing an idealized, natural world. For most of us, nature is still the earth, sky, rock, soil, water, landforms, plants, and animals we can see, hear, smell, and touch. These remain the surface signs we assemble in various ways to refer to the ever-expanding core mysteries of nature as science reveals them to us. Topophilia requires tangible objects and places, and landscapes, being the venues for human expression of this affection, have personified both the intensities and the ironies of our attachment to nature. The rise of technology did not threaten to eliminate tangible symbols of nature. It has, however, placed boundaries around them, cordoning off separate domains of the machine and domains of nature. Land use zoning only formally institutionalized what was perceptually and cognitively inevitable in the growing ability of industrial, mechanized life to compete on equal footing with more organic, traditionally religious world views. Modern landscapes are characterized by boundaries, containerized parks and front yards wherein nature is presumed to reside, and industrial zones (or industrial "parks"), auto strips, and superhighways which serve as the domain of technophilia. Such an ideologically territorialized landscape allowed symbols of nature to survive and to still represent an idealized, organic universe, in spite of the increasingly dominating and fragmenting effect of technology. Although the modern landscape which evolved during the nineteenth and early twentieth century was increasingly driven by technology, at least nature had a tangible place within it, and the notion of "place," whether natural or human-dominated, was still important. There were official lines drawn around neighborhood parks, national forests, wilderness areas, and national parks; official policies followed which were intended to protect these physical manifestations of nature. Thus the American psyche was segmented according to the dual gods of topophilia and technophilia, and as long as each construct could be constrained to its own zone, the system worked. It was only when we began to redefine nature as a system without boundaries; when we discovered that the effects of technology were not localized; when we invented invisible technologies, and when we realized that we had the potential to make replacement copies of nature by technological means, did this system show signs of collapsing.

Likewise, the technologies of the industrial revolution—the steam engine, mechanized looms, mills, and forges; the cutting and threshing machines of agriculture; the railroad, steamboat, motorcar, and eventually, the airplane—certainly completed Postman's transition from a tool-using culture to a true technocracy. However, these machines still had one important thing in common with their nonmechanized predecessors; they were highly *visible*. A resident of the nineteenth century might not know what particular technology would emerge next or from what particular sector of society it would appear, but at least he could see it coming and know when it arrived. The railroad, Leo Marx's symbolic machine, could not be ignored or camouflaged as it entered the garden. The technologies that swept over the western world and transformed the European and American continents were highly *conspicuous*.

Their effects were undeniably real and tangible. Nineteenth and early twentieth century landscapes became ideological battlefields between the highly tangible titans of technology and the traditional icons of nature. The clash between the two could be seen, heard, felt, breathed, and smelled. Whatever could be said in favor of or against the technological onslaught, one could not ignore it. Whatever its negative effects, one could put them in place on the land.

America as a Technological Theme Park

The conspicuous clash between the forces of nature and technology in the eighteenth, nineteenth, and early twentieth centuries has been a pivotal theme in American history, and the singularly most formative influence on the American landscape. The blend of gross land resource exploitation, transcendental reverence for nature, and love–hate ironies of the wilderness frontier are peculiarly unique to America. But until recently, the economic necessity of extractive industry and highly consumptive manufacturing technology led to a myopic sense of guilt; we beat hell out of the land to get at its resources, and turned the other way at the obvious horror of it all. The twentieth century exportation of extractive and manufacturing industries "offshore" to other countries coupled with the rise in the landscape-invisible "information" technologies at home allowed us some perspective on our technological heritage. The National Park Service has now formalized this perspective; a large section of southwestern Pennsylvania is being preserved as an American Industrial Heritage Site. The former iron ore mining and steel mill towns of Altoona and Johnstown, the industrial landscape corridors between them, and the historic structures associated with them have been designated for preservation as a technology-driven historic landscape. The National Park Service states the twofold purpose of the project:

> The first purpose is to commemorate the significant contribution of the region's iron and steel, coal, and transportation industries, which helped fuel and move America's industrial growth and development and establish her standing among nations of the world . . . Second, the project will use related historic sites and cultural resources within the nine counties as focal points for a tourism promotion program.
>
> *National Park Service, 1991*

This designation by the National Park service signals two things; first, that a shift in the national psyche has occurred which acknowledges that American hegemony in mining and manufacturing is now over, and second, that the central socioeconomic force which has arisen to replace consumptive, transformative technology is tourism and entertainment. America is now a technological theme park where, as William Irwin Thompson (1991) puts it, an "industrial economy of commerce" is being replaced by an "information econ-

(a)

AMERICA'S INDUSTRIAL HERITAGE PROJECT

UNITED STATES DEPARTMENT OF THE INTERIOR
NATIONAL PARK SERVICE
SOUTHWESTERN PENNSYLVANIA
HERITAGE PRESERVATION COMMISSION

(b)

Images from this National Park Service American Industrial Heritage Route Guide mark the passage from an economy dominated by mining and manufacturing to one dominated by entertainment and tourism. Courtesy of the U.S. Department of the Interior, National Park Service.

omy of commercials." In defense of the National Park Service, it is certainly appropriate that we enshrine those industrial landscapes so vital to how America became what it is. But the official, cultural admission that consumptive technological landscapes have already metamorphosed into the "nostalgic" category has a sad ring to it. It marks the transition from a visible, utilitarian, conspicuous, and genuine battle between nature and technology characteristic of the Industrial Revolution to a less-visible, superficial simulation. In the process, our landscapes become the repositories of entertainment imagery rather than essential providers of the physical necessities for life. The battleground between nature and technology has moved beyond the visible to another venue, leaving only the silent, surface glorification of a formerly serious and formative confrontation.

Nature as Number and "Fact"

Perhaps the transition of nature at the hand of technology was inevitable. By the early twentieth century, nature was being scrutinized by mathematicians who began to see a parallel mathematical structure in both the living and nonliving world. As the common, concrete language of the scientific movement, mathematics did not differentiate between life and nonlife. Structure in bone could be defined and measured in similar fashion to structure in rock. Hardison uses the work of British biologist D'Arcy Thompson to illustrate the effect of mathematics on images of nature. In 1917 Thompson published his book *Of Growth and Form,* wherein he mathematically measured and analyzed the sizes and shapes of animals and developed a system of conclusions and hypotheses about their dimensions in response to formative influences in the environment. His work employed some of the same mathematical techniques that were being applied to the design of bridges, ships, and airplanes. By graphing the shape of fish on an x–y grid and then mathematically distorting the grid, he was able to demonstrate rather startling relationships between the anatomical forms of different fish species, presumably in response to differing contexts for Darwinian selection.

Embedded in Thompson's work was the next step in a line of questioning in the tradition of science dating back to Copernicus; the conclusions drawn only added the next nail in the coffin of traditional, organic vitalism as the dominant world view. Writ between the lines of Thompson's conclusions was a loss of the difference between living and nonliving reality, and the source of the dissolution of that boundary was the language of mathematics as it approached universal stature in science. Organic vitalism—the notion that life is a vital and dynamic force separate from all physical and chemical forces—has been almost completely replaced by the "dead" science so accursed by Carolyn Merchant. Vitalism is fighting a last desperate battle over the nature of the human brain: Is consciousness merely the sum total of molecular scale,

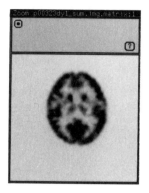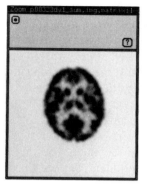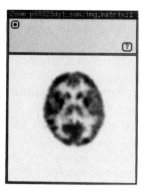

Positron emission tomography (PET) images of a normal human brain. PET scans use radioactively produced, electrically charged particles to map the "geography" of biochemical activity within the brain. Although highly useful for diagnosing brain disease and dysfunction, PET scans intensify the debate over whether the notion of "mind" can be considered anything more than precision biochemistry. Courtesy of Northern California P.E.T. Imaging Center, Sacramento, CA.

electrochemical neuron firings predisposed by specific DNA codes, and triggered by chemical signals, or are mental processes something ultimately more essential, unique, and fundamental? Indeed, when mathematics and scientific reduction increasingly dissolve distinctions between the building blocks of living and nonliving matter, Merchant's metaphor of "death" embodied in the Newtonian, Cartesian, Euclidian seizure of science seems evermore fitting.

Nature as a Necessary Fiction

Ironically, it is the same language of mathematics that is leading to the remystification of science after it had been nearly pronounced dead. Physics—the academic discipline which all sciences seek to emulate in its concreteness—soon arrived at the inevitable dead end of Newtonian, mechanistic reductionism. After Newton's world failed to explain what the physicists had been finding in their astonishing experimentation, they had to literally reinvent the rules under which they viewed the universe. The subsequent "paradigm shift" in physics which sprang forth from the work of Planck, Bohr, Heisenberg, Schrodinger, and Einstein has been popularized ad nauseum by Capra, Kuhn, and Prigogine and dozens of other authors, and in itself has become a new metaphoric world view. However, Hardison's (1989) treatment of the subject emphasizes a little-known but absolutely essential component of this transformation of modern physics. Hardison writes:

. . . the dominant movement of the twentieth-century theoretical science, especially mathematics, physics, and cosmology, has been away from certainties and toward masks and games. This is undoubtedly the result of the involvement of modern science with the unimaginably small and the impossibly large. The main impetus, however, is a widespread sense that the world as it is known is a construct. If there is an absolute reality—a *real* reality—it is known only as a tantalizing, ever-receding goal. (p. 49)

Hardison's main point is that after the dead-end of Newtonian theory, the disciplines of physics and astronomy (the very smallest and very largest horizons of nature) found it necessary to become more playful and arbitrary in constructing their fundamental presumptions about the universe. Currently the most fundamental subatomic particles presumed by physicists are called "quarks," the name coming from a line in James Joyce's *Finnegan's Wake* ("Three quarks for Murster Mark"). As building blocks of such "larger particles" as electrons, protons, and neutrons, quarks were supposed to lead to a simpler, more elegant atomic theory. However, upon continuous and rigorous investigation, quarks have been classified by quite serious, Nobel-caliber physicists as having three "colors," three "anticolors," six "flavors," a property called "charm" and varying degrees of a property they call "strangeness." Says Hardison: "Quarks are arranged in an eightfold way, a phrase borrowed from Zen. They are combined by particles called gluons because they glue quarks together. When gluons stick to other gluons they are called glueballs." (p. 52). A most amusing, yet serious conclusion has now been reached by physicists; while the mathematics points with veracity toward the existence of quarks, the theory itself also suggests that quarks may be permanently undetectable and inaccessible. Hence subatomic physicists probing the absolute innermost bracket of natural phenomena seemed to have arrived at a convoluted, "irrational," and somewhat humorous conclusion; the fundamental building blocks of the universe exist but can never be observed.

Physicists seriously hypothesize and mathematically prove other astonishing twists to our image of reality and nature. Einstein, of course, showed us that time and space were not discreet and independent, but relative and inextricable from one another, as were mass and energy. Recent theory also suggests that there are subatomic particles much smaller than a proton called "superstrings." Superstrings, which are in constant motion, are everywhere, and cannot be "located." They form a "worldsheet" fundamental to the universe. Theoretical mathematicians and physicists ponder the "form" of this worldsheet, referring to it like a "doughnut with an arbitrary number of holes" or like the "foam on a glass of beer" (Hardison, 1989). Superstrings are thought to have 10 dimensions, of which four (three Cartesian dimensions plus time) have "uncurled," while the other six remain "curled" as they have been since the dawn of physical creation.

At the other end of the spectrum of size or scale, scientists explore the origins of the universe and try to synthesize astrophysics (which is based upon relativity) and subatomic theory (which is based upon quantum mechanics) into a "unified theory" capable of explaining the all of physical nature. Such astounding concepts as black holes—the "negative" stars with such high density (i.e., localized mass) and gravitational attraction that even photons (particles of light) cannot escape—are now taken for granted. Controversy centers around the notion of the "Big Bang"—a theory which assumes an essential, creative, explosive origin for the universe. The Big Bang supposedly took place 10 to 20 billion years ago, yet it is the first 10^{-30} second of that 20-billion year period that is in question. An "inflationary theory" has been proposed to explain physical phenomena during this immensely short period which presumes that mass is a positive form of energy and gravity is a negative form of energy. Inflationary theory

> . . . assumes that immediately after the big bang, a transition occurred during which the universe took shape more or less as a hole forms in Swiss Cheese or a bubble in a glass of ginger ale. Our universe is one of many bubble universes which may continue to form forever. For a time, the bubble expanded rapidly. It is this period of "inflation"—rapid growth—that gives the theory its name. After the inflationary period another transition occurred. Matter precipitated out of the vacuum inside the bubble, and the universe was irreversibly on the way to becoming its familiar self.

> *Hardison, 1989, p. 55*

Inflationary theory has a similar essential drawback to quark theory; it suggests its own undetectability. On the other hand, it presumes that everything that exists (e.g., energy) cancels out something else that exists (e.g., matter). The obvious and concluding condition: zero or nothing. The world's most brilliant physical theorists have been working toward astounding conclusions; that the universe evolved as a quantum fluctuation from literally nothing. Such conclusions often seem like a long and circuitous way of arriving at the same end point as certain nihilists or, if one adopts a different point of view, religious fundamentalists. But world-renowned physicist Steven Hawking has so far concluded that the universe has no beginning and no end in time, no edge in space, and as paraphrased by Carl Sagan in the book's introduction, "nothing for a Creator to do." (Hawking, 1988, p. x).

Glueballs? "Foamy" universes? Quarks with "charm?" Uncurled dimensions

---

Theories predict three possible shapes to the universe: (a) *a closed, spherical universe which will eventually contract and collapse,* (b) *a saddle-shaped, open universe which will expand (as it is expanding now) forever, and* (c) *a flat universe predicted by inflationary theory which is perfectly balanced between open and closed, and will slow down to a zero expansion rate. Unlike these two-dimensional artist's renderings, however, the universe has no edges. Courtesy of Lawrence Berkeley Laboratory.*

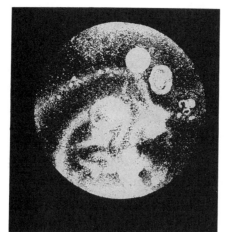

(a)

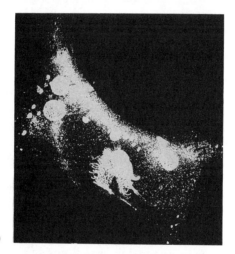

(b)

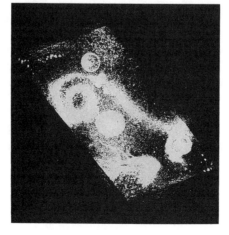

(c)

of superstrings? Everything from absolutely nothing? No beginning, no end, no boundaries? Taken to its utmost extreme, the physical exploration of inner and outer space by the most brilliant and highly specialized scientists working in the most exalted and emulated of academic disciplines results in a world view resembling something from ancient mythology, Alice in Wonderland, or eastern religious philosophy. One wonders how a process building upon such concrete, mechanistic origins could result in conclusions so mystical and slippery. Perhaps the universe is nothing at all, or perhaps we have arrived at the ultimate boundaries of human ability to know the unknowable. Whatever conclusion one draws depends on one's position with respect to teleology versus existentialism—whether the universe has "purpose" or merely "exists." However, one thing is for certain. Science, starting with the most rational excursions into the "real" phenomena of nature, has led us into a realm of "reality" that is highly unrecognizable, unfathomable, and "unrealistic." Nature has, indeed, changed.

Technology As a Means to the Core of Nature

In the evolution of the construct of nature, technology, of course, has played the critical role. The devices used by scientists to observe and prove or disprove hypotheses about the nature of reality were in themselves practical applications of proven scientific hypotheses. They were human creations, and are not humans part of nature? Are particle accelerators, electron microscopes, and radio telescopes "natural?" By developing more and more sophisticated measuring and observing devices, technology has given humans extra "eyes" to study nature on the fringes of normal human perception. The scientists would like us to believe that the findings made by such highly sophisticated technological devices are merely extensions of the range of everyday human perception, and therefore, of unquestionable veracity. They are not. Use of these devices, in their increasing complexity, has become the privilege of a select few and are rarely available to the common person. Furthermore, the use of such devices requires translation to and from mathematics and other highly technical, proprietary "languages" which few lay people "speak." When forced to take as truth a scientist's claim that the atoms in our bodies are made up of quarks, or that the universe consists of foamy sheets of superstrings, our perceptions fail to validate the claim. We find little in the accessible, perceptual surface of our experience that would be congruent with what we are being asked to believe. As some of us seem to know more and more about the core of nature, most of us know less and less.

"Old" nature, of course, has not disappeared. We can still see the trees and sky outside our windows; we still smell the fresh, salty air at the ocean. We can dig our hands into loamy soil and feel its dampness. Always reassuring, these tangible interactions are, of course, readily available to most of us, but their meanings have been diluted by the expanding complexity and scale of what we must now consider "nature." It is the perceptual *boundaries* of an expanding construct of nature which have disappeared, like explorers' sailing ships dropping below the distant horizon. The tangible "center" of nature struggles to hold meaning as the boundaries expand into the invisible realm.

Another evolutionary line of technologies—those involved in the processing and dispersal of *information*—are discussed in greater detail in Chapter 8. Information "technologies" have played a fundamental role in formulating the constructs of "nature" and the communication of "reality" since the dawn of time. When faced with the seemingly impossible task of accepting what the scientists now tell us about the expanding frontiers of nature, we won't believe it unless we "see" it on television as part of the unfolding, electronic media construct of reality.

Technopoly and Technological Determinism

More and more scholars and social critics begrudgingly admitting that our technologies may be getting the best of us. Neil Postman defines a third stage of technological culture as *technopoly*—the disappearance of the traditional world view left over from the tool-using culture at the hands of technology. The means by which technology accomplishes this is none other than Hardison's notion of "disappearance:"

> Technopoly eliminates alternatives to itself in precisely the same way Aldous Huxley outlined in *Brave New World*. . . It does not make them illegal. It does not make them immoral. It does not even make them unpopular. It makes them invisible and therefore irrelevant. And it does so by redefining what we mean by religion, by art, by family, by politics, by history, by truth, by privacy, by intelligence, so that our definitions fit its new requirements. Technopoly, in other words, is totalitarian technocracy.
>
> *Postman, 1992, p. 48*

Postman's coining of the term "technopoly" was preceded by Langdon Winner's notion of "autonomous technology." In his seminal book of the same name, Winner stops short of embracing technological determinism—the idea that advances in technology directly determine the outcome of cultural evolution, believing that such a rigid theory precludes willful cultural or contextual change. Instead, he puts forth the notions of technological "drift" and technological "imperative." Technological drift, as he views it, describes processes for which "a multiplicity of technologies, developed and applied under a very narrow range of considerations, act and interact in countless ways beyond the anticipations of any person or institution . . . with almost no existing means for controlling or regulating the products of this chain of events" (Winner,

1977, p. 89). Winner also suggests the existence of a technological "imperative," defining technologies as "structures whose conditions of operation demand the restructuring of their environments" (p. 100). Looking about, we can see the extent to which technologies have restructured our environments. Highways, roads, and parking lots are the skeletal landscape of America; industrial zones, commercial shopping centers, and housing subdivisions are its flesh. The motorcar, mechanized economic production and distribution, and video-based home entertainment have certainly expressed their imperatives.

Although the idea of a completely "deterministic" technology is ultimately rejected by Winner, he does emphasize that technologies are not inert, but instead contain their own political implications and change their cultural and physical milieux accordingly and often with little possibility of deliberate control by humans. Postman, who writes 15 years later than Winner, is not so kind. The United States, he says, is the only culture as yet to have become a technopoly (he observes that Europe and Japan are close behind), where the influence of technology on culture is paramount, having replaced its closest competitor, the traditional values associated with religion. In the works of Frederick Taylor, the progenitor of modern scientific management, Postman finds the "event that signaled the beginning of a technological theory." Taylor's work was nothing short of a mechanistic formula for humans in the work place—one that espoused technical calculation over human judgment; things that could be measured over those that could not; the opinions of trained experts over those of everyday participants.

> In the work of Frederick Taylor we have, I believe, the first clear statement of the idea that society is best served when human beings are placed at the disposal of their techniques and technology, that human beings are, in a sense, worth less than their machinery.
>
> *Postman, 1992, p. 52*

Postman argues that technopoly took route in America because of a series of unique and interrelated reasons: the unique American character which saw everything in constant motion and "no limits placed by nature to human endeavor;" the frontier mentality and the abundance of natural resources; the tradition of religious freedom, and the American skepticism toward culture itself; the genius of American inventor/capitalists like Bell, Edison, Rockefeller, Astor, Ford, and Carnegie and their willingness to dismiss past models; the technological alternatives for old world habits or beliefs (penicillin instead of prayer, mobility instead of family roots, television instead of reading, etc.).

Old systems of belief came under siege from all directions: Nietzsche announced the death of God; Darwin made the question of God a moot point; Marx argued that history had its own agenda, irrespective of our wishes. Freud taught us to distrust reason, Watson showed that free will was an illusion, and Einstein told us that everything was relative. "Amid the conceptual debris" writes Postman, "there remained one sure thing to believe in—technology" (p. 55).

Science, Technology, and the Expanding Core of Nature

The quantum theories of subatomic physics and the relativistic theories of astrophysics are not the only influences on the expansion of the core of nature. In addition to the frontiers of the very small and very large, other dimensions of scientific exploration are enlarging the domain to be included within the boundaries of nature. The emergence in recent years of an entire classification of phenomena popularized as "Chaos Theory" (Gleick, 1987) has shaken the foundations of many scientific disciplines seeking to reveal natural phenomena. Until recently, most disciplinary scientific research has been based upon finite mathematical reduction, linear equations, and computer algorithms which were thought to "model" reality; in the tradition of Newtonian physics, one set of input variables would predictably produce a single set of output conditions. But a number of inquisitive scientists looked at the natural landscape and *knew* that something else must be going on; how could linear equations predict the infinitely varying shapes of clouds, the patterns of ocean shorelines, the branching of trees, or the swirling hydraulic currents in a whitewater rapids? Visible "nature" was far too unpredictable and varied to be explained by the Euclidian geometry of squares, circles, and regular polygons and the rational, convergent notions of linear mathematics. Yet we could always recognize vague patterns in nature. Clouds were clouds even if no two were alike. Trees of the same species could be identified by laymen by "reducing" certain leaf patterns to the realm of predictability. Economies did not work as economists predicted. Nature was obviously some magical combination of disorder within order, or vice versa.

At the Santa Fe Institute, an unusual amalgamation of scientists is exploring a set of spontaneous, self-organizing phenomena they call "emergence"—the patterns that begin to emerge and dissolve as many copies of a singular element begin to assemble and exhibit complex group behavior which could not have been predicted by examining the singular element by itself. For example, a steady trickle of sand from above a table builds up a sand pile with a relatively predictable angle of repose. But occasionally, the addition of one more grain of sand becomes critical, causing a large slide as the sand pile adjusts. Other times, smaller slides occur more frequently, all in a recognizable, yet unpredictably random pattern. To the uninitiated, emergence sounds very much like the essential notion of "life," and to the religious or primitive person, that part of existence which could only be described as "spirit." After the Big Bang, molecules somehow assembled in cells; cells amalgamated and formed complex organisms; ultimately, conscious "mind" somehow emerged. And many conscious minds together interact in strange ways at the edge of chaos, such as the sudden collapse of a 40-year communist hegemony in Eastern Europe, or a 500-point, one-day dip in the American stock market. At the Santa Fe Institute, scientists have developed computer programs that simulate emergence principles. On the computer screen, individual "organisms" grow, multiply, change "genetic" structure, collect into flocks, exhibit recognizable flock behavior and motion, and suffer population crashes. By examining these and other highly complex, unpredictable phenomena in the real world which appear related across formerly unrelated academic disciplines, the physicists, economists, artificial intelligence specialists, and others at the Santa Fe Institute are molding a unified concept of science in which old disciplinary barriers break down, and from which the true stuff of "life" is to be coaxed forth (Waldrop, 1992).

French-born Mathematician Benoit Mandelbrot discovered a simple mathematical concept—*fractal* geometry—which was to illustrate and serve as a referent for the entire realm of nonlinear, "naturalistic" phenomena now referred to as "chaos" or "complexity." "Fractal" referred to the notion of fractional dimensions. Mandelbrot boldly hypothesized that spatial dimensions in nature might be better classified as fractions of integers rather than whole numbers. Instead of *one-, two-,* or *three*-dimensional reality, he suggested that form could be classified as having, for example, 1.37 or 2.76 dimensions. Mandelbrot began with simple equations which assumed a fractional dimension as a coefficient. Assuming a starting value as an input variable, calculating an end value, and using the end value as the new input value in another iteration of the same equation, Mandelbrot began to plot the end values of his iterative equations on the new supercomputer graphic terminals available to him at the IBM Research Corporation where he was employed as a Research Fellow. What emerged from the screens of the supercomputers were visible patterns and forms the likes of which the world had never seen, but which immediately revealed a likeness to visible natural phenomena which could not be denied.

If, according to Mandelbrot, a straight line were of dimension 1.0 and a smooth, complete plane were of dimension 2.0, then a line of, say, dimension 1.67 would begin to meander indefinitely about the surface with an iterative complexity which began to fill most of the area. Complex "shorelines" and "island archipelagos" appeared. The higher the fractional dimension, the more "space" the lines filled and the more complex the patterns. By using fractal dimensions between 2.0 and 3.0, Mandelbrot—and a host of inspired mathematicians and followers—were able to produce likenesses of surfaces which mimicked the varying intricacy of mountain ranges after various degrees of erosion, or planetary surfaces under various degrees of pocking by asteroids or meteor showers.

Fractals have personified and made visible a host of related "chaotic" or highly nonlinear, complex phenomena which have served to break down barriers between scientific disciplines. By plotting input and output conditions of various natural systems and by examining the graphic results from the per-

A fractal image produced at the IBM labs at Böblingen, Germany. Fractal images are self-similar at larger or smaller scales. As formerly unknown, "concrete," originally meaningless forms, fractals have come to symbolize the complexity and near-chaotic order of nature. Image by H.-O. Peitgen, P. Richter, W. Hehl, and D. Wollschlager from Peitgen and Richter (1986).

spective of chaos theory, scientists have begun to cross the forbidden boundaries of their disciplines to "talk" to other scientists. Atmospheric scientists have found commonalties with cardiological physiologists; ecologists find patterns in population dynamics similar to those found by vibration experts in applied mechanics. Chaos theory has cracked the safe box of disciplinary isolation and has, in essence, served notice to those who felt that scientific reduction could reveal the most fundamental properties of nature separately within each discipline. But more importantly for our discussion, fractal geometry has offered a powerful new technology in the *simulation* of nature; George Lucas' famed motion picture special effects laboratory—Industrial Light and Magic—is producing some of the most advanced work in fractal-related mathematics, producing imaginary landscapes for future worlds and far-off planets.

The importance of chaotian mathematics, emergence, and fractal geometry to the landscape is twofold, yet far-reaching. The history of environmental design has been one of seizing upon patterns from painting and the arts to *inform* the self-consciously designed cityscapes and landscapes which were its principal output. First, with the advent of the supercomputer, which can perform millions of calculations to reveal formerly invisible patterns and shapes which somehow resemble those of nature, fractal geometry and other abstract manifestations of complex, lifelike patterns may yet find a way to replace the worn-out, modernist shapes of Euclidian geometry which have been the formal building blocks of architects and landscape architects for several decades. By revealing a seemingly "deeper" mathematical structure of nature which is not entirely predictable and precise, fractal geometry and its cousins may capture the spirit of a rebellious, new scientific paradigm and allow a degree of philosophical mediation between science, technology, and nature.

On the other hand, the highly evolved forms derived from fractal geometry and emergence patterns may make it easier for artists and technicians to make *replacements* of nature which are increasingly indistinguishable from the real—a subject discussed at length in the next chapter. While consumptive, landscape-scale industrial technologies could be perceived as direct, frontal assaults on nature, fractal geometry and the computer games of the emergence scientists have taken on an ability to simulate nature to the point where very ponderous questions must be asked: Is all "life" natural, or can "life" be synthesized by humans? Or, is this even a reasonable question to ask?

Nature, Deep Ecology, and Gaia

Fractal geometry, chaos, and complexity theory primarily address the perceptual or "concrete" level of natural phenomena with limited concern for functional or symbolic levels of significance. At the opposite, most abstract, or symbolic level, nature is undergoing a similarly revolutionary transformation. With the arrival of the discipline of ecology in the past 40 years, nature as a system of symbolic and transcendental *objects* has been expanded if not supplanted by attention to the *relationships between* natural objects and components. Ecology is the science of inclusion and connection rather than of isolation and individual analysis. Ecology now represents the very heart of the *core* of landscape—the ultimately systematic set of functional connections between *organisms* (both human and otherwise) and *contexts*. In the past few years, ecological science has increasingly focused upon the *landscape* scale or level; landscape ecology is now a *bona fide* subdiscipline of ecology. While originally a social construct derived from notions in painting, "landscape" structure and function now serve as a principal foundation for the study of ecology (Forman and Godron, 1986). The rapid expansion of the *landscape* scale of focus in ecological science has already begun to alter the public meaning of the term away from its preoccupation with surface and toward *core* considerations.

At first, ecology emerged in the tradition of other so-called "pure" sciences which attempted to turn an objective eye toward nature and, without value-laden bias, reveal its secrets as if they were entirely objective fact. But from Aldo Leopold and Rachel Carson on, ecology would only play at being value neutral. Implicit within the structures and functions of ecosystems as they emerged under the light of scientific scrutiny were the seeds of a dramatic change of values by now so familiar to readers: ecology was the first science with potential (borrowing Eckbo's terminology from the beginning of the chapter) to *put the pieces of the scientific world back together again*. Environmental and ecological science, while somewhat facilitated by technology, has only served to undermine the naive world view and quasi-religious stature of technological determinism to the point that the "ecological paradigm" serves as the major, value-laden alternative to the technological world view. The only major accomplishments of the 1992 Rio "Earth Summit" were a treaty on preservation of biodiversity and the agreement to curb global climate change; the former speaks to the ascendancy of ecology as the emerging, paramount value system; the latter marks the first glimmers of the twilight of the technological order.

As the mountain range of ecology thrusts upwards and grinds against the tectonic plate of technological determinism, two mysterious peaks have appeared which have drawn considerable controversy, marking the extreme discomfort which society must endure in making such monumental transitions. The first is *deep ecology* and the second is the *Gaia hypothesis*.

Deep Ecology

Deep ecology is a term first coined by Norwegian philosopher Arne Naess to describe an ecology guided by a deep sense of normative philosophical values. Primary among these values is a sense of self as indistinguishable from and united with the natural world, which goes beyond the typical Western idea of the *self* as *independent* from the environment. Deep ecology proclaimed that other living beings had intrinsic value for their own sake, independent of their practical utility to humans. The richness of other life forms and ecosystems was to be considered a necessary contributing influence to the realization of self-as-part-of-nature. Other values were espoused by the founders of deep ecology as well: a reduction in human species population; a lessening of the level of human interferences with the nonhuman world; and an emphasis on life qualities rather than quantities (Naess and Rothenberg, 1989; Devall and Sessions, 1985).

Deep ecology first found resistance among traditional resource managers whose idea of "conservation" implied eventual consumption of the "conserved" resources for the utility of humans; among humanists who found in the writings of deep ecologists strains of misanthropy; and even among ecologists who still believed they were conducting value-free, "objective" science.

Ultimately the study and practice of ecology could not be kept separate from the values latent and implicit within it. Although the early ecologists considered themselves heirs to the objective scientific tradition (Dubos, 1980), they themselves unselfconsciously laid the basis for the eventual infusion of value. By articulating their scientific theories of the *connectedness* of nature, they were reawakening and giving credence to the long-buried values of organic vitalism and universal holism still residing in the mythology of primal peoples, in eastern philosophies, and in western mysticism. Philosophers, humanistic scholars, and the general public saw this potential even before the scientists themselves. As a holistic, integrative science, ecology proved much too strong a threat to the dominance of reductionist technological determinism, and much too potent a paradigm for explaining and ordering human life within the context of other living and nonliving entities. Deep ecology soon became "ecology with a conscience." Borrowing and building upon a set of normative moral values from philosophical and mystical religious traditions which included, rather than ignored, other human life forms, deep ecology soon incurred the anger of religious dogmatists and the backlash of technophiles, whose rigid embrace of technological determinism had become a kind of religion unto itself.

Even landscape architects were slow to espouse deep ecology, believing (quite correctly) that it might demonstrate that their formal notions of designed landscape held insufficient moral basis for existence. Indeed, in spite of the works and writings of several famous landscape architects (following the lead of Ian McHarg), much of today's designed landscape cannot be justified by a value system which seeks parity between humans and other species and seeks less human interference rather than more.

As of this writing, deep ecology is still considered an extreme position. But it is well on its way to becoming a bona fide cornerstone of a new and dominant international social paradigm. The significance of deep ecology to the expanding nature of nature cannot be underestimated. With ecological science expanding the more traditional notions of "nature," the emphasis shifts from perceivable *objects* to often imperceptible *systems of relationships*. The addition of deep ecology's set of normative values on top of these new systematic relationships fundamentally has begun to alter the way in which nature serves its transcendent function. As long as nature was primarily, as Hardison says, a "collection of visible objects set firmly in the middle distance," the transcendental, moral value of nature such as that espoused by Emerson was easily facilitated; a picturesque nature composed of water, trees, rocks, and soil could readily "absorb" spiritual meaning and easily refer to or stand for a set of higher spiritual and moral values. The moral values of deep ecology, however, are based less on visible objects and more on barely visible relationships, and relationships make less sharply defined symbols than do objects.

Deep ecology, therefore, only makes nature that much more difficult to visualize, and requires a stronger act of faith by the participating public. It is no wonder that Spotted Owls and rainforests, both perceptually *visible* images, have been captured and used by the media as symbols to represent the relative invisibility and expanding complexity of "ecological" nature.

The Gaia Hypothesis

If deep ecology widens the necessary leap of faith in the transcendent value of nature, the Gaia hypothesis opens up a virtual chasm. Pioneered by eclectic and independent atmospheric chemist James Lovelock and biologist Lynn Margulis, the Gaia hypothesis presumes that "the Earth's climate and surface environment are controlled by the plants, animals, and microorganisms that inhabit it. That taken as a whole, the planet behaves not as an inanimate sphere of rock and soil, sustained by the automatic and accidental processes of geology as traditional earth science has long maintained, but more as a biological superorganism—a planetary body—that adjusts and regulates itself." (Joseph, 1990, p. 1). Named after the ancient Greek goddess of Earth, Gaia has prompted intense reactions, from vicious assault to ecstatic endorsement. Critics fault the theory as being teleological and quasi-religious (hard-core science abhors teleology, or the notion that the earth or universe might have a higher "purpose"). Adherents see in Gaia a scientific basis for a "green" cosmology where humans share the earth rather than dominate it.

Lovelock first found evidence for the theory while working on NASA grants searching for ways to detect life on other planets by means of chemical sampling of atmospheric elements. Independently wealthy from having invented the electron capture detector (a device useful for sampling the chemical composition of sparse atmospheres), Lovelock used his new device to first detect that CFCs were building up in the earth's atmosphere, and therefore can justly claim to be the progenitor of the now widespread public concern over ozone depletion. The essence of Gaian theory states that certain chemical cycles between the earth's crust and atmosphere, notably the carbon, oxygen, and methane cycles, are collectively regulated by the living organisms which depend upon them. In the earth's atmosphere, free oxygen and free methane coexist in significant proportions, whereas on a sterile planet without life they would rapidly combine to form other compounds in the presence of sunlight. Earth's atmosphere contains 21% oxygen. At 23% oxygen, vegetation would literally burn up in massive fires. At 19%, anaerobic bacteria would replace the predominantly aerobic organisms that now dominate the plant and animal kingdoms. For 3 billion years the average temperature of the Earth has been held relatively constant (plus or minus a few degrees centigrade), while it has been scientifically presumed that the radiant energy output of the sun during that time has increased by about 30%. Lovelock concludes that only the cybernetic regulation of temperature conditions by life itself could account for the stability of surface temperature over the increasing radiant energy of a warming sun. In his view, earthly life regulates the ideal conditions for its own existence.

Lovelock's assumptions threatened the scientists working in more narrow realms for whom the idea of a unified, self-regulatory biosphere/atmosphere necessitated a reinvention of the foundations of their own disciplines. But Lovelock has come under fire from environmentalists too. Those who believe humans should reduce the level of technological interference and fossil fuel consumption to avoid global warming were disappointed by Lovelock's theory. They criticized his conclusion that human generation of carbon dioxide from the industrial processes of urbanization and technological development were far less damaging to the supposed Gaian cybernetic balance than were the degraded conditions of the rainforests, grasslands, and methane-producing wetlands as a result of human agricultural activity. For many of these critics, industrial technology was the real culprit, while agricultural technologies deserved their romanticized status; for them, Lovelock's hypothesis was getting it all backward.

Ultimately, as Joseph (1990) writes, the Gaia hypothesis has developed a multiple persona:

Gaia is: a scientific hypothesis that our planet behaves as a living organism, and a biogeochemical theory of how that system has evolved; a planet-sized creature some 3.5 billion years old; a planetary patina sustained by microbial symbiosis; a necessary overstatement on the power and influence of life on Earth; a wishful trivialization of the vast mechanical power of geological systems; a profoundly erroneous supposition that nature works for the good of all; a brilliant intellectual organizing principle; an ecological world view for the twenty-first century; a romantic metaphor for oneness; a unified symbol for pantheism; a whole lot of hot air; a travesty against both secular humanism and organized religion; and even a pop star, duly dubbed by *People* magazine, which declared her one of the twenty-five most intriguing characters of 1989.

Joseph, 1990, pp. 248–249

For now, the Gaia hypothesis holds the dubious distinction of being perhaps the "largest" and most comprehensive of all scientific hypotheses about life on earth, while at the same time serving as an overarching spiritual metaphor. Gaia is profoundly attractive to the public for the same reasons it is profoundly threatening to hard-core, atheistic scientists; it offers the glimpse of a bridge between science and religion, and, like some of the end conclusions of particle and astrophysics, seems to arrive at the same metaphysical conclusions espoused by ancient and primitive peoples and eastern religious philosophies while emanating from distinctively western, empirical, scientific traditions.

In ironic fashion, mathematics, science, and technology have expanded the construct of nature to include a vastly increased philosophical territory, from the very small, quantum world of quarks to the very large theories of cosmic origin; from the very concrete, perceptual levels of fractal geometry and non-linear mathematics to the very abstract, and ultrasymbolic levels of deep

Landscape architect and artist Jonathan Hammond's conception for a Temple of Gaia, *shown as sited in a rice field during a rain storm near Fukuoka, Japan. Gaia is a profoundly controversial yet inspirational hypothesis about nature at the planetary scale.*

ecology and the Gaia hypothesis. This is an incredibly vast empire of beliefs—one which the old pictorial symbols of nature find increasingly difficult to represent in the landscape. So much of this ideological empire of nature is beyond the horizon of visibility that no one vantage point has the power to survey the entire realm. Nature is now subatomic, cosmic, fractal, electronic, complex, emergent, and Gaian. It is deeper, farther, broader, larger, smaller, more concrete, and more abstract than ever before.

The New Invisible Technologies

Technology has not only facilitated the expansion of nature beyond the boundaries of perception, but it is also evolving out of sight itself. Although technological devices have provided new "eyes" for the study of natural phenomena, the technological "tools" by which American society aims to earn a living are increasingly invisible as well. While we have certainly moved from the "machine" age through the "jet" and "space" ages and into the "information" age, we must also conclude we have entered the "biological" age, and may even be "seeing" glimpses of a "postbiological" world. The highly visible, mechanical, energy-consuming devices of the past century have thoroughly and conspicuously structured today's American landscape. However, many of the technologies now emerging which show potential for economic development and cultural influence are inconspicuous if not totally invisible, and will affect the landscape in a completely different manner than the previous conspicuously consumptive technologies.

Genetic engineering (or, euphemistically, biotechnology) is the deliberate, laboratory-based manipulation of the DNA of living plants and animals to alter their structure, function, and contextual response to the environment. Bill McKibben (1989) laments that genetically altered organisms signal the end of the notion of nature as independent, obviously wild, and devoid of human influence. Like many other critics of genetic engineering, McKibben emphasizes the ethical and moral concerns it has raised: the questionability of playing God; the efficacy of "defying" nature; the perpetuation of an attitude of human dominance over the environment rather than acceptance of limits; the danger that some altered organism might go out of control. Jerry Mander (1991) echoes similar concerns, identifying six negative points about genetic engineering: (1) newly engineered organisms or "bugs" may escape into the environment, and we have inadequate safety standards and preventative measures and no means to stop such organisms once released; (2) the evolution of mandatory genetic screening of humans prior to conception and birthing could lead to new levels of race and genetic discrimination; (3) the patenting of new animals may lead to corporate control of "life forms" and the reduction of life to a corporate commodity; (4) "market" mechanisms leading to "designer babies" with human genetic tendencies which could be bought and sold and which aim the human gene pool toward superficial, cosmetic cultural ideals; (5) an overall reduction of the genetic diversity of all life forms could result, and (6) genetically altered or created organisms could potentially be used as weapons of war and destruction.

Genetic engineering has indeed opened up a new avenue in the history of technology, and its social implications are many and serious. Genetic engineering's potential effect upon the landscape is unique and crucial to the theme of this book: *it is a basically imperceptible or opaque technology.* Genetically altered strawberries which resist frost damage look just like ordinary strawberries. Corn tolerant of saline irrigation water looks like any other corn. The new biotechnology offers few if any clues to the altered relationship between surface properties and core functions; its utility to humans is based upon the opposite spatial premise to that of mechanical devices. Fossil fuel machines *conspicuously change the environment to fit the organism* (i.e., humans), while genetic engineering *inconspicuously changes the organism to fit the environment.* The result will be a relative inability of the landscape to reflect the essential structure and function of the technology, or to serve as a mediating device between "nature" and the new technology. With the machine age, we knew what was coming at us. The landscape was the index of our scientific culture and the bellwether of our technological innovations, and "nature" was a visible, baseline condition against which we could contrast the "progress" of technology. In the biotechnological age, the line between nature and technology will be invisible and may literally dissolve altogether. We will notice nothing, except perhaps that the strawberries in the field won't die after a hard frost. The perceptual feedback or "visual ecology" from biotechnology will be barely perceptible and often misleading. People may scarcely be able to notice corn growing in saline water or grape vineyards in far northern climates. Genetically altered plants and animals will diffuse invisibly into our ecosystems and subtly change our expectations of what is "natural." We will have no sure way of detecting the presence of biotechnically altered organisms among us. Like so many other emerging technologies, genetic engineering will contribute to the fundamental cultural blurring of what is "real" and what is not.

It is a short distance up (or down) from biotechnology to *nanotechnology*. The term, popularized by K. Eric Drexler (1986), implies machines and devices which build new creations *molecule by molecule,* on the scale of *nano*meters a thousand times smaller than a micrometer, or 10^{-9} meters. As Drexler envisions this future technology, nanomachines will be made from proteins and synthesized DNA which will be used as *assemblers* of more complex molecules. "Biochips"—computing devices made from organic molecules— will control the processes, using electron "currents" as small as a few electrons. *Replicator* molecules will make larger volumes of the desired material. Nanomachines and assemblers will ultimately be able to work with inorganic, hard substances other than proteins. Nanotechnology might be used for molecular-scale surgery, localized cell repair, advanced anesthesia, and a host of other medical applications. Drexler admits the potential for the misuses of nanotechnology in biological warfare, and the potential for a synthesized molecular substance to replicate dangerously out of control. In spite of obvious limitations and possible pitfalls, Drexler, a former National Science Foundation Graduate Fellow of MIT, is convinced of the inevitable development of nanotechnology.

Some pieces of Drexler's bold vision have already come true. Scientists are turning protein molecules into nanoscale chemical processing plants (Freedman, 1991). Protein "switches" have been developed which act more than a thousand times faster than those made from silicon or gallium semiconductors (Kiely, 1990). Chemists have developed a fully optical computer memory from bacterial proteins which can be "read" by a tiny laser; the prototype is already faster than the fastest semiconductor memory. Devices with features of little more than 100 atoms across have been produced to study the wavelike (or quantum mechanical) behaviors of electrons confined to small areas (Smith, 1990). Drexler himself, responding to the challenge to substantiate his claims, has produced an impressive and scientifically grounded first volume on molecular machinery, manufacturing, and computation (Drexler, 1992). Nanotechnology appears to be off and running.

When nanotechnological "bio-chips," propulsion molecules, molecular-scale machines, and DNA building blocks can be physically and functionally combined, we will have succeeded in taking from nature the basic ingredients

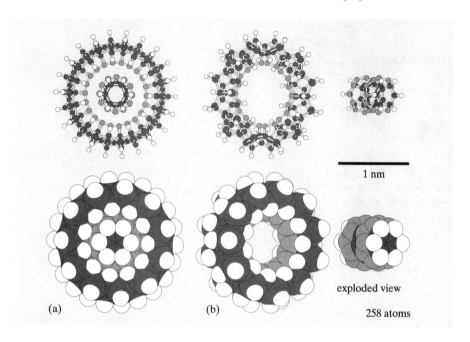

Conceptual design of "nanotechnology" bearings less than 5 × 10⁻⁹ meters in diameter. Individual atoms which make up the bearings are clearly identifiable as spheres in the drawings. From Drexler (1992).

for making truly new forms of "living" beings from biological "machine" parts: cellular automata with "living" tissues, artificial "intelligence," and the ability to move independently. If and when nanotechnology succeeds in this task, the boundary between the machine and nature will be effectively, if not frighteningly, erased.

The Disappearing Battlefield

I have only scratched the surface of today's scientific thresholds and cutting edge technologies, and I have saved the bulk of discussion on information and communication technology for Chapter 8. What is most critical to the discussion of the landscape, however, is that *the developing edges of both nature and technology have now moved beyond the visible realm.* With few exceptions, the unfolding dimensions of nature are now well outside the boundaries of everyday human perception. Likewise, the technologies with the most potential to drive our economy in the very near future (without some radical shift in social priorities) are equally invisible. Finally, the locus of conflict between technology and nature is moving rapidly toward invisibility as well. The major arenas of environmental degradation caused by our technological lifestyles are often atmospheric, global, underground, diffused over imperceptibly large areas, too small to "see," or located away from major population areas. True, the old visible conflicts are still there—traffic congestion, trash buildup, urban smog, and clear-cut forests. But the worst potential crises are turning out to be the ones which, for the reasons given above, we cannot see.

Acid rain silently and invisibly kills fish in Canadian lakes, leaving little perceptible trace of its devastating effect on ecological food chains. Ozone, an essentially colorless gas, builds up in excess at the surface levels of the earth's atmosphere but thins out dramatically and invisibly in the stratosphere, leaving only the potential of increasing sunburn and skin cancer as its visible trace. No one can see the 20% increase in carbon dioxide in the Earth's atmosphere since 1950. Likewise, we can't see the ambient increases in nuclear radiation which still pervade Europe from the Chernobyl accident. Radioactive milk looks just like any other milk. The incredible amount of groundwater pollution from chemical sources is hidden from sight; estimates of the relative amount of all filling stations which have leaked gasoline into the ground reach as high as 75%. The devastation of rainforests so often mentioned in the media takes place in landscapes far away from the population centers whose residents consume the byproducts of such devastation. Since few of us have actually visited the Amazonian rainforests, we rely on our imaginations and media imagery to make sense of these effects.

Among the newly discovered crises involving technology and landscape are the growing number of scientific studies reporting the negative health effects of ELF (extremely low frequency) electromagnetic energy, such as that found near power lines and step-down electrical transformers (Hester, 1992). Extremely low frequency electromagnetic energy is now thought to be linked with increased incidences of carcinogenesis, including childhood leukemia. The research, in its infancy, is similar to the early years of study on the effects of cigarette smoking. Should the research trends continue to find increasing evidence of ELF health risks, the millions of Americans living and working near high-voltage power lines, power substations, or other ELF sources will need to fundamentally reassess the meanings of the places they live and work. While power line rights of way have never been popular or deliberately favored as residential or commercial locations, they have mostly been considered to be mildly unattractive and functionally constrained by the need for utility company access. If ELF research establishes more definitive health risks, there will still be added negative *visual* meaning. The *core* meaning of power line rights of way will change, but the surface imagery will not change to reflect any newer, more dangerous status.

The Crisis of Surface and Core and the Loss of the Middle Landscape

The landscape has always been the arena of compromise between nature and technology. But how is landscape, which is a visible, tangible, experiential

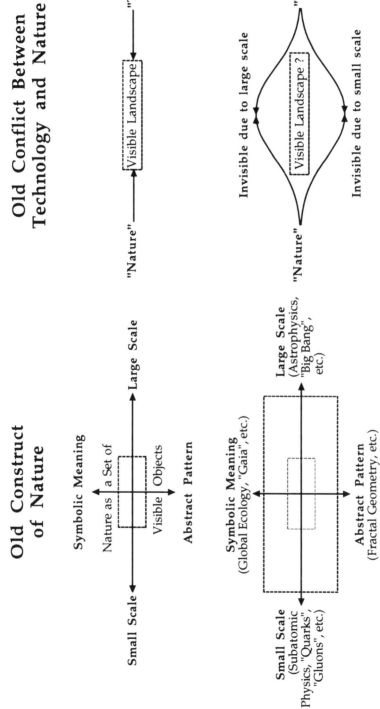

Old Conflict Between
Technology and Nature

"Nature" → Visible Landscape → "Technology"

New, Less Visible Conflict
Between Technology and Nature

"Nature"

Invisible due to large scale

Visible Landscape ?

Invisible due to small scale

"Technology"

Old Construct
of Nature

Symbolic Meaning

Large Scale

Nature as a Set of

Visible Objects

Abstract Pattern

Small Scale

New, Expanding
Construct of Nature

Large Scale
(Astrophysics,
"Big Bang",
etc.)

Symbolic Meaning
(Global Ecology, "Gaia", etc.)

Abstract Pattern
(Fractal Geometry, etc.)

Small Scale
(Subatomic
Physics, "Quarks",
"Gluons", etc.)

The changing nature of nature, technology, and their interrelationship. By "disappearing" from the visible realm, nature and technology threaten to make the tangible landscape irrelevant as an ideological battleground or conceptual mediating device.

medium, now supposed to capture the essence of compromise between nature and technology which are no longer visible? The problem seems obvious: landscape is visible, tangible, and locationally or spatially specific; technology and nature are increasingly intangible, invisible, and ubiquitously nonlocal. Therefore, the role of landscape as a mediating device between technology and nature is seriously jeopardized.

In Chapter 1 I mentioned the symbolic ideal of a "middle" landscape where nature and artifice seem to meet in peaceful compromise. For 200 years, the pastoral tradition of mildly agrarian landscape forms in rural, "natural" contexts has served that symbolic purpose, driving the landscape tastes and desires of Americans as no other landscape concept could. But Americans have always needed to reconfigure this symbolic landscape of compromise and make tangible manifestations on the land itself. Various versions of the pastoral tradition have sufficed to fill this symbolic need simply because the two extremes requiring compromise were highly visible. The anthropocentric horrors of the city and the pleasantries of rural lands or wild nature could be seen and felt. Like primary colors of yellow and blue mixing to make green; butter and garlic combining in a tasty chef's sauce, or violin and cello harmonizing in a musical composition, a pastoral, "middle" landscape which mixed wild nature and civilized artifice produced a tangible, often tasteful result. But when the colors mixed are beyond the perception of the human eye, the musical sounds combined beyond the pitch range of the human ear, or the tastes beyond the sensation of the human tongue, the attempt at synthesis, mediation, and compromise is fruitless and imperceptible.

This is the situation in which we find landscape today; the characteristics it might otherwise mediate seem beyond its capacity to serve as a referent. What can a suburban streetscape possible say about quarks or the Big Bang? How should rural landscapes interpret the struggle over genetic engineering or nanotechnology? Can Gaia be addressed by a landscape? How about ELF radiation? For the first time in history, the landscape struggles for relevancy at the newly invisible edges of nature and human artifice, and upon reaching this threshold of disappearance, turns increasingly to trivial simulations of human-scale nature. With the moving of both technology and nature beyond the visible horizon, the traditional pastoral landscape is a vacuous and hollow symbol destined for the dusty storage shelves of history or the memory banks of the emerging electronic mythology.

Conclusion

In his book of poetry entitled *No Nature*, Gary Snyder (1992) provides an introductory comment on the illusiveness of nature:

> *No Nature.* Human societies each have their own nutty fads, mass delusions, and enabling mythologies. Daily life still gets done. Wild nature is probably equally goofy,

with a stunning variety of creatures somehow getting by in all these landscapes. Nature also means the physical universe, including the urban, industrial, and toxic. But we do not easily *know* nature, or even know ourselves. Whatever it actually is, it will not fulfill our conceptions or assumptions. It will dodge our expectations and theoretical models. There is no single or set "nature" either as "the natural world" or "the nature of things." The greatest respect we can pay to nature is not to trap it, but to acknowledge that it eludes us and that our own nature is also fluid, open, and conditional.

Snyder, 1992, p. v

So, in mystic fashion, we are destined to track nature but never capture it; to constantly reinvent nature but never get it patented. Our previous constructions of nature, like ethereal, animate spirits, seem to spring forth from our former landscapes and vanish, leaving them disempowered and disenchanted. With the disappearance of both nature and technology beyond our view and their potential reunion at the atomic scale, we confront a void which yearns to be filled, yet the conflict is still crying for resolution. How can we resolve tensions we can no longer perceive? If the combatants are beyond the horizon, is the battle still being fought? We *need* landscape to help us literally "make sense" out of the dilemma of nature and technology. But as we search ever deeper into nature's expanding core, and as we chase technological development into the invisible realm, the visible surface of the landscape seems less and less relevant, and the center does not hold. Landscape, we fear, may become irrelevant. Like the world during the Cold War, we grew accustomed to a visible stand-off between nature and technology as experienced through and mediated by landscape. Like the world after the melting of the Iron Curtain, we struggle to make sense out of the disorder occurring with the disappearance of old adversaries. Like modern-day politicians, we try to invent a replacement opposition; a tangible villain-and-hero duality. To address a resolution of tensions between topophilia and technophilia, we must first make them visible again. This is the most important and often overlooked challenge of "sustainable" landscapes, and it is discussed in detail in Chapters 9 and 10.

Meanwhile, the tension between nature and technology, having dropped out of sight, gives the false impression of being resolved. While sustainability addresses *core* relationships between nature and technology, postmodern society is rapidly evolving a "reality" made up only of surfaces and simulations. With the aid of information technology, a surface construction of nature is being generated which threatens to replace the core of nature in the collective consciousness. This is the topic of Chapter 8.

8

Reality, Unreality, and Hyperreality

> *The very definition of the real has become:* that of which it is possible to give an equivalent reproduction . . . *The real is not only what can be reproduced,* but that which is always already reproduced: *that is, the hyperreal . . . which is entirely in simulation.*
>
> JEAN BAUDRILLARD

> *Fifty-seven channels and nothin' on.*
>
> BRUCE SPRINGSTEEN

As if the changes in nature and technology were not enough, most readers have undoubtedly noticed even more puzzling changes occurring in the culture around them. Imagination is now done for us by MTV, Disney, Spielberg, and the advertising industry. Image is the substance of political life. Sex has become a matter of public policy. A "volcano" in Las Vegas erupts every 15 minutes on schedule. NASA spends billions to have astronauts recover a satellite with their hands. After riots, Los Angeles the police are simultaneously criticized for being too forceful and too weak. Smart bombs with video eyes guide themselves down Iraqi air-conditioning vents, then the TV picture goes blank. World leaders gather to discuss global environmental problems in Rio de Janeiro, where thousands of children were murdered the previous year. "Not in my backyard" is *de facto* regional planning policy across the United States, while Mickey Mouse and Donald Duck are significant export commodities.

As if to signify that reality had indeed become strange, the telephone rang while I was in the midst of writing this chapter, and I picked it up only to hear a machine-dialed, prerecorded advertisement for a financial service—the first call I had ever received from a non-human. I normally respond to commercial calls from "real" people by saying: "I'm sorry, we do not accept telephone solicitations." I had gotten half way through my rote, mechanistic response

195

The Information Landscape: In this fantasy TV commercial, the figure in the billboard on the left reaches across the road to grasp a bottle of beer from the other billboard. Courtesy of Miller Brewing Company.

when I realized that I was being addressed by a "real" machine which could not hear me. Bewildered, I hung up.

Whatever we once considered reality has certainly changed, and it is still changing faster than ever. But to assume there was ever one "reality" would be absurdly naive. Reality is a social construction we continually reinvent to make sense out of our environment and to give baseline meaning to our personal lives. However, in the postmodern world, we find that many of the various meanings of reality have lost their anchors. Like balloons whose strings escape the hands of children, traditional signs and symbols shed their earthly referents and float freely in the media-saturated, electronic atmosphere of society. The old balloons seem to escape as fast as we can blow up new ones.

An enlightening philosopher of the peculiarities of this postmodern era is French social critic Jean Baudrillard. Struggling through his analysis of our information-saturated Western world is like looking for peals at the depth of the ocean; the effort is great, but so are the rewards. Baudrillard's pearls of wisdom are his perceptions of radical change in social theory and political economy in response to consumer behavior, media, information, and cybernetic technology. For Baudrillard, genuine social interaction (what he calls "the social") has ended, and society has "imploded." Increasingly frantic attempts by media, advertising, and politics to have people *react* have resulted only in *inactive,* truly "silent majorities"—a nonresponse Baudrillard sees as a new form of radical social rebellion in its own right. The postmodern world of Baudrillard is characterized by "hyperreality" and simulation, where the copies of physical environments and social events have *replaced* the original, genuine referents. Core concerns are quickly converted by the media-drenched society to become surface spectacles and, after a very short half-life, disappear.

Walter Truet Anderson (1990) chronicles the contemporary social movement away from a search for ultimate, objective truths toward one of multiple, socially constructed "realities" and the general societal loss of belief in belief itself. From the perspective of either Baudrillard, Anderson, or numerous other contemporary critics (Umberto Eco, Ian Mitroff and Warren Bennis, Neil Postman, Joshua Meyrowitz, and Jerry Mander), the postmodern world is characterized by radical abandonment of the former boundaries of reality and the emergence of an era in which simulation and surface spectacle are rapidly becoming the norm. As a bellwether of normative values, the landscape is changing as well.

Media Saturation and The Postmodern World

Surprisingly, the so-called "information technologies" and the evolution of the "Information Age" are especially crucial to the study of landscape. I would not have made this comment 10 years ago when I began to examine the landscape manifestations of technology. *Information,* it seemed at the time and still does, was basically a nonspatial entity. It does not occupy space; it need not have a specific location. It can be transmitted invisibly from one point to another, and even from one point to *every* other. How could such an illusory, invisible entity be harmful or even disruptive to the landscape? I soon realized that the principal influences of information technology on landscape are not primary, but of the second or third order.

Information can be considered formally or colloquially. Most of us have a reasonably clear idea of what constitutes everyday information. A more fundamental, academic, yet operative theory of information evolved from the early 1930s through the early 1960s in the work of Claude Shannon, Warren Weaver, and Norbert Wiener. Shannon and Weaver saw in the operation of binary, "on–off" switches the foundations for logical thought. Their mathematical analysis, based upon multiple binary choices between singular "yes–no" or "true–false" logical positions, established and explained the information "bit" now so familiar in the computer era; the bit became to the information scientists what the quark has become to the subatomic physicists: the building block for the rest of theory. Another mathematician, Norbert Wiener, coined the term *cybernetics* in 1948 to describe an emerging theory of control and communication, whether in animals or machines. Wiener's mathematics helped

"Information is information, not matter or energy."

-Norbert Wiener

A

```
1100 1001 1110 1110 1110 0110 1110 1111 1111 0010 1110 1101
1110 0001 1111 0100 1110 1001 1110 1111 1110 1110 1110

1110 1001 1111 0001

1100 1001 1110 1110 1110 0110 1110 1111 1111 0010 1110 1101
1110 0001 1111 0100 1110 1001 1110 1111 1110 1110 1110

1110 1110 1110 1111 1111 0100

1110 1101 1110 0001 1111 0100 1111 0100 1110 0101 1111 0010

1110 1111 1111 0010

1110 0101 1110 1110 1110 0101 1111 0010 1110 0111 1111 1001
```

B

```
1100100111101110111001101110111111110010111011011110000111111010
0111010011101011111110111011101101001111100011100100111101110111
1001101110111111110010111011011101110000111110100111010011110111110
1101110111011101110111011110100011101101111000011111101001111
0100111001011111001011101111111100101110010111101111011100101111
100101110011011111111001
```

(a) *Binary code for a portion of the quote ("Information is information, not matter or energy.") by Norbert Weiner, written in the machine language of a Macintosh computer.* (b) *The computer "reads" the language as a binary stream of zeroes and ones.*

to explain the idea that in its most fundamental form, information could be mathematically defined as a signal—a change in the mathematical "pattern" (representable by binary numbers)—distinguishable from background "noise." Most important to our discussion, however, is that Shannon, Weaver, and Wiener established a mathematically based concept of information which could be considered *independent* of the sending or receiving *devices,* the particular *channel,* and even the *meaning,* which only made the information effective or useful by means of a language or *code.*

> Information is information, not matter or energy. No materialism which does not admit this can survive at the present day.

> *Wiener, 1961, p. 132*

By revealing the essential nature of information as independent of source, channel, and receiver, and separable from meaning by code or language,

Wiener revealed an elemental fact of immense importance to the future landscape: in its most rarified form, *information does not require a place.*

Prior to the emergence of modern electronics, however, communication did most directly involve the landscape. Until the advent of the telegraph, information required the accompaniment of a human being to get from one place to another. Messages were taken by some human courier who walked, rode a horse, took a sailboat, or rode in a stagecoach, train, or other vehicle. Communication was, therefore, intimately linked to people, place, and the time it took people to travel to, from, and through places (Meyrowitz, 1985). Because it was difficult and time consuming for humans to physically move through space accompanied by their messages, preelectronic communication had a stripped-down utilitarian character to it; frivolous messages were a waste of effort and resources, so messages were constrained to that which was deemed important and likely to result in some appropriate action. *People, place, message, utility, action:* these words describe an elemental communication system very different from what we live with today and what is being described by modern social critics.

When the telegraph and later the telephone were widely diffused into common use, things began to change. Telegraphs and telephones still required

Electronic media eliminate the emphasis on landscapes, places, and distances between sources and receivers of messages inherent in earlier communication technologies. Thus deemphasized, these landscapes and technologies of the past retreat into an "electronic" mythology. Courtesy of Wells Fargo Bank.

physical wires, which, in turn, required humans to select the routes, lay the wiring, and keep the lines operating. Place was still somewhat important. But the speed of messages had increased to the point of simultaneity, and the efficiency of communications had lost a critical link to the land; messages were no longer constrained by the burden of human effort in getting from one place to another. For the first time in history, communication was no longer entirely dependent upon transportation: the movement of information was separated from the movement of goods and people. The spaces between people communicating became less important, and the messages communicated could afford to be more frivolous.

With the advent of transatlantic submerged cable, radio, microwave towers, satellites, and video technology, human involvement in the land and spaces between communicators dropped away from perception, necessity, or concern. Direct human effort and necessarily slow-paced involvement with the land or sea in taking information from one place to another had disappeared. In its place were the video/audio images only of the sources of information or the locations where it was received. The common image of electronic media creating a "network" of communication "links" in space is actually a misconception; by making the landscapes between sources and receivers irrelevant to the communication process, electronic media have created something more like an infinite series of isolated dots. Recently, AT&T, the dominant long-distance telephone company, purchased a large share in Cellular One, the largest provider of wireless remote "car" phone services and hardware. With this combination, the future of telephone communication becomes rather obvious: totally wireless, mobile phones which attach themselves (literally) to people as they move about, rather than to structures which, of course, are fixed in place. In this probable scenario may lie the end of telephone numbers attached to places. Instead, they will be *replaced* by numbers associated with persons. You will be able to be reached at your own phone number whether you are in Houston or Honolulu. The communication value of places, the distances and actual physical landscapes between senders and receivers of messages are quite literally becoming "meaningless," and the so-called communication "net" is being snipped into a series of knots with no strands between them. The result will be an immense mass of communication sender and receiver "dots" on an electronic simulation of the world's surface. Over time, as mobile phones replace stationary ones, those communication "dots" will begin to move about, making time, distance, location—and the landscapes in between—even more irrelevant.

The importance of this characteristic of information on the loss of a sense of place in the American landscape cannot be overstated. "Place" is not only a sense of physical intimacy and locational uniqueness, it is also a sense of *connectedness*—a physical relationship to other places in a contextual web or matrix. Electronic communication has played a fundamental role in divorcing us from our immediate landscape context. We know more about Baghdad, Sarajevo, and Barcelona than we do about cities in our home state. We know more about the personal lives of celebrities than we do about our neighbors down the street. The landscapes of Disneyland, Pebble Beach, or Yellowstone may be more familiar to us than some local or regional parks.

Joshua Meyrowitz, in his award-winning book *No Sense of Place* (1985), discusses in great detail the impact of electronic media on social relations in the United States. The most fundamental change he describes is the dissolution of spatial boundaries for the appropriateness of specific behaviors. Prior to electronic media, Americans prayed in church, engaged in political debate in public squares and buildings, sought solace, adventure, or economic resources in the wilderness, learned in school, courted, made love, argued, and died in private. Place and behavior were strongly linked, and it was as inappropriate to laugh in church as it was to pray at the county fair or get drunk at school. Few of these behaviors seen unusual to us anymore, however. With the saturation of television, any possible juxtaposition of places and behaviors has already occurred and is no longer surprising to us. The images and sound bites which are quickly and sometimes carelessly assembled into the collages of electronic information which pass for "reality" could hardly be more shocking.

One evening during the writing of this chapter, as my wife and I watched the national news on television, a story prompted by Russian president Boris Yeltsin's U.S. visit was aired which involved the congressional debate about the possibility that POW's from Vietnam, Korea, and even World War II were still alive and what, if anything, the U.S. government should do about them. As the TV commentator was talking, the camera slowly panned to the footage being shown on the backdrop behind the news commentator's head. It was file footage (filmed in black and white) during the Vietnam war, and focussed on an infantry soldier's face as he was shot by enemy fire. This was definitely not acting, but real war. The troops around him continued firing, while the wounded soldier turned his head awkwardly toward the cameraman; his eyelids grew heavy, and he slumped and died. For a moment, the television news shifted back to a closeup of the nicely dressed, pleasant-looking news commentator as he talked matter of factly about the possibility of a U.S. effort to find prisoners of war. The camera then panned back to again include the black and white file footage. The soldiers were still firing away, while the G.I.'s now dead eyes seemed to stare askew into space. The television station then went on to coverage of the upcoming Olympics in Barcelona.

My wife and I found this casual inclusion of such horrifying personally tragic, out-of-taste-and-context video "bites" abhorrent, but I soon realized that this not only happens every day millions of times over in America, but also that it represents the virtual status quo of television's relationship between landscape places and cultural events. Television takes the various forms of human behavior and the numerous physical venues in which this behavior might normally occur, scrambles them up, and shakes them out before our eyes like scattered playing cards, so that any relationship or juxtaposition is not only possible but appears directly before us. We are now so accustomed to "channel surfing" with the remote controller that any formerly strange relationships between places and behaviors is possible and few even catch our attention. Meyrowitz (1985) comments: "By merging discrete communities of discourse, television has made nearly every topic and issue a valid subject of interest and concern for virtually every member of the public. . . . By revealing previously backstage areas to audiences, television has served as an instrument of demystification. It has led to a decline in the image and prestige of political leaders, it has demystified adults for children, and demystified men and women for each other" (p. 308).

Our world may now seem senseless to many of us simply because it has first become placeless, and the normally expected bonds between landscapes or buildings and the feelings and actions we would take in these places is no longer constrained by tradition. Television tends to reduce everything to its own terms. With the possible exception of food, the most sought after items by looters in the 1992 Los Angeles riots were television sets and camcorders. When captured on video tape by news teams, many rioters seemed to act up for the camera and relish their newly found celebrity status. In a world whose values were established (or, some would say, dissolved) by television, "citizens" could now steal televisions and become television "stars" at the same time. No bookstores were looted at all.

In a certain sense, however, the Los Angeles riots were less typical and more of an aberration in the effects of television simply because, for once, people *acted* in response to the Rodney King verdict they heard about on television. In the overwhelming majority of cases, however, television's barrage of strangely juxtaposed news events, places, and advertising images serves to deaden public response and purpose. The imagination, discussion, and action which might otherwise engage us all seem to be done for us on the screen, so why should we take the effort of debating with one another or getting up from the couch? In the case of Los Angeles, the spiritual center of the media society, when action finally came, it was catastrophic and sad.

A fundamental characteristic of today's saturated media condition is that, to paraphrase Jerry Mander, technology and the information media no longer merely *affect* the environment, they have *become* the environment itself (Mander, 1991). When one acknowledges the degree to which media are controlled by wealthy corporations, the fact that those corporations are desperately trying to sell us products, and that the average American witnesses 21,000 television commercials per year (58 per day) sponsored by these corporations and each with its own elaborately controlled, stylized, and idealized images of landscapes, people, products, and events, we begin to understand the extent to which media imagery has supplanted the physical environment in the creation of mental images of reality. Humans interact or "transact" with the physical landscape by means of mental maps or spatial and cognitive schemata which they develop through previous experience with the world. But increasingly, much of that experience is vicarious, passive, and obtained through exposure to the simulations or technologically "mediated" situations "experienced" on television.

Television creates an idealized world in several ways. First, by saturated, bizarre, and repetitious exposure to the most hideous of places and the most heinous of human behaviors, television deadens our response to the unpleasantness of the world. No desecration of place or moral character is too unbelievable any more; no Sarajevos or Love Canals bombed out or polluted enough; no Somalias starved or emaciated enough; no Baghdads or Beiruts violent enough; no Harlems or Los Angeles' desperate enough; and few political candidates feckless or foolish enough to try to provoke a *real* response. After desensitization toward the more unpleasant aspects of reality by the "news," television attempts to replace this deadened sensation with a new American Nirvana of idealized lives and landscapes: bronzed, beautiful men and women drinking beer, playing volleyball, and laughing on golden, unpolluted beaches; four-wheel drive vehicles solitarily driving all-American families into dramatic mountain landscapes amid profusions of multicolored wildflowers; chipper senior citizens with steel-blue hair teaching wide-eyed, respectful children the techniques of fly casting at the old country lake at sunset; a stylishly dressed group of young, good-looking African-, Asian-, Latin-, and Euro-American business executives meeting for a power lunch in the rainforest atrium lobby of a fancy, downtown hotel.

Wouldn't it be nice? What is most interesting about the deliberate fabrication of an idealized world by a rapidly accelerating media technology is that the more elaborate the electronic fantasy becomes, the more things "out there" seem to deteriorate. We sense an inverse qualitative relationship between the imaginary electronic landscape "in the box" and the earthen, tangible landscape outside, but we are unsure which is the cause and which the effect. One thing seems clear, however—the fantastic landscapes of television advertising and the electronic media are *doing our imagination for us*. What the human imagination once did in response to real landscapes (i.e., the mental creation of a better world) is now being done by the media with electronic simulations of landscapes. In *The Wake of Imagination*, philosopher Richard Kearney (1988) ponders whether the postmodern culture is being accompanied by the "death" of the human imagination.

As experience of "place" becomes less physically tangible and more electronically vicarious, the American public is literally "holing up." Venturing out into real landscapes to engage in real experiences can be life threatening (as it always has), and requires us to take physical and social risks. We might actually have to interact with or be confronted by people of different socioeconomic, racial, religious, or political backgrounds; we might get shot by a gang in the city or an irate driver on the freeway, or arrested and beaten by a prejudiced or brutal police officer; we might get Lyme's disease, poison oak, Giardia, or a rattlesnake bite. Depending on where we live, we might risk a hurricane, earthquake, wildfire, tornado, flash flood, or lightning storm. Increasingly, these hazards make fine thematic material for TV shows and movies, but people are less and less willing to confront them in reality.

Television as a Dissipative Structure

Imagination and creativity, of course, have not died. As anyone who watches television knows, there is an immense amount of time, effort, money, and imagination spent on creating the dramatic media effects that bombard us daily. Jeff Robbins (1990) has suggested that television, taken together with its entire systems of producers, transmitters, and consumers, acts like a *dissipative structure.* The term, coined by Chemistry Nobel laureate Ilya Prigogine, refers to the second law of thermodynamics, which states that for any real process or event taking place in the universe, the entropy, or overall disorder, of the universe must always be greater after the event than before. Entropy is increased when energy dissipates and systems move from an ordered state to a disordered state. A dissipative structure, then, maintains or increases its own order by transferring the entropy or disorder which must result from its processes into the surrounding environment. By suggesting that television is a dissipative structure, Robbins implies that *as the producing system of television grows in the potency of its energy, the entropy or disorder produced is displaced into the consuming system—its viewing public.* In short, creativity, structure, imagination, and energy at the input or producing side of television results in lethargy, disorder, and inaction at the output or consuming side. The entire input end of television invests extreme amounts of order and energy: advertising agencies put immense creativity and imagination into television commercials; corporate sponsors structure their entire sales efforts and product development campaigns around the advertising imagery; broadcasters structure entire programs around market segments; politicians stake their futures on television advertising. The entire input sector creates a fanaticized, imaginary reality, while at the receiving end of television, less and less public *action* results. Viewers seem to watch more and pay less attention. "Signals" become "noise," as individual ads get lost in a blur of thousands of other advertisements and no one product prevails. Even the physical response of viewers seems to be to "sit" more and "move" less.

When television first evolved into a widespread social phenomenon, its original critics worried more about the effects of its messages than the characteristics of the medium itself. By some sort of Orwellian nightmare, it was feared that television might uniformly brainwash the masses by a singular, monolithic, and malevolent message *content,* much as Hitler and Stalin had done during World War II without television. It was not until Marshall McLuhan's pivotal work (1964) that the more subtle influences of the *medium* itself—irrespective of content—were shown to be the more potent influence on society. Far from monolithically molding the "masses" into a singularly responding body politic, television has turned out to have a highly fragmenting effect resulting in infinite splinter groups and massive inaction. Television analysts are now predicting the multiplication of specifically aimed cable channels and the rapid splintering of audiences into smaller subgroups, so that viewers need only watch precisely those programs that match their interests. We will have wet-fly fishing channels, overweight person channels, dog show channels, and rose gardening channels. Advertisers will be able to further target their products to specific audience segments as entertainment blends indistinguishably with consumerism. Any vestige of broadly shared, common experience with fellow citizens will be lost, and the electronically constructed, idealized landscapes in the minds of viewers will shrink that much more.

Jean Baudrillard discusses the response of society to the electronic media in terms of the "loss of the Social" or, in lay terms, the loss of any genuine, passionate social *involvement* with everyday life. Baudrillard (1983) and many others (Kellner, 1989; Thompson, 1989) claim that we are in an age where media, cybernetics, entertainment, television, computers, and all forms of "information" manipulation have replaced industrial production and political economy as the organizing principles of our society. Consequently, physical "*modes* of production" have been replaced by "*codes* of production" (Kellner, p. 62). The Marxist–capitalist opposition which concerned itself with the means of production of real goods has been replaced by a new "order" which places supreme value in the codes or various symbolic languages of meanings irrespective of physical reality. What serves as the ultimate measure of power is not how much a person or organization's prestige is grounded in actual material wealth, land, resources, or money, but how much their "image" stock sells for on the public market of meanings and ideas. Today, being popular and celebrated in the media is better than being wealthy and ignored by the media.

> For a long time capital only had to produce goods; consumption ran by itself. Today it is necessary to produce consumers, to produce demand, and this production is infinitely more costly than that of goods. For a long time it was enough for power to produce meaning (political, ideological, cultural, and sexual), and the demand followed; it absorbed supply and still surpassed it. . . . Today, everything has changed: no longer is meaning in short supply, it is produced everywhere, in ever increasing quantities—it is demand that is weakening."
>
> *Baudrillard, 1983, p. 27*

Now we face a situation where more and more meanings are required to produce less and less physical production. The ultimate conclusion to this trend is media saturation at the expense of physical goods and places. Much more of the budgets of corporations are now dedicated to producing, rather than meeting, market demand. The price or "cost" of commodities like cars and beer reflects the vastly increased effort in selling them as opposed to making them. In response, the symbolic meanings of commodities and consumer items are becoming more important and the actual use of them less important. Teen gangs sell drugs and literally kill for the ability to wear footwear with subculturally correct meanings. According to Baudrillard, meanings are now starting to float freely with less reference to the actual uses of things. With little mental effort, we could soon imagine a time when the meanings formerly attached to products are electronically bought and sold like grain or pig futures on a commodities market with no need for the physical objects to change hands, or even be tangibly produced. During the final years of the Cold War, it mattered less whether the grand, strategic weapon systems worked or were eventually deployed. What mattered most was the political gravity of the likelihood that they could even be technically developed; the *meanings* of the weapons became the actual weapons.

Hyperreality and Simulacra

News "media" first evolved as a mirror of reality; events happened which were recorded and interpreted by scribes and later, by newspapers. Mediated recording of the events by oral or written means stayed reasonably close to the form of the original event. Although humans have always engaged in certain concrete actions intended largely for their surface effects, like the territorial threats and courtship displays of all higher animals, action preceded image; there was a grounding of the surface impression in a core of "real" action. There has occurred a fundamental change in reality caused by the explosion of technological media, where surface images are no longer grounded in physical, real reference. Instead of mirroring real events, media *precede,* or drive real events. This is what Baudrillard calls the "precession of simulacra:" the fact that mediated copies of objects and events no longer grow from a grounded reality, but instead, refer only to other simulations, codes, and copies, and have, in essence, created a *hyperreality*—a system of copies of simulations of events, objects, and environments which are more "real" than the real itself.

Baudrillard's concepts of hyperreality and simulation are difficult but essential to the discussion of what is happening to society—and ultimately to the landscape—under the overwhelming influence of information technology. Landscapes, whether intentional or vernacular, reveal the degree to which our world is now woven of simulations and hyperreality. The trade magazines of the landscape architecture and landscape contracting industries are loaded with advertisements for simulated rock work, waterfalls, fake coral reefs, fiberglass animals, artificial fog devices, concrete pavers that simulate bricks, ceramic tile, or cobblestone, and even plastic turfgrass and plastic trees, shrubs, and flowers. These various simulacra are so thoroughly integrated into deliberate landscape design and installation as to raise few eyebrows. Competition is now over which company makes the most realistic imitations.

A simulated rockscape dominates this vendor's booth at the 1990 American Society of Landscape Architect's annual meeting and exhibition. An increasing number of vendors and advertisers in landscape architecture exhibit halls and publications are selling simulations of rock, stone, brick, water, plants, coral reefs, and so on.

Bomanite™, the original producer of poured-in-place, stamped concrete which imitates stone, brick, and other paving materials, took out a full-page advertisement in *Landscape Architecture Magazine* (Vol. 79, No. 8, p. 31, October 1989) which stated boldly: "If it doesn't say Bomanite™, . . . it's not the real thing." What the advertisement didn't say was that even if it *did* say Bomanite™, it wasn't the *real* thing either—not brick, granite, or cobblestone, but a concrete simulation.

In this industry-wide competition, the core reality has disappeared, and the simulacra have begun to refer only to each other and to create an entire, surface network of expected landscape imagery. It can easily be argued that intentionally designed landscape has always been a simulation of reality. Historically and etymologically, "landscape' was an idealization of the "garden" which, originally meant "paradise" in Persian.

But what Baudrillard refers to as the "orders of simulacra" shed some light on the historical evolution of the relationship between the real and the copy. Baudrillard describes three such sequential "orders:" *counterfeit, production, and simulation.* In archaic and feudal societies, rigid social caste and rank prevented impersonation beyond one's status, and each material object of daily life was authentically and individually copied for practical use from its artifactual predecessor. It was not until the Renaissance, when the relaxation of rigid caste structures created the notion of fashion and the possibility of fluidity in social status, that the notion of a *counterfeit* evolved—an intentional copy of some object (event, place, or person) of status, with the intent to deceive or defraud. This is Baudrillard's first order of simulacra. The counterfeit marked the ascension of objects and events to widespread symbolic/social value *separable* from the utility of the objects or events themselves. Hence, by being the subject of a counterfeit, the *original* was imbued with more value. But prior to the machine age, even counterfeit copies were difficult and time consuming to make, and so their numbers were few enough not to constitute much of a change in the value or nature of the original. In the newly developed material of stucco, however, Baudrillard finds a hint of a future world of simulations. Renaissance and Baroque period craftsmen molded the malleable new stucco material into representations of animals, plants, furniture, marble, and even water. In retrospect, however, stucco imitations were taken less seriously as threats to some natural order, since the perceptual boundary between real object and stucco copy is usually quite clear.

Baudrillard's second order of simulacra is the pure series of identical objects mass produced for consumption, and the corresponding series of mass-produced places, social behaviors and structures. With the industrial revolution came the deliberate melding of the concepts of "original" and "copy," since the intent of the artistry was to be replicated innumerable times by machinery—what Baudrillard refers to as the "pure series." By relinquishing its claim to represent a real, natural order (such as that claimed by the original artifact of the Renaissance), the pure series announced the ascendancy of market value and commercial equivalency as social directions replacing the "natural law of value."

In the digital, cybernetic world of today, Baudrillard finds the third order of simulacra, where the notion of naturally valued, physical "originals" has been further permuted and degraded, and simulations or copies have taken over and become the world. He uses the analogy of the genetic code and DNA to describe the social dynamics of codes, models, and simulations, each of which contains the information necessary to replicate itself many times over. Such codes and models precede and collectively create a form of reality— *hyperreality*—like maps that are drawn prior to the physical territory they are ultimately to represent. Kellner (1989) writes:

> In the society of coded simulation, urban planners, for example, modulate codes of city planning and architecture in creating urban systems, in much the same way that television producers modulate television codes to produce programs. Models and codes come to constitute everyday life, and modulation of the code comes to structure a system of differences and social relations in the society of simulations. (p. 80)

> In a hyperreal world, "the model comes first," and its constitutive role is invisible, because all one sees are instantiations of models . . . such a hyperreal society of

simulations includes such things as interstate highway and urban freeway transportation systems, fashion, media, architecture and housing developments, shopping malls and products which are reproductions of models, instantiations of codes . . . (p. 83)

It is this world of landscape, fashion, architecture, and media simulations that has replaced the "real" and become the hyperreal: a vast network of semidetached and floating references and images without grounding in a naturally established, real order. Subdivisions are copies of formalized zoning and building codes as well as unwritten but strict social codes; so are freeways, shopping malls, front yards, and cul de sacs. Each is an idealization of a preceding code. No "original" can be found. Simulation has become "reality" by violating the reality principal: that the line between original and fake, or between reality and fantasy, be kept clear. In traditional theater, for example, a member of the audience enters through a doorway into a fantasy landscape of characters, sets, and dramatic events. Afterward, the theater-goer recrosses the threshold back into reality of the street. Today, the walls of the theater have melted, and all the world is indeed the stage from which we can no longer escape.

Many contemporary social critics refer to Disneyland and Epcot Center as the cultural epicenters of hyperreality. Other authors point to various World's Fairs, Mall of America, or the West Edmonton Mall, which "re-creates Bourbon Street and Polynesia in a domed environment in the freezing north of Canada" (Mander, 1991, p. 158). I prefer the Mirage Hotel Casino, previously described in Chapter 6, as the best example of how the reality principal of a perceptual line between simulacrum and original is so ingeniously and deliberately erased. But by mentioning such specific, isolated landscapes, I do not intend to imply that the world of simulacra and hyperreality is constrained to the various fantasy or theme parks which come to mind. We are in the midst of the "theming" of the entire country. Simulation and hyperreality have escaped the boundaries of Disneyland and other entertainment centers and have diffused into the American heartland. As the national economic pastime gradually shifts from production of goods to management of the information of entertainment, America becomes a high-tech theme park which simulates and packages a formerly essential utilitarian relationship to and for entertainment and fantasy. Come to Long Beach, where a steamship is a hotel and an oil terminal looks like tropical resort, or to Colorado, where cattle ranches and silver mines have been replaced by dude ranches, casinos, and ski resorts. In the new hyperreality, core landscape concerns melt away and leave only a network of surface preoccupations, like the shapes children once made from balloons by wrapping them with string, covering them with glue, and popping the balloon to leave only the lattice surface.

Remaking authentic communities into packaged forms of themselves, re-creating environments in one place that actually belong somewhere else, creating theme

parks and lifestyle-segregated communities, and space travel and colonization—all
are symptomatic of the same modern malaise: a disconnection from a place on Earth
that we can call Home. With the natural world—our true home—removed from our
lives, we have built on top of the pavement a new world, a new Eden, perhaps; a
mental world of creative dreams. We then live within these fantasies of our own
creation; we live within our own minds. Though we are still on the planet Earth, we
are disconnected from it, afloat on pavement, in the same way the astronauts float in
space.

   That our culture has taken this step into artificial worlds on and off the planet is a
huge risk, for the logical result is disorientation and madness, and . . . the obsessive
need to attempt to re-create nature and life.

Mander, 1991, p. 158

The Virtual Landscape

In the manner by which simulation can devour and digest the reality it
purports to simulate, interactive computer graphics is revealing itself to have
an enormous appetite. The fledgling industry of "virtual reality" is well on its
way. Virtual reality can be defined as the "new interactive technology that
creates the completely convincing illusion that one is immersed in a landscape that exists only inside a computer" (Rheingold, 1991). Hence "VR" (the
nickname given it by its proponents) is a technology that combines a highly
sophisticated, simulated three-dimensional environment of some sort (i.e., a
new shopping center design, battlefield landscape, or another human body)
and a set of computer controls and sensory feedback devices which enable the
operators (or participants) to enter the virtual environment, sense where they
are, see, hear, touch, and manipulate various components of the virtual environment, and otherwise undergo a total perceptual and sensory experience
without having to interact with the virtual environment's real counterpart
at all.

   Virtual reality evolved directly from the simulators used to train pilots of
military and civilian aircraft, who have a special need for developing the
utmost skill at guiding their real machines (airplanes) through real landscapes
(airports, battlefield terrain). In the early days of flight simulation, the "wind-
shields" of the cockpit simulators were the principal visual/spatial displays,
and these were coupled to rather awkwardly mounted cockpits which mechanically jerked the pilot about in a crude fashion similar to some amusement
park rides. Today's technology of total sensory input/output devices is aston-
ishingly more sophisticated, sensitive, and realistic, as are the simulated environments developed with the most powerful supercomputers. By coupling the
latest in electronic simulation with advanced robotics, the most advanced VR
input/output devices copy all of the human perceptual/sensory apparatus.
Treadmill-type devices with electronic sensors now simulate walking. Jump-

Mall of America, near Minneapolis, is the world's largest enclosed shopping environment and doubles as a theme park and tourist destination for overseas visitors. Photographs by Bob Perzel. Courtesy of Mall of America.

suit devices pick up the motion of arms, legs, and torso directly through electronic sensors. Gloves act as surrogates of human hands, electronically mediating hand sensations and movements. Goggles, helmets, and earphones have been integrated into combination display and input/output devices, so that once a participant has donned such an apparatus, he or she perceptually "enters" the virtual space. Moving the head up, down, or to the side creates a corresponding change in the virtual displays. Moving hands and "touching" can result in manipulation of parts of the virtual environment.

The "environments," of course, are mathematical algorithms of their real counterparts, created with the high levels of sophistication one might now expect having seen the special effects done by major studios in popular films. One may "walk" through the lobby of a proposed office building and up the stairs, and even fly out the window and above the building. Virtual reality analyst and author Howard Rheingold reports having commanded repair robots in virtual outer space at NASA, gone "fishing" for simulated fish with an electronic "fishing pole," undergone an "out of body" experience by taking a simulated tour around his own body by means of a robotic camera linked to his own eyeglasses, felt virtual "sandpaper" by means of an electronic glove, and finally, in Silicon Valley, used various bodily input/output devices, and danced with a woman (in virtual space) who had taken the form of a 12-foot tall purple lobster.

Virtual reality reveals an astonishing, fascinating, and frightening level of possible technologically based "mediations" between the environment and the human participant. Real physical environments can now be transformed mathematically and electronically in virtual displays, but the possibilities for manipulation of the real conditions are endless. Technology allowing pilots to see through fog or clouds to the "real" landscape beneath and to rehearse missions prior to combat is now routinely available. In the Persian Gulf War, F-117 Stealth pilots spent hours "practicing" their attack runs on virtual simulators until they knew every key landmark along their route and precisely where and when to turn, dive, climb, speed up or down, and release their weapons.

The process of mediation of actual landscapes by VR simulation, however, also allows any or all of the real characteristics of actual places to be changed, modified, or screened out. Entirely new "landscapes" unlike anything actually on the ground can be generated electronically. Virtual reality breaks the link of veracity between original place and simulation. For multisports fans of the future, ski slopes can be "placed" right next to surfing beaches and golf courses. New "sports," requiring new "landscapes" as venues, can be created at will. Virtual golf games, already in existence, are popular in many American cities. Virtual reality takes Baudrillard's third-order simulacra to its most frightening conclusion: we will soon be able to simulate, enter, and interact with—with a very high and rapidly increasing degree of realism—virtually any landscape we can imagine.

Even more astounding are the technological mediation possibilities surrounding the input/output devices of the human body. Soon, entire percep-

Virtual Reality

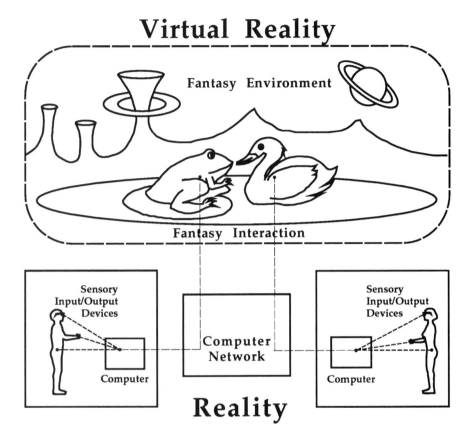

Reality

Virtual reality takes the art of simulation into new dimensions; participants can cavort in computer-generated "cyberscapes," altogether removed from real physical landscape and tangible social interaction.

tual/sensory "envelope" suits may be developed which, when donned by participants, will connect all the bodily sensations of sight, sound, touch, movement, smell, and hearing directly to the computer. According to Rheingold, an Italian engineer has developed an artificial human skin:

> De Rossi's artificial dermis is made of a water-swollen conducting gel sandwiched between two layers of electrodes that monitor the flow of electricity through the squishy middle. Like the all-natural human version, this dermis senses the overall pressure being exerted on an object. As pressure deforms the gel, the voltage between the electrodes changes; the harder the object being pressed, the greater the information. By keeping tabs on how the voltage is changing, a skin-clad robot could distinguish between a rubber ball and a rock. (1991, pp. 347–348)

It is not a long technological distance from De Rossi's artificial skin to rather complete sensory "body suits" that act as both input and output devices. The temptation to extrapolate beyond this point to telecommunicated, "virtual" sexual encounter is irresistible, and dramatically illustrates both the power and danger of such a technological mediation between participant and environment. A person in Illinois puts on a skin tight body suit complete with gloves, hood, and glasses, turns on a minicomputer, and searches various virtual landscapes for a suitable partner. Finding another cybernaut from Rhode Island with similar needs and intentions, they explore a fantasy landscape together, cavorting in the electronic foreplay of virtual, computerized space, exchanging actual body sensations through their body suits. However, instead of being limited to sending exact visual replications of themselves as one might do for computer dating games, they may (out of insecurity, negative self image, or just plain curiosity) choose instead to electronically transform themselves into mermaids, weight lifters, movie stars, or tigers. One can only imagine how many different ways such entirely possible future scenarios might play out. In an age of increasing fear of AIDS, intimacy, rejection, or commitment, VR represents both the ultimate in "safe sex" and the ultimate disconnection between place, body, and sensation.

Landscape is the sensory skin of the Earth. The dramatic extent to which VR technology mediates the sensory relationship between human participants and the landscape itself *renders the core condition of earthly ecosystems irrelevant to sensory participation.* If Yellowstone National Park gets too crowded and polluted, or burns down altogether, we may be able to "visit" it (in its cybernetically idealized version) in virtual space. Virtual reality changes the basic possibilities of the landscape/human transaction and raises a specter of total severance between dirt, rock, water, and flesh. We may still "feel," "see," and "hear" landscape surfaces, but they may have little relationship with the actual ecological role of landscape as the core venue for nourishment, refuge, and survival. In the virtual landscape, the need for the genuine has disappeared; the new electronic "landscape," although highly sensory, is totally opaque; the core is irrelevant.

The Reversal of Fantasy and Reality

With science expanding the concept of nature through increasingly astonishing and unbelievable conclusions; with core technologies everywhere attacking the core of nature beyond our sight; with simulations of nature and landscape forming the new surface continuum, the new core realities of science and nature seem more unreal, while the electronic simulations of landscapes and nature seem ever more real. Science no longer reveals the "real," but the increasingly unbelievable and unfathomable. Yet, with primal minds, we rely on our perceptions to determine what is real. "Real" is what we can see, sense, and experience. Nature and technology are no longer transparent, and we can only see the hyperreal replications of nature's surfaces amid the simulacra of material culture. Quarks, black holes, the Big Bang, global warming, ozone holes, and acid rain are invisible, unfathomable, and therefore, *unreal.* Shopping malls, the landscapes of movies and TV commercials, the Mirage Volcano, Disneyland, virtual golf courses and Nintendo can be seen, sensed, and "experienced," and are therefore *real. In the postmodern world, reality and unreality have switched places.*

Electronic Mythology and the New "Medial" Landscape

In Chapter 7 I discussed the movement of the frontiers of nature and technology beyond the boundary of visibility. In this chapter I suggest that the traditional positions of the "real" and the "unreal" have been reversed, and that we are beginning to live in a world of surface simulations while core concerns are neglected. These may seem to be rather cavalier and sweeping generalizations. "But there is a tangible, real landscape, with real, 'natural' trees just outside my door!" the reader might exclaim. Indeed, wherever we go, we are in a "real" landscape. Landscape still surrounds and involves us; we may still touch, it, feel it, *be* in it. Furthermore, we still *see* the evidence of contemporary technology about us. Many of us are still extremely concerned with the core condition of our landscape and ecosystems, and many of us are taking specific actions to bring about change in the core relationships between nature and human nature. I do not wish to deny these obvious counterpoints; in fact, they form the very basis for the expanding notion of sustainability which is the focus of the remainder of the book. My main points here are that the *social meanings* of nature, technology, reality, and unreality have changed, the relationships between these constructs have changed, and in the process, the *meaning of landscape* is changing as well.

The dilemma of technology and nature is a drama whose main characters often change personalities and roles like chameleons. Consider that in the past 20 years, deserts and wetlands have moved from being considered useless wastelands to be altered recklessly or avoided altogether, to become symbols of nature's delicate ecological order, fecundity, or fragility. In the same time period, nuclear power plants have changed from benevolent, bottled genies to looming specters of potential ecological disaster. The social "stock" of the railroad is rising again (after dropping considerably during the ascendency of air travel); the social stock of the freeway, however, is declining. With the explosion in media technology and the supersaturation of information in postmodern society, the meaning values of many landscapes, both "natural" and technological, fluctuate ever more widely according to whatever various bits of information we may receive, whether from hard scientific evidence or entertainment-world trivia.

In Chapter 7 I suggested that the cliche of the tangible, pastoral ideal is no longer an adequate symbol of the *Middle Landscape*—that traditional venue of compromise between nature and technology. The saturation of electronic imagery in today's society, the reversal of reality and unreality, and the disappearance of the core of nature and technology may have rendered useless the notion that *any* physical landscape can adequately serve as the venue of compromise. We are moving to a point where the conflict of nature and technology is not resolved symbolically on land, but in *the simulated world of the electronic media,* where imagining is done for us. Leo Marx's original notion of a "middle" landscape implies a certain spatial position between two physical poles. As a concept, it grew out of the association of city landscapes with the ills of society, the wilderness with raw nature and spiritual transcendence, and humanized, rural land as the ideal which lay in between. In the age of electronic media, however, actual positions on an urban-wild spectrum become less meaningful concepts. Electronic media, as we have seen, make any formerly established relationship between place and meaning null and void. Information technology now allows the positive and negative social meanings formerly associated with cities, rural lands, industries, or wilderness to float on an open market. The electronic media have made of landscapes a new mythology of their own; video and computers can turn city, countryside, or wilderness images into beasts or beauties according to their own electronic whims; the anchors to established meanings have been cast aside.

Since more of our storehouse of salient landscape imagery comes to us electronically mediated and less from our actual experience in physical landscapes, perhaps it is now fitting to discard the notion of a "middle" landscape and replace it with a *"medial"* landscape. The nature–technology conflict has been seized by the electronic media and has become convoluted and self-referential, and is in danger of becoming a mere simulacrum of itself. The information media absorbs the core ecological concerns of the world and diffuses them back to us via a plethora of short-lived video bites. Environmental issues and crises have become big-time entertainment. It is much easier (and for many, more fun) to watch a television show about the problem of the destruction of the rainforest than it is to do anything about it. Unfortunately, *it is also becoming easier to create pleasant, illusory environments than it is to heal the problems in real environments.* While outwardly "informing" us about impending ecological deterioration, the subliminal message of the electronic media is: "What problem?" In the electronic surface of the New Age, technology and nature have been recombined and fused. After centuries of warfare between nature and human artifice, and after so much time yearning to reenter Eden and atone for our sins against nature, the media provide us with an electronic placebo complete with prepackaged imagination and predigested ideological struggle.

Although the electronic media offer the impression that nature and technology are becoming one, we sense that the apparent resolution of tension is on the surface only; that the core conflict has merely been stuffed further from view. What allows us this hint of vision through the media fog? The *physical landscape,* of course. But while landscape provides a sense of real context, it has always been a slippery medium in terms of meaning.

Landscape Architecture and the Unreality Industry

Landscape architecture, the profession most directly involved in shaping the surface imagery of specific land areas such as gardens, parks, and plazas, finds itself being swept along by the social currents of the information age. As society responds to the advancing impact of the media, planners and designers of landscapes are faced with an increasing social preoccupation with the surface phenomena of entertainment, illusion, fantasy, and escape. By and large they maintain a professional sense of responsibility toward the core relationships of function and ecology. Ultimately, however, professions like landscape architecture, architecture, and city planning respond to, rather than drive, the main thrusts of social evolution, and today, those are in the direction of surface image and deliberate manipulation of meaning rather than substance. Authors Ian Mitroff and Walter Bennis write in *The Unreality Industry* that the reality of the outside world has become much more complex since the end of World War II, and that we have now developed a near-psychopathic preoccupation with unreality to avoid coping with this increasing complexity. These authors note:

> The "industry" part of unreality turns on the fact that, as a society, we no longer leave the invention of unreality to random chance or accident. No way. Unreality is big business. It involves the expenditure of billions of dollars annually. It is deliberately manufactured and sold on a gigantic scale. The end result is a society less and less able to face its true problems directly, honestly, and intelligently.
>
> *Mitroff and Bennis, 1989, p. xii*

The "unreality industry" already extends beyond television, advertising, and politics to environmental design, landscape architecture, architecture, and land development in general. An increasing proportion of design and development business is intertwined with the expanding social preoccupation with entertainment, image, status, and short-term economic gain. The real estate and environmental design industries both emphasize an idealized, simulated environment which ignores or glosses over core ecological and social problems. Theme parks and other simulated landscapes constitute an increasing percentage of landscape architectural work. The world's largest landscape architecture firm recently completed work on EuroDisney in France. Recent buildings by Antoine Predock, Frank Gehry, Michael Graves, and Robert Stern have served to place the Disney Corporation on the pinnacle of popular culture and architectural high style (Painton, 1991; McGuigan, 1991). In an age of simulation, big business follows illusion, and both architecture and landscape architecture follow big business. Architectural criticism has been reduced to the fine art of discussing which buildings most successfully capture the essence of fantasy and illusion—Baudrillard's third order of simulacra gone wild. Landscape architecture professor and anthropologist Dan Rose (1990) says of this new trend:

Theme parks are approaching a total experiential environment . . . Perhaps the most pressing issue confronting landscape designers is not that of intermedia referencing or finding marketable meanings in a locale, but the need to recover nature from the ever-more-pervasive electronic imagery and messages found at many entertainment sites. Beyond recovery, we need active resistance, for increasingly we must take water, soil, vegetation and even climate back from their simulations by advanced technology; with more sophisticated cultural values, we must find a way to recoup a lost nature. (p. 112)

Here Rose states in restrained fashion what William Irwin Thompson asserts vigorously in *The American Replacement of Nature* (1991): that the main American export is now simulation, illusion, and entertainment, and that the implicit effect of such an export is nothing less than the annihilation of indigenous regional and national cultures. Americans, with some degree of racism, complain that Japanese imports and investments erode American culture. However, while the Japanese readily import our culture, they do not deliberately superimpose theirs along with the products and investments they pour into the United States. In contrast, the "new Disneyland being constructed near Paris represents the largest foreign investment in France in its entire history" (Thompson, 1991, p. 58). *American culture,* in this case, is the intentionally exported product.

The profession of landscape architecture has always dealt with the edges of illusion and reality, nature and artifice. From the Roman villas described by Pliny the Elder, to Frederick Law Olmsted's Central Park, to the modern urban works of Lawrence Halprin, landscape architecture wrestled with the ideological questions of what is natural and what is appropriate in the way of form and context to provide humans a respite from the pressures of their self-imposed technological evolution. I (and several other fellow landscape architects) believe we may be reaching a fork in the ideological path of our profession which, in essence, may force us to choose between two competing paradigms: simulation or sustainability.

A Reaction: Art, Landscape, and Awareness

Any mounting social tension is fair game for exploitation by artists. The opposition of the free-floating, simulated world of technology and the topophilic reaction toward sustainability is fuel for a new cadre of landscape artists, who deftly and often ironically exploit the earthy medium of the landscape as a means of interpreting and expressing this tension. For the most part, artists raise public awareness along the fault lines of social oppositions, commenting and offering alternative visions, but stopping short of advocating action toward resolution. The 1960s era earthwork artists Robert Smithson and Michael Heizer articulated an "antiaesthetic" which attempted to point

Landscape architecture has always been concerned with idealized relationships between nature and artifice, but the profession now faces increasing pressure from the growing national preoccupation with entertainment and simulation. Courtesy of American Society of Landscape Architects. Magazine cover photograph ©The Walt Disney Company.

out the shallowness and hypocrisy of the modern world, which adhered to a nineteenth century romantic illusion of nature while gouging, scraping, and consuming the earth with twentieth century technology. Their large-scale, often remotely sited earthwork sculptures, like Smithson's "Spiral Jetty" and Heizer's "Double Negative," were themselves scraped out of pristine desert landscapes in Utah and Nevada by bulldozers, and jarred the public's sense of what was "appropriate" and beautiful in the landscape (Schenker, 1992). Early earthworks were often deliberately aimed commentaries on technological society. As the environmental art movement matured in the 1970s–1990s, however, artists felt more at liberty (or perhaps compelled) to move away from the early abstractions of Smithson and Heizer toward the more deliberate, content-laden messages of Nancy Holt, Helen Mayer Harrison, and Newton Harrison. Nancy Holt manipulates familiar structural elements and technical systems in the landscape to reveal and comment upon our reliance on technology as a means of interpreting, simulating, or assaulting nature. Her sculptural landscapes point in both directions—out to the cosmic truths of solar angles and geometry ("Sun Tunnels") and inward to the modern necessity of engineered storm drainage ("Catch Basin"). Says Holt: "My work is about exposing those basic systems of our existence and owning up to them . . . Most want to hide them away and many have notions about 'being natural' while living in air-conditioned environments . . ." (quoted in Hess, 1992). Like an environmental CAT scan, Holt's work penetrates the landscape surface and reveals the inner workings of our technological dependency, leaving us to arrive at our own official diagnoses and possible cures for ecological ills.

The Harrisons move deeper into the activist role; they have been treating their large-scale commissioned art pieces as revolutionary statements and demands for environmental action since the early 1970s. Their work often involves landscape restoration, biodiversity habitats, wetlands, waste or spoil piles, or other artistic displays aimed at the very idea of *survival* for all species as well as humans (Harrison and Harrison, 1990). For the Harrisons, there are no boundaries between art, environmentalism, and action. Their intent is nothing less than the rewelding of surface to core. Increasingly, artists are following in their footsteps, feeling compelled toward more provocative comment about the crisis of technology and nature in collision. Indeed, environmental restoration may become the art movement of the twenty-first century, as artists sense a growing social bifurcation between economy and ecology too wide to ignore.

Another art movement of significance is the growing manipulation of abstract computer imagery made possible by supercomputers and nonlinear mathematics. This totally new medium has greatly contributed, of course, to the world of simulation and has obviously led to the blurring of boundaries between the real and the fake. However, most artists who explore this medium of fractals, fly-bys, ray tracing, and special effects are less interested in deliberate public deception, but more interested in probing the depth and power of the medium or the "soul of the machine." It is likely that a branch of this new computer art (with its immense power to create imaginary new landscapes) will evolve which questions the ethical limits to making such landscape surrogates. We may yet see an intersection between the high-tech simulations of the supercomputer artists with the environmental souls of the Harrisons in some artistic attempt to make sense out of the nature–technology opposition. Until computer graphic artists begin to question and challenge the negative impacts of their powerful new medium, the advances in supercomputer graphic simulation and VR technology will only continue to blur the boundary between reality and fantasy.

"Catch Basin" (1982), by Nancy Holt, St. James Park, Toronto. Photograph courtesy of Nancy Holt.

Revenge of the Core: In Desperate Defense of the Genuine

Any social movement is first defined by growth at the fringes, and the information media are drawn toward the edges of issues, for that is where the action is. But the central core of nature has not vanished. It has only been overshadowed by the attention directed at the expanding fringe. The actual vernacular landscape is still there. It is still not too late to focus the center of the conflict— the degradation of core ecological properties of specific landscapes at the hand of technology. There is a significant, subconscious backlash—the knowledge that ecological issues are more serious than ever—that leads increasing numbers of people to mount a staunch defense of core concerns and a continuing attempt to blast through the layers of hype and simulation to hold the center ground. In the face of seemingly irresistible pressure by the postmodern media society to create a world of simulations, replications, and fakery, a growing minority are demanding the *genuine*. It is a difficult battle. Defenders of the environment soon realize they must resort to the same media weapons used by their adversaries. "Deep" ecologists frantically utilize all known channels to keep core environmental concerns in the public consciousness, while the world of simulation and media technology turns every symbol into surface spectacle. Spotted Owls and rainforests become media stars which are treated as heroically and as superficially as any other celebrity. We will most certainly see even more ingenious responses by the environmental movement to avoid the attenuation of core environmental issues into the slithery, ethereal surfaces of the electronic "mediacracy."

The most tangible vehicle for radical resistance to the tyranny of autonomous technology is the old-fashioned "natural" landscape itself: soil, rock, sunlight, wind, water, wood, chlorophyll, protein, and the essential forces that organize these components into living entities. These primal landscape elements are, and always have been, the essence of the "real" and "genuine." Humans still base their constructed images of reality first upon sensory interaction with the physical environment, as perceptual psychologist J. Gibson has argued cogently for decades. Only by careful, transparent, and congruent manipulation of the surfaces and core relationships of genuine, tangible elements can we create landscapes that reassure us that we are living in a real world. The relatively recent capability of the media to provide surrogate, sensory simulations of environments, the replacement of primal landscape forms by carpentered ones, and the visible devastation of ecosystems by consumptive technologies all combine to alter our perceptions of reality. The antidote for the effects of a high-technology, manufactured, controlled, and electronically simulated environment is one which is none of the above. The primal, organic landscape itself holds considerable power if it can be substantially "demediated."

Technology has placed so many layers between our perceptions and the core realities of landscapes that surface and core no longer relate: what we often see is the opposite of what we get. Beautiful landscapes may threaten our health; apparently "natural" landscapes may be ecologically impoverished. The movement toward a sustainable world must include the peeling away of intervening images between landscape *function* and landscape *experience*. The wilderness movement, of course, attempts to do just that—strip away social mediation to obtain raw experience directly from nature. But the wilderness movement is not enough. It is a necessary outer edge to our relation to nature; a parenthesis but not a complete thesis. By rejecting all forms of technology and human intervention on specific, isolated parcels of land, the wilderness movement risks being defined as a misanthropic flight from reality.

The notion of sustainability, on the other hand, asks not that we reject other humans and their artifacts altogether, but rather that we make *responsible* artifactual connections to the ecosystems we touch and occupy, and that we connect these ecosystems *directly* to our experience in a transparent, congruent, and lasting manner. It is this kind of wildness—wildness by creative, yet responsible *action,* rather than by selective overreaction—which has been missing in our everyday world.

Galactic Simulation versus Earthly Sustainability

Isolated, officially containerized wilderness parcels may represent one form of escape from reality but, ultimately, the trend toward technological simulation and environmental fantasy reaches its opposite extreme in the proposed exploration of space. Space exploration carries with it an assumption of yet another untapped resource and a perpetuation of the same forces of exploitation, exhaustion, and eventual departure which technological humanity has been using on wild frontiers for centuries.

In 1970 I came face to face with the ethical conflict implicit in future space exploration. In 1969 I was employed as a designer for the Advanced Space Systems Group of Grumman Aerospace Corporation. Grumman had designed and produced the Lunar Module, the spacecraft which later landed on the Moon. With the likely success of the Lunar Module, Grumman expected to receive many more government contracts for future spacecraft. My new job was the conceptual design of crew living environments for long-duration space missions. I developed design concepts for crew quarters, cabin mobility and restraint, personal hygiene, food preparation and communal meals, privacy and sleeping systems, and recreation—all in an ambient environment of "zero gravity." I also developed concepts for crew living and working modules that could be reused and assembled like modular space architecture for various missions. It was exciting and unprecedented design work. On July 21, 1969, as my Grumman co-workers and I watched the TV from our drafting tables, Neil Armstrong stepped off the Lunar Module onto the surface of the Moon, and the building rocked with cheers, applause, and handshakes.

To many, this was the moment of absolute apogee in American technology. We had put a human on the moon—we could do anything with technology that we pleased, or so we thought. But in spite of a flawless performance record for the Lunar Module, Grumman never received another major spacecraft contact. Within one year, employees were leaving the company in droves. Although I had enjoyed the exciting work, something had been wrong with my connection to Grumman all along. I later realized that in the aerospace industry I had lost a sense of connection to the earth—that my design work, although challenging, seemed a form of escape from responsibility. While the astronauts were landing on the Moon, American pilots were napalming the jungles in Vietnam. The first Earth Day came in 1970, awakening us all. Soon I had left my aerospace career, eventually to turn to landscape architecture, where I could continue my creative design work while still exercising stewardship and concern for the welfare of the environment. I had, at last, found a workplace for the soul as well as the brain and hands.

Since the first moon walks, the space industry has waxed and waned. After the first distant views of planet Earth were beamed back home from the Moon, a strange dualism gripped American society. The perpetual human urge to advance technology, explore frontiers, and simulate earthly systems in lonely outposts was now to be counterbalanced by an indelible image of a small, compact, blue-green planet which, for all we knew, contained all the life in the universe. By stepping back from the planet itself, we had gained a holistic vision of what we had, and what we had better take care of. This irony of the space movement has never dissipated. There are still those who argue strongly for space exploration—for taking the human spirit to the "high frontier," arguing that it is in our human nature to do so. As far back as 1897, Russian philosopher Konstantin Tsiolkovsky was quoted as saying: "Earth is the cradle of humanity, but one cannot live in the cradle forever" (Hartmann et al. 1984). Several voluntary societies exist to promote space exploration; some of the members are otherwise quite ardent environmentalists.

But the fundamental question remains as to whether we can have it both ways—whether we can expend the immense financial and energy resources necessary to leave the earth, while claiming to heal it and take care of it at the same time. The Space Shuttle is an extremely polluting device; the tremendous exhaust emissions from the booster rockets contributes to the degradation of the ozone layer and the buildup of greenhouse gases in the earth's atmosphere. Each launch represents a gross consumption of nonrenewable energy resources that might be used for more beneficial, earthly pursuits. But more than the utilitarian impacts of space exploration, it is the implicit *philosophical* position—that we must continue exploring and exploiting frontiers if we are to survive—which crowds out and precludes the opposite position—that we can no longer afford to squander the resources of the home land or home planet and live off the spoils captured from the frontier.

Europeans first left to exploit the "new world" of North America, then moved westward across the continent after eastern resources and land were depleted. Soon we had exploited the western forests and dammed most of the western rivers, found most of the fossil fuel, and begun to wear out the rich midwestern soils and deplete the aquifers. Later, we turned to the oceans, which we thought were inexhaustible food sources. It is now apparent that fish and other aquatic organisms are not infinite, but are imperiled like other resources we have used up. Now we contemplate space exploration, lunar mining, and space disposal of wastes. The frontier ethic is being pushed farther out without questioning the archaic human pattern of consumption, depletion, and departure.

In his recent book, *In The Absence of the Sacred*, Jerry Mander refers to the proliferation of World's Fairs, entertainment "worlds" such as Disneyland and EPCOT Center, enclosed shopping malls, and so on as "domed environments" which represent the fact that we have already psychologically "left" the Earth and are now preparing to depart from it physically. In Mander's view, "New Age" thinking and plans for long-range space colonization are but the latest expressions of the tendency to kill nature and then make simulations of it:

> . . . space travel is not new; it is only the final stage of a departure process that actually began long ago. Our society really "left home" when we placed boundaries between ourselves and the earth, when we moved en masse inside totally artificial, reconstructed, 'mediated' worlds—huge concrete cities and suburbs—and we aggressively ripped up and redesigned the natural world. By now, nature has literally receded from our view and diminished in size. We have lost contact with our roots. As a culture, we don't know where we came from; we're not aware we are part of something larger than ourselves
>
> *Mander, 1991, p. 148*

The Biosphere 2 project in the Arizona desert serves as a new manifestation to Mander's assumptions, and represents new heights (or depths) in environmental simulation, but this time with a twist. Biosphere 2 (so named because the Earth is Biosphere 1) is a closed-system simulation of seven ecosystems under a three-acre, airtight glass roof in which a "crew" of eight "biospherians"—four men and four women—live for a period of two years, growing their own food, recycling their own wastes, and studying the dynamic interaction of the plant, animal, air, water, and waste systems at close range. An article coauthored by Mark Nelson, the project's CEO, chief architect, and publicist, stated that "Development and mastery of biospherics will be critical to developing a sustainable way of life on planet Earth and to the future evolution of life into the Solar System" (Nelson et al., 1990, p. 61). The parent organization for Biosphere 2 is called Space Biosphere Ventures. Nelson himself seems to straddle both sides of the philosophical fence, acting as Director of Space Applications as well as consulting on "echotechnics," or "total systems ecological management." Nelson has also experimented with innovative arid-land agricultural methods and pasture and plantation techniques for tropical regions.

At first glance, the Biosphere 2 project appears as a genuine attempt to fuse technophilia with topophilia—to straddle the philosophical fence and weld the innate technological tendencies and achievements of humans to the necessity of ecosystem preservation, and to simultaneously incorporate both stewardship and frontier values. But several aspects of the Biosphere 2 project cloud its supposed purpose. It is a private venture, funded by self-proclaimed "ecopreneur" Ed Bass (Davis Enterprise, 1992), complete with souvenir shop, restaurant, inn, and viewing windows for visitors. Certain features of the simulated ecosystems are much like zoo or aquarium exhibits, with fake rocks, electrically powered misting devices, and artificially induced tides. The jumpsuit-and-logo garb worn by the "crew" strongly resemble those of Star Trek characters or NASA astronauts. One crew member, who had to leave the facility briefly, smuggled back treats to the crew. And technically, although

A portion of the Biosphere 2 site near Oracle, Arizona awaits landscape construction. As a "human habitat" and destination resort, Biosphere 2 is a questionable blend of science and simulation. Photograph by Patrick T. Miller.

intended to be a closed ecosystem, Biosphere 2 is powered by external hookups to the local electric utility. An overseeing committee headed by famed ecologist Thomas E. Lovejoy formally criticized Biosphere 2 for its lack of scientific rigor (*New York Times*, 1992), then finally resigned. Architectural writer Michael Crosbie went even further: "Biosphere 2 isn't meant to live in harmony with nature, but to bottle it for export" (Crosbie, 1991, p. 142). Biosphere 2 is now advertised in airline flight magazines as a destination resort. Advertisements show the Biosphere 2 structure against a desert landscape backdrop and a caption enticing readers to "Spend 24 hours that are out of this world."

In short, Biosphere 2 is the ultimate Baudrillardesque simulacrum: a totally encapsulated zoo display, with humans looking back at each other across glass boundaries. We would like to believe that the project earnestly hopes to discover secrets that will help us live more lightly on Earth; however, we cannot determine whether the Biosphereans really want to stay home and try to make a better world out of the remnants of a posttechnological society, or to jump into the first intergalactic vehicle and strike out for a new home in outer space. In Biosphere 2 we see disturbing evidence that even the relatively noble ideas of stewardship, recycling, closed resource loops, and self-perpetuating ecosystems can be slurred into the world of media phenomena, quick profits, fantasy entertainment, technological gimmicks, and surface simulations.

Emergent Trends in Landscape Evolution and Landscape Architecture

Some of the trends I have described in this chapter are already evident as we look about the American landscape; others are emerging on the horizon of technological development. Not only does the creation of new technology proceed unchecked, but so does the creation of new, technologically simulated worlds. As this transformation occurs, we are less able to relate image to substance, or surface to core. When unreality consumes and becomes the reality, we will have lost our bearings as dwellers on the surface of the earth; we will be unable to tell what is ultimately good for us, or what is good for our companion species. With senses that react automatically to what looks, sounds, smells, feels, and *seems* real, and a mind skeptical of an increasingly strange and invisible "reality" forged for us by expanding science and hidden technology, we will believe only what we can sense, which may be an electronic fantasy or a technological simulation. When this happens, we may be lulled into thinking that technology and nature have fused, and their former dissonance is no longer necessary. We will be wrong, but we may not be aware that we are mistaken. No matter how illusive, "nature" is a core concept; we are a core concept; survival is a core concept. If our landscapes address only surface concerns, they will cease to be either nurturing or sustainable.

One may look about the American landscape and see two trends, one dominant, the other nascent and still relatively insignificant but growing. The major trend is toward increased technologically facilitated simulation of nature's surfaces and the creation of sophisticated, idealized environments that ignore the social and environmental problems that challenge us. This is the Landscape of Simulacra, and it can be identified by its emerging archetypes, surface preoccupations, relative opacity and incongruity, high energy and entropy, reliance on consumptive and information technology, and its avoidance of responsibility in relation to the dilemma of nature and technology. In reaction to this dominant landscape, a second, fledgling, Sustainable Landscape is emerging. This Sustainable Landscape will be associated with its own archetypes, and will be identified by its transparent relationship between surface and core, its grounding in real world issues and concerns, its use of fantasy only to support and enrich its own base in reality, its low energy, low entropy, and use of regenerative technology, its individual authenticity and uniqueness, its emphasis on qualitative values rather than quantitative measures, and its acceptance of responsibility for conflict between technology and nature.

Emergent Trends in Landscape Evolution and Landscape Architecture

	The Landscape of Simulacra	The Sustainable Landscape
Archetypes:	Mirage Hotel, Orlando, Disneyland, Mall of America	Village Homes Solar Community Arcata Wastewater Lagoons Montezuma Hills Wind Farm
Surface:	surface hides core	surface allows view into core
Core:	hidden, consumptive, incongruent w/surface	regenerative, expressed, and congruent w/surface
Fantasy:	prime organizing principle	limited and constructive
Reality:	reality consumed by fantasy preoccupation	concerned with core function and ecology
Nature:	imitates natural surfaces, simulates "appearance" of nature	attempts to include sustainable technology in a revised meaning of nature.
Technology:	consumptive and information technologies dominate ecosystem	regenerative technology serves and preserves ecosystem
Energy/ Entropy:	high energy high entropy	low energy low entropy
Authenticity:	unconcerned with authenticity	seeks authenticity
Economy:	economy based on growth, creation of demand, fantasy	economy based on sustained resource regeneration and community values
Posture w/r Nature/Tech.	denial, avoidance of known conflict	acceptance, action to resolve conflict

Two competing trends in landscape evolution and landscape architecture; the first and most dominant trend is based on a "hyperreal/technological" paradigm, the other on a "sustainable/ecological" paradigm.

A Probable, Mixed Future

These two trends are occurring simultaneously, one as the overwhelmingly dominant social movement, the other as a necessary reaction to it. The sustainable "stay home and take care of the planet" ethic now begins to seriously challenge the "simulation/high technology/frontier" ethic in a vigorous competition for the soul of American culture. The end result of this cultural conflict is unknown. The most notable predictions of the future by the most respected authors of the past have proven only partially true; we did not get *1984* in 1984, and the *Brave New World* wasn't much of either. The *Population Bomb* hasn't detonated quite yet. However, neither do we live in a cybernetic, automated heaven with ample leisure time, little disease, and widespread social justice as technology has implicitly promised us. When considering the two landscape trends described above, the most likely scenario is a unique mixture of the two.

Several ironies come to light in the wake of this rather unrevolutionary prediction. First, as the concept of nature "disappears" from the visible, tangible realm, we will need it more than ever, and a growing and vocal minority will fight hard to prevent it from totally slipping away. Second, as the *surface* images of nature and technology merge into simulated harmony in the expanding world of electronic media, the *core* impacts of our technologies will continue to wage war on our fundamental ecological relationships. Third, as the simulated surface resolution progresses, we may find it necessary to preserve what remains of the classic nature–technology opposition, for in some essential way, our gut reaction to the negative effects of technology is all we have as a check on runaway technological determinism. We feel an urgency to narrow the chasm between our operative notions of nature and technology, but not by relinquishing reality altogether.

It is important to extend the trends toward simulacra and sustainability to their logical conclusive ends in order that we may dramatize the alternative future worlds they represent. On the one hand is a vision of continued degradation of the core of nature, with hyperreal, electronically assisted and technologically manipulated simulations of nature's surfaces. In this vision, a population "drugged" silent and passive by oversaturated media accepts the emerging electronic mythology as the new "reality," while artificially intelligent, invisible, genetically engineered life forms emerge unnoticed from the laboratories of the nanotechnologists. Meanwhile, hidden from our perception, extractive, consumptive technologies degrade our ecosystems with increasing rapidity and violence. Maudlin science fiction? Perhaps, but not farfetched, given the alarming technological trends of today.

On the other hand, one could visualize a world where a fundamental awakening of perceptions occurs which sees beyond the superficial resolution of nature and technology, curbs the use of runaway simulation, and instead begins to incorporate regenerative technologies and sustainable ecosystem management strategies in a deep and transparent manner. In this vision, what we see in the landscape is what we get, and what we get is beneficial to all living organisms as well as ourselves.

Ultimately, these two visions imply completely different types of landscapes as fundamentally opposed as the Mirage Volcano is to Arcata Marsh. We will have a mixture of these two scenarios for a while, but I am convinced that the long-term coexistence of two such fundamentally opposed paradigms is inherently unstable. Like a ball balanced on a fence, culture will fall toward one vision or the other. We will either surrender our real landscapes to the world of electronic simulation and our intelligence and humanness to a generation of post-biological beings, and forsake our planetary home for a search of the next galactic frontier to exploit—or we will learn to live responsibly, sustainably, and firmly planted on the blue, brown, and green landscapes of Earth. Section 3 of this book argues vigorously in favor of the latter scenario.

III

Sustainable
Landscapes:
One
Way
Out

*B*uzzword or not, the central idea of sustainability—as a characteristic of a process or state that can be maintained indefinitely— makes sense. Although the label may change, the essential notion is here to stay, and it has come none too soon. Sustainability emerged as an inevitable response to the dynamic and increasingly dissonant tension between nature and technology in contemporary society. In essence, sustainability is a notion by which we intend to allow ourselves once more to become part of nature; to see ourselves subordinate to a larger context of universal life. The concept of sustainability is beginning to find use as a filter to separate technological alternatives and to choose only those that reinforce rather than destroy existing ecological and social values. If it can be physically demonstrated that certain ways and means of organizing human living systems result in living lightly, sensitively, and perpet-

Old and new wind energy technology, Montezuma Hills, California.

ually on the land with our companion species, then we may rightfully claim to have created—or rediscovered—sustainable landscapes.

In the remaining chapters I concentrate on the sustainable *landscape*. Landscape is where the current conflict between technology and nature is most easily sensed; it is also the place where any attempt at resolution of the conflict must be tested and proven. For now, sustainable landscape is a promising vision, which, although somewhat fuzzy, is sharpening quickly. This vision may be brought into clearer focus by understanding it as a multidimensional response to a complex cultural conflict. We may envision:

In response to the present tyranny of unchecked technology, an alternative landscape where natural systems are dominant.

In response to the squandering of energy and resources, a landscape where resources are regenerated and energy is conserved.

In response to an ideological battle between increasingly invisible forces of technology and nature, a landscape which allows us to see, understand, and resolve the conflict.

In response to a world preoccupied with entertainment, simulation, and fantasy, a landscape where essential life functions are undertaken, revealed, and celebrated.

In response to dependence on technology and guilt over its environmental impacts, a landscape where the technology incorporated is sustainable, is the best of all possible choices, and can be considered a part of nature.

In response to a frontier ethic of discovery, exploitation, exhaustion, and abandonment, a landscape where we plant ourselves firmly, nurture the land, and prevent ecological impoverishment.

In response to loss of the importance of place, a landscape which relies on local resources, celebrates local cultures, and preserves local ecosystems.

In response to an electronic media world where the very idea of landscape is becoming irrelevant, a *physical* landscape pivotal to our existence.

Although utopian in origin, this vision of a sustainable landscape has begun to take on specific characteristics for which evidence can be found on the land itself. As the vision emerges, however, questions arise: What do sustainable landscapes look like? How will we know one when we see one? Are sustainable landscapes important? How do they work? How do we *make* sustainable landscapes from scratch when few existing precedents can be found? Will they make a difference to human existence or experience?

In the remaining chapters, I offer answers to these questions. In Chapter 9 I examine the basic function of sustainable landscapes. I first discuss the evolution of sustainability as a concept and describe 12 "living systems" by which humans are tied to the physical environment and by which sustainability can be generated and measured. I describe several existing, specific landscapes which, in one or more dimensions, already embody and demonstrate sustainable principles. I conclude by offering a comprehensive vision of a more sustainable world—a vision which is cautiously optimistic, yet tempered by realistic constraints.

In Chapter 10 I discuss the interactive role and importance of sustainable landscapes to human experience as both practical and perceptual solutions to the nature–technology conflict. I also suggest that the resolution of the nature–technology conflict is a matter of prioritizing our affections and taking action.

The Epilogue admits a completely personal and totally subjective immersion into my topic, but hopefully sends the reader into the world with a sense of expanded possibility.

9

New Symbols of Possibility

To change the situation we require new symbols of possibility, and although the creation of those symbols is in some measure the responsibility of artists, it is in greater measure the responsibility of society.

LEO MARX

The landscape most acutely reflects the current conflict between nature and technology, and it is in the landscape that a resolution of that conflict can most easily be found. Landscape represents a testing ground for the validity of the emerging social and political call for sustainability—the possibility that we might be able to restructure technology to serve ecological and human values rather than overwhelm them. Attempts at this restructuring can already be found in many American landscapes. Similar evidence can be found, albeit in nascent form, in the rapid growth of sustainability as a political and social concept.

Sustainability: The Growth of a Concept

In Chapter 4 *sustainability* was defined as "a characteristic of a process or state that can be maintained indefinitely," and *sustainable development* as "improving the quality of human life while living within the carrying capacity of supporting ecosystems." Likewise, I repeat here my earlier definition of a *sustainable landscape* as "a physical place where human communities, resource uses, and the carrying capacities of surrounding ecosystems can all be perpetually maintained."

The history of the term "sustainability" as it currently applies to environmental issues probably goes back at least to the idea of "sustained-yield" forestry, if not further back into the lexicon of agriculture. Until recently, agriculture had been considered the symbolic archetype of the sustained fer-

"Sun Tree"—a solar apartment complex in Davis, California.

tility and recurrent productivity of the land. Prior to the 1960s, forestry was also guided by the idea that a sustained yield of timber could be taken from forests by means of uneven-age management and selective thinning and harvesting of trees. For the classic forester, taking only what the forest could provide continually over time was plain common sense. Because of their supposedly similar focus on sustainable yields of harvestable products, forestry and agriculture are managed under the same federal agency, the U. S. Department of Agriculture.

In the last few decades, however, the timber industry and the U. S. Forest Service have largely abandoned sustained-yield forestry in favor of clear cutting and even-age management, a practice which is more increasingly criticized, even by Forest Service employees themselves (Robinson, 1988). Likewise, during a similar period of time, agriculture evolved to such extremely high levels of chemical, energy, and water inputs that crop harvests now often produce only a fraction of the caloric energy in food value compared to the energy embodied by fertilizer, water, pesticides, and herbicides required for their growth. (Lovins et al., 1984). In some areas, more bushels of soil are lost per acre than bushels of food crops produced. Although they played a role in the evolution of sustainability as a concept, neither forestry nor agriculture as typically practiced live up to the term today.

More recently, the term "sustainable development" has emerged in response to the debate centered in the United Nations between the technologically developed countries wishing to address global environmental problems and developing "third world" countries who desperately need economic development of their own natural resources to provide for their citizens and pay off foreign debt. The term "sustainable development" was first coined in the *World Conservation Strategy* (WCS), published jointly in 1980 by the International Union for the Conservation of Nature and Natural Resources (IUCN), the United Nations Environmental Programme (UNEP), and the Worldwide Fund for Nature (WWF). The *World Conservation Strategy* is an influential and often-quoted document emphasizing three objectives which have now become widely accepted as fundamental to sustainable development: (a) that essential ecological processes and life-support systems must be maintained; (b) that genetic diversity must be preserved; and (c) that any use of species or ecosystems must be sustainable.

The United Nations-sponsored World Commission on Environment and Development (1987) defined "sustainable development" as "development that meets the needs of the present without compromising the ability of future generations to meet their own needs." A more recent United Nations-sponsored publication, *Caring for the Earth: A Strategy for Sustainable Living* (IUCN/UNEP/WWF, 1991), clarifies this terminology somewhat:

> If an activity is sustainable, for all practical purposes it can continue forever. The term [sustainable development] has been criticized as ambiguous and open to a wide range of interpretations, many of which are contradictory. The confusion has been caused because "sustainable development," "sustainable growth," and "sustainable use" have been used interchangeably, as if their meanings were the same. They are not. "Sustainable growth" is a contradiction in terms: nothing physical can grow indefinitely. "Sustainable use" is applicable only to renewable resources: it means using them at rates within their capacity for renewal.
>
> "Sustainable development" is used in this Strategy to mean: improving the quality of human life while living within the carrying capacity of supporting ecosystems.
>
> A "sustainable economy" is the product of sustainable development. It maintains its natural resource base. It can continue to develop by adapting, and through improvements in knowledge, organization, technical efficiency, and wisdom. (p. 10)

Others have interpreted the concept of sustainability to fit practical and specific situations. Landscape architects have previously referred to "sustainable landscapes" as those that contribute to human well-being, work with native landscape conditions, do not deplete or damage other ecosystems, conserve valuable resources such as water, soil nutrients, energy, and species diversity, and generally are in "harmony with the natural environment" (CELA, 1988). City planners have defined sustainability as a dynamic balance between protection and enhancement of ecosystems and resources, economic productivity, and provision of social infrastructure such as jobs, housing, education, and medical care, citing the need to minimize the amount of physical *growth* required for *development* (Dominski et al., 1992). The influential Worldwatch Institute routinely incorporates the concept of sustainability into its frequent publications.

A fundamental attribute of the new concept of sustainability is its ability to gather under one philosophical and practical umbrella a number of formerly separate environmental movements. Solar energy, appropriate technology, resource conservation, organic farming, wildlife management, wilderness protection, bioregionalism, and local economic development now share use of the terminology of sustainability to describe their common goals. In one form or another, all wish to reverse the engine of technological determinism and replace it with an alternative approach more respectful of ecological and human values. This is not an insignificant turn of events. Instead, it represents a basic broadening of public thinking, governmental and economic policy, and a recognition that humans are ecosystemically connected to all other living things. When the United Nations, the Vice President of the United States, and numerous world leaders endorse a concept, it has acquired political respectability and must be taken seriously (Gore, 1992).

Whether the word "sustainability" and its etymological relatives will survive is hard to tell. Jargon may change as all surface phenomena do these days, but the substance of the concept is likely to contribute to both worldwide environmental policy and localized action from now on. The concept of sustainability is far too powerful, too necessary, too well diffused into common usage, and too useful to ignore.

Sustainable Landscapes: Some Fundamental Properties

As a place on the land which allows human community, resources, and surrounding ecosystems to coexist in perpetuity, a sustainable landscape must embody certain fundamental properties relating to *time, landscape structure* and *function,* and the *flow of energy* and *physical materials.* Landscapes that are capable of lasting over time imply two things: first, a reduction in the *rates* of consumption of energy, water, food, and other resources not to exceed the rates at which they can be renewed or regenerated, and second, a closing of *resource loops* at all possible points. Material outputs and byproducts from one system or process must be used as input material for other constructive processes and not be deposited into waste "sinks." Waste is merely the inefficient recycling of resources. Often, the ideas are connected. In certain ecosystems, if processes involving certain components and their rates of consumption are merely slowed down enough, resource regeneration and recycling can occur naturally where such regeneration would not occur at accelerated rates.

As the venues for all life, landscapes have *structure* and *function.* Landscapes are formed by the systems that perpetuate life: the energy paths through various organisms; the building of food chains from primitive micro-

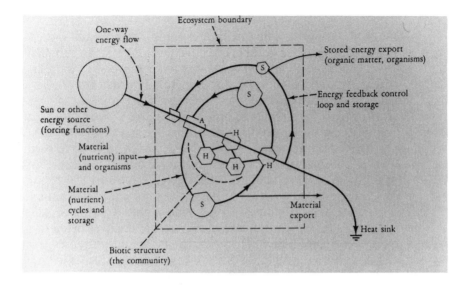

A functional diagram of an ecosystem, with emphasis on internal dynamics involving energy flow, material cycles, storage, and food webs. A sustainable landscape maximizes stored energy and material recycling within ecosystem boundaries, and minimizes losses to external "sinks." Reprinted from Ecology and Our Endangered Life-Support Systems, *by Eugene Odum (1989).*

organisms through more complex trophic levels of plants, animals, and humans, and the biological and geological processes that serve to make resources available and aid in their continually recycled movement throughout ecosystems. Structure results from the ecological function of a landscape in a particular physiographic and geologic context. In a stable, "natural" ecosystem, the landscape efficiently recycles water, nutrients, and energy throughout the various ecosystem components and organisms so that little energy is wasted as heat, and few physical resources end up in unusable forms or locations. *Entropy* is the universal physical tendency of things to move from highly energetic and ordered states to states of low energy and high disorder. Ecosystems are the principal agents on earth that curtail entropy, achieving the most amount of structural and dynamic order, the most amount of recycling of materials, the highest complexity of systems, and the least amount of wasted energy. While it is physically impossible to stop or reverse entropy, the *human-influenced* landscapes that are sustainable reduce entropy to a minimum by maintaining the structure and function of the landscape as an ordered, efficient, regenerative system. Sustainable landscapes need not copy the surface *appearance* of nature, but must emulate the interdependent and efficient *structure* and *function* of natural systems.

"Vertical" and "Horizontal" Energy

Physics tells us that energy and matter must be conserved in the universe, but energy only flows through our world in one direction. All energy to sustain life comes from the sun, and all eventually returns to the universe as waste heat radiated outward into space. When energy is captured by the earth, however, much of it can be efficiently passed from state to state and from living organism to living organism. In essence, all our earthly energy is solar energy, and its path from the sun to the earth's surface, through the earth's living and nonliving systems and ultimately, to waste heat, is often referred to as the energy "cascade." All such energy is "renewable;" even oil and coal come from the energy stored in plants and animals which were deposited and consolidated in the earth's crust over billions of years; if we were able to wait around a few billion years more, we could observe fossil fuels being regenerated, albeit at extremely slow rates. Wes Jackson and others refer to this type of energy as *vertical* energy (Jackson, 1987). Vertical energy is, for our purposes, nonrenewable; it takes exceptionally long times to accumulate and exists in highly concentrated and localized forms, making it both highly useful and irresistible to "spend" in a hurry. Using vertical energy is like squandering in one day a savings account that took years to build up; the rate of spending (the money or energy) is not equivalent to the rate of accumulation. This is the very definition of an *un*sustainable condition.

On the other hand, there is a more or less constant rate of sunlight, or useful solar energy, falling upon the surface of the earth at any given time. This can be thought of as *horizontal* energy. Direct solar energy is impacting half of the earth's surface atmosphere at any given time. Being relatively low-density (i.e., low-temperature or "cool") energy, solar energy's ability to do work at any one location is limited. Some solar energy is reflected or reradiated back into space; much is converted directly into heat, keeping the planet warm enough for life to persist. Some of the incident energy drives the hydrological cycle, while some causes other weather phenomena such as wind and ocean currents. A small amount is fixed by photosynthesis of plants. This relatively tiny amount (less than 1% of the total solar flux entering earth's atmosphere at any given time) not only provides the food for all organisms including humans, but also accounts for the tiny, accumulated layers of detritus, which, over billions of years, are consolidated and transformed into oil, coal, and natural gas.

Horizontal energy is "contemporary" energy (Jackson, 1987), or energy in the "here and now." The amount of useful energy falling upon the earth's surface at any given time is a kind of natural speed limit—an earthly metabolic threshold beyond which life in its present form cannot be sustained. For most ecosystem components and living organisms (except humans), the amount of energy used is strictly regulated by the amount falling on the earth's surface and taken up in its surface processes. Sunlight fixed by photosynthesis is the basis for all living organisms, yet some scientific estimates

Direct solar energy is "horizontal" energy, which can only be captured in the "here and now" over a specific land surface area, as in this LUZ solar-thermal powerplant in southern California. Photograph by Robert Sommer.

place the portion of this primary production from photosynthesis controlled by human activity to be 40% (Meadows et al., 1992). Humans consume 3% of this photosynthesis directly through food, fuel wood, and animal feeds. Another 36% is used up by crop waste, forest clearing and burning, desertification, and destruction of natural areas for settlements. Some is also lost to pollution. There are limits to the proportion of horizontal energy humans can commandeer before impoverishment of other species takes place. The greater the percentage of global photosynthesis captured by humans, the less is available to maintain other life forms or earthly processes. In short, there is only so much sunlight to go around. High energy consumption by humans, whether horizontal or vertical, leads directly to the decline of other species.

Horizontal energy is low-intensity, widely dispersed, renewable energy in the form of wind, sunlight, water moving by tides or gravity, and energy fixed by plants (food for metabolic energy or fuel wood). Although capable of regenerating easily, some horizontal energy forms can be unsustainably used; food can be consumed too rapidly, wood burned too quickly, or water run out of hydroelectric reservoirs too fast to allow forests, agricultural soils, or reservoirs to naturally regenerate or reaccumulate. *Sustainable landscapes use horizontal, renewable energy, and are necessarily limited by the rates and locations at which horizontal energy can be regenerated.* This has serious implications. The current level of energy use per capita in the United States and other developed countries now relying on vertical energy cannot be sustained worldwide. It is therefore a grave mistake to assume that renewable energy use can replace vertical or fossil fuel use without an overall, significant scaling back of the "metabolism" of human infrastructure. Sustainability will require a significant, global *reduction* in energy use among the highest-end users. However, with increased energy *efficiency* (i.e., less energy wasted as useless heat to the atmosphere), much more "work" can be accomplished to preserve the quality of human life. *Sustainable landscapes, therefore, use energy only at rates that regenerate in "real" time,* and imply a greatly increased capacity for energy efficiency. In energy terms, unsustainable landscapes imply a shift from the "business-as-usual" assumptions of fossil fuel and nuclear power. Use of vertical energy, therefore, is an illusion—a temporary (on the order of hundreds of years) extravaganza which will be short-lived in the ultimate, future reflection of the millions of years of human history.

Sustainable Technologies

From examining the fundamentals of sustainable landscapes, we can envision the technologies required to bring them about. In Chapter 4 I defined a *sustainable technology* as a utilitarian technique or system which, when employed productively by humans, results in no loss of ecosystem carrying capacity, resource availability, or cultural integrity. Sustainable technologies are those developed and utilized because of their relatively benign or stabilizing effects on human cultures and surrounding ecosystems. All technologies have environmental impacts. However, the technologies likely to be considered sustainable may rely on renewable resources and more locally available materials, may be smaller in scale and more dispersed throughout the landscape rather than concentrated in a few centralized locations, and will likely emit only outputs and byproducts that are easily reabsorbed and utilized by surrounding ecosystems. Sustainable technologies may abandon the tendency to save time by rapidly consuming energy and wasting resources in favor of preserving ecological stability, human community, self-sufficiency, and essential quality of life.

There are, of course, many unresolved questions. For example, is information technology sustainable? One argument is that only by increasing the flow of information between parts of the complex, global industrial "machine" we have built can we make it run more efficiently and with less environmental impact. This is the "cybernetic noosphere" argument; that the recent explosion of information technology is merely our attempt to bring the global "control system" up to par in sophistication and effectiveness with the horsepower of the world's engine of industrial technology. The essential presumption here is that once the information system becomes complex and responsive enough, we will be able to continue to enjoy the same or greater level of technologically-induced, global "metabolism" as we have been, yet with less pollution and waste.

Others question, however, whether information-based technology is necessary or sustainable if its only reasons for existence are merely to sell relatively useless information to each other resulting in little action, or to create additional imagery, symbolism, and market demand for manufactured products we don't need, but sell to one another only for the image quality and secondary economic benefits (Papanek, 1984; Mander, 1991). I am convinced that there is currently too little technological development based on genuine need and too much aimed at creating new markets for unnecessary technological gadgets. In an age of underemployment and demonstrated impacts of information technology in displacing workers, there is little justification for time-saving electronic devices and duplicative systems beyond the narrow competitive advantages of certain segments of business. Do we really *need* an electronic, pocket-sized device that replaces our car keys, wallet, and even the pictures of our children, as Microsoft mogul Bill Gates has suggested? Will not such devices exacerbate the already severed relationship we have with our environment? Truly sustainable technologies will allow us closer, more direct contact with and greater understanding of the natural systems we must protect.

Characteristics of Sustainable Landscapes

From the previous discussion, some generalizable characteristics of sustainable landscapes emerge. Sustainable landscapes will:

1. Use primarily renewable, horizontal energy at rates which can be regenerated without ecological destabilization
2. Maximize the recycling of resources, nutrients, and byproducts and produce minimum "waste," or conversion of materials to unusable locations or forms
3. Maintain local structure and function, and not reduce the diversity or stability of the surrounding ecosystems
4. Preserve and serve local human communities rather than change or destroy them
5. Incorporate technologies that support these goals. In the sustainable landscape, technology is secondary and subservient, not primary and dominating

I concur with John Lyle (1993), who emphasizes that sustainability depends primarily on *environmental design*. Creation of new landscapes and renovation of existing landscapes based on the general characteristics previously mentioned is necessary to give form and function to a newly emerging, sustainable world view. This chapter presents one way to structure the analysis of existing landscapes or to approach the planning and design of future landscapes with sustainability in mind. The process, of course, must start with a clear analysis and understanding of the ecological context of the landscape under consideration. Within a certain site of existing or proposed human activity, what are the overarching structure, function, and dynamics of the ecosystem enveloping that site? Human activity alters what might otherwise be considered a "natural" baseline. Although the ecological conditions may change considerably under human influence, knowledge of that baseline ecosystem is necessary to properly design the human modifications and adaptations to that ecosystem.

Humans, of course, can be considered natural players in the dynamics of the ecosystems they inhabit and change. When analyzing a human-influenced ecosystem, it is most important to keep in mind that humans are only part of, and not the center of a greater system of structure, order, and operation. However, since humans must take responsibility for their interactions and make conscious decisions about the nature and degree of their own modifications to their ecosystems, it is helpful to think of human interaction as a multidimensional set of connections, like a spider web attached at key points to a greater and more intricate web.

Living Systems

In my teaching and private practice regarding sustainable landscape planning, I have found it useful to consider a dozen "points of attachment" where humans interact with the greater ecosystem to survive. Far from being mysterious or puzzling, these points of human/ecosystem dependence are quite familiar—food, shelter, energy, water, transportation, materials, waste, and so on. Each of these dimensions is really a system of "give and take" with respect to a greater system. Each can be considered in terms of what is taken (i.e., either borrowed or consumed) from the greater system and what is given back. I refer to these two-way, dynamic dimensions as "living systems." Living systems not only are the points of reciprocal connection between humans and their activities on the land, but also between each system and other living systems. When dealing with human communities and landscapes, I often consider the following twelve systems: (1) landscape ecology and biodiversity; (2) culture, education, and community values; (3) urban design, housing, built form/structure; (4) transportation and circulation; (5) agriculture (including forestry and material fiber); (6) water supply and use; (7) wastewater treatment; (8) stormwater management; (9) energy supply, use and conservation; (10) processed material flows and recycling; (11) industry, employment, and economy; and (12) recreation.

Many other ways of categorizing living systems are possible, and the 12 categories I use overlap considerably. For example, transportation relates to energy use as well as urban design. Water supply, stormwater, and wastewater

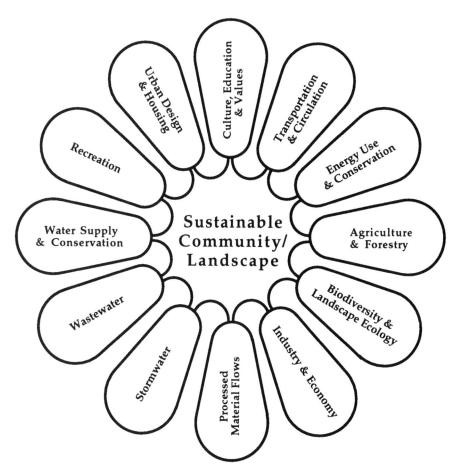

A "Living Systems" approach to sustainable community/landscape planning. The twelve systems or dimensions shown in the diagram interact and contribute to the overall sustainability of any landscape, community, or region.

treatment form a triumvirate of related systems. Agriculture is entwined with landscape ecology and biodiversity as well as water supply and energy. My choice in presenting these particular categories is based upon how the systems often present themselves in land planning and development projects.

Each living system is a potential consumer of resources and energy and a potential generator of entropy or disorder. However, most living systems are also sources of reclaimable, reusable materials, and in many cases, retrievable energy and order. Readers may find these 12 dimensions useful in evaluating their personal behaviors and physical impacts with respect to their own land-scape contexts—to where they live, work, and play. One can think of the many technologies used in each living system in the vernacular landscape, and how few of these technologies can actually be considered sustainable: gas-guzzling recreational vehicles, sophisticated farm machinery, synthetic chemical pesticides and herbicides, fossil fuel power plants, and so forth. In a majority of cases, the technologies by which our culture has chosen to support itself result in *taking* too much in the way of concentrated energy and nonrenewable materials, dispersing or *diffusing* too much energy without accomplishing enough work, *returning* too much useless material to inaccessible locations, and *dissipating* too much in the way of organizational structure.

In our society, very few durable goods serve a useful purpose over long periods; most are converted into residual waste nearly as fast as the material can be extracted, processed, and manufactured (Fisk and Vittori, 1991). For example, we take large quantities of metal or plastic and after using them briefly as cars, refrigerators, or televisions, we return them to the earth in a state of extreme disorder. Contemporary living systems are either too *consumptive,* their outputs too disconnected from inputs of other systems, or they operate too *fast* for the unaided, natural rates of regeneration to occur.

More often than not we forget to consider how the "return" or output end of one living system can attach to the input end of another system. We forget that human wastes can be inputs for other biological organisms to the benefit of all involved, or that like blood, water can be cleansed and reused over and over again. We often structure our own *recreation* such that it results in the *destruction* of the context in which we are recreating. By substituting an abstraction like money for direct, personal survival use of resources, much of our economy creates jobs for today largely by robbing the future. By accelerating the consumption of vertical energy for a temporary financial gain in the present, our economy builds up a backlog of entropy or disorder which will become evermore acute and problematic in the near future.

Any attempt to identify separate classes of connections between humans, resources, ecosystems, natural processes, technics, and metabolics runs the risk of reductionism. As Kenneth Boulding implied with the title of his book, *The World as a Total System* (Boulding, 1985), everything on earth is indeed connected to everything else, and viewing any portion in isolation risks losing perspective on important connections between elements. Few people have grasped the integrated nature of "human" and "natural" systems more cogently than Pliny Fisk, architect, sustainable development theorist, and founder of the Center for Maximum Potential Building Systems in Austin, Texas. Fisk emphasizes that the cycling of essential elements in any ecosystem indicates life's basic need for a continual flow of physical materials. Energy conservation results from highly efficient systems working together, rather than as independent, single-purpose machines (Fisk and Vittori, 1991).

When considering whether a landscape is sustainable, we must ask several questions; first, whether each living system, when examined independently, can be expected to continue indefinitely without detriment to other system components; and second, whether the connections of input, output, and throughput of energy and materials *between* systems is efficient and produces little physical waste, disorder, or dissipated energy. We must also ask: do any or all of the living systems to be considered within a human-influenced landscape harm the baseline landscape ecology or threaten biodiversity?

Each landscape proposed for development or modification has a different set of contextual conditions; no two landscapes are identical. While it is dangerous to suggest formulaic, preconstructed "solutions" to the challenge of sustainable community and landscape planning, there are enough examples of progress toward sustainability to be able to describe some general tendencies or patterns as to what those landscapes might include. In the pages that follow, I offer a necessarily sequential discussion of the twelve living systems which combine and interact with one another to form the basis for a sustainable landscape.

Biodiversity and Landscape Ecology

In America, technological development has had an obvious, widespread, and generally negative impact on biodiversity, with the result that many species of plants and animals vanish each year. We have most often structured our own, humanized landscape as the primary background for our activity, leaving only patches of habitat for other species in the form of parks, remote wilderness, forgotten riparian or grassland fragments, and occasional (and most often too small) "nature" or wildlife preserves. We have unfortunately convinced ourselves, whether consciously or unconsciously, that our human habitat should be the dominant landscape, with small exceptions carved out for other species. Clearly, we have it backward. To paraphrase Bob Schneider, builder/developer and Sierra Club chapter officer, we don't need more habitat preserves in the context of urban development; we need "developer preserves" in the overall context of habitat for biodiversity.

Perhaps two of the most critical aspects of conservation biology are to maintain habitats large enough to support critical species and ecosystems and to ensure a system of landscape linkages between these large habitats. The resultant pattern resembles a net of habitats with very large knots or nodes connected by unbroken corridors. Contemporary technological development often violates both of these biodiversity requirements; highways frequently sever wildlife migratory corridors. Sprawled development eats up, fragmentizes, and isolates habitats into areas too small, scattered, and disconnected to support the original ecosystems and species.

Schneider's comment is directly applicable to a sustainable solution. We must consider the greater natural landscape as a continuous, physical web of linkages and large habitats, and ourselves and our own human landscape needs as subordinate and just one of many uses of the same landscape by many different species. Where existing development has severed linkages and fragmentized habitats for other species, we must reconnect and reconstruct them. Where new development is proposed, it must be contained and concentrated

Riparian corridors, as depicted in this view of the Putah Creek Reserve at the University of California, Davis, are critical to the network of habitat reserves and linkages required to maintain biodiversity in the face of encroaching urban, recreational, and agricultural land uses. Photograph by Mark Francis.

within reasonable bounds, and the linkages that *we humans* need (highways, rail lines, etc.) must allow the linkages needed by other species to pass under, over, or through them without interference. Wherever possible, we should include habitat values for other species as a joint use of land we need. Most importantly, we must learn not to consume such large blocks of land in the first place for our own purposes. In most cases, higher-density human development with considerable remaining open space results in less damage to biodiversity than if the same human population were spread evenly over the entire landscape. By consciously thinking of *our own* land patterns as patches of human habitat with nondestructive linkages between them, our physical landscape "web" can coexist with those of other species in a less destructive manner.

To make our land use patterns more capable of sustained biodiversity, we may begin by protecting, reconstructing, and reconnecting riparian habitats in virtually every stream and river. Where we are able to increase the density of our own land use patterns to serve the same human population, larger habitat areas can be preserved for other species. We can arrange our own land uses so that agricultural or recreational buffers surround primary wildlife habitat reserves. Fundamentally, we must recognize that the land areas and configurations *we* need should not deprive the thousands of other species of life who share our landscapes of the networks of habitats and linkages *they* need.

It will be difficult to accomplish these goals; to start on a solution will require loosening up our anthropocentric spatial frameworks. We must rethink and reconfigure our own habitat patterns on the land to include the habitat patterns of other species.

Culture, Education, and Community Values

In terms of human ecology, "sustainability" is a hollow buzzword unless there is a cultural code of common human values and behaviors which can itself be sustained. Far from being a solely technological solution, sustainability is only possible if there are stable and continuing human cultures and subcultures that value the regenerative use of resources and the longevity of dynamic but stable ecosystems. Landscapes that are considered the most sustainable in the world have most often evolved from rather well-established human cultures persisting over hundreds of years. The Amish farming country of Pennsylvania, for example, would cease to be sustainable if the Amish culture of soil conservation, land stewardship, resourcefulness, frugality, and strict codes of social behavior faltered.

Much of American culture, however, has evolved in just the opposite direction; a quickly changing value system of consumerism, frequent relocation, lifestyle fads, resource wastage, fossil fuel addiction, and anthropocentrism. If we are to deliberately *design* sustainable landscapes, we will also need to *educate* each other and deliberately "design" or foster the *stable social structures* that guide human activity in those landscapes. Without sustainable values, landscapes designed to be sustainable will be misused, become unsustainable, and fail.

In an essay entitled *"Don't Move!,"* Gary Snyder sees the first necessary step toward living sustainably as a resolution to remain in one's region, learn the local ecology, make it home, and make it work (Snyder, 1991). Once a set of cultural roots can be established, care, and ultimately, sustainability, will follow. I have lived in the flat, hot, agricultural Central Valley of California for 20 years—longer than I have lived anywhere else. While I might not have originally chosen such a landscape out of a catalog of alternatives, this is where I live, and I have grown fond of it. I know its resident and migratory animals; its native, introduced, and threatened plants; its weather modes and moods; its baking heat, beautiful sunsets, and muddy sloughs; its benign as well as its destructive technologies; and most of all, its people. With each additional year of residence, I learn more about how to take care of this place, and what we collectively ought to do to make it right and keep it that way. I *belong* here now, and perhaps this place needs me too.

Sustainable landscapes require concurrent social structures and cultural values which support sustainability, as in this farmers' market in Evanston, Illinois, where organic, locally grown produce is directly marketed to the consumer. Photograph by Robert Sommer.

Human culture, of course, is an immensely complex system of codes, behaviors, signs, and symbols. Today there are strong indicators of an increasing desire for sustainable living: intentional communities built upon sustainable values; watershed associations and citizen-initiated planning advisory groups; Audubon society chapters and bicycle commuting clubs. More people have begun to realize that we can't have our environmental cake and eat it too. In terms of culture and society, sustainability implies *"not* business as usual," but a rather substantial and fundamental shift in attitudes and cultural longevity. As little as 10 years ago, for one to speak of the need for a change in the highly consumptive American lifestyle meant being dismissed as an outrageous "granola-head" or environmental radical. No longer. Recently, at a Renewable Natural Resources Foundation congress I attended in Colorado, I was pleased to discover the general consensus among well-established resource managers, professionals, and federal bureaucrats was that we *must* begin to reduce the intensity of our consumer-oriented life style. "*Not* business as usual" is becoming more common and culturally palatable as a first step toward real social change and an eventual, sustainable society. It will require both changing values and deliberate education to do so.

Urban Design, Housing, and Built Form

American regions, suburbs, and cities have been shaped by consumptive technologies and economies. Digging into the earth's savings of fossil fuels, metals, soils, and aggregates has enabled a broad pattern of built form to spread across our landscapes. Such a pattern can last only until the limited supply is exhausted. Automobiles have temporarily extended the time in which we could try to live in the imaginary, idealized middle landscape between rural nature and urban culture. Fossil fuel fertilizers, pesticides, and herbicides have allowed us to grow more crops on less land and build more houses on the land we took out of farming. More recently, information technologies have allowed us to turn inward and away from the perceived problems of the world into isolated, gated subdivisions connected to the global "community" by satellite and fiber optics but disconnected from the former social discourse of the neighborhood. Information technology and a service-based economy have allowed a ring of suburbs to become disconnected from the former center city, leaving its lower-income neighborhoods forgotten and abandoned.

Several prototypic responses to these unsustainable conditions have arisen. The Ecocity movement, spearheaded by Richard Register (1987), seeks to resurrect the physical ecology of the city, bringing piped and channelized streams back to their former riparian surface character and function. Intentional communities like Village Homes (see page 287) reestablish genuine human interaction and community through innovative site planning, while reducing energy and automobile use, and encouraging neighborhood food production. Cohousing, the intentional association of small cottage owners in resident-owned cooperative clusters is growing in the United States, following the lead of the Scandinavians. On top of it all, the so-called "Solar Age" never really died, but merely hibernated through the winter of Reaganomics and is showing signs of renewed life. Visions of more sustainable built environments grow clearer, with more compact, efficient structures, friendlier, more gregarious site planning, more fine-grained and diverse land use mixtures, and more connection and penetration of wild corridors into urban fabric. By no means, unfortunately, are such patterns becoming the norm; there is simply too much short-term thinking and long-term cultural investment in the typical unsustainable patterns of land development. On the positive side, however, the real estate industry in California has now recognized the need for a more sustainable type of development, and has begun to listen to the concerns of its critics. (Inman, 1993).

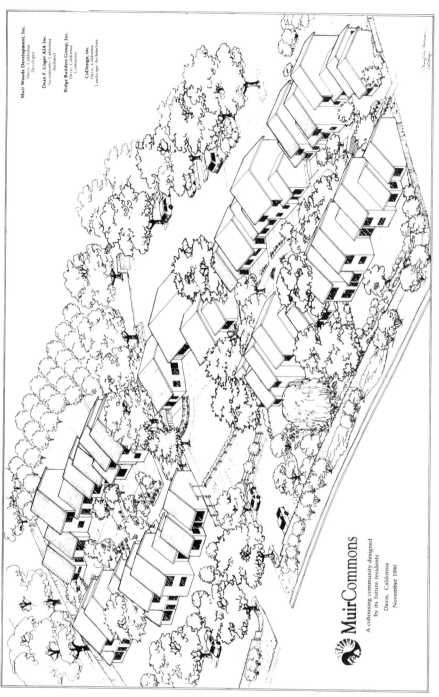

MuirCommons

A cohousing community designed
by its future residents

Davis, California
November 1990

Muir Woods Development, Inc.
Davis, California
Developer

Dean F. Unger AIA Inc.
Sacramento, California
Architect

Ridge Builders Group, Inc.
Davis, California
Contractor

CoDesign, inc.
Davis, California
Landscape Architecture

Muir Commons, the first cohousing community built in the United States. Designed and cooperatively owned by its 26 households, Muir Commons includes small, attached, solar homes, a community house with kitchen, dining, recreation, and meeting rooms, day care, an organically productive garden, and orchards. Courtesy of CoDesign, Inc. Drawing by

Sustainable Food and Fiber

American agriculture has evolved from the prevalence of the single family farm to the dominance of the large corporate/conglomerate *grower*. In the process of this transition, agriculture has largely traded small-scale steward-ship and labor intensive practices for megascale, mechanized operations with high inputs of chemical pesticides, herbicides, and fertilizers. My own university campus is known for having invented the tomato-harvesting machines that put thousands of migratory field hands out of work, and also for developing varieties of tomatoes capable of withstanding the physical abuse that comes with a highly mechanized harvesting and transport system.

Author Mark Kramer (1987) describes the "farmerless" farms in the southern San Joaquin Valley of California operated by enormous real estate conglomerates like the Tejon Ranch Corporation. These giant land-holding and growing operations aim toward the utopian farms portrayed in the Kraft Foods pavilion at Epcot Center. At Epcot, large robotic, space-age vehicles resembling a cross between lunar rovers and combines patrol the fields, while white-collar controllers manage the "farming" operations from a high-tech, computerized control tower overlooking an agrotechnical valley devoid of humans or communities.

In spite of such trends and visions of the future, countering trends in agriculture are more enlightened. "Low-input" and "sustainable" are two terms which first filtered down from theory into practice in the realm of agriculture. Integrated pest management (IPM) aims to replace chemicals with natural predators for insect pests. Drip/trickle and subsurface irrigation, water recycling, and minimum-tillage practices have begun to take hold, reducing water and soil wastage. Organic farmers are proliferating, having established certification procedures in many states. Direct marketing of produce is become more widespread, especially near large metropolitan areas. My wife and I "subscribe" each year to the Fiddler's Green organic vegetable farm in the Capay Valley near our home in Yolo County, California. For a yearly fee we pay in advance, Fiddler's Green provides us and other families with a great variety of weekly vegetables delivered to a common destination central to a number of subscribers in our neighborhood. We are typical of a rapidly growing number of families willing to pay slightly more for organic produce. Certain farming regions have become profitable by catering to increased concern for food quality and increasingly sophisticated culinary tastes in the cities by growing wholesome, speciality vegetables, such as bok-choy, shallots, capers, numerous lettuce and mushroom varieties, and so forth.

Research at agricultural universities shows signs of turning away from increasing yields at the expense of energy and environmental quality to decreasing energy and chemical inputs and exploring ecologically sensitive and socially viable means of producing food. Farmers are trying to live up to the once proud but recently faltering image that "farmers were the first true environmentalists." It is in the realm of agriculture that the highest prolifera-

Asian greens, mustard, and bok choy grow at Fiddlers Green Farm near Capay, California. Fiddler's Green is typical of many new, organic farms supported directly by consumer subscriptions. Courtesy of Fiddler's Green Farm.

tion of sustainable practices can be identified. Reduction of chemical inputs, symbiotic cropping patterns, agroforestry (intermixing tree and row crops), establishment of biodiversity hedgerows, wildlife corridors, windbreaks, beneficial insect strips, organically raised beef, grains, vegetables and fruits, recycled water, reduced soil tillage, and an increasing consumer awareness and concern for food quality have marked a strong trend toward a more sustainable agriculture. Other human living systems can learn much from agriculture's experience and progress toward sustainability.

Processed Material Flows and Recycling

America has become a throw-away society. Consumption of material goods is driven by advertising, planned obsolescence, technophilia, and a style-conscious culture. The amount of physical material, energy expenditures, and costs to produce the packaging "required" for marketing purposes often far exceeds that needed for the product itself. Packaging material has a short lifespan; after successfully enticing the consumer to buy the product, it goes directly to the landfill. Often the product is not far behind. Consumer products themselves are often intended to go out of style or fall apart rapidly, encouraging replacement purchases. Material "newness" is worshipped. In

1988, Americans discarded 662 kilograms (roughly three-quarters of a ton) of solid waste per person (Young, 1991). There is now a widely acknowledged solid waste crisis in America, with well-publicized odysseys of garbage-laden trains, ships, and barges from New York and other major cities wandering around America looking for disposal sites. In a perversion of NIMBY, some states pass legislation prohibiting the interment of solid waste from other states while they themselves seek out-of-state disposal sites for their own garbage.

Solid waste not only consumes land, but wastes energy as well, and the prices of consumer goods do not include the real costs of this entropy, wasted energy, land consumption, and ecosystem disruption. Reduction of consumption, reuse of products, and recycling of discarded materials are all steps toward a more sustainable material flow through American culture and landscape. In Marin County, a sophisticated waste recovery system reclaims 95% of the solid waste stream for reuse or conversion to usable byproducts. Sewage sludge becomes fertilizer. Glass, aluminum, paper, cardboard, a growing number of plastic types, motor oil, and even paint can be recycled. A Berkeley firm, Urban Ore, recovers, repairs, and sells useful items such as building materials, refrigerators, televisions, and appliances which are often prematurely discarded at the city's municipal waste transfer station for want of minor repairs.

Organic solid wastes can be burned to create electricity, but the process is

Hedgerow Farms near Winters, California. Fields of about forty acres are framed by hedgerows of plants chosen as habitat for beneficial insect and bird species for crop pest control. In the right-center foreground is an irrigation tailwater pond, which mitigates pollution from irrigation run-off, allows recapture of eroded soil and provides habitat for waterfowl. Photograph by John Anderson.

(a) *Daniel Knapp, PhD, founder of Urban Ore, a Berkeley recycling firm, helps a customer look for a window. Dr. Knapp believes that the only remaining obstacles to total recycling are legal and social, not technological.* (b) *Recycled sinks and tubs for sale at Urban Ore. Courtesy of Urban Ore, Inc. Photographs by Mary Lou Van Deventer.*

not a particularly clean one, and still produces greenhouse gasses. Hard-core solid waste specialists also insist that burning wastes to produce energy only counteracts the growing social responsibility to recycle and reuse, and NIMBY responses have frequently prevented the siting of solid waste incinerator power plants. Sacramento and other cities are now establishing "enterprise zones" to encourage the establishment of industries based on recycling and reprocessing of discarded materials. But since these zones are centralized "sinks" for various discarded products, and since the recycling and resource recovery processes create their own environmental hazards, people do not often welcome a resource recovery plant moving in next door. However, although few human recycling processes are 100% efficient, the net result of a transition to recycling and resource recovery industries will be of tremendous overall bene-fit to both landscapes and ecosystems. Ultimately, each region will have to take responsibility for reconverting the wastes generated within its own bound-aries. As this begins to happen, public guilt and avoidance will decrease and consumer responsibility will increase, and sustainable treatment of material flows on and in the land may then begin to provide a source of pride rather than shame.

Water Supply, Use, and Conservation

In the arid western part of the United States, water is scarce, and agriculture accounts for over 80% of all human water use. Of the water used by urban development, more than half is spent on irrigating ornamental landscapes, and most often this water is of potable, drinkable quality. Even many areas of the presumably well-watered eastern U.S. have reached the end of their water supplies. The age of creating large, federally subsidized dams and reservoirs has come to an end owing to tighter budgetary controls and staunch opposi-tion from environmental groups. Increasingly, water utility companies and governmental agencies realize that the best "new" source of water is conserva-tion. California recently passed Assembly Bill 325, The Water Conservation in Landscaping Act, which requires local governments to enact and enforce land-scape water conservation ordinances. After experiencing six continuous years of drought, California is also experimenting with water "banking," or allowing agricultural water not needed by farmers for crops to be sold back to the state for resale transfer to urban communities with insufficient water supplies. While widespread water transfers from agricultural uses to urban uses in the arid western states raises an immensely complex set of legal, social, environ-mental, and economic questions (Reisner, 1986, 1990), many experts now agree that more water once used for low-cash-producing agricultural crops, crops subsidized and sold at a net loss, or crops grown in regions where saline buildup threatens to make agricultural infeasible, should be saved and redi-rected toward the cities. The major questions are "how?," "who pays?" and "who benefits?"

However, providing cities with agriculture's formerly wasted water should not permit a lack of conservation by urban communities. An American house-hold of four people typically uses about one acre-foot of water per year (or a football-field-sized reservoir a foot deep). This quantity of water could be substantially reduced by conservation and by choosing appropriate interior and exterior technologies, such as water-efficient toilets, faucets, shower heads, and drip-landscape irrigation systems. Not only can so-called "orna-mental" landscapes be reconfigured to emphasize "hydrozoning" (the creation of zones of landscape water use commensurate with expected levels of human use), but they can also be made to more closely resemble natural ecosystems

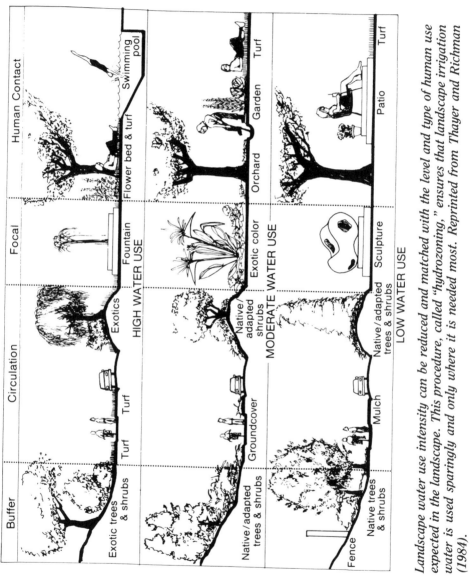

Landscape water use intensity can be reduced and matched with the level and type of human use expected in the landscape. This procedure, called "hydrozoning," ensures that landscape irrigation water is used sparingly and only where it is needed most. Reprinted from Thayer and Richman (1984).

and utilize plants that are either native or well-adapted to a particular region's natural climate, soil, and rainfall.

Most importantly, there is no need for high-quality, potable water to be applied to exterior landscapes. Water for landscape irrigation can be reclaimed and partially treated if necessary for landscape use after being used initially for "higher quality" functions in kitchen and bathroom sinks. With the passage of a state law allowing "gray water" (e.g., water from sinks and bath tubs) plumbing systems, California communities and developments have begun to install dual plumbing to handle reclaimed water for irrigation of landscapes.

With more efficiency of indoor and outdoor uses, strict hydrozoning and ecosystemic planning of outdoor landscapes, reuse of gray water for landscape irrigation and environmental enhancement, and a well-conceived policy of water transfers and appropriate water pricing, community development can reverse the unsustainable water gluttony which has plagued the United States for decades.

Wastewater Treatment

The typical technology of urban water supply and wastewater treatment is to take water from surface or ground sources, purify and chlorinate it to potable quality (if it is not pure already), use it inefficiently (i.e., once) in either the house, garden, store or factory, return it to sanitary sewers, and process it by mechanical, chemical, and energy-consumptive means in highly engineered treatment plants located out of sight and as far from the center of town as possible, hopefully somewhere people rarely go. It is no wonder that few people, when asked, can tell you where their wastewater goes once their washing machine cycle is operated or their toilet is flushed. "Out-of-sight, out-of-mind" is the guiding principle, reinforced by a host of necessary but uncreatively interpreted health and safety laws concerning water quality.

Recently, however, the ability of multipurpose, natural biological systems to treat water has been recognized (such as the successful Arcata wastewater treatment system discussed in Chapter 6). Wetland and estuarine ecosystems have been nature's wastewater treatment system for millions of years, with little else needed but the sun's energy, sufficient land, and the right combination of microbial organisms, plants, and animals, and water. Various wetland configurations have been constructed to process not only urban sewage, but mine tailing runoff and various other highly toxic effluents (Hammer, 1989). However, not all urban areas have enough land for full-fledged constructed wetlands for wastewater treatment. John Todd, founder of the New Alchemy Institute in Massachusetts, has developed a space-saving, greenhouse-based, intensive water treatment system which relies on sunlight and natural organisms to process wastewater and produce useful organic byproducts. Wastewater engineering companies have seen the benefits of a more ecologically based

Low-cost, multipurpose wetlands can process human wastewater and double as wildlife habitats. Two major types are subsurface flow systems and free-water surface systems, as shown in this Denham Springs, Louisiana wetland. Courtesy of Nolte and Associates, Sacramento. Photographs by Ron Crites.

approach to water treatment as well. Ron Crites of Nolte Engineering in Sacramento, California has developed a gravel and reed bed marsh system for small communities. While Ron and I were both consulting on a proposed sustainable new town plan (see Nance Canyon on page 294), we worked on plans for six "neighborhood-scale" gravel/reed bed systems for on-site processing of all human wastes, each with a gray-water system. All wastewater effluent treated by these systems would be reclaimed and reused for irrigation or environmental enhancement.

After decades of a wasteful, "once through" attitude toward urban water use and treatment, we have begun to realize that as the lifeblood of ecosystems, water can easily be cleansed and reused without great energy, mechanical, or chemical inputs, and the resultant wetland environments have multipurpose benefits as wildlife refuges and even scenic or recreational amenities. Arcata's

"Flush with Pride" slogan is indeed gaining new significance as resource loops are closed, ecosystems are enhanced, and humans finally begin to see their organic wastes as what they really are—natural resources.

Stormwater Management

Urban development typically presents a far less permeable and more "hardened" surface to the rain than the land it covers up. A drop of rain falling on an urban roof in America is apt to roll down the roof into a gutter, fall through a downspout onto a paved driveway, flow along a concrete curb and gutter into a concrete drop inlet in the street, drop into an underground concrete or ceramic storm sewer pipe, and travel to a "daylight" outflow in a channelized, often concrete-covered urban stream corridor miles from where the drop originally fell. In some cities, raindrops touch only engineered materials en route from rooftop to ocean. The path this water droplet takes has grave consequences, both for the ecological function of the land and for the environmental awareness and perception of the urban dweller. First, hardened surfaces mean the water has little chance of returning to earth near where it fell, thereby depriving the local groundwater of its ability to naturally recharge. Second, as water accumulates from all the other roofs and streets and flows through hardened pipes and channels, it has more volume and higher speed, creating higher flood dangers. Third, since most of this path of urban stormwater runoff is in artificially impervious channels, few organisms, plants, or animals will benefit from or share use of this water while it is being conducted away from people. Finally, being largely out of human vision, the public gets little or no visual feedback as to the multifaceted role of water in sustaining ecosystems and other life forms.

What are the consequences of an overly hardened landscape and an over-engineered stormwater system? Increased flooding, dropping water tables, impoverished ecosystems, less diverse visual environments, and worst of all, a deadening of the public's perception of where they are in relation to the natural world.

Let us reexamine the path of this water droplet and suggest what might be done differently to remedy the situation. First, runoff from the roof might be directed into planter beds or porous, gravel-filled dry wells so as much rainwater as possible returns to the soil very near where it fell. Second, the water that does run off can be conducted along open drainage swales resembling intermittent stream channels, which can be planted with native plants and intermittently dammed by small weirs, thereby creating percolation ponds, habitats for birds, frogs, beneficial insects, and other formerly resident wildlife. Third, larger concentrations of stormwater runoff can be directed to larger overflow areas, retention ponds, and constructed wetlands. These can provide shelter and forage for fish, aquatic and migratory birds, small mammals, and

West Davis Ponds. What was once a bare, trapezoidal storm water basin is now also a managed wetland wildlife habitat and well-loved local spot for bird watching and strolling. Since the reconfiguration of the ponds, adjacent property values have increased sharply.

other typical ephemeral wetland organisms, and may also double as basins for groundwater recharge.

One hundred yards to the north of the office where I am writing this book is such a retention pond. Once a crudely engineered, flat-bottomed stormwater basin, the West Davis Ponds have been skilfully designed, recontoured and planted with native plants. While the total flood storage capacity remains unchanged, a small, residual amount of water is kept year round in the organically patterned, contoured basin floor of islands, deeper pools, and narrow channels. After typical rain storms, the water level rises to temporarily flood shallow mud flats, later receding back down to the level of permanent water storage elevation as water evaporates, transpires, or percolates away. In the three years since its reconfiguration, the West Davis Ponds have attracted a rich population of Canada Geese, Avocets, Black-necked Stilts, Great White and Snowy Egrets, Blue Herons, Green Herons, Night Herons, Harriers, Burrowing Owls, Mallards, Coots, Kildeer, Muskrats, Jackrabbits, Mice, and countless other species. What was once a dreary and forgotten void is now alive with life, ringed by observation decks, and accessed by bicycle and pedestrian paths.

By bringing the urban stormwater system back to the surface of our landscapes, we literally bring our communities back to life. To do so still requires skilled, creative engineering and a concern for runoff water quality, of course. But by weaving the ecological structure and function of the micro- and meso-scale watershed back into our neighborhoods, we are able not only to reinforce the community of humans, but also to rebuild the wider and truer community of all living creatures, many of whom had long since fled the hardened, sterile worlds which we had unfortunately created for ourselves. Among all the living systems discussed in this chapter, the stormwater system offers us perhaps the easiest and most direct path away from a technological fixation toward a more sustainable, ecologically vibrant landscape.

Energy Supply, Use, and Conservation

Our current addiction to vertical, nonrenewable energy is, of necessity, only temporary. Soon we will have consumed all of the principal in the time-deposited "bank account" of fossil fuels, and we will be forced to reconfigure our landscapes to take advantage of solar energy, which arrives in finite, limited quantity and is distributed over the entire Earth's surface. The idea that we may merely switch from fossil to solar energy without affecting our extravagant lifestyles or existing economic structures is an illusion. There is only one, real, possible future energy policy; one that emphasizes conservation, utilizes solar energy, and respects the essential fact that most of the solar energy falling on the earth must be used to drive essential, earthly life-support systems.

Looking at our typically "developed" landscapes, however, gives us many clues as to where to start implementing this meritorious energy policy choice. The millions of acres of rooftops and parking lots now covering the land offer us immense opportunity for solar collection. These surfaces now operate as thermally inefficient structures, and serve only to create "urban heat islands" during hot summers when we do not need additional heat. By directly harvesting solar energy falling on built surfaces through the use of passive, direct-gain windows in winter, solar photovoltaic electricity in summer, direct heating of water for domestic, industrial, space heating, and other uses, and by harvesting less direct forms of solar energy (wind, ocean currents, etc.) we will be creating a much more purposeful, efficient, and sustainable urban landscape.

We all know how hot the car gets in the shopping center parking lot in summer (and we all know how many cars are parked in the shopping center parking lots in summer!). Imagine if we could capture that energy, turn it directly and benignly into electricity to run our air conditioners and other "essential" appliances. We can. Here is one instance where we only need to employ the ample solar and wind energy technologies already in existence; employ the utmost in energy conservation behaviors and techniques; tie these solar systems into a greater integration of living systems, and give ourselves the necessary visual *permission* to reconfigure our community landscapes to effectively harvest this energy. Under these conditions a sustainable energy landscape becomes entirely possible. Although our lifestyles will change accordingly and must reduce the amount of energy expended per person per year, there is currently enough wastage of energy and enough potential solar energy to provide us with a more than adequate level of comfort and convenience.

There will inevitably be impediments to such a radical shift toward a sustainable, solar energy-based living system, the most obvious of which is the artificially low price of oil, which does not take into account either its finite supply or its devastating global and local environmental impacts. Transitional phases will be needed before we can restructure our energy living systems along sustainable lines: a restructured economic system with accurate price signals reflecting environmental realities and constraints; a revamped energy delivery system which may first substitute cleaner natural gas for "dirty" gasoline before finally using hydrogen as the cleanest means of dispersing and delivering solar energy; and most importantly, an enlightened human value system which comes to terms with both the true need for energy and the necessity of conserving it. Ultimately we must overcome our extreme guilt and begin to accept personal responsibility for the environmental impacts of the energy we personally consume. For a society steeped in environmental guilt,

Sustainable energy at work. Direct solar energy (sunlight) is heating this passive solar house in Davis, California.

NIMBY, and having our cake and eating it too, this is the most difficult transition we face.

A significant number of changes can be made to one's home, simply and without great effort or expense, but with significant results. Our family lives in a solar house, where the interior is heated directly by an architectural sunspace in winter, and cooled by the natural drop in summer air temperatures at night. Our domestic water is preheated by solar collectors on the roof. We own one car, and ride bicycles or walk to work and back virtually every day. We often tow our bicycle cart to the market for food. We have installed the long-life, low-energy, high-output compact fluorescent light fixtures throughout our house. With these types of techniques and a constant level of energy awareness for turning out lights, driving the car a bit less, taking the bus and train occasionally, we are able to consume half the energy of the typical California residents, yet I would hardly describe our lifestyle as deprived, nor our house or landscape as uncomfortable or ugly.

The ability to reconfigure energy landscapes and living systems toward sustainability will go a long way toward making people feel less threatened by technology in general and less in need of covering up their energy technologies or putting them in someone else's back yard.

Transportation and Circulation

With simultaneous addictions to both motion and individual self-determination, Americans have structured their current landscape around the automobile—the "random access, personal privacy, self-expression" mode of transportation. No other technology captures the essence of the American persona so effectively as the car. Using fossil fuel, it has allowed us each to create our own, vast, decentralized network of home, job, social activity, essential (and frivolous) shopping, recreation, and worship. With the automobile, none of these venues of modern life need be located close together. Consequently, we are each "free" to create as large a daily or weekly spatial orbit as the car, cheap gasoline, and lack of traffic jams will allow. Furthermore, we need not allow strangers or "undesirable" social elements to enter our protected, mobile, personal space, and we can listen to music, make deals on the phone, and even watch TV while travelling down the road. It is no wonder that we find the automobile difficult or impossible to give up.

However, to build on a fact Ivan Illich (1974) once pointed out, if we took the real costs of the automobile into account—how long we must work each day to earn the money to pay for the car, its gasoline, repair, storage, and parking—and how long we would have to work each day to pay for our own share of the global and local environmental desecration caused by our cars—it would constitute such a large portion of our available time and potential earnings that we would be better off walking to our destinations.

Fortunately, planners have begun to awaken to the need for a more pedestrian- and bicycle-friendly, transit-dominated, automobile-tamed world. Unfortunately, the public, and especially the real estate developers, are lagging behind. Although certain well-intentioned city planners (e.g., Andreas Duany and Peter Calthorpe) have made sincere attempts to provide neo-traditional and transit-oriented urban development alternatives to suburban auto sprawl, few projects have successfully moved beyond the design stage to serve as models for others to follow. However, the emerging theory is straightforward: provide dense, village-sized neighborhoods with narrow streets, less parking, and full pedestrian access to essential neighborhood services within a 10-minute walk, while locating job opportunities, recreational amenities, and necessary services close together along mass transit corridors connecting these villages. In other words, make it easy, fun, and necessary to walk, while making it slightly more difficult and far less necessary to drive. The results are friendlier and more socially cohesive neighborhoods, cleaner air, less land covered with asphalt, safer streets and play venues for children, and healthier, less sedentary people.

It is possible for these goals to be realized; I live in a neighborhood where where auto use per capita is 40% lower than the average for the rest of our city

Bicycling, walking, rail, and bus systems are the most sustainable transit alternatives worldwide. Davis, California uses renovated London buses and has more bicycles per capita than any other American city. Photograph by Robert Sommer.

(Lenz, 1990). Perhaps the main obstacle in the transition to pedestrian/transit communities is the difficulty in removing Americans from their private cars and placing them next to one another in buses or trolleys at a time when they seem most isolated from each other by electronic media and most fearful of possible interaction with other social groups they perceive as either different or threatening. Perhaps the best we can hope for is that the number of autos per family, the auto miles traveled per person, and the size of the automobile will decrease, the fuel consumption will decrease, and the fuel used (hydrogen, perhaps) will be less environmentally damaging. Even if we could achieve a situation more like that of the Europeans, where cars are smaller, fewer, and more of a luxury used for recreational travel and less for the necessities of everyday living, we will be taking steps toward a more sustainable transportation and circulation system. To do this however, requires not merely changes to the technology itself, but a dramatic reversal of the way we build our community landscapes. Ideally, the two will mutually reinforce each other in the transition; as cars change, so will their requisite landscapes, and vice versa.

Regenerative Industry and Economy

The nineteenth and early twentieth century saw the burgeoning of centralized manufacturing, rapidly accelerating use of fossil fuels and consumption of renewable and nonrenewable resources, and swift transformation of the American landscape first by railroad, then by auto and airplane transportation. The late twentieth century has seen the destruction of physical places by invisible electronic means, the shipping "offshore" of the manufacturing of consumer goods, and the rise of the "service" and "information" sectors of the economy. There is increasing unemployment, yet more Americans are working harder and longer hours than ever before.

For a brief period during America's transition from a manufacturing-based economy to an information/service-based economy, it was possible to entertain the illusion that the condition of the environment would improve because most of us were no longer working in grimy steel mills, coal mines, and polluting factories. This much was true, but we were still *consuming* ever greater quantities of manufactured goods. However, these goods were now being made in foreign countries like Taiwan, Japan, Korea, and Mexico. We had merely exported the immediate environmental consequences of our consumer demand overseas.

Even the illusion that information technology was "clean" has burst and, as discussed in Chapter 8, the negative social and environmental consequences of the so-called Information Age have begun to be felt. The production of semiconductors chips is accompanied by some of the most toxic byproducts known to humanity, and pollution by computer firms such as those located in Silicon Valley is a serious and well-documented problem (Siegel and Markoff, 1985).

The question of paramount importance to the creation of the sustainable landscape is: "What does (or *should*) a sustainable society *do for a living?*" Such a question cannot be answered simplistically or narrowly. The nature of jobs and workplaces will both *respond to* and *help drive* an overall social transformation to a society where quality of life has superseded *quantity* of possessions as the first and best measure of self-worth. Such a transformation, obviously, will not happen overnight. However, several trends mark the beginning of a possible, fundamental restructuring of the economy and, in particular, the nature of work itself (Robertson, 1985):

1. A loss of faith in the myth that only economic growth can produce full employment (unemployment is rising worldwide)
2. An increase in self-employment and persons using home venues for at least part of their work
3. An increase in part-time jobs, job sharing, and cooperatives
4. More people electing early retirement
5. An increase in bioregional affiliation
6. Increased pressure and opportunity to reuse, recycle, and reprocess what were once considered waste products

What is emerging is a vision of a more *regenerative* economy—one in which both the worker's sense of self-worth and job satisfaction is regenerated along with the physical goods, lands, resources, and social institutions involved. An economic structure can only be sustainable if it regenerates order, stability, health, self-worth, social structure, and ecosystem richness and viability.

Although the growth-dominated economic paradigm will be among the last hurdles to be surmounted en route to a sustainable society, there is enough widespread and well-publicized dissatisfaction with the current economic paradigm among economists themselves to mark the beginning of a fundamental structural shift (Boulding, 1968; Costanza, 1991; Daly and Cobb, 1989; Power, 1988).

What will such a shift mean to the new landscapes of industry, economy, and employment? First, there are likely to be more home offices and local neighborhood opportunities for sharing office spaces and support services, although not necessarily with one's industry or professional co-workers. When I began to write this book, my house sustained some freeze damage and was uninhabitable for three months. Being on sabbatical, I was also unable to use my University office. Instead, I rented a small space in a cluster of offices above a local shopping center near the temporary apartment we rented while our house was being repaired. My office was one of many small offices, most used by professionals involved in some information or service sector. My working neighbors included a small jazz radio station, a real estate trade specialist, a civil engineering firm, a grain export broker, a lawyer, a psychologist, and a paper products distributor. Most of us "communicated" with our respective professions and clients by phone and computer, but we shared secretarial and reception services, voice mail, meeting rooms, photocopying, a lounge, and other office amenities. I found it nearly an ideal way to work, since I could avoid the social isolation of the home office while not getting caught up in the daily "politics and interruption" cycles one usually experiences after commuting to a central office. Furthermore, I saved resources by sharing office equipment and by walking five minutes to work. Neighborhood work centers like the one just described may become a salient feature of the new pedestrian villages now being planned.

Other manifestations of a new economic paradigm can be glimpsed in future landscapes: more localized, dispersed service and entertainment facilities such as groceries, day care centers, postal and parcel dispatch sites, neighborhood convenience stores, video rentals, and eating establishments are likely to form the backbone of a movement towards pedestrian-scale neighborhoods. This is not really a new condition, but a return to the logic and efficiency of older urban neighborhoods formed before the days of cheap energy and auto domination.

Communities are also looking toward designating specific "enterprise zones" where businesses based upon reusing, recycling, and remanufacturing are established to reprocess byproducts of local industry. In my region, which is dominated by agriculture, businesses have been established to process rice hulls and walnut shells into useful products, to make ethanol from agricultural wastes, to manufacture fertilizer from sewage sludge, and to produce energy from landfill gases.

While the landscape of industry and employment will evolve very slowly toward sustainability as the dominant economy changes, virtually every community or regional plan offers possibilities to regenerate local physical resources and to develop localized social skills and markets in a more sustainable fashion.

Recreation

The idea that recreation might be a sustainable living system just like the others previously mentioned may strike some readers as peculiar. However, recreation is an essential focus of modern life, and an industry worth many billions of dollars, with tremendous impact on resources and ecosystems. The word *recreation* implies a regeneration or rebuilding. However, the many energy-consuming recreation gadgets we now play with, the thousands of miles we often travel, and the goods we consume in order to relax and refresh our outlook can hardly be considered sustainable. By recreating in these ways, we are consuming some of the earth's "body" to feed our "heads."

It is possible to take a fresh tack by considering recreation from the standpoint of sustainability. Are there ways we can reinvigorate our souls while not destroying the earth? Of course. In one of my university class discussions, a number of us informally proposed a simple index based on the assumption that outdoor exercise was healthful and beneficial and that motorized or resource-consumptive recreation was not, and that the more high-tech equipment one needed, the more resources and energy were consumed and more entropy produced. Our index basically stated that a recreation activity or device could be considered "sustainable" if it resulted in the operator or participant exerting more physical energy during the life cycle of the device than the amount of energy consumed to both manufacture and operate the device. Recreation activities and devices were considered sustainable if this ratio, or index, was greater than one—not sustainable if less than one. Lacking time and in-depth information about life-cycle costs and embodied energy expenditures, we were not able to pursue this line of thought much further. However, I bet that I have spent far more energy staying fit by riding my eight-year-old racing bicycle than the bicycle "cost" in terms of manufacturing or "embodied" energy. In contrast, someone who tows a jet ski behind his car to a distant reservoir every weekend is likely to burn far less energy in body metabolism than that needed to manufacture and operate the car and jet ski.

Of course, such an index is too simplistic, too impatient with motorized recreation aficionados, and too harsh on existing American recreation patterns. But one can easily imagine the kinds of recreation landscapes possible if sustainability is considered an important planning and design consideration. First, the closer to home one recreates, the less fossil fuel one is likely to consume in getting to the recreation site. This makes a case for ensuring ample recreational opportunities close to home through proper regional planning. Perhaps of most importance is planning for *nearby nature* (Kaplan and Kaplan, 1989; Francis, 1987), or for unstructured, nature-based recreational corridors and areas near populated zones. Often we drive for hours to escape the oppression of our built environments, whereas if our built environments were less oppressive to begin with and included some of the qualities we seek in the natural environment, we would be more content recreating in or near our own neighborhoods. For example, the East Bay Regional Park District near Berkeley and Oakland, California places thousands of acres of wildland recreational trails, parks, picnics areas, scenic overlooks, reservoirs, and other amenities within walking and bicycling distance of several million residents, and serves as a stellar example of sustainable recreation planning. As I mentioned in Chapter 2, our technologically driven society has led us to consider our many recreational machines and gadgets as symbols of our affection for land and nature. In some ways, recreational technophilia has built upon and threatens to replace topophilia. If the fishing is lousy we can always go out to the shop and play with our new high-tech, graphite spinning gear. In spite of this trend, there is evidence that recreation may be undergoing a transforma-

The East Bay Regional Park District in northern California places "nearby nature" recreation opportunities within immediate walking and cycling distance of millions of urban residents. The EBRPD significantly reduces the energy which might otherwise be spent travelling to more remote natural recreation sites. Courtesy of the East Bay Regional Park District. Photograph © by Bob Walter.

tion toward more sustainable values. Already the concept of *ecotourism* has emerged, where tourists travel to resorts that are nondestructive of local habitats and that preserve authentic local culture and strive to protect local ecosystems. Ecotourism has risen to become a significant movement within the tourist industry, and resorts are finding that more people consider ecological factors in choosing vacation venues. Finding pool-side sunbathing or pleasure driving meaningless, some recreators will pay to travel to remote sites to volunteer in landscape restoration activities or to aid in the preservation of endangered species (Ocko, 1990).

Travel by train, a more energy-efficient form of transportation than driving, is undergoing a resurgence in the United States. Hydrocarbon, nitrous oxide, and carbon monoxide emissions per passenger mile are lower for passenger train travel than for any other form of motorized transportation (Lowe, 1990). If recreational and passenger trains were to make special concessions for bike-and-train travellers, such as easy and convenient boarding and detraining with bicycles (as is common in Europe), a whole new era of more sustainable recreation travel, even for families, would be feasible.

Living Systems Integration: Case Studies of Sustainable Landscapes

The 12 living systems previously outlined offer a framework for approaching sustainable community planning and design at any scale from the home landscape to the entire region and beyond. A general approach to such community planning can be sketched which:

1. Seeks to build upon a baseline landscape ecology, with minimum disruption to the ecological processes and dynamic equilibria which existed prior to the landscape project or community being developed.
2. Examines each living system by itself in terms of the ecosystems it protects or destabilizes, the technologies it uses, the resources it conserves or wastes, and the behaviors it engenders.
3. Looks for linkages between living systems which make use of output from one system as input for another, and minimizes total entropy and total throughput of materials, water, and energy.
4. Rejects consumptive, destructive, destabilizing technologies in favor of regenerative, sustainable technologies.
5. Nurtures and reinforces social structures and cultures that perpetuate sustainable values and ethical behaviors.
6. Begins to ease the visual/environmental *guilt* inherent in our attitudes toward technology and allows truly sustainable technologies a more visible, respected place *closer to home*.

Even within the suggested living system framework, it is extremely difficult to plan a landscape or community that will achieve a high degree of sustainability within a reasonable length of time. The current growth-oriented economy based on consumption of resources is still the foundation of most of contemporary American society, and carries with it a momentum that resists change. The right of private land owners to develop their own land for their own economic welfare is a deeply held principle of the American political economy. It is also a legal principle frequently upheld by the Supreme Court as constitutional against a number of litigations brought by plaintiffs arguing in favor of a greater, "public" good (Fulton, 1991). Legally sanctioned, private-sector development of land for short-term economic return is the norm in America, and perhaps the single most significant barrier against which any attempt at sustainable development usually seems powerless. Many Americans understandably believe that our landscapes and communities are actually planned by private developers, and in spite of public outcry and supposed protection by mandated local planning, there is little that individuals may do to prevent it.

The discomfort individuals now feel between technology and nature, however, has allowed an alternative landscape model to emerge, made clearer by a new visionary literature and the beginnings of political legitimacy. A problem we now face is a lack of enough tangible landscape examples—enough new symbols of possibility—which can help us resist entrapment by hopelessness, techno-fantasy, electronic simulation, and avoidance of environmental issues. Technological determinism has so thoroughly dominated and molded the American landscape that one must constantly seek out patterns by which living systems and landscapes *can* be assembled and structured in a more sustainable fashion.

Speaking of the relationship between form and a new philosophy, John Lyle asks metaphorically, "Can floating seeds make new forms?" (Lyle, 1989). Many ideas and design concepts now emerging have the potential to guide the form of planning, design, and development in more a sustainable, regenerative direction; they are like seed-kernels of ecological wisdom looking for fertile soil in which to grow. Unfortunately, many projects with immense potential to improve on the status quo are killed by circumstance, entrenched political positions, or changing economic winds. Some never evolve past conceptual design (such as Nance Canyon, discussed further below). Some, like Oregon's Cerro Gordo (Town Forum, Inc., 1982) are planned and partially built, but fail to flourish. Some die altogether. A few take root and thrive long enough to contribute to the process of social change toward sustainability.

Fortunately, although few landscapes live up to the multidimensional promise of sustainability, a number of landscapes fulfil one or more dimensions. The examples described below will hopefully allow the reader to assemble the various pieces of the sustainable community puzzle—renewable energy development, pedestrian emphasis, water conservation, community open space, habitat corridors, and so forth—into a composite image of what might be possible in the next generation of American landscapes.

Harvesting the Wind (Montezuma Hills Windfarm)

Perhaps more than any "new" technology, contemporary wind-generated electrical power plants have evolved to symbolize a new relationship between humans, energy, and land. Wind, of course, has been powering human activity for thousands of years. By the twentieth century, with the exception of the rural windmills of the American west and the rustic windmills of the European low countries, cheap fossil fuel put a temporary halt to the use of wind power. In the late 1970s, favorable political and tax structures fostered the development of the fledgling American wind power industry, with significant advances in turbine design, technical reliability, and siting. The wind turbines now seen as icons in films and commercials are actually quite simple designs: rotor blades attached to 60 cycle per second generators with mechanical or electrical devices that allow for a constant rotation speed over various wind speeds. Mounted on towers or pylons that allow yawing, or swiveling, into and away from the wind, arrays of these turbines are now directly competitive with all other sources of electrical power production (Brower, 1992). At present, many of the world's electric utilities are seriously attempting to site new wind power plants.

The Montezuma Hills, an area of rolling livestock grazing land on the north shore of the Sacramento River in Solano County, California is home to one of America's most environmentally responsible and technically advanced wind farms. Here 350 turbines are arrayed in ordered rows on the tops of the ridges of the hills to harvest the strong and steady winds that blow up from San Francisco and San Pablo Bay via the Sacramento River valley into the great Central Valley of California. The turbines, roads, and other human alterations to the landscape occupy less than 5% of the total land area, allowing the remaining 95% to remain as grazing land for sheep and cattle. Care has been taken to minimize erosion from the grading of tower pads or access roads. While early wind power plants have occasionally resulted in the deaths of foraging raptors, at the Montezuma Hills plant, bird deaths are minimal and pose no threat to population stability.

Electrical power generated from the Montezuma Hills wind plant and others like it has many advantages. It is nearly environmentally benign, and entirely renewable. Rather than driving development, it secures land in perpetual open space for other multiple, compatible uses, such as stock grazing, row crops, or outdoor recreation trails. The wind turbines, however, are highly conspicuous—they must be sited on ridge tops where winds are highest and visibility from the surrounding land is greatest. When the large California wind plants were first established, they caused a portion of the public to react negatively, with a significant minority feeling that the turbines represented a violation of the "rural" landscape character and pastoral beauty. But wind energy's visibility can also be seen as an advantage if functional transparency is valued. With wind energy plants, "what you see is what you get." When the wind blows, turbines spin, and electricity is generated. When the wind doesn't blow, the turbines are idle. This rather direct expression of function serves to reinforce wind energy's sense of landscape appropriateness, clarity, and comprehensibility. In the long run, wind energy will contribute highly to a unique sense of place.

During the early stages of wind energy development, however, not all installations were carefully sited or well maintained, and at times turbines broke down or did not spin when other landscape cues revealed that strong winds were blowing. Abandoned and inoperative turbines became the pivotal public relations problem for the wind industry. As the industry has matured, however, it has begun to realize that the direct, dialectic way by which wind turbines "inform" the viewer is important. Sitting techniques have improved so that turbines are no longer placed in areas of less wind, and inoperative turbines are quickly repaired or replaced. In the final analysis, the public would much rather deal with the forthright visual expression and benign function of a wind farm than worry about what is going on behind the mysterious, 20-foot thick concrete walls of a nuclear reactor (Thayer and Hansen, 1989). The pinwheel-like motion of the new wind plants is a source of playful

The Montezuma Hills Wind Farm in Solano County, California. Wind energy developments such as this offer a renewable, benign source of clean energy while allowing agricultural or open space land uses to continue.

visual interest to many, and fortunately, has become an essential part of wind energy's symbolic status.

The research I have done indicates that the vast majority of citizens of Solano County, California (a fast-growing exurban county) vastly prefer wind energy over fossil fuel and nuclear energy production. As the wind industry has been tried and tested, people have begun to conclude that, while not perfect, wind power represents a better choice than building more nuclear, coal, or gas-fired plants, all of which present much more severe and damaging environmental costs (Thayer and Hansen, 1989).

Tapping fossil fuels allows highly concentrated energy to be used, but at far too fast a rate to be replaced by natural processes. Wind energy, on the other hand, is a "horizontal" energy source; wind energy can only be harvested by humans in the here and now, and so, like hydroelectric energy, there is a natural limit on the amount of energy per land area which can be harvested. Planners estimate that California and the United States as a whole have enough lands suitable for wind energy development—areas of constant, strong wind away from scenic or sensitive ecological areas—to provide about 10% of the current amount of electrical energy needed in the United States (Gipe, 1991). Wind energy now provides about 1% of California's electrical power. Wind power plants secure multiple-use open space from other development, occupy less than 5% of the land surface taken, and transparently communicate the benefits of horizontal energy. By doing so, wind energy represents and embodies a shift in the relationship between landscape and technology, with positive implications for energy policy and long-term sustainability.

Conservation, of course, is still the most important national energy policy we must establish; the Montezuma Hills wind plant, however, represents an energy technology on the land which serves rather than dominates humankind.

Reinventing the Suburbs (Laguna West)

As the environmental sins of automobilia become more and more evident, a groundswell of enthusiasm has developed among planners for rethinking suburban sprawl. Most of this enthusiasm centers on a general set of principles previously described and ultimately aimed at weaning people away from the automobile: denser neighborhoods centered around light rail or mass transit, humanized, pedestrian-friendly streets, and a mixture of shops, offices, schools, and day care centers within a quarter-mile radius. Foremost among the designers of such alternative, postsuburban communities are Peter Calthorpe of San Francisco and Andres Duany and Elizabeth Plater-Zyberk (DPZ Architects) of Miami. DPZ's's master plans often resemble clusters of nineteenth century villages, which Duany and Plater-Zyberk call TNDs (traditional neighborhood developments). An avowed historicist, Duany relies heavily on traditional architectural forms, narrow streets, and a return to the geometric grids of the nineteenth century town centers. Cul-de-sac streets, in Duany's view, are "dead worms"—symbols of auto-dominated decadence and a loss of traditional community.

Calthorpe's concepts, which he calls "pedestrian pockets," although less wedded to the grid and to traditional-period architecture, are also dense, transit-oriented, mixed-use developments with narrow, pedestrian-friendly streets. Central to the pedestrian pocket concept is the intent to provide a level of amenity and convenience in all departments of life—employment, school, day care, grocery stores, and recreation all within immediate walking distance and linked to other such pockets by mass transit. Calthorpe points out that 75% of suburban auto trips are noncommuter trips, and by "capturing" local trips via other circulation means such as biking or walking, the automobile beast can be effectively tamed.

Calthorpe's ideas were seized upon by developer Phil Angelides, who hired Calthorpe to design Laguna West, arguably the nations first intentionally and comprehensively designed pedestrian pocket community near Sacramento, California. The project has received much press—almost too much—for it has been unable to live up to the high expectations set for it by all parties involved. However, the community has broken new ground, both literally and figuratively.

The Laguna West plan calls for locating 3300 housing units on 1000 acres surrounding an artificial lake, with a mix of every type of housing, including apartments, town houses, single-family neighborhoods and grandiose "lake front" mansions. A 100-acre town center joins the lake to a retail commercial center abutted by industrial space. Apple Computer selected the site just across the street from the Laguna West Community for its new assembly plant; Apple was impressed with the Laguna West plan and wanted its workers to be able to walk to work. With such a reputable anchor in place, Laguna West can look forward to attracting the other office, commercial, industrial, and retail businesses that might allow it to live up to its much-heralded status as a complete community in microcosm.

However, for being a prototypic "pedestrian pocket," the project leaves much to be desired. Although the streets are narrower than most suburban communities, the plan still decidedly favors the automobile. With few exceptions, traditional sidewalks (many of them fairly narrow) share automobile corridors as the primary means for walking about in the community, making the danger of children crossing the street little better than in the average community (in contrast to Village Homes, described below). A look at the pedestrian system reveals that the pedestrian connections still play second fiddle to the automobile system as the formative skeleton of the community. The siting of housing around an artificial lake (the subdivider's standard attraction, even in semiarid, drought-stricken California) has the effect of further diluting the pedestrian quality of Calthorpe's original pedestrian pocket purity. Furthermore, the lake is shaped like the leftover dough sheet after all of the cookies are stamped out, with no identifiable character at all. Although the lake will serve as a stormwater receptacle and source of landscape irrigation water, its location, shape, and shoreline character make it more of a sales gimmick and less of a recreational or ecological amenity.

Some of the development's housing is a modestly successful attempt at curing suburbia's ills: narrower streets; homes sited closer to the streets with less wasted front yard space; rear garage alleys and plenty of shade trees. These features indeed breathe fresh air into the stale automobile sprawl we have come to expect. But Laguna West is also to have its share of conspicuous consumption; a "Street of Dreams" demo by custom home builders features houses of 3000–4600 square feet, each built on lake-side lots and each with a three-car garage.

While Sacramento Regional Transit's Light Rail system is unlikely to extend southward to connect with Laguna West for some time, the Laguna West Town Center is designed as a Regional Transit bus layover facility, and buses have now begun to run between the Laguna West development and downtown Sacramento.

As with any innovation in community design and planning, Calthorpe's original pedestrian pocket concept was considerably watered down by the

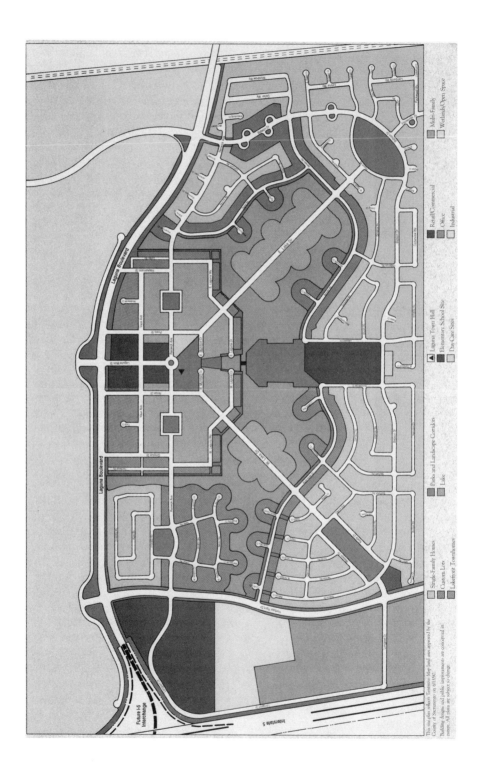

Residential streets in Laguna West are narrower and houses are placed closer to the street, creating a more intimate urban feeling with higher density and less wasted space. This configuration will result in calmer auto traffic and more pedestrian "control" of the tempo of the street.

expected resistance of the plan approval process and by the economic and political realities of development. The developer, Phil Angelides, should receive much credit for being willing to change the plan for the better; he had already received approval for a more traditional suburban development on the site, yet chose to spend the considerable extra funds necessary to revise the plan along Calthorpe's ideas. In spite of its failure to live up to the full potential of the pedestrian pocket concept, as the pioneering attempt at the concept, Laguna West is a step forward in making suburbia more sustainable. By upping the ante for developers concerned with auto and transit issues, Laguna West will continue to be an important laboratory for learning how to shed the tyranny of automobilia in working and reworking American communities.

The approved plan for Laguna West shows the town center (upper center) with retail/commercial areas, a town hall, and central plaza connected to a park (center) and elementary school site (lower center) by a pedestrian landscape corridor across the artificial lake. Multifamily housing surrounds the town center and occupies the islands, while larger custom homes and townhomes ring the "lake." An Apple Computer facility has located just across Laguna Boulevard (top) from the town center. Plan courtesy of River West Developments, Sacramento.

Planning Around Mass Transit (Del Norte Place Transit Village)

While considerable attention has focused on building new communities which reduce auto dependence, opportunities abound in existing cities and suburbs to create "transit villages" which place high-density housing, offices, shopping, and service amenities all within walking distance of established mass transit lines. The Eastern U.S. has lead the way in the use of mass transit as an organizing principle for high-density urban development. Western U.S. cities, however, have been slow to adopt mass transit, and even slower to accept the concept of planning high-density residential projects near transit stops. Northern California's suburban communities have traditionally spurned high-density residential projects, and the Bay Area Rapid Transit (BART) system, completed in 1972, had continually rejected proposals for housing near its stations, favoring instead plans to develop stations as commercial centers which would provide employment.

Recently, the BART Board of Directors has admitted the failure of this policy (McCloud, 1992). With increasing highway gridlock and overloaded suburban arterials, both BART and several of the suburban communities it services have begun to plan more complete mixed use developments near BART stations, with high density housing reaching nearly 50 units per acre in some instances.

Del Norte Place is just such a project. Designed by San Francisco architects Sandy & Babcock for the Ibex investment group and the City of El Cerrito Redevelopment Agency, the 35 unit-per-acre, four-story project is one block from the El Cerrito Del Norte BART station and directly adjacent to the elevated BART lines, and consists of 135 units of apartments on the higher floors, with street level floor space containing a mix of retail and commercial uses, including a grocery store, offices, restaurants, and a health clinic. Parking for 175 cars is placed under the adjacent, elevated BART superstructure.

About a third of the Del Norte Place apartments are occupied by seniors, while twelve percent of the occupants are students. Twenty seven units are set aside for low to moderate income households. Half of the occupants commute to work or school regularly on BART, while 71% use BART routinely for local trips within the Bay Area (Stewart, 1993).

The project has served as a catalyst—the first of its kind to mix high density housing and commercial uses so close to any BART station. As of this writing, the Del Norte Place project appears as a conspicuous gamble, contrasting with the somewhat deteriorated surroundings in an optimistic gesture of confidence that the area will develop into a *bona fide* transit village. That optimism seems to be paying off. The El Cerrito Redevelopment agency is now negotiating with other developers to provide 92 units of high-density condominums on the parcel between Del Norte Place and the BART station, and BART itself is planning a 210 unit residential project in addition to other mixed uses on the station property itself. Although the area around Del Norte Station is also adjacent to a freeway and a heavily used arterial boulevard which parallel the

The makings of a transit village. Del Norte Place, a mixed use development including commercial space, offices, and high-density multi-family housing, adjoins the Bay Area Rapid Transit lines in El Cerrito, California. The Ohlone Greenbelt bikeway (in the lower right shadows of the BART line) connects the project to nearby parks, coastal access, schools, and shopping.

BART tracks, it is also accessible via the Ohlone Greenbelt, a bicycle corridor leading to parks and nearby coastal open space accesses.

In the mass-transit- reticent Western U.S., Del Norte Place is a bellwether of change toward a more sustainable relationship between suburban living and transportation, offering hope that genuine alternatives to auto-dominated sprawl can be coaxed from existing suburban fabric through enlightened planning and redevelopment.

Sustaining a Watershed (Trexler Park)

There are innumerable instances in recent American planning history where development has swallowed up and obliterated the naturally sustaining functions of small watersheds. Land development upstream "hardens" the land surfaces, increasing stormwater runoff volumes and decreasing the time between initial rainfall and peak stream flows. Downstream, water courses are channelized to safely handle the new flood dangers, thereby eliminating their ecological functions altogether.

Trexler Memorial Park in Allentown, Pennsylvania is a small but significant example in the movement to regenerate our urban watersheds. Little Cedar

Creek, a Pennsylvania State "Class A Wild Stream" with a population of wild brown trout, was being degraded by development as it coursed eastward through Trexler Memorial Park. A stormwater outfall built by the city in the mid-1980s channeled increasing urban runoff into the stream. This urban runoff water arrived sooner than water from the outlying watershed and caused a hydraulic dam effect which eroded the streams banks and removed native vegetation, soil, and a valuable fish spawning habitat. The stream gradually widened, warmed, and became shallower, further degrading conditions necessary for ecological stability as a trout stream.

Andropogon Associates of Philadelphia prepared a master plan for the park which, among other things, reinforced and stabilized the stream bank, detained floodwaters, recharged local groundwater, restored stream side vegetation, and upgraded the aquatic conditions for fisheries. Earth grading created backwater channels and retention basins off-stream to absorb and quiet floodwaters. The principal stream channel was deepened, while floodplain terraces were regraded to resemble their original profile and roughness to retain and absorb water and control erosion. Large, rolled, coco fiber mats called "fiberolls" by their German inventor, Lothar Bestmann, were affixed to the edges of the stream bank with wooden stakes. The coco matting deteriorates slowly and provides an interim substrate for young herbaceous plants. The rolls, which look like 20-foot long sausages, also trap and hold sediment until plants can become established. Fiber carpets of similar coco material were staked up the stream bank from the fiberolls to provide a similar sediment-trapping plant medium.

Through a combination of sensitive site grading, ingeniously low-tech bank and flood plain erosion control methods, skilled choice of native plantings, and good field supervision, Andropogon personnel were able to encourage a colder, swifter, less turbid, and more ecologically rich and productive stream from what once had been a degraded and dying ecosystem.

With examples like Allentown's Trexler Park, Arcata's Wastewater Wildlife Marsh, and the West Davis Ponds, it is possible for any community to gain both clear direction and inspiration to reclaim the ecological integrity and sustainability of the water that courses through its riparian surface and buried pipe "veins." Teams of ecologists, landscape architects, and engineers have now produced enough good examples of success in water conservation, reuse, aquifer recharge, flood control, recreation, and wildlife enhancement that the old, nonsustainable planning methods and overly hardened engineering solutions typical of the last 50 years now seem absurdly unsatisfactory.

Rethinking the Ecology of Materials (Laredo Blueprint Farm)

In the search for examples of sustainable community planning and design, the actual landscapes or built structures found are often like small flecks of gold

(a) *Construction crews place organic fiber rolls as part of the process of creek restoration in Trexler Park, Allentown, Pennsylvania.* (b) *The restored banks and native vegetation have curtailed erosion, cooled and clarified the water, and improved aquatic habitat. Photographs courtesy of Carol Franklin, Andropogon Associates.*

marking a much deeper and richer vein of valuable knowledge and potential. Such is the case with Blueprint Farm in Laredo, Texas and its designer, Pliny Fisk III.

Fisk, with degrees in architecture and landscape architecture, is an original environmental theorist synthesizer of sustainable regional and community planning methods, and an unconventional, yet skilled designer. With his partner and codirector Gail Vittori, Fisk operates the Center for Maximum Potential Building Systems in Austin, Texas or Max Pot, for short. Fisk's calls his guiding conceptual framework for sustainable planning and design "Biommetrics™", which he has registered as a trademark (Fisk and Vittori, 1992). In essence, it is a means of accounting for and guiding the life-cycle flow of materials, resources, and energy needed for human communities from source through process, use, and ultimate recycling, from the global scale down to

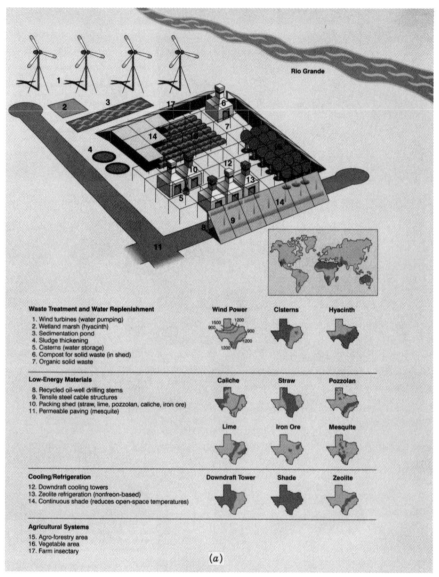

Waste Treatment and Water Replenishment

1. Wind turbines (water pumping)
2. Wetland marsh (hyacinth)
3. Sedimentation pond
4. Sludge thickening
5. Cisterns (water storage)
6. Compost for solid waste (in shed)
7. Organic solid waste

Low-Energy Materials

8. Recycled oil-well drilling stems
9. Tensile steel cable structures
10. Packing shed (straw, lime, pozzolan, caliche, iron ore)
11. Permeable paving (mesquite)

Cooling/Refrigeration

12. Downdraft cooling towers
13. Zeolite refrigeration (nonfreon-based)
14. Continuous shade (reduces open-space temperatures)

Agricultural Systems

15. Agro-forestry area
16. Vegetable area
17. Farm insectary

Wind Power   Cisterns   Hyacinth

Caliche   Straw   Pozzolan

Lime   Iron Ore   Mesquite

Downdraft Tower   Shade   Zeolite

(a)

(a) *Pliny Fisk mapped available building materials and technologies and incorporated this analysis with more traditional planning parameters to arrive at his design for Blueprint Farm near Laredo, Texas. Fisk's latest planning methods include a graphic icon-based "accounting" system which identifies regionally appropriate materials and sustainable technologies. Reprinted by permission (Tilley, 1991).*

the regional, building, and component scales. The process begins by examining a project within its biome, or regional ecological context. Indigenous, original, and recycled materials typically available and commonly used within the biome are identified. Then, using a graphic icon-based system of design symbols, the optimum interrelationships between the various materials, environmental constraints, and opportunities for recycling and regenerative industry are synthesized and illustrated. In this fashion, Fisk extends the visible parameters of his architecture or planning projects into the entire life-cycle accounting of the materials essential to human communities—a kind of visual, accounting system for regenerative materials.

Fisk advocates a new view of technology as "industrial metabolism" and "industrial ecology." In his view, industrial processes are considered as both essential to human activity and a necessary part of the design challenge. Where Fisk departs from tradition is his determination that the source, manufacture, transport, installation, management, byproducts, reuse, and recycling of materials be constrained to the ecological limits and potentials of the biome, region, and local community. Fisk intends for Biom-metrics™ to replace the narrow, microeconomic view of manufacturing. Using the maxim that the best scale at which material life cycles can be integrated with ecological constraints is the smallest, Fisk and Vittori have recently expanded the City of Austin's energy conservation program into a more comprehensive ecological accounting system for water, waste, and building materials as well as energy.

Blueprint Farm is where Fisk's ideas of ecologically based material flows, recycling, regional economic development, ecological architecture, and sustainable building strategies have taken form on the land. Fisk and Vittori have mapped not only expected physiographic factors like climatic conditions, geological formations, vegetation, and hydrological patterns, but have also included in their spatial analysis sources of virgin and waste materials, natural cooling potentials, agricultural crops, byproducts, and low-energy materials. Sitting on the cusp between southwestern desert and prairie grassland, Blueprint Farm sought to optimize climate control strategies for both building and farming through ingenious use of shading, natural building ventilation, and recycled materials. A fabric shade structure over the growing plots squeezes an extra summer growing season from the otherwise too hot and bright south Texas climate. Wind turbines provide electrical power to the remote site, while scarce rainwater is captured in cisterns. Wastewater is used and reused, and processed on site by natural means, including a sedimentation pond and natural wetland marsh (Tilley, 1991).

Much of the building utilized salvaged local materials, including recycled bits of old steel oil-well drilling rigs. Every material, whether original or recycled, was selected by carefully analyzing its role in a greater biome-based ecosystem. For example, aluminum was avoided for its high embodied energy and remote origins. Hay bales from the surrounding grassland biome became fillers for stuccoed curtain walls on the Farm's five simple buildings. Flyash, a

(b) *Prototype shed buildings at Blueprint Farm are made from local straw bales covered with sprayed on cement. An awning reduces summer daytime temperatures by 10 to 15 degrees, while downdraft towers provide natural cooling. Photograph courtesy of Pliny Fisk, III.*

discarded byproduct of the local coal-mining industry, was used as part of the building stucco surface material. Flyash, when mixed with lime slag, another coal-processing by-product, produces a concrete which is as strong, yet cheaper and far less energy-intensive than typical cement concrete. Corrugated metal towers with water-dampened intake pads provided the buildings with natural thermosiphon cooling—a system indigenous to Iran (which occupies a biome similar to that of Laredo).

As a demonstration project, Blueprint Farm has been constrained by political changes in sponsorship. However, the ideas embodied in Blueprint Farm—architectural regionalism, sustainable planning and design, life cycle consideration of material flows, economic development which matches local material sources with local processes and uses, and ecological constraints on material choices—are too important to be ignored. They will no doubt resurface in future projects by Max Pot and others who realize the need for a revolutionary view of industrial technology and ecology which, in Fisk's words, "breaks down the artificial boundary between technology and nature that we have managed to create" (Fisk and Vittori, 1991). With his attempt to weld the processes and flows of materials for building human communities with the constraints inherent in natural communities, Fisk is a pioneer in the resolution of the nature–technology conflict.

Living in a Solar Community (Village Homes)

Perhaps more than any other example, the community of Village Homes in Davis, California represents a convergence of several dimensions of sustainability in one 70-acre landscape. First conceived by Mike and Judy Corbett in 1973, Village Homes broke ground in 1976. Much has been written about this community of 220 clustered solar homes, naturally drained open space, community gardens, orchards, and vineyards. My wife and I both moved into Village Homes as singles in 1976, were married in 1980, and have lived here ever since. This book has been written from the second floor window of our study, looking out at the neighbors' sun rooms, solar collectors, vegetable gardens, and our commonly owned, natural drainage open space.

Every conceivable type of solar house has been built here (Bainbridge et al., 1979), from small passive solar cottages with little more than good south-facing glass and ample insulation, to sophisticated, hybridized, active–passive solar homes that use air or water as a heat storage and dispersal medium for both winter heating and summer cooling. My friend and neighbor Jim Zanetto is an architect and the owner of what is undoubtedly the most energy efficient house in Village Homes, the City of Davis, or our entire county. It is an earth-sheltered, 1110-square foot house, with thick earth berms against the east and west walls, and eight inches of soil on the waterproofed roof. His landscape is entirely planted in drip-irrigated California native or similarly water-efficient Mediterranean plants, with the exception of table-grape vines on a trellis over his south facade and blackberry vines growing in his front yard. I frequently take visitors to Village Homes on walking tours up the stairs to Jim's rooftop, where drought-tolerant groundcovers and low shrubs grow in the shallow soil. Two things are revealing about the Zanetto house—first, it can barely be detected from the air because of it's vegetal roof and walls, thereby totally minimizing its contribution to the urban "heat island" effect. Second, since it is buffered from the extreme daily changes in the local summer temperature (typically from 65 in the morning to 100 or greater in the afternoon) by the native soil, it requires very little heating and no air-conditioning energy. Jim is proud of the fact that he has never paid one penny to the local utility company for energy to heat or cool his house. On the very rare occasions he has needed

Village Homes in Davis, California combines a number of sustainable systems in one community. This aerial view shows solar houses, narrow streets, common open spaces, pedestrian/bike paths, community orchards, and vineyards. Photograph by Mike Corbett.

supplemental heating in our generally mild winter, he feeds a few construction wood scraps he gathers into his tiny parlor stove. With its solar orientation and earth sheltering, native, drought tolerant, and food-producing plants, the Zanetto house presents the pinnacle of sustainable housing.

Although all the houses in Village Homes face due south as if in reverent respect to the sun, the variability of housing types and the undulating east–west streets and pedestrian paths give the site plan a refreshing variety. Houses rest on tiny private lots. Each group of eight households owns a contiguous "common area" away from the street, which might typically contain a small grassy area, fire pit, toddler's play area, vegetable gardens, fruit trees, and percolation ponds for storm runoff. A third category of land ownership is the "greenbelt"—jointly owned by all 220 households, which includes a solar community center building and swimming pool complex, central play field, large orchards, vineyards, playground, garden center, and many acres of community garden plots available to any resident without charge (there is a homeowner's fee which pays for a generally organic landscape maintenance regime, pool upkeep, and other community maintenance). Open spaces are planted in many fruit and nut trees. Delineation of where private, common area, and greenbelt land ownership ends or begins is unclear to the visitor, and, unfortunately, people will often "cruise" through the community picking the ample fruit, thinking that the lack of fences or other spatial delineation implies that it is public domain.

Circulation to, from, and about Village Homes is dominated by the bicycle–pedestrian paths. The Corbetts deliberately designed Village Homes to make it easier to visit between houses by walking or biking than by driving. Also, there is a policy that houses maintain a transparent boundary between private lots and common areas. Opaque fences are discouraged,—maximizing the chance encounters and conversations with one's neighbors that build a sense of community far beyond that of most fenced American suburbs. Streets are all dead-end cul de sacs, most with pedestrian connections, and those people attempting to drive fast into, out of, or through the community are yelled to a stop by neighbors highly protective of their pedestrian dominance. Consequently, Village Homes is a pedestrian paradise, and a safe haven for children who want to

Architect Jim Zanetto's earth-sheltered solar house in Village Homes. Native and drought-tolerant plants on earth-covered walls and roof help stabilize the interior temperature in summer, while sun heats the house in winter.

visit friends in the Village. The innate pedestrian safety enables parents to allow their children nearly free reign within Village Homes. Because of this, children have great social access to one another, and form congenial bands of playmates who, at times, seem like they are being raised communally.

The pedestrian and bicycle paths lend themselves to evening strolls, toddler bicycle training, roller skating, and lemonade stands, while the greenbelt open spaces and common areas facilitate much social interaction. Our house is one of 20 or so within a stone's throw of a football-field size chunk of greenbelt. On spring and summer weekends, a resident may put up the red "potluck" flag, and neighbors come flocking out of their houses with various dishes and sit on the lawn, picnic-style, for dinner and socializing. Evening potluck attendance in our greenbelt typically numbers between 20 and 60, and usually features the children and teens bolting their food and quickly organizing into pick-up stickball or soccer games. Even the neighborhood dogs have come to establish their own hierarchy and play patterns, with amazingly few dogfights. Neighborhood "pooper-scoopers" are made available by some residents and used by all.

My wife and I realize that we might never achieve this kind of neighborhood quality and sense of community in any other location. Most of our best friends live in our neighborhood, and we know a large portion of the Village Home residents by name and most everyone at least by sight. Our three children (10, 10, and 12 years old) also recognize the quality of their neighborhood, and steadfastly inform us that we are *never* to move away (not even for a year's sabbatical!)

In addition to taming the automobile and saving household energy, Village Homes has a highly successful open or "natural" drainage system. Instead of buried storm drains, frequent curb cuts in the streets empty water into common area swales interrupted by numerous check dams or weirs. This system allows winter stormwater to collect and percolate into the local soil profile and allows an ephemeral riparian planting regime to take hold. After rains, the retention ponds fill up, but percolate down within a matter of hours. Combined with the general deemphasis on chemical herbicides and pesticides, the open drainage system allows for a rich ecological diversity—there are toads, lady beetles, owls, doves, mockingbirds, kildeer, cedar waxwings, crows, magpies, owls, and numerous flocks of migratory birds which visit each year, and an occasional resident possum or skunk. The open drainage system is a haven for small children who enjoy the ability to directly interact with the water, sand, and mud. In summer, when the rains have gone, many percolation ponds double as sandboxes and excavation sites for toy trucks and sandcastles. Other percolation zones are in lawns, and allow shady venues for camping out under the stars.

A large portion of the Village Homes landscape is "edible." Homeowners grow food in front yards, common areas, and the community-wide garden plots. Instead of an ornamental landscape buffer on the adjacent city street, Village Homes has a working almond orchard. A community agricultural

The natural drainage system of Village Homes allows storm water to collect behind small weirs (a) *and percolate into the soil in small, temporary ponds* (b). *Open drainage systems can reduce site development material costs, improve habitat, add visual diversity and provide places for children to experience nature firsthand.*

board guides who grows and harvests what and when. Community members may pick the fruit and nut crops without charge. Compost piles abound, and weeds are tolerated to a degree unheard of in more typical, manicured American subdivisions. Research by former UC Davis graduate student Thomas Lenz shows that Village Homes residents use 36% less energy for vehicular driving, 47% less electricity and 31% less natural gas per household, grow a higher percentage of their own food, and have more close friends in their neighborhood than a conventional neighborhood control group in Davis (Lenz, 1990).

Village Homes, of course, is not *absolutely* sustainable. Most residents own two cars per family, buy food at grocery stores, have VCRs, and otherwise behave like typical American suburbanites. Homes range in size from small 600 square foot attached units to 3000 square foot luxury homes, often mixed together on the same streets. Some neighbors use too much water, some own too many cars, and some leave too many lights on. Some don't choose to take advantage of the potential for community interaction. By its very design, however, Village Homes encourages its residents toward sustainable behavior in energy use, food production, water management, pedestrian and bicycle transportation, maintenance of wildlife habitat, commuting habits, and overall community interaction.

To me, perhaps the most significant attribute of Village Homes is the ability to live in a community whose values are so closely intertwined with my

A community almond harvest in Village Homes. This productive almond orchard doubles as the "ornamental" street landscape. Photograph by Mike Corbett.

Work parties have constructed many of the landscape features of Village Homes. Here residents plant shade trees near a future playground. Photograph by Mike Corbett.

research, teaching, professional practice, and lifestyle. I acknowledge that most American families may not share our luck in being able to get by with one car, ride bikes or walk to work, and live in such an environmentally visionary and socially fulfilling community. Few developers have had the courage to try to duplicate the successful, sustainable features of Village Homes. However, Village Homes has enabled me to integrate work, philosophy, recreation, and family values. It is fair to say that had I not moved here 17 years ago, this book would not exist.

Putting the Pieces Together

I am often asked why there are not more places like Village Homes, where pieces of the sustainable solution begin to fit together. It is a difficult question which eludes simple answers. Village Homes resulted from a convergence of the right people, the right place, the right time, and the right economic and political conditions. This type of convergence happens very infrequently. The metaphoric "floating seeds" to which John Lyle (1989) refers do not often find fertile ground in the entrenched political, economic, and technical realities of everyday life. Traditional land development patterns, although often insensitive to ecological systems and long-term environmental effects, have worked well enough to respond to short-term market demands, meet basic and immediate public needs, and provide steady profitability for developers. Change involves risks that most people are unwilling to take. We have based our communities on automotive technology, cheap energy, and resource waste for so long that change toward sustainability requires the major readjustment of most of our social institutions. Philosophical acceptance of the need for "sustainability"—or something just like it—is the greatest risk of all.

Nance Canyon

Occasionally, conditions seem to evolve where movement toward integrated, sustainable development seems possible. In 1990 our firm assisted DPZ Architects in the planning for Nance Canyon, a proposed sustainable new town on a 6500-acre low-foothill site in Butte County near Chico, California (Thayer, 1991). From the outset, the owners and potential developers of the site committed themselves to produce the most environmentally responsible town plan possible. The site lay on poor soil unsuitable for agriculture, yet it abutted a major highway and an unused railroad right-of-way. An extensive, open charrette process brought together planners, environmental consultants, engineers, clients, county representatives, opposition groups, and potential builders for two weeks of round-the-clock planning and design, punctuated by frequent goal-setting sessions and philosophical debates.

The resultant plan defined eight dense, tightly clustered villages linked together adjacent to a future rail connection to Chico. Five thousand acres were to be placed in permanent open space. Stormwater was to be captured on site, used for wildlife habitat and recreation, and allowed to percolate and evaporate, while all human wastewater was to be treated by constructed wetlands doubling as wildlife habitat, and recycled for use in irrigated landscapes. Architecture and building design was based on solar orientation and passive strategies for climate modification. Housing favored pedestrians and community life. Each neighborhood was designed so that essential services could be reached from all houses within a one-quarter mile radius—a 10-minute walk. The canyon itself, occupying about half of the site, was to be dedicated to the county as a regional park and nature preserve, with a gradient of available recreational opportunities from organized sports and picnicking in the lowlands to a wildlife preserve protected from human entry in the higher elevations.

The economic plan for the project proposed a balance between housing provided and jobs generated on site by "incubating" environmentally based industries and attracting existing "clean" industry. A site for an auxiliary research campus was offered to Chico State University. Since the Nance Can-

The plan for Nance Canyon, a proposed, sustainable new community in Butte County near Chico, California called for dense pedestrian-oriented villages, on-site storm water and wastewater treatment, and the preservation of three-quarters of the site in open space. Drawing © courtesy of DPZ Architects, Miami.

yon town site also abutted a near-capacity county landfill, our firm proposed the establishment of a "Regenerative Industrial Park" adjacent to the landfill site. Our proposal suggested new industries that could be developed based on long-term material recovery and reprocessing to provide local employment, and included production of methane from the landfill and from sewage sludge produced on site. We also proposed the production of solar-photovoltaic energy to produce hydrogen for future vehicular and transportation use. Since thousands of volcanic rocks peppered the surface of the site, we also proposed a small-scale rock and crushed gravel enterprise for processing the boulders gathered from construction sites for resale and redistribution to local home buyers and businesses as a landscape rock for retaining walls and walkways.

Had Nance Canyon been built as planned, it might have been the foremost example of integrated sustainable community planning and design in North America. However, the severe 1991–1992 recession forced the developers to abandon the project after investing hundreds of thousands of dollars in the planning process.

Nance Canyon has had its positive impact however. Those involved in the process came away convinced that fundamental change toward sustainable development was not only necessary, but possible, and closer to reality than many of us had thought. We had brought our concern and expertise together to form a clear vision of future possibilities—a vision where all living systems were woven together in a new standard for sustainable community development and a new phase in the relationship between nature and technology as it is revealed on the land.

A Growing Vision

The vision of an expanded sense of community among humans, ecosystems, resources, and technologies is more possible, necessary, and urgent than ever before. However inevitable this growing vision may seem, it requires deliberate articulation. Before sustainable patterns spread across society and into the landscape, they must willfully occur at specific *places* upon it. Before sustainable principles are embodied in a physical place, they must coalesce as a vision in the mind. What *could* the landscape be like if we are even modestly successful at incorporating this difficult but necessary concept of sustainability?

I close this chapter by offering a personal vision of what could be. Although I have criticized the excesses of fantasy in previous chapters, I reiterate my contention that fantasy is only as beneficial as the reality it can inform, enrich, and improve. Today, our unsustainable relationships between nature and technology need considerable improvement. Please join me in a constructive and necessary fantasy, as I take an optimistic look at where *I* hope to be— and the kind of landscape I hope to be in—nearly 40 years hence.

. . . Bless her gray-haired soul. For my 83rd birthday, Lacey arranged this shuttle trip with our friends to Cold Canyon Nature Reserve in our home region of Yolo County. For a couple of hours, 12 of us seniors shuffled up and down the dirt trail, aiming our binoculars at a coyote, three eagles, two Peregrine falcons, and numerous other species of birds who have returned to this area in the past few decades. 2030 has been another good year for birding, and all of us feel grateful for these harbingers of a healthy environment. Although Lacey and I have ridden our bicycles these 16 miles from our home in Davis countless times, I'm content to let this hydrogen-powered shuttle carry my old body here and back in the congenial company of our surviving friends. Ready for a rest, we settle into the seats, chatting and gazing out the window as we head onto the road and down the canyon.

I've been asked to speak on campus about the landscape changes that I've witnessed the past 35 years in our region. As the shuttle putts down the road, I'm writing (or scrawling—yes, still using a pencil!) notes for my upcoming talk in this old-fashioned notebook when most folks would bring their electronic notebooks instead—my fingers are just too unsteady to press the keys, and talking into a machine would be unsociable!

Cold Canyon is a part of the Yolo Biodiversity Network, a system of interconnected habitat reserves, buffers, and corridors woven throughout the county from the Coast Range on the west to the Yolo Basin Reserve along the Sacramento River to the east. The Network has evolved slowly since 1995, but now forms the backbone of our natural world here, and ties the diverse parts of our region together with a system of foot, horse, and bike trails, and occasional observation decks and picnic shelters. Thank God for it! As we ride down the Putah Creek Canyon to the plains, the school kids are out in force on this November day. As part of their curriculum, sixth graders take care of the trails, interpretive signs, burrowing owl nests, quail refuges, fish spawning gravels, and so on. Between these youngsters and the "Greenies"—U.S. Environmental Corps workers doing their year of mandatory federal service—the Biodiversity Network is kept in good shape for humans and critters alike.

I'm looking at the sky. It is a fine day—so clear that even I can see the birds without my glasses. My weakening vision has been more than compensated for by the improvement in air quality—it is now so clear that it's mostly taken for granted. Before 2000, the rice growers burned their fields to control fungus, and autos and trucks ran on gasoline. Now agricultural burning is outlawed, and the rice growers that are left no longer burn their fields, but manage them by the "roll-and-flood" method as wildlife habitats. Vehicles burn mostly hydrogen, and the local air quality has improved substantially. In Spring though I still sneeze from the pollen of the willow and cottonwoods which have come charging back along our sloughs and streams.

The roads look a bit different now too. Each lane has a long stain line caused by the water dribbling out of the exhaust pipes of these hydrogen-powered vehicles. They make a strange, quieter, puttering sound unlike that of the old gas-powered piston engines. You still see the old gas guzzlers now and then, but there are fewer of them around. Filling stations mostly sell hydrogen, and natural gas is available for the older "transition" vehicles of the 2010s and 2020s. Occasionally a gasoline pump can be found for the real old clunkers.

I'm not allergic to oaks, fortunately, and the controls on grazing have allowed the Blue and Valley Oaks to return to the foothills in force, bringing with them acorn woodpeckers, ground squirrels, and their associated animal and plant friends. Some cattle still graze on the hillsides, but they are far fewer in number and those wasteful and polluting feedlots are mostly gone now. Range-fed beef has replaced "fat" beef, and is now a specialty entree in most restaurants, more exotic in taste, but much more expensive than the old "hamburger" folks used to eat so much of. I'm looking for evidence of soil erosion on the hillsides, but finding little. I haven't seen nearly as much hillside erosion in the last 15 years or so since the oaks have come back. The ravines are crowded with Live Oak, Toyon, and Manzanita where the highly protected Biodiversity Corridors snake up to the top of Blue Ridge.

We now pass through the small city of Winters on the cusp between the foothills and the great valley. I remember what a tiny town Winters once was—just a few thousand people or so in 1990. Fortunately, much of Winters' growth in last 40 years was handled in a decent fashion; development mostly off the most productive agricultural land; densely packed neighborhoods of townhouses and cohousing away from the floodplains, creek, and sloughs; and most neighborhoods linked directly to the Biodiversity Network and Open Space System by footpaths and trails. With some help from University of California

*Ecological Extension Specialists, Winters has become an
internationally known showcase of agroecology. Long recognized for its
orchard crops, the area is now surrounded by polycultural
combinations of tree, perennial, and mixed annual row crops—all
grown in carefully researched combinations, where each crop plays a
valuable symbiotic role in relation to the others. The interspersed
almonds, apricots, walnuts, soybeans, vegetables, and perennial grains
create an almost musical rhythm out the shuttle window as we pass
by.*

*Winters has also built a thriving regional economy based on
regeneration of orchard and crop wastes. We just passed two small
plants which process agricultural byproducts into ethanol, methane,
natural insect-suppressing mulches, various natural soil amendments,
biodegradable soaps, cleansers, and lotions. Wouldn't have been a bad
place to live, Winters. . .*

*Heading eastward, our shuttle crosses Interstate Transitway 505
near the Winters Station. This was the old six-lane I-505, and now
features Regional Transit light rail lines carved from the old median
and the two innermost car lanes. 505 is typical of most former
interstate highways in the state. Mass transit has finally taken hold,
and auto travel has declined by over half. Hydrogen is a great fuel for
cars, but with the "green" taxes added in, God, is it expensive,
especially on a fixed income. And gasoline? It got so scarce and
expensive, most dealers stopped supplying it as the cars switched over
to cleaner fuels. Lacey and I drive our only car less and less as we get
older—it's so much easier to take the shuttle with our friends or pack
our fold-up bikes on the transitways or railway.*

*As we pass into the flat rich farmland of Yolo County, hawks circle
lazily overhead. The old, monotonous, one-crop agricultural fields of
the 1990s come back to mind, where once you could see for miles
across laser-planed fields with few trees. Skyrocketing fuel costs and
the revelations about pesticides, herbicides, and cancer put a quick end
to this type of farming. Now the line of sight is pleasantly interrupted
by windrows of oak, walnut, and native shrubs with bunch grass verges
to the sides. The fields are further dissected by shrub and perennial
hedgerows and "pin-stripes" of forbs and grasses which serve as
beneficial insect strips for the biological control of crop pests. In
response to the Farm Bill of 2005 and the Agricultural Ecology and*

Farmland Protection Act of 2008, the average county field size has dropped from well over 100 acres to around 40. For a decade or two farmers have received both federal and state subsidies to incorporate windrows, hedgerows, biodiversity corridors, habitat reserves, and integrated pest management strips on their lands. Todays Yolo "farmers" are now really land stewards as well as business folks, and these farms I see out the window now have a patchy, ecologically diverse appearance nothing like those old flat expanses of plowed dirt 30 years ago. I guess in some ways the patterns of agriculture are going backward to the old days—with smaller scale and higher complexity, only with a lot more ecological sophistication this time around.

On the route home we've just gone by John Anderson's "Hedgerow Farms," where the whole agroecology movement first found a definitive style and form back in the early 1990s. It's now a State Historic Site and teaching laboratory for the University as well as a field station for the Greenies and other stewardship groups. One thing you see in the county farmlands these days is **more people.** After the ecological transformation of 2010–2020, farming gained popularity among job seekers. Food stopped being taken for granted in the early 2000s. The computer-overkill of the late 1990's temporarily stalled the manufacturing sector, but compared to some of the trivial occupational pursuits of the old "entertainment era" 20 years ago, rural ecology and farming became more meaningful and sought-after occupations. Two of our children are involved in agroecology right now—one right here in Yolo County.

The most conspicuous change in the rural landscape over the last 30 years is the proliferation of consumer-subscription vegetable and fruit farms. Over half the county's residents buy shares and get their vegetables and fruits delivered weekly to their doors. Some of these farms look as close to paradise gardens as you could imagine, and Lacey "oohs" and "aahs" at them as we go by, craning her neck around and risking a flareup of her arthritis again. Folks are always snapping video shots of the many-colored and textured vegetable rows, small hothouses, neatly organized composting systems, and tidy water-recycling cisterns. I guess there's just something magical about making food in the country that folks have always found irresistibly beautiful.

As we near Davis and Woodland, the county's two biggest cities, I'm thinking of how close they came to merging. Once 10 miles apart, their

borders grew toward one another in the late 1990s, only to be halted
by the Farmland Protection Act and the final political compromise on
the Willow Slough Reserve, an X-shaped biodiversity habitat centered
around the intersection of Willow and Dry Sloughs. Like Winters, all of
the county towns tightened up their housing densities after the axe fell
on future development in productive farmland.

Having entered the Davis city limits, we're now passing through
several cohousing neighborhoods, each with their "common house" and
densely clustered, attached cottages. Just about every type of single,
detached house site plan was tried by developers as they increased
density in response to the mounting environmentalism and steady-state
economy. Finally, they came around to the inevitability of the attached
house as the best environmental solution. Many of the newest parts of
Davis remind me of some of the medieval countryside towns Lacey and
I saw cycling through the English countryside on our honeymoon 50
years ago. Streets have really gotten narrow, and the houses crowd the
street, making it a more pleasant, less dangerous place for us oldsters
and kids alike. Hardly any two-car garages these days, and a lot fewer
cars . . . shuttle lanes, bike lanes, and bike parking take up about half
the existing pavement in town.

Just about every conceivable kind of bicycle and human-powered
vehicle now appears on the streets of Davis: singles, tandems, triples,
quads, two-place pedal cars, pedal cars with convertible tops, combo
pedal and electric commuter vehicles, bikes with trailers, bike pick-up
trucks, bikes that fold into suitcases for traveling on the local trains,
busses, and shuttles. There are even bikes that couple together for
tandem, side-by-side riding. Bikes are now so much lighter than they
were 40 years ago. They are more expensive, too, but nothing
compared to the cost of a large, powered vehicle. Lacey and I have five
different bikes and a pedal vehicle between the two of us—such blatant
consumerism for a couple of old-timers!

Nearly all of the new houses built in Davis since about 2005 are
solar in some way or another. Most of the latest ones have photovoltaic
roof tiles which plug together in modular fashion and hook to a
centralized storage cell in the utility core of the house or apartment.
Larger apartment complexes and commercial buildings with enough
roof area actually sell electricity back to the Pacific Gas and Electric
Company. The Davis Street Tree program, after a long period of
decline, took a more active policy toward cooling house walls and

paved areas with trees in our hot summers, while allowing sun to reach the vital photovoltaic rooftops all year round. The City's Pavement Shading Ordinance, passed 10 years ago, required all parking lots and streets to be 60% shaded (by trees or built elements) within 10 years of construction, or to incorporate some sort of energy-producing feature. Parking lots have now become sources of useful energy, where they once were heat islands. Some developers cover every surface with photovoltaic shade structures, figuring the receipts from producing electricity into their bottom-line building costs. Since photovoltaic electricity became cost effective, urban development has become a major producer of much of the power it consumes.

As the shuttle makes its rounds, I gaze at the older neighborhoods and realize how much they have changed. Protection of farmland has turned most urban development inward. Density has increased greatly, with much more in-fill development, and many "granny flats" tucked into the corners of those huge, older lots. We're considering living in one behind our son's house, starting as early as next year. The 40-year-old, formerly wide streets are now leaner and greener, much of the pavement having been reclaimed for bicycle and shuttle lanes, torn up for shade tree planting strips, or designated for community open space. The bare-asphalt street glare which burned our eyes on summer days years ago is nearly gone as a result of the pressures to densify older neighborhoods, yet make them cooler and more livable.

Hardly any newer home has a large front yard anymore; many townhouse developments feature the Play–Park concept, where cars access housing clusters by way of landscaped community plazas. As "guests" in this pedestrian and recreation-dominated environment, vehicles share the courtyards with kids playing basketball and all the other new games I can barely keep track of. Everyone likes this concept; the plazas are designed for people first; kids can play safely, and old folks can walk down the middle of the street without risking being run over and killed. Car speed limits are 5 mph. Guest parking is outside the multipurpose play courtyards, and speed-limit violating neighbors are yelled to a standstill by angry residents. Not as much parking is needed these days either, since most families only own one powered vehicle.

I'm amazed at the progress in residential street construction too. Streets used to be wide, impervious, and made of asphalt which had to be jackhammered up to get to the buried sewer, water, gas, and electrical lines. Now most low-speed paving in residential areas is porous for increased water infiltration, and is laid dry on subgrades of compacted gravel and crushed, recycled concrete. The new pavers are made in each local region, and interlock like puzzle pieces. They are very light for their strength, being made from of an amazing combination of recycled plastic, fly ash, and reclaimed local soil, all bonded together by a kind of organic, high-strength silicon "glue" made from—of all things—recycled glass.

Utility lines are also modular and arranged in conspicuous, well-designed, prefabricated, covered channels running down the exact middle of the streets. Workers have only to lift the modular channel tops, make the necessary utility repairs, and replace the tops. No fuss, and no jackhammer noise. People also have a sense of how they are hooked into all those technical umbilicals we still depend on—it's all right in the concrete channels in the middle of the street, and any third grader can easily recognize how the water, power, and information arrives at their house. City engineers have even built a demonstration called "The Living Home," where students and citizens can look through transparent walls, pavement, and piping to see how the typical house is linked to the biosphere.

What I find most fascinating about today's new neighborhoods is the extent to which the systems we used to hide are now such an integral part of the architecture—a far cry from the old "environmental guilt" days of screening garbage cans, coloring cable TV pedestals to look like grass, and hiding the electric meter. After years of aimless preoccupation with fantasy, Mickey Mouse, post-structuralism, and whimsy, architects finally figured out that the exterior form of a building ought to respond to the surrounding ecology and climate, and the interior to the social life inside. It's a lot easier to figure out "where we all are" now that roofs aim respectfully south to pick up sunlight, recycling receptacles have proudly come "out of the closet" to replace the old out-of-sight "garbage" cans, and people don't screen antennae anymore. Roofs seem so pleasantly logical—gathering both water and energy for use inside the home. It's even easier to see the damned houses, too, since there are fewer cars in the way!

I guess what was most difficult to finally get through the heads of city officials and developers was the need for all neighborhoods to be connected in some fashion to an open space and wildlife habitat corridor. With all this new high-density development, seniors like me *get to feeling packed in, and if we couldn't take our morning walks out to see the birds, water, trees, and terrain, we'd go crazy (or crazier!) When the new pedestrian-style urban development really took hold in the late 1990s, it took nearly 10 years for landscape architects to get developers to realize how much more critical "nearby nature" had become as a payoff for all that extra density. Finally, they came around.*

Today, in 2030, many neighborhoods of Davis have taken cues from the original drainage plan for Village Homes, and are now linked to the surrounding region by a network of open, natural drainages, much of it existing as part of the city-owned Davis Greenway. In several regions of the city it is possible to walk from one's house along these small surface swales into the naturally draining Greenway and on out to the Yolo Bypass and the Sacramento River, following a path nearly parallel to that taken by a drop of rain rolling from one's roof. These natural drainage corridors have done a great deal to bring our formerly buried and overengineered, urban watershed back to the surface. They remind me of where I am in the natural order— somewhere between the foothills and the river—and it all started with the humble open drainages of Village Homes like those right outside our door.

The shuttle is nearly empty now. We've said our goodbyes, and only Bob and Diane remain on board. They live out east of town now in a retirement community overlooking the edge of the Yolo Basin Reserve. We asked George, who drives the shuttle for the Senior Center, to take us out to Bob and Diane's house. Former residents of Village Homes, they have deeded their house to their son Charlie, and his wife. As the shuttle putters eastward, we pass along the Willow Slough Reserve, where many Swainson's Hawks, once endangered, now perch in readiness for their southern migration, delayed by the beautiful weather we've been having and the abundant prey available amid the reserve's acres of wild habitat. Willow Slough Reserve is a major node in the Yolo Biodiversity Network—a large area of riparian forest, upland, and ephemeral drainage nursed back from former impoverishment and obscurity to serve as a major habitat for birds, amphibians, reptiles, and mammals of the region. It's one of our favorite destinations—a place for local recreators from both Woodland and Davis, who picnic at the shade shelters along the perimeter of the refuge and enjoy the richness of life within from a respectful distance.

We travel eastward past the Davis Regenerative Industry Park, where egrets, herons, geese, canvasbacks, stilts, and avocets share the shallow waters of the wetlands which convert our local, human wastes into a complex food web of plants, microorganisms, and creatures. These multipurpose wetland areas have totally replaced the old, mechanized, "concrete dinosaur" sewage treatment plants across the U.S. It's inconceivable to young people these days how we could have ever wasted that energy, water, and nitrogen without turning it into something desirable in the form of ecological richness or recycled byproducts.

The Regenerative Industrial Park is a sight to see. Once the overflowing county "dump" sight, it is now a beehive of activity, as materials are separated, collected, processed, and converted into a myriad of useful things. For about 10 years now the size of the landfill has actually receded, as "mining" of the formerly buried materials takes place. Organic material is placed into methane generators for conversion to electrical power. At least 10 separate resource recovery industries now are visible at the park, and employees keep the place tidy as can be. Gone are the vast hordes of gulls that once clouded the skies behind those behemoth caterpillar tractors as they mashed discarded refrigerators and lawn chairs into the landfill. Now small conveyor belts feed hoppers of reclaimed materials from drop-off stalls into a large, low building where the material stream is sorted into several smaller streams of different materials. Out of this regenerative complex comes mulch, plastic pellets, shredded wood, alcohol, methane, compost, scrap metals, hydrogen, and electricity. What on earth took us so long to figure these processes out?

We reach our easternmost point: the Basin View Terrace complex where Bob and Diane invite Lacey and I and the shuttle driver for tea on their deck overlooking the vast Yolo Basin Wildlife Reserve. There is a rather large, 20-power, swiveling spotting scope mounted on their deck to watch the millions of birds who are now their most populous and energetic neighbors. Once, more than a hundred years ago, the Sacramento River flooded this area naturally, but in the mid-twentieth century an immense engineering effort placed the flood waters within controlled levees, and the land became a seasonal site of mechanized, high-input, cash-crop farming. Over the past 20 years, however, efforts to release the Sacramento's nourishing floodwaters from their engineering straightjacket have born fruit. Plans first conceived in 1990

*have resulted in a several-thousand acre system of permanent pools,
seasonal flood basins, channels, riparian shrubs, perimeter
cottonwoods, willows, and upland terraces spotted with oak and
covered with bunch grasses. Small-scale patches of land are farmed
with selected crops which provide field residue of food value to the
many species of local birds. Into this newly reconstructed home have
come geese, ducks, pelicans, tundra swans, egrets, barriers, pheasants,
tricolored blackbirds, kestrels, osprey, giant garter snakes, blackfish,
suckers, catfish, and even striped bass in the permanent sloughs. Bob
and Diane have the nicest neighbors!*

*We laugh and say goodbye, following George back to the shuttle.
He'll drop us off at home and return the vehicle to the Senior Center
on "A" Street. Back in Village Homes (where we've lived for over 50
years . . . I can hardly believe it!), I'm flooded with memories of where
we used to be and where we are now. Although we have stayed in one
place, I am enriched by how far we have come. Village Homes is an
anachronism now, but a well-loved one—almost sacred to Lacey and I
and our eldest son, Doug, who lives on the next street over, refusing to
ever leave the place where he grew up. We've watched this bioregion
grow, change, and become reenchanted, helping out in whatever small
ways we could. My obsession with the relationship between humans,
technologies, landscapes, and the rest of nature has both plagued me
and sparked my interest since graduate school. But here, in the Yolo
bioregion of California, USA, planet Earth, in the year 2030, an 83-
year-old man feels at home—content in the belief that after so much
time, we may be starting to get it right.*

10

The Experience of Sustainable Landscapes

*Yet there is hope. On a hotter planet, with lost deltas and shrunken coastlines,
under a more dangerous sun, with less arable land, more people, fewer species of
living things, a legacy of poisonous wastes, and much beauty irrevocably lost,
there will still be the possibility that our children's children will learn at last to
live as a community among communities. Perhaps they will learn also to forgive
this generation its blind commitment to ever greater consumption. Perhaps they
will even appreciate its belated efforts to leave them a planet still capable of
supporting life in community."*

HERMAN DALY AND JOHN COBB (1989)

From a scattering of crudely chipped flint tools to a near-complete transformation of the earth's surface and climate, technology has presented human nature with an ever-widening paradox: we developed technology as a means of survival in nature, and now it is killing other life forms and threatening us as well. Yet technology is the "nature" of human nature. In spite of a green heart, we have made an ambivalent gray world; with a creative vision of paradise, we have begun to create a hell on earth. Our intent was not malicious, only nearsighted. As if caught by the curve of space-time, our good intentions went out freely, yet came back to hit us from behind.

The conflict between nature and technology has become large, oppressive, and inescapable. Like being stuck between floors in a small elevator with a menacing stranger, escape seems desperately necessary, yet highly unlikely. Our only hope is to confront the situation. The size of the problem may seem more manageable when we fully understand both the threat and the opportunities it may present.

In Chapter 8 I suggested that our gut-level technophobia may be not only very persistent, but perhaps even useful as our only defense in a world of electronic simulation which glosses over the nature–technology conflict with sweet surface imagery, while the core of nature reels from continued and deep technological assault. Perhaps a basic skepticism of technology is healthy in the long run, and if this is true, the landscape is bound to continue to manifest the guilt we feel over technology. However, guilt is not a static emotion; it can be productive and healthy when it leads toward fundamental change. We must learn, then, to examine the cognitive dissonance of the technophilia–topophilia–technophobia triangle and evaluate when this inherent tension is constructive and when it is not.

How Important Are Sustainable Landscapes?

Can a few conspicuous solar houses, constructed wetlands, bike paths, recycling industries, wildlife habitat corridors, organic agriculture plots, and wind

Sustainable technologies contribute to a reintegration of nature and human nature.

farms really be the key to saving the world? Isn't a much greater transformation needed in global economic, political, and social institutions? The answer to the last question is, of course, yes. But the new institutions needed for a transition to a sustainable world must ultimately be based upon the perception and comprehension of the ordinary people who will create them. In turn, *their* ultimate reality is in the land and spaces around them. The small steps taken to build sustainability into the local landscape in discreet, manageable chunks which people can observe, try out, experience, and improve are actually large steps for humankind. In the 18 years I have lived in my current house in our solar neighborhood, there have been countless bus loads of visitors from many states and foreign countries passing through, asking questions, and taking pictures. I have given innumerable house tours and minilectures on the solar, water, and open space features of the neighborhood myself. In spite of the frequent interruptions, I realize that this is the way it should be; a critical purpose of the sustainable landscape is the demonstration and diffusion of environmentally and socially sustaining principles into common usage in the everyday world.

This kind of direct experiential role for sustainable landscapes can not be overemphasized. An *acceptance of sustainable techniques and technologies into our concept of nature and human nature* is an essential part of the process toward remaking global institutions. French President Francois Mitterand once toured Village Homes, landing on the big greenbelt in his French military helicopter. Vice presidents, senators, and other VIPs have joined the ranks of everyday folk touring the Village. While it is difficult to measure precisely the impact of such visits, it is clear that sustainable landscapes offer visual and experiential proof that humans and certain certain technologies *can* live together without guilt, and that growing vegetables in your front yard, parking your bike cart in the driveway, and having a flat-plate solar water heater visible from the street is not cause for guilt-ridden camouflage or censure by design review boards or other arms of the "thought-and-taste police."

In the struggle to reconcile technophobia with topophilia, we as individuals search for ways of resolving the conflicts we feel between the technology we have always considered ugly and the various symbols for nature and pastoralism we have always revered. There is a natural tendency for individuals to want to make sense of their worlds. Landscape is a principle vehicle for making sense (Kaplan and Kaplan, 1982a.) If landscapes cease to help individuals make sense, landscapes are not fulfilling one of their most important functions. Air conditioning is a typical example. When we enter any public building (or higher-priced home) in the mid-to-lower latitudes in the United States in summer, we walk into a different climate zone with no idea whatsoever of the price we pay for such technological magic. Style-conscious architects of the status quo, spurred on by unenlightened clients, fail to design buildings which are naturally or passively heated or cooled. Overdesigned, electro-mechanical air conditioning is inevitably provided, hidden well behind screen fences or roof parapets so as not to spoil "the aesthetic." Far away somewhere beyond our view is a coal, gas, or nuclear power plant consuming the earth's stored energy to provide us with that interior climatic illusion. If the particular power plant running your air conditioners happens to be the Four Corners Plant in Farmington, New Mexico, or any one of four or five others nearby which burn coal from the Four Corners area,[1] then Navajo and Hopi people are literally dying of black lung disease to provide you with this climatic illusion (Matthiessen, 1984; Mander, 1991).

Landscapes that create an illusion of a better world while depriving us of the actual means of achieving it are not sustainable. If the *perceptual* function of a technology is to convince us the world is a more pleasant place, while the *practical* dimensions of the technology functionally contribute to making the world worse, something is critically out of balance. Air conditioners powered by fossil fuels create the illusion of coolness in one place by making the entire planet hotter through their contribution to global warming. Sustainable landscapes, therefore, are an essential grounding element in the transition to a new philosophical framework—the antidote to a runaway world of consumption and fantasy where technology is destroying nature and making a lifeless replica.

Using the power plant/air conditioning scenario as a jumping off point, let us redesign the entire relationship. Instead of walking into a postmodern building like the library on our campus, for example, whose glass-block, west-facing wall absorbs considerable heat during precisely the wrong time of day and year (hot summer afternoons)—we instead walk into the north side entrance of a new, passively cooled building. In our new scenario, solar thermosiphon towers would bring cool nighttime air down into the building between the hours of 2 and 6 in the morning, powered by fans that receive electrical energy from batteries that store electricity from photovoltaic cells visibly mounted on the roof. Massive internal walls of water and masonry store the coolness of the night air, absorbing excess interior heat during the day. A tall, partially roofed, shaded interior courtyard adds natural cooling. Outside the building, tall rows of deciduous shade trees screen the building surfaces from the hot western summer sun. In winter, low southern sun warms the building directly through the windowed south facade shaded by architectural "eyebrows" that block high summer sun. A display in the library lobby explains how the building conserves energy, and where that energy comes from. All the working parts of the building are visible and easy to understand by the university students who, after all, have come to the library to learn about the world.

Transparency: Expressing the Unseen

Transparency—the ability to see into and understand the inner workings of a landscape—is an absolutely essential ingredient to sustainability. In a world where more and more of the technology controlling our lives is not only beyond our individual control but is also invisible and incomprehensible to the average person, the landscape serves not only as the foundation for our only genuinely "tangible" reality, but as the only mechanism by which we can really know *where* we are—and *how* and *why* as well. It can be argued that as humans we have a *right* to know where we are, how we are connected, and *how we are doing.*

Not all transparent landscapes will be beneficial, nurturing, or sustainable. However, I argue that it is much better in the long run to *see* what is consumptive, dangerous, or wrong with our built environment than to *not* see it (Strang, 1992). In the case of wind energy generation, as mentioned in Chapter 9, the natural transparency of wind turbines themselves is a double-edged sword which allows the public to see into the system, whether the wind industry would like it that way or not. The tendency for American culture to place its so-called "necessary" technologies beyond the realm of public view or experience is jointly caused by a technophobic public and a political structure that is more than willing not to have their exercise of power blatantly revealed to the public. The current chemical, mining, forestry, and manufacturing industries are actually glad you don't want to see them in your neighborhoods, for if you did, you might not agree with their methods, and they might have to clean up their act. I will not go so far as to suggest a conspiracy to conceal (Wood, 1989), but there may well be a "don't rock the boat" attitude of corporate convenience inherent in public landscape guilt over technology.

Visual Ecology

Without being able to see into the workings of our own landscapes, we may be unable to make necessary adjustments to changing environmental conditions. The feedback of experience between habitat and organism which guides environmental behavior is a cornerstone of ecology. In transparent landscapes, a *visual ecology,* where we are able to assess the conditions affecting us and make cogent environmental decisions, is both possible and necessary (Thayer, 1976). Since humans are symbolic animals who interpret the world through abstraction, deduction, and discourse, the feedback we receive from the environment is, of course, laden with symbolic meaning. But positive meanings (and hence constructive action) accrue more steadfastly to things that can be seen and experienced. That which is not seen is often viewed with fear and exaggeration. The first step toward building a sustainable world then is to open up our landscapes to view, such that we may learn from them where we are, how we are doing, and what we need to do to make the world better. Opacity and fakery in the landscape ultimately only serves to perpetuate the unsustainable status quo.

This "Archimedes screw" uses the natural hydraulic power of the river to raise water into a water feature at Flint Riverbank Park, Flint, Michigan. In this case, the technology is sustainable, visible, and easy to understand. Photograph courtesy of Bill Hull and Sat Nishita.

Congruency: Complexity *without* Contradiction

While occasional surprise, contradiction, feint, and whimsy are ingredients of humor (and humor makes life worth living), by and large people strive for *congruency* between various departments of their daily lives and between their various emotional, behavioral, and cognitive states. I have already discussed cognitive dissonance as the emotional state where an individual's beliefs, feelings, and actions are incongruous and uncomfortable. The natural tendency of humans is toward consistency between emotions, thoughts, and actions. This should be the natural, normal tendency in our landscapes as well. When—as in the landscapes of today—the opposite tendency toward surprise, contradiction, simulation, and irony moves beyond the boundaries of art and entertainment into the absolute mainstream of human existence, something is fundamentally wrong.

The second major point regarding the experience of sustainable landscapes is that once made transparent, sustainable landscapes must ultimately be *congruent*. In other words, the emotional state provoked by the landscape's *surfaces* should be congruent with and not contradictory to the manner in which the *core* properties of the same landscape provide for our functional needs and well-being. If an air-conditioned building that allows one group of people to feel like spring in the middle of summer simultaneously contributes to the painful death of others, the various levels of meaning and experience represented by the building cannot be congruent. On the other hand, if a constructed wetland not only safely processes the human wastes it receives but also provides safe habitat for birds and a recreational venue for humans, it is most certainly a congruent and sustainable landscape.

There is, of course, a natural relationship between transparency and congruency. Congruency is often prevented by opaqueness—if we can't see how a landscape functions, we are unable to detect the possible incongruities. Merely by an increase in landscape transparency, the natural human tendency toward congruity between thought, feeling, and action, or between surface and core, will foster the remaking of a more sustainable environment.

Fantasy is Necessary, But So is the Boundary Between It and Reality

The sustainable landscape should not herald an era devoid of fun, fantasy, or imagination. Fantasy and imagination are necessary for human survival. In today's world saturated by entertainment and illusion, the danger is not as much in the *amount* of fantasy itself but in the *blurring of the line between fantasy and reality* (Mitroff and Bennis, 1989). Sustainable landscapes need not be austere, solemn, dictatorial X rays of ecological processes blaring across our consciousness. On the other hand, Baudrillard's *reality principle* should be kept in mind; landscapes should give strong cues when one is leaving reality and entering the realm of fantasy and entertainment. Much has been written about "entertaining ourselves to death" (Postman, 1985), but entertainment and death are fundamentally in opposition. When landscapes contribute to the excessive blurring of reality and fantasy, they are contributing to unsustainable conditions for human life.

Fantasy and ritual are clearly necessary for survival, and both fantasy and ritual require landscape venues. We can learn by a simple example from ancient Hawaiian culture that a sharp boundary between the real and imaginary is beneficial and necessary. On the big island of Hawaii is a sacred Hawaiian site now administered as an historic national park—*Puuhonua-o-Honaunau*, the City of Refuge. When an ancient Hawaiian broke a fundamental law or *kapu*, he or she was often subject to punishment by death. If, however, the kapu violator could escape, resist capture, and arrive at Puuhonua-o-Honaunau, a secluded village sheltered by a lagoon where certain *kahunas* or shamans presided, the accused would be declared safe and after a certain time, purified, forgiven, and allowed to return to everyday life. The ritual journey and ultimate salvation were clearly marked by an invisible but well-

Spirit figures guard Puuhonua-o-Honaunau, *the ancient Hawaiian City of Refuge, now a national park on Hawaii's Big Island.*

known spatial boundary around the City of Refuge. The world without and the world within were sharply separate and defined landscapes, and the entire arrangement served the social and ecological advantage of both guiding human behavior toward respect for the kapus and allowing the social group to keep its members alive (Dudley, 1990).

There is much room in a sustainable world for fantasy, imagination, and ritual. In fact, like the ancient Hawaiians, most primal societies existed sustainably for thousands of years within rich traditions of storytelling, mythology, pageantry, and imaginative art. What differentiates their world from ours is that the relationship between mythology and real-world behavior among primal peoples was clearly understood and linked to an essential human ecology. Myth and ritual allowed a high degree of *control* over the use of tools and technologies; boundaries of behavior and place were well defined and coordinated, and consequences for crossing these boundaries were well established.

In our world, boundaries have dissolved, behaviors can take place anywhere, and technology is not *constrained* by imagination—only *created* by it.

Some scholars—Jerry Mander (1991) is one—advocate that the runaway technological determinism among modern, western societies has failed, and that we would do well to reexamine our own deteriorated mythical, ritual framework using primal native cultures as possible models for positive change. In some ways, sustainable landscapes provide venues for us to test Mander's hypothesis. It is not enough for our landscapes to merely communicate a transparent and congruent ecology; they should also serve to reenchant our world through imagination, sensation, and ritual. However, this enchantment must serve to guide and direct our behaviors toward a sustainable human ecology, rather than destroy it. In Hawaiian religious mythology, the volcano-goddess Pele is the creator (Kane, 1987). She is much more than a volcano; she is the spiritual force responsible for moving from island to island, creating the land, and keeping it intact and sacred. She is continually at work adding new land, and her domain extends from deep beneath the ocean and includes the water as well as the earth. Recently, a power plant and heavy industrial complex were proposed near Kilauea, the active volcano on Hawaii's Big Island. The project called for geothermal drilling on Kilauea's eastern flanks, processing of ocean-mined ores, elimination of a large area of rainforest, and production of highly toxic waste. Native Hawaiians viewed the project as a sacrilege against Pele and the ancient Hawaiian traditions of land stewardship and, through a vocal and vigorous political resistance, defeated the proposal (Mander, 1991).

In this instance, we see how intensely connected and positively beneficial the relationship between a landscape (the Hawaiian volcanoes, ocean, and rainforest), mythology (Pele), and stewardship behavior can be. Contrast this to the technological fakery and deceit of the Mirage Casino "Volcano" and the misplacement of fantasy in American environmental design and culture becomes self evident.

Beyond Aesthetics: The Style of No Style

The postmodern preoccupation with simulation, fantasy, irony, contradiction, vague historical reference, boundary warping, and lack of guiding principles will not last long, simply because "postmodern" style attempts to "deconstruct" or make a mockery of all former, form-giving influences and assumptions. It has given up seeking an underlying "truth." I argue, however, that an underlying truth is rapidly revealing itself to us in the birth of the notion of sustainability, however "trendy" the word has become. A need to put flesh (in the form of physical landscapes) on the skeletal philosophy of sustainability has become too powerful to resist.

Yet even when sustainable and regenerative values can be embodied in landscape form, they are unlikely to collectively result in any one particular "style." Instead, sustainable landscapes are likely to express a unique sense of visual and spatial pluralism. Sustainable landscapes can vary from humanized farm country to rough-looking wetlands to precisely ordered arrays of wind turbines. Some sustainable landscapes are those in which people live, while others are relatively devoid of human presence. Because of the infinite relationships possible between humans, ecosystems, and natural resources, no two sustainable landscapes are apt to look alike, particularly if they occur in different regions or evolve with different baseline ecosystems or cultures. The movement toward bioregionalism deliberately attempts to exploit the *uniqueness* of local cultures and landscapes in creating a sustainable future, and runs counter to the idea of a widely dispersed, externally imposed aesthetic style.

In some sense, the new forms of the sustainable landscape will have certain commonalties with modernism, but with several key differences. There may be a partial return to a version of "form follows function," but this time the "function" is not mechanistic (in the narrow, modernist sense), but *ecological* (in the *post*-postmodern sense). Form will follow a highly complex, evolving notion of the core interrelationships of nature, and will be expressed uniquely in the surfaces of local landscapes as experienced by local cultures. Sustainable landscape form and content will seek to reveal this ecological order through an interplay of surface and core *unique* to both place and culture. Consequently, there may be no distinct style, since "style" itself necessarily separates surface from core.

Art and Creativity are Critical

The unlikeliness of a common "style," of course, does not imply the lack of a role for art and creativity. Artful interpretation is necessary to offer alternative visions and to explore and make sense out of the unseen. Bringing core ecologies to the surface will be an important role of landscape artists and designers. The continually unfolding complexity of the natural world and the inability of traditional forms to represent these changes will result in the evolution of new, unfamiliar surface-core relationships. A critical function of landscape architecture and environmental art will be to continually interpret the relationship of human beings to their environment in spatial, visual terms. Since the change in relationship between people and nature is accelerating, new formal interpretations are required at an ever-increasing rate. Here is where artistic creation plays a key role. Art has the ability to anticipate society. Genuinely artful interpretation offers a range of possible futures by which sustainable landscapes can be identified, emphasized, evaluated, and made visible.

Conspicuous Experiential Quality Speeds Acceptance

There may be two or more groups of actors relating to any sustainable landscape: those "within" the landscape itself and those who observe it from without. As such, different sets of meanings may evolve for the same landscape. But for either the internal "players" or the external observers, the visibility of the sustainable landscape and its ability to form images in the human mind is critical to its experiential impact and the rate at which it will be adopted by society and emulated in common use. Theory on the diffusion of innovations (Rogers and Shoemaker, 1971) suggests that *complexity* impedes the rate of adoption of an innovation (like sustainable technologies or landscape processes), whereas *observability* speeds the adoption rate. Since they represent a higher level of system complexity than "cosmetic" landscapes and incorporate ecological relationships that may be invisible or difficult to observe, sustainable landscapes present obstacles to their own acceptance. However, making sustainable landscapes *observable* can help to counteract this problem. Fourteen years ago I argued that solar energy systems should never be regulated out of sight because their high visibility—however controversial by contemporaneous aesthetic standards—was crucial to their widespread adoption by society. Sustainable technologies and landscape features like natural storm drainage and visible solar collector systems symbolize "conspicuous nonconsumption" and are essential markers along the road to a more sustainable world (Thayer, 1980).

Sustainability, Culture, and Community

Ultimately, the goal of sustainable landscapes is the transformation of *culture*—the taming of technology, the emergence of a new environmental ethic, a new measure of life quality, and a substantially broadened sense of *community* including not only humans, but all life. If this sounds like a manifesto or a grandiose political wish, I suppose it is. What I have written in this book implies the need for "*not* business as usual," and I believe more decision makers and social critics are accepting this implication each day. Therefore, it is important to look at sustainable landscapes in terms of the nature and degree of social change they imply.

In the search for prototypes for sustainable landscapes we often focus on established, nonindustrial cultures that have practiced regenerative agricultural or other resource-harvesting techniques over a long period of time (Jackson et al., 1984). A potential criticism leveled at the movement toward a sustainable landscape is that it appears to depend upon human labor rather than energy inputs, coupled with the obvious limitation and reluctance of modern society to revert to labor-intensive agricultural and industrial prac-

"City Boundary," by landscape architect Steve Martino and artist Jody Pinto, marks the boundary between two modern Arizona cities (Phoenix and Scottsdale). The project (a), built of rejected local quarry stone and aligned to the summer solstice, expresses an ancient means of desert survival—harvesting rainwater. Seven terraces with notched stone check dams capture and concentrate stormwater (b) to irrigate and regenerate a portion of the desert itself. Photographs by Steve Martino.

tices (Nash, 1979). Although we admire and often romanticize the Amish culture of Pennsylvania and the 900-year-old productivity of the Hopi mesa landscapes in Arizona, for example, it is naive to assume that the majority of Americans would intentionally adopt the austere social structure and involvement with the land implicit in both of these cultures. However, sustainable landscapes need not be heavily peopled nor labor intensive. Wind farms generally lack human dwellers, and multipurpose constructed wetlands can and do exist a stone's throw away from places like the Los Angeles International Airport (*Landscape Architecture,* 1988). While a sustainable world will not be able to support the excessive resource consumption levels of our western

"Conspicuous nonconsumption" is the implicit message of this solar house in Portland, Oregon.

societies, it will depend a great deal upon renewable energy sources and labor-saving devices we recognize today.

There will, however, be limits. In fact, recognizing the limits of our techno-logical lifestyles and landscapes is what this book and many others (e.g., Meadows, et al., 1992) are all about. However, both the landscape venues and the cultures that animate them will evolve gradually toward sustainability in concert, each influencing the other in mutual cause and effect. We created the conflict between nature and technology slowly over a long period of time, and we are likely to climb out of it steadily and incrementally as well. To some extent, sustainable culture will *evolve,* but if we are to make a more sustain-able world, we must do so by *intentional design*. This implies that we will not usually have the advantage of an existing culture or subculture upon which to build. We may, quite literally, need to design and build the cultural elements necessary to accompany and actualize new sustainable landscapes as we build the landscapes themselves.

There are many encouraging examples of sustainable subcultures evolving along with the evolution of physically identifiable sustainable landscapes. Cohousing groups, bioregional councils, watershed associations, renewable energy societies, ad hoc citizen's planning advisory boards, "defenders" of various animals, plants, and environments, and even the NIMBY resisters of technological or threatening land uses are all manifestations of the birth of a

Animal traction and strip cropping are two of many sustainable techniques used by Amish farmers in Pennsylvania. A strong, traditional culture has guided Amish use of farming technology and allowed continued soil productivity for over two hundred years.

subculture of sustainability running counter to the inertial resistance of the "silent majority." Recently, California's Resources Agency secretary, Douglas Wheeler, made the profoundly radical, landmark decision to reorganize the management of California's natural resources along bioregional lines related to the ecological character of the land rather than "irrational" political boundaries. Wheeler's action, which he supported by a public speaking and meeting tour in California's rural hinterlands, set the stage for local citizens, often from both sides of controversial environmental issues, to sit down together and work out a means of sustaining their own regional resources themselves (McHugh, 1992). In this dramatic policy change, Wheeler, a Republican, was influenced by a number of people, including Gary Snyder, who had been a former logging industry worker himself. In this case, the subculture of bioregionalism had worked its way up to influence the dominant political culture of California.

Living with Inconsistency and Managing Landscape Guilt

While sustainable subcultures and their corresponding landscapes are evolving together, there is still much in the dominant culture which seems inconsistent, unreal, and out of control. By and large, landscapes are getting more opaque as society entangles itself further in the veil of technologically aided simulation, avoidance, and fantasy. As a consequence, our sense of what is real is becoming as fragmented as the landscape itself. In this state of affairs, we will have to learn to live with inconsistency for a quite a long while. Environmental guilt, the sense of dissonance we feel about technology's impact on the land, will likely increase as we struggle to reinvent a more regenerative landscape in the face of cultural momentum to the contrary. The colliding tendencies toward simulation on the one hand and sustainability on the other will be the dominant tension affecting the landscape for some years to come.

Instead of striving for complete and total resolution of tension, we are better off learning how to manage the dissonance between nature and technology constructively to create a more sustainable landscape. Topophilia and technophobia interact in both constructive and destructive ways. For example, natural aversion to technology affords society some caution in allowing uncontrolled development of the earth's ecosystems. The environmental impact review processes now common in planning practice resulted from technophobic/topophilic reactions to the 1970 oil spill off the Santa Barbara coastline. As a result, the National Environmental Policy Act (NEPA) and the California Environmental Quality Act (CEQA), were passed—evidence of constructive use of the tension between topophilia and technophobia. While neither NEPA or CEQA have proven to be ideal planning tools, both have been instrumental in setting new public standards for environmental quality.

On the other hand, fear of anything technological may prevent beneficial and sustainable technologies from being implemented because of guilt by association. Los Angeles County Supervisors voted against a proposed wind power plant which, although largely out of sight of the freeway, would have reduced local carbon emissions and provided direct benefits for local residents. Instead, their actions opened the door to more low-density, rural "ranchette" housing development which will only add to carbon emissions and local smog by increasing energy demand and encouraging automobile commuting.

Our affection for land and nature can likewise form constructive as well as destructive relationships to technophilia as well. The natural tendency to tinker and solve problems through technology has led to a number of sustainable management tools, such as computerized natural systems data base planning, geographic information systems (GIS), environmental impact forecasting, and ecological modeling. In planning, landscape architecture, and ecology programs at American universities, GIS is seen as an increasingly necessary research tool and popular skill to acquire among students and faculty alike.

At Muir Commons cohousing in Davis, a subculture of sustainable living has co-evolved with the design. Assisted by the architect and builder, prospective neighbors design their own shared community (a), and share evening meals in a Common House (b) which also contains meeting rooms and a day care center. Cohousing recaptures and sustains the sense of community lost in more conventional American development patterns. Satisfaction among Muir Commons residents is high. Similar cohousing projects are now underway all over the country. Photographs by Chuck Durrett and Virginia Thigpen.

	Topophilia w/r Technophilia:	Topophilia w/r Technophobia:
Constructive Relationship:	Natural tendency to tinker and improve the situation:	Natural skepticism of technological effect on nature:
	- Computer GIS data systems for ecological studies	- National Environmental Policy Act to assess environmental impact
Destructive Relationship:	Over-dependence on technological fixes:	Paranoia over "surface" concerns blocks out "core" advantages:
	- Over-irrigation of the desert: 100+ golf courses in Coachella Valley, CA	- Defeat of Gorman Wind Farm project for Tejon Pass, Los Angeles County

Topophilia, technophilia, and technophobia interact in both constructive and destructive ways. Constructively managing these often-conflicting human emotions is the key to building a more sustainable world.

Similar technophilic predispositions have also resulted in more sustainable technical systems like solar photovoltaics, by which we may wean ourselves of more consumptive and destructive technologies. Our innate desire to create and solve problems through technology is not the entire answer to the challenge of building a sustainable world, but, if used with forethought, will certainly help.

In contrast, blind infatuation with technology can lead to ever more consumptive and extravagant use of fossil fuels and other primary resources. In the Coachella Valley of California, a desert region with less than five inches of annual rainfall, over 100 irrigated golf courses are draining the aquifers and changing the mesoclimate. Each golf course in this region annually consumes a quantity of irrigation water equivalent to the volume of a reservoir 11 feet deep over the entire surface area of the course. Defenders of these golf courses will point to the increasing efficiencies of the irrigation technologies—more accurate soil moisture sensors, more efficient spray heads, better computerized valve control, and reclaimed water, as if to tell us that fine tuning the technology can make the immense environmental impact go away. Often what is needed are not technological fixes, but substantial reversals of environmental policy to correct gross mismatches between human expectations (e.g., lush turf) and environmental contexts (e.g., deserts).

Ultimately, we must accept the fact that guilt over the impacts of technology on nature may never completely disappear, and manifestations of this guilt will be revealed in the landscape well into the future. Perhaps it is just as well, for our intuitive adverse reaction to technology is a baseline check against its autonomy. However, when guilt over technology results in a landscape of opacity, concealment, and illusion, it is not constructive. To arrive at a more sustainable world, we will need to make clear choices in favor of certain technologies and against others. The choice to employ and express a more sustainable technology in place of a less sustainable one should not be paralyzed by technophobia, but only guided by it.

Taming the Technological Tyrant

The evolution of nature, technology, and their conflicting interrelationship demands movement toward resolution. We created the dilemma of topophilia, technophilia, and technophobia, and we must strive to resolve it. The sustainable landscape is a natural step in the transformation toward resolution; we cannot kill the technological tyrant, only tame it. There is a parallel here between the evolution of sustainable landscapes and David Rains Wallace's metaphor of the Klamath giants. Mythical or not, the Klamath giants symbolize a nontechnological, peaceful, human-like animal capable of complete and totally nondestructive integration with nature. Likewise, sustainable landscapes represent a turnabout in the direction of fundamental human tinkering away from dominance of nature toward reverence for and subservience to it. Like the Klamath giants, if sustainable landscapes had not begun to emerge, it would have been necessary for us to invent them. We may never actually see the Klamath giants, but we can certainly *build* sustainable landscapes. In essence, to tame the technological tyrant, it has become extremely necessary to reinvent both culture and environment—to reconfigure both our landscapes and ourselves.

Taking Action

So far, I have aimed the discussion in this chapter at the unique role of sustainable landscapes in relation to human experience; we create them and they create us. By far the most critical aspect in our experience of sustainable landscapes is *taking action* to bring about their existence. It is easy to talk about sustainable landscapes, and although frustrating at times, it is still relatively easy to write books about them. What is most difficult is *making* them. Sustainable landscapes imply a different set of ground rules, yet the game must go on in order for the rules to change, like a child's sand-lot baseball game where players share the role of umpire and argue over the calls. We must *make* sustainable landscapes to know *how* to make them, and we must make them in order to know *what* they really are. Taking action will involve considerable commitment to change in "business as usual," faith that viable alternatives to the status quo are possible and effective, and resiliency to put up with inevitable and innumerable failures. Above all, action requires unbridled optimism and enthusiasm.

I recommend that citizen activists, planners, and designers of sustainable landscapes set a limited number of achievable goals within the scope of each project, and try to reach at least one or two of them. Learning will take place in the attempt, even if all goals are not reached. In one recent 100-acre neighborhood design project, for example, my consulting partners and I were successful in providing solar access, calming a major auto street, structuring an open space network with pedestrian and bicycle linkages, providing a natural storm drainage system, and designing a water-efficient landscape. We were unable to persuade our clients to provide a community garden, common areas, cohousing, a critical wildlife habitat connection, or a dense, mixed-use neighborhood/commercial area which might have reduced auto use even further. However, we accepted these limited accomplishments and moved on.

Each concrete action to make a specific landscape more functionally sustainable will involve several outward, symbolic dimensions: reinforcement of personal values; maintenance of a sense of self, place, and community; influence on the attitudes and behaviors of one's immediate peer group; and evidence of political feasibility or economic viability. For the next several years, every planning or landscape architectural project intended to move toward sustainability will necessarily be a "demonstration," or "pilot" project. As in the case of Laguna West, the potential is great for each of these projects to achieve too little in the way of measurable reduction in the impact of consumptive technology, and too much in the way of media exposure and superficial success. While the *experiential* qualities of sustainable landscapes are critical, without *functionally* contributing to actual environmental solutions, supposedly sustainable landscapes degenerate into mere simulations (Kahrl, 1993). Continual effort must be made to ensure that the actions taken toward more sustainable design be concrete and measurable at the core as well as informative and meaningful on the surface.

Action toward sustainable community planning and design of specific landscapes should take place simultaneously on many fronts. While working on site-specific design solutions that respond to existing political and economic constraints, planners and designers may be inspired to work on changing the constraints by attending public meetings, writing letters, teaching workshops and courses, giving lectures, and so forth. Furthermore, each planner, designer, or involved government official is also a private citizen of the neighborhood, bioregion, and planet. I believe that those involved in structuring a community or landscape should do so as if they were going to live, play, or work there themselves, whether they intend to or not. In my daily life and work, hardly a day goes by when I do not question whether I am truly "practicing what I preach." This self-reflection may result in something as simple as riding a bicycle to a business meeting with a client whom I hope to persuade to accept a less auto-dominated neighborhood plan. There is always some discrepancy between personal beliefs, intentions, and actions. However, by building congruity between one's public actions, personal beliefs, and private behaviors, both the limitations and potentials of sustainable design become clearer.

Each person also votes, not only with ballots, but also with their wallets, checkbooks, and credit cards. We are all consumers of the products of technology, much of which are simply unsustainable and unnecessary. Like other American excesses, buying is best done in moderation, and with some forethought about environmental consequences, both personal as well as public. However, occasionally actions and beliefs become disjointed. My wife and I recently bought a new car, temporarily violating our long-standing goal of being a one-car family until we sold the older vehicle. While we waited for the phone to ring with a prospective buyer for the second car, I began to feel uncomfortable and inconsistent; I had plunked down thousands of dollars for a new technological dragon without slaying the old one and, with my money, I felt I had voted to perpetuate the excesses of the automotive infrastructure. This cognitive dissonance subsided after selling the second car, but during that period of time I was reminded that each personal financial decision or consumer purchase one makes, when combined with similar actions of many others, constitutes a tacit influence on environmental policy. Money not only talks, but *acts*.

Voting by ballot, of course, is often the most powerful form of action an individual can take. Voting patterns are often strange admixtures of image and substance, reaction and action, selfishness and altruism, and fear and hope. On rare occasions, political *substance* emerges out of the baseline of media imagery and hype, and glimmers of constructive change appear on the horizon. Vice President Albert Gore's excellent book, *Earth in the Balance,* written before his election in 1992, espouses a philosophy and course of action complimentary and compatible to that of this book. Gore's book was widely read prior to the election, even by his opponent. Although not a political scientist, I would like to believe that the realistic policies espoused by Vice President Gore contributed substantially to the outcome of the election. While we can only hope that the political accomplishments of the Clinton–Gore administration will follow and closely embody the positions outlined in Gore's book, the fact that the Clinton–Gore team was elected is in some small part a testimony to the willingness of the American people to vote for change toward a more sustainable environment.

How to plan and design sustainable landscapes is a topic better handled in existing (Lyle, 1993) and, hopefully, future books. Likewise, the economic and political dimensions of the transition to sustainable communities and landscapes have been offered more cogently elsewhere: political implications in Vice President Gore's book, global and national policy alternatives in works by the Worldwatch Institute and by the United Nations, and economic implications in books by Herman Daly and John Cobb (1989) and Robert Costanza (1991), to which I enthusiastically refer interested readers. It is my contention, however, that the perceptions, beliefs, and many small *actions* of individual citizens, residents, volunteers, activists, designers, and planners—acting out of a need to resolve the conflict experienced in their own personal worlds from the inside out—constitute the most potent agents of change. In the present era, information and opinion flows in torrents, while concrete action trickles along. In the future, I hope that Jean Baudrillard will be proven wrong—that the so-called "silent" majority will not just speak out, but ultimately, *act*. In this fashion, I consider each bicycle commuter, solar house, recycling bin, constructed wetland, reclaimed stream or river, wind turbine, and wildlife habitat reserve as a marker along a path we should continue to follow.

Small Victories and a Large Question

Finally, we must learn the *joy* of working on the solution—not to be consumed by despair over the immensity of the task—but enriched by the steps to be taken, one at a time. In the words of Gandhi, "What you do may seem unimportant, but it is terribly important that you do it" (Attenborough, 1982). Each additional piece of the sustainable landscape is a small victory, and should be celebrated as such. Fundamental change in the relationship between nature, technology, and landscape will come from the incremental experiences of thousands of individuals in the actual places where they live, work, play, and touch. In a world where development is still heavily constrained by the limitations of market economics, landscape change is risky

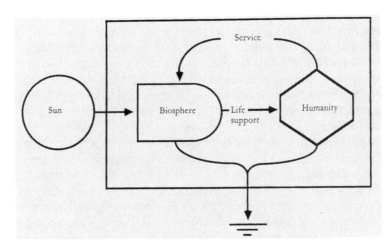

A life-support model reprinted from Ecology and Our Endangered Life-Support Systems *by Eugene Odum (1989). The original caption reads: "Humanity must service (i.e., preserve, maintain, and repair) the biosphere if we expect to continue to receive high-quality life-support goods and services."*

Photograph by Mike Corbett.

business. Few developers can muster the courage to follow their own hunches toward constraining technology more in the service of nature than in traditional models of profitability. However, millions of Americans together possess far more resolve. As more people express their discontent with the technological overkill inherent in their immediate lifestyles and landscapes and begin to change each accordingly, they apply increasing pressure on the world of development, industry, and politics to respond in kind.

Perhaps the greatest obstacle to be overcome by everyday people trying to establish a more sustainable world is the corporate marketing pressure to consume without purpose, meaning, or ethical control other than that provided by advertising. I am convinced however, that there is a vast, relatively untapped public "market" (in both the strict economic as well as broad philosophical sense) for a new means of combining technology and ecology in the landscape where the former serves the latter, but does not overwhelm it. The media, of course, have discovered this fact, and attempts to turn environmentalism into a media spectacle and to package it for profit are well under way. Landscapes that *function* sustainably on and in the ground, however, are the antidote for media trivialization. Each actual sustainable landscape attempted, then, is a concrete step toward a desirable, if not distant destination.

The affection for nature we hold in our hearts is still capable of standing up to the ambivalent world our technologies have made, but the framework by which to mount a resistance is open to question. It would be possible to consider the relationship of technology and nature as an unending drama played out with landscape as its stage, and as each new act unfolds, we would develop the characters, rewrite the script, and change the props. It would also be possible to consider the conflict between technology and nature as an eternal clash of Titans, and we would merely referee their colossal struggle in the arena of political economy. Neither of these metaphoric frameworks is satisfactory.

Ultimately, the conflict between nature and technology—the triangular tension of topophilia, technophilia, and technophobia—is a dilemma of *love*. Humans have an immense capacity for love, but as any lover knows, affection and commitment often require painful prioritization. Hidden behind the layers of our profligate material culture, between extravagant gardens and electronic gadgets, beyond wilderness areas and theme-park shopping malls, is the paramount dilemma of our very most fundamental, emotional priorities. Is our *deepest* attachment to technological culture, or is it to Earth? We might ask: Which could we ultimately not do without?

The earth existed before the explosion of human technology, and it will remain afterward. Our infatuation with technology is a brief, distracting affair, but we are wedded to the earth for life. Sustainability asks not for the banishment of technology from the landscape, but only for its servitude on behalf of a more fundamental, paramount, ecological ethic. Through a constant and unfolding process of experiment and experience, we may finally come to place our love of nature and our affection for technology in the right order upon the land.

NOTES

1. The Four Corners plant near Farmington has been called the single greatest source of air pollution in the United States—greater than the entire city of Los Angeles. Its plume was the only man-made phenomenon to be seen from space by astronauts in 1966. It and four other plants burn coal from the surrounding region to provide electricity via the power grid to an area from southern California to Texas (Matthiessen, 1984).

Epilogue

I rode my bicycle 20 miles out and back in the farm country today, as I have done many days for well over a year while writing this book. It is a brief half mile or so from my home to a distinct town edge, after which the brown, gold, and green patchwork unfolds before me out to the summer-dry foothills. I ride, mostly head down, toward the west. I often pause at the apogee—a humble, weedy verge at the corner of a field next to an irrigation pump. The view is indelible in my mind; the soil, the changing crops, a farm machine or two in the distance, followed by the inevitable plume of dust; dry foothills and the Vaca ridge farther to the west, with its tiny whiskerlike protrusions of microwave antennae; the big powerline crossing the view three miles away; a lone house to my right with no trees and a boat parked in the gravel driveway. Usually at least one airplane lands or takes off at the local county airport and one or two hawks sit on the wires behind me.

Today the view is sharp, clear, and still. I can see individual trees on the ridge 10 miles away. Balloons from the Napa Valley (which is probably fogged in) course overhead, occasionally firing their natural gas blowers and metaphorically mimicking life with their restricted ability to control their own direction. Suddenly a pheasant flushes from the dry weeds in front of me, followed by another, and then many others down the roadside edge. Blackbirds chirp in the irrigation ditch by the pump. A Northern Harrier glides over the alfalfa, looking for prey. Soon it is quiet. I have caught my breath, and my body tells me to hop back on, buckle my helmet, and pedal.

I have fussed with the adjustments so many times that my bicycle fits me perfectly, and being a compulsive squeak-and-rattle exterminator, my trip home is smooth and silent, save for my own heartbeat, the air rushing in and out of my lungs and past my ears, and the hiss of the narrow tires meeting the road.

I am often hit hard with profound thoughts on these rides, and today, once again, I am wrestling with this technology, nature, and landscape relationship all over again. I have realized that perhaps *I* have unconsciously been the subject of my own book—I am both the protagonist and the antagonist, the problem and the solution, the bad examples and the good. My inconsistencies yell out at me. Perhaps that is the case with each of us. On these rides, however, the thoughts are often confusing, but the *emotions* are not. I am joyously riding my bicycle in the country, powered by cereal, milk, and bananas, wheels touching ground on the billion-year old, hardened, crushed plant-and-animal ooze we now call asphalt. I am smugly gloating over moving through space so efficiently, using less energy per mile than any other form of human motion, including walking. I am a 46-year old child of nature, smiling as I play with a simple machine in a landscape totally altered by an odd collection of human devices, yet possessing a resilient, common beauty and a distinct richness of life, both human and nonhuman.

I love this bike, but I think I have my priorities straight. It is the living world through which I ride—the sudden break of a pheasant, the cry of a Swainson's Hawk overhead, the crisp blue sky, the faraway oak ridge, the awareness that I am riding through the very land which could provide my breakfast and the motion in my legs—that matters most. I have already tried one of those stationary bicycle trainers in front of the television set, and soon abandoned both. If it came down to an absolute choice between nature and technology, I would give up my bicycle and walk out into the country.

Fortunately, an absolute choice is not necessary. Resting my arms on the handlebars, I lean toward the distant line of trees and pedal for home.

References

Amato, I. 1991. "The Apostle of Nanotechnology." *Science,* **254**:1310–1311.

Anderson, W. 1990. *Reality Isn't What It Used To Be.* New York. Harper & Row.

Appleton, J. 1986. *The Experience of Landscape.* New York. John Wiley & Sons.

Appleyard, B. 1992. *Understanding the Present—Science and the Soul of Modern Man.* New York. Doubleday.

Arieti, S. 1976. *Creativity—The Magic Synthesis.* New York. Basic Books.

Attenborough, R. 1982. *The Words of Gandhi.* New York. Newmarket Press.

Bainbridge, D., J. Corbett, and J. Hofacre. 1979. *Village Homes' Solar House Designs.* Emmaus, Pennsylvania. Rodale Press.

Balling, J. and J. Falk, 1982. "Development of Visual Preference for Natural Environments." *Environment and Behavior,* 14:5–38.

Bateson, G. 1979. *Mind and Nature—A Necessary Unity.* New York. Bantam Books.

Baudrillard, J. 1983. *In the Shadow of the Silent Majorities,* or *The End of the Social and Other Essays.* New York. Semiotext(e), Inc.

Baudrillard, J. 1983. *Simulations.* New York. Semiotext(e), Inc.

Baxter, V. 1982. "CHACO/Pueblo Bonito: A Computer Analysis Applied to an Ancient Solar Dwelling." *Landscape Journal,* 1(2): 85–91.

Berry, T. 1988. *The Dream of the Earth.* San Francisco. Sierra Club Books.

Berry, W., Jr. 1991. "Look What They Did To My Canyon." *Sacramento Bee, Forum.* Sunday, October 13, pp. 1, 6.

Bohm, D. and M. Edwards. 1991. *Changing Consciousness.* San Francisco. Harper Collins.

Boulding, K. 1956. *The Image—Knowledge in Life and Society.* Ann Arbor. University of Michigan Press.

Boulding, K. 1968. *Beyond Economics.* Ann Arbor. University of Michigan Press.

Boulding, K. 1981. *Evolutionary Economics.* Beverly Hills. Sage Publications.

Boulding, K. 1985. *The World as a Total System.* Beverly Hills. Sage Publications.

Boyd, R. and P. Richerson. 1985. *Culture and the Evolutionary Process.* Chicago. The University of Chicago Press.

Brand, S. 1987. *The Media Lab—Inventing the Future at M.I.T.* New York. Penguin Books.

Brion, D. 1991. *Essential Industry and the NIMBY Phenomenon.* New York. Quorum Books.

Broder, B. 1979. *The Sacred Hoop.* San Francisco. Sierra Club Books.

Brooks, A. 1989. "The Office File Box—Emanations from the Battlefield." In *Zoning and the American Dream.* C. Haar and J. Kayden, Eds. Chicago. American Planning Association, pp. 3–30.

Brower, M. 1992. *Cool Energy: Renewable Solutions to Environmental Problems.* Cambridge. MIT Press.

Brown, L. 1981. *Building a Sustainable Society.* New York. Norton & Company.

Brown, L., C. Flavin, and C. Norman. 1979. *Running on Empty—The Future of the Automobile in an Oil-Short World.* New York. Norton & Company.

Brown, L., C. Flavin, and S. Postel. 1991. *Saving the Planet—How to Shape an Environmentally Sustainable Global Economy.* New York. Norton & Company.

Brush, R. and E. Shafer. 1975. "Application of a Landscape-Preference Model to Land Management." In *Landscape Assessment: Values, Perceptions and Resources.* E. Zube, R. Brush, and J. Fabos, Eds. Stroudsburg, Pennsylvania. Dowden, Hutchinson and Ross, Inc.

Capra, F. 1975. *The Tao of Physics.* Berkely. Shambala.

Capra, F. 1982. *The Turning Point—Science, Society, and the Rising Culture.* New York. Bantam Books.

Carlson, A. 1985. "On Appreciating Agricultural Landscapes." *Journal of Aesthetics and Art Criticism,* pp. 301–312.

Center for Maximum Potential Building Systems, Inc. 1992. "Biom-Metric Planning and Design: Operating Principles Towards Sustainable Communities." Austin, Texas.

Chase, A. 1987. *Playing God in Yellowstone—The Destruction of America's First National Park.* Orlando, Florida. Harcourt Brace Jovanovich.

Chenoweth, R. and P. Gobster. 1990. "The Nature and Ecology of Aesthetic Experiences in the Landscape." *Landscape Journal* 9(1):1–8.

Cole, T. 1836. "Essay on American Scenery." *American Monthly Magazine,* I:4–5.

Costanza, R., Ed. 1991. *Ecological Economics—the Science and Management of Sustainability.* New York. Columbia University Press.

Council of Educators in Landscape Architecture. 1988. "Sustainable Landscapes—Call for Papers." Department of Landscape Architecture, California Polytechnic State University, Pomona, California.

Crosbie, M. 1991. "Desert Shield." *Architecture,* May, pp. 76–81, 142.

Daly, H. and J. Cobb, Jr. 1989. *For the Common Good.* Boston. Beacon Press.

Davis Enterprise. 1992. "Advisers: Biosphere Needs to Pay Attention to Science." New York Times News Service. Monday, July 27.

Denig, N. 1985. "'On Values' Revisited: A Judeo-Christian Theology of Man and Nature." *Landscape Journal,* 4(2):96–105.

Devall, W. and G. Sessions. 1985. *Deep Ecology—Living as if Nature Mattered.* Salt Lake City. Peregrine Smith Books.

Dominski, A., J. Clark, and J. Fox. 1992. *Building the Sustainable City.* Santa Barbara. Community Environmental Council.

Dominski, A., J. Clark, and P. Relis. 1990. *The Bottom Line: Restructuring for Sustainability.* Santa Barbara. Community Environmental Council.

Drexler, K. 1992. *Nanosystems.* New York. Wiley, p. 298.

Drexler, K. 1986. *Engines of Creation—The Coming Era of Nanotechnology.* New York. Anchor Press/Doubleday.

Dubos, R. 1965. *Man Adapting.* New Haven. Yale University Press.

Dubos, R. 1980. *The Wooing of Earth.* New York. Scribners.

Dudley, M. 1990. *Man, Gods, and Nature.* Honolulu. Na Kane O Ka Malo Press.

Eco, U. 1986. *Travels in Hyperreality.* San Diego. Harcourt, Brace, Jovanovich.

Ellul, J. 1964. *The Technological Society.* New York. Vintage Books.

Festinger, L. 1963. "The Theory of Cognitive Dissonance." In *The Science of Human Communication.* W. Schramm, Ed. New York. Basic Books.

Fisk, P. and G. Vittori. 1991. "Sustainable Cities as a Part of a Global Ecology - a Conceptual Framework." In *A Better Place to Live—Visions of a Sustainable Future.* Conference Proceedings. Sarasota, Florida. Cooperative Extension Service for Sarasota County and the Florida House Foundation.

Fisk, P. and G. Vittori. 1992. "Towards a Theory and Practice of Sustainable Design." Paper presented at the National Convention of the American Institute of Architects, Boston, Massachusetts, June 21.

Forman, R. and M. Godron. 1986. *Landscape Ecology.* New York. John Wiley & Sons.

Francis, M. 1987. "Urban Open Spaces." In *Advances in Environment, Behavior, and Design* (Vol. 1). E. Zube and G. Moore, Eds. New York. Plenum.

Francis, M. and R. Hester, Eds. 1990. *The Meaning of Gardens: Idea, Place and Action.* Cambridge. MIT Press.

Freedman, D. 1991. "Exploiting the Nanotechnology of Life." *Science,* 254:1308–1310.

Fulton, W. 1991. *Guide to California Planning.* Point Arena, California. Solano Press.

Gane, M. 1991. *Baudrillard's Bestiary.* New York. Routledge.

Gardner, H. 1985. *The Mind's New Science—A History of the Cognitive Revolution.* New York. Basic Books.

Gendron, B. 1977. *Technology and the Human Condition.* New York. St. Martin's Press.

Gibson, J. 1979. *The Ecological Approach to Visual Perception.* Boston. Houghton Mifflin.

Gillespie, W. 1984. "The Environment of the Chaco Anasazis." In *New Light on Chaco Canyon.* D. Noble, Ed. Santa Fe. School of American Research Press.

Gipe, P. 1991. "Wind Energy Comes of Age." *Energy Policy.* October, pp. 756–768.

Glacken, C. 1967. *Traces on the Rhodian Shore.* Berkeley. University of California Press.

Gleick, J. 1987. *Chaos—Making a New Science.* New York. Viking.

Glick, F. 1985. "Going Places." *Landscape Architecture,* 75(2):42–51.

Gore, A. 1992. *Earth in the Balance.* Boston. Houghton Mifflin.

Gresham, Oregon, City of. 1992. Site Design Review guidelines for Commercial, Industrial, and Community Services.

Haar, C. and J. Kayden, Eds. 1989. *Zoning and the American Dream.* Chicago. American Planning Association.

Hammer, D., ed. 1989. *Constructed Wetlands for Wastewater Treatment.* Ann Arbor. Lewis Publishers.

Hammond, J., J. Zanetto, and C. Adams. 1981. *Planning Solar Neighborhoods.* Sacramento. California Energy Commission.

Hansen, H. 1989. *Energy in Our Backyard?* Unpublished Master of Science Thesis. University of California, Davis.

Hardison, O. B., Jr. 1989. *Disappearing Through the Skylight: Culture and Technology in the Twentieth Century.* New York. Viking.

Harrison, N., and H. Harrison. 1990. "Breathing Space for the Sava River." *IS Journal,* 5(2):42–58.

Hartmann, W., R. Miller, and P. Lee. 1984. *Out of the Cradle—Exploring the Frontiers Beyond Earth.* New York. Workman Publishing Company.

Hawking, S. 1988. *A Brief History of Time.* New York. Bantam Books.

Heiman, M. 1990. "From 'Not In My Backyard!' to 'Not in Anybody's Backyard!'" *APA Journal,* Summer, pp. 359–362.

Hess, A. 1992. "Technology Exposed—Toward a New Aesthetic for Technology in the Landscape." *Landscape Architecture,* 82(5):38–49.

Hester, G. 1992. "Electric and Magnetic Fields: Managing an Uncertain Risk." *Environment* 34(1) pp. 6–11.

Hodgson, R. and R. Thayer. 1980. "Implied Human Influence Reduces Landscape Beauty." *Landscape Planning,* 7:171–179.

Horning, B. 1991. "Language Busters." *Technology Review,* 94(7):51–57.

Hough, M. 1984. *City Form and Natural Process.* New York. Van Nostrand Reinhold.

Hough, M. 1990. *Out of Place—Restoring Identity to the Regional Landscape.* New Haven. Yale.

Hughes, T. and A. Hughes. 1990. *Lewis Mumford—Public Intellectual.* New York. Oxford University Press.

Illich, I. 1974. *Energy and Equity.* London. Calden and Bryars.

Inman, B. 1993. " 'Sustainable' Cities." San Francisco. *San Francisco Examiner,* January 31, pp. F-5, 6.

IUCN/UNEP/WWF. 1991. *Caring for the Earth—A Strategy for Sustainable Living.* Gland, Switzerland.

Jackson, J. B. 1984. *Discovering the Vernacular Landscape.* New Haven. Yale University Press.

Jackson, W. 1987. *Altars of Unhewn Stone.* San Francisco. North Point Press.

Jackson, W., W. Berry, and B. Colman, Eds. 1984. *Meeting the Expectations of the Land.* San Francisco. North Point Press.

Jefferson, T. 1814. Personal letter to William Short, Nov. 28. *Writings, XIV,* p. 214.

Jellicoe, G. 1985. "The Search for a Paradise Garden." In *1985/86 IFLA Yearbook.* Paris. International Federation of Landscape Architects.

Joseph, L. 1990. *Gaia—The Growth of an Idea.* New York. St. Martin's Press.

Kahrl, W. 1993. "Ersatz Environmentalists." *Sacramento Bee—Forum Section.* January 10, p. 4.

Kane, H. 1987. *Pele—Goddess of Hawaii's Volcanoes.* Captain Cook, Hawaii. Kawainai Press.

Kaplan, R. and S. Kaplan. 1989. *The Experience of Nature—A Psychological Perspective.* New York. Cambridge University Press.

Kaplan, S. and R. Kaplan. 1982a. *Cognition and Environment.* New York. Praeger Publishers.

Kaplan, S. and R. Kaplan, Eds. 1982b. *Humanscape—Environments for People.* Ann Arbor. University of Michigan Press.

Kearny, R. 1988. *The Wake of Imagination.* Minneapolis. University of Minnesota Press.

Kellner, D. 1989. *Jean Baudrillard—From Marxism to Postmodernism and Beyond.* Stanford University Press.

Kiely, T. 1990. "Biocomputing." *Technology Review,* 93(2):23.

Knowles, R. 1974. *Energy and Form.* Cambridge, Massachusetts. MIT Press.

Koffka, K. 1935. *Principles of Gestalt Psychology.* New York. Harcourt.

Kraft, M. and B. Clary. 1991. "Citizen Participation and the NIMBY Syndrome: Public Response to Radioactive Waste Disposal." *The Western Political Quarterly* 44(2):299–328.

Kramer, M. 1987. *Three Farms—Making Milk, Meat, and Money from the American Soil.* Cambridge, Massachusetts. Harvard University Press.

Krohe, J. 1990. "You Call This a National Park?" *Planning,* 56(8):4–10.

Kuhn, T. 1970. *The Structure of Scientific Revolutions.* Chicago. University of Chicago Press.

Lang, J. 1987. *Creating Architectural Theory: The Role of the Behavioral Sciences in Environmental Design.* New York. Van Nostrand Rinehold.

Leccese, M. 1990. "Next Stop: Transit-Friendly Towns." *Landscape Architecture,* 80(7):47–53.

Leopold, A. 1949. *A Sand County Almanac.* New York. Oxford University Press.

Lenz, T. 1990. *A Post-Occupancy Evaluation of Village Homes, Davis, California.* Unpublished Masters Thesis. Department of Geography. University of California, Davis.

Lewis, P. 1990. "Questions of Taste". Unpublished paper. Department of Geography. Pennsylvania State University.

Lovelock, J. 1979. *Gaia—A New Look at Life on Earth.* New York. Oxford University Press.

Lovelock, J. 1988. *The Ages of Gaia.* New York. W. W. Norton & Company.

Lovins, A., L. Hunter Lovins and M. Bendor. 1984. "Energy and Agriculture." In *Meeting the Expectations of the Land.* W. Jackson, W. Berry, and B. Colman, eds. San Francisco. North Point Press. Pp. 68–86.

Lowe, M. 1990. "Alternatives to the Automobile: Transport for Livable Cities." *Worldwatch Paper #98.* Washington, D.C. Worldwatch Institute.

Lucas, R. 1970. "User Concepts of Wilderness and Their Implications for Resource Management." In *Environmental Psychology—Man and His Physical Setting.* H. Proshansky, W. Ittelson, and L. Rivlin, Eds. New York. Holt, Rinehart and Winston, pp. 297–303.

Lumsden, C. and E. Wilson. 1983. *Promethian Fire—Reflections on the Origin of Mind.* Cambridge, Massachusetts. Harvard University Press.

Lyle, J. 1985. *Design for Human Ecosystems.* New York. Van Nostrand Reinhold Company.

Lyle, J. 1989. "Can Floating Seeds Make Deep Forms?" Keynote address, *The Avante Garde and the Landscape* Conference. Minneapolis. University of Minnesota. April 15.

Lyle, J. 1994. *Regenerative Design for Sustainable Development.* New York. Wiley.

Lynch, K. and M. Southworth. *Wasting Away.* San Francisco. Sierra Club Books.

Mandelbrot, B. 1977. *The Fractal Geometry of Nature.* New York. W. H. Freeman & Company.

Mander, J. 1991. *In the Absence of the Sacred—The Failure of Technology and the Survival of the Indian Nations.* San Francisco. Sierra Club Books.

Marx, L. 1963. *The Machine in the Garden.* New York. Oxford University Press.

Marx, L. 1990. "Lewis Mumford: Prophet of Organicism." In *Lewis Mumford—Public Intellectual,* T. Hughes and A. Hughes, Eds. New York. Oxford University Press.

Matthiessen, P. 1984. *Indian Country.* New York. Viking.

McBeath, G. and T. Morehouse. 1987. *Alaska State Government and Politics.* Anchorage. University of Alaska Press.

McCloud, J. 1992. "High-Density Housing Near San Francisco." New York Times, Real Estate, Sunday, July 5.

McCormick, Kathleen. 1991. "We Don't 'Do' Wetlands." *Landscape Architecture* 81(10):88–90.

McGuigan, C. 1992. "Apres Mickey, le Deluge." *Newsweek* 119(15):64–66.

McHarg, I. 1969. *Design with Nature.* Washington. Natural History Press.

McHugh, P. 1992. "Rumble in the Sierra" and "Reinventing the Map." *San Francisco Chronicle, This World* section, September 13, 7.

McKibben, W. 1989. *The End of Nature.* New York. Random House.

McLuhan, M. 1964. *Understanding Media.* New York. McGraw-Hill.

Meadows, D. H., D. L. Meadows, and J. Randers. 1992. *Beyond the Limits.* Post Hills, Vermont. Chelsea Publishing Company.

Meinig, D., Ed. 1979. *The Interpretation of Ordinary Landscapes.* New York. Oxford University Press.

Merchant, C. 1980. *The Death of Nature*. New York. Harper Collins.

Meyrowitz, J. 1985. *No Sense of Place*. New York. Oxford University Press.

Milbrath, L. 1989. *Envisioning a Sustainable Society*. Albany, New York. State University of New York Press.

Miller, D., Ed. 1986. *The Lewis Mumford Reader*. New York. Pantheon Books.

Mitroff, I. and W. Bennis. 1989. *The Unreality Industry*. New York. Birch Lane Press.

Mumford, L. 1967. *The Myth of the Machine*, Vol. 1, *Technics and Human Development*. New York. Harcourt, Brace and World.

Naess, A. 1973. "The Shallow and the Deep, Long-Range Ecology Movement." *Inquiry* 16: pp. 95–100.

Naess, A. and D. Rothenberg. 1989. *Ecology, Community and Lifestyle*. New York. Cambridge University Press.

Naisbitt, J. 1982. *Megatrends*. New York. Warner Books.

Nash, R. 1967. *Wilderness and the American Mind*. New Haven. Yale University Press.

Nash, R. 1979. "Problems in Paradise." *Environment*, 20(6):25–40.

Naske, C-M. and H. Slotnick. 1987. *Alaska—A History of the 49th State*, 2nd ed., Norman, Oklahoma. University of Oklahoma Press.

Nelson, M., P. Hawes, and K. Dyhr. 1990. "Biosphere 2: Laboratory, Architecture, Paradigm, and Symbol." *International Synergy Journal*, 5(2):59–75.

New York Times News Service. 1992. "Advisers: Biosphere Needs to Pay Attention to Science." Davis, California. *Davis Enterprise*, July 27, 1992, p. A-4.

Noble, D., Ed. 1984. *New Light on Chaco Canyon*. Sante Fe. School of American Research Press.

Ocko, S. 1990. *Environmental Vacations: Volunteer Projects to Save the Planet*. Santa Fe. John Muir Publications.

Odum, E. 1989. *Ecology and Our Endangered Life Support Systems*. Sunderland, Massachusetts. Sinauer Associates.

O'Hare, M., L. Bacow, and D. Sanderson. *Facility Siting and Public Opposition*. 1983. New York. Van Nostrand Reinhold

Ornstein, R. and P. Erlich. 1989. *New World, New Mind*. New York. Doubleday.

Otway, H., D. Mauer, and K. Thomas. 1978. "Nuclear Power: The Questions of Public Acceptance." *Futures*, 10:109–118.

Painton, P. 1991. "Fantasy's Reality." *Time*, 137(21):52–59.

Pitt, D. 1982. "Are Landscape Preferences Genotypical or Phenotypical? An Investigation of Evolutionarily-Based Hypotheses of Aesthetic Preference for Landscapes." Unpublished paper. Minneapolis. University of Minnesota.

Postman, N. 1985. *Amusing Ourselves to Death—Public Discourse in the Age of Show Business*. New York. Penguin Books.

Postman, N. 1992. *Technopoly—The Surrender of Culture to Technology*. New York. Alfred A. Knopf.

Power, T. 1988. *The Economic Pursuit of Quality*. Armonk, New York. Sharp.

Powers, R. 1984. "Outliers and Roads in the Chaco System." In *New Light on Chaco Canyon*, D. Noble, Ed. Santa Fe. School of American Research Press.

Prigogine, I. 1984. *Order Out of Chaos—Man's New Dialogue With Nature*. New York. Bantam Books.

Ralston, H. 1988. *Environmental Ethics*. Philadelphia. Temple University Press.

Rapoport, A. 1977. *Human Aspects of Urban Form*. New York. Pergamon Press.

Rees, W., Ed. 1988. *Planning for Sustainable Development: A Resource Book*. Vancouver. Center for Human Settlements, University of British Columbia.

Register, R. 1987. *Ecocity Berkeley—Building Cities for a Healthy Future.* Berkeley. North Atlantic Books.

Reisner, M. 1986. *Cadillac Desert.* New York. Penguin Books.

Reisner, M. 1990. *Overtapped Oasis—Reform or Revolution for Western Water.* Washington, D.C. Island Press.

Rheingold, H. 1991. *Virtual Reality.* New York. Summit Books.

Rifkin, J. 1989. *Entropy—Into the Greenhouse World.* New York. Bantam Books.

Robbins, J. 1990. "To School for an Image of Television." In *A Delicate Balance: Technics, Culture and Consequences,* Proceedings of the Society for Social Implications of Technology Conference, Institute of Electrical and Electronic Engineers, Los Angeles. pp. 285–291.

Robertson, J. 1985. *Future Work; Jobs, Self-Employment, and Leisure After the Industrial Age.* New York. Universe Books.

Robinson, G. 1988. *The Forest and the Trees—A Guide to Excellent Forestry.* Washington, DC. Island Press.

Rogers, E. and F. Shoemaker. 1971. *Communication of Innovations.* New York. Macmillan.

Rogers, M. and N. Warren, Eds. 1990. *A Delicate Balance: Technics, Culture, and Consequences.* Los Angeles. The Institute of Electrical and Electronics Engineers, Society on Social Implications of Technology.

Rose, D. 1990. "Prospect: Theme Parks are Approaching a Total Experiential Environment." *Landscape Architecture,* 80(6):112.

Samuelson, R. 1992. "How Our American Dream Unraveled." *Newsweek,* March 2, pp. 32–39.

Schenker, H. 1988. Unpublished Masters Thesis, Department of Art and Art History. University of California, Davis.

Schick, K., and N. Toth. 1993. *Making Silent Stones Speak—Human Evolution and the Dawn of Technology.* New York. Simon & Schuster.

Schweickart, R. 1982. *Earth's Answer, Exploration of Planetary Culture at the Lindisfarne Conferences.* New York. Harper and Row. Quoted in album notes for *Missa Gaia—Earth Mass,* Paul Winter. Litchfield, Connecticut. Living Music Records. Inc.

Segal, H. 1985. *Technological Utopianism in American Culture.* Chicago. University of Chicago Press.

Shannon, C. 1938. "A Symbolic Analysis of Relay and Switching Circuits." *Transactions of the American Institute of Electrical Engineers,* 57:1–11.

Shannon, C. and W. Weaver. 1964. *The Mathematical Theory of Communication.* Urbana. University of Illinois Press.

Siegal, L. and J. Markoff. 1985. *The High Cost of High Tech—The Dark Side of the Chip.* New York. Harper and Row.

Siler, T. 1990. *Breaking the Mind Barrier.* New York. Simon and Schuster.

Smith, H. 1990. "Seeking a Radically New Electronics." *Technology Review,* 93(3):26–40.

Smith, J., J. Broberg, and T. Dominski. 1991. *Ecological Planning Principals for Sustainable Living in Ventura County.* Thousand Oaks, California. The Citizen Planners Project.

Snyder, G. 1974. *Turtle Island.* New York. New Directions Publishing Corporation.

Snyder, G. 1989. *The Practice of the Wild.* Berkeley. North Point Press.

Snyder, G. 1991. "Don't Move!" *Earthword,* 2(2):45.

Snyder, G. 1992. *No Nature.* San Francisco. Pantheon.

Sommer, R. 1978. *Mind's Eye—Imagery in Everyday Life.* New York. Delta Publishing Company.

Springsteen, B. 1992. "Fifty Seven Channels." On the *Human Touch* album. Warner Music.

Stewart, D. 1990. "Nothing Goes to Waste in Arcata's Teeming Marshes." *Smithsonian,* April, pp. 175–179.

Stewart, J., 1993. "Del Norte Place Resident Profile." John Stewart Company, San Francisco.

Stilgoe, J. 1984. "Popular Photography, Scenery Values, and Visual Assessment." *Landscape Journal,* 3(2):111–122.

Stone, C. 1987. *Earth and Other Ethics—The Case for Moral Pluralism.* New York. Harper and Row.

Strang, G. 1992. "Infrastructure as Landscape." Paper presented at the Council of Educators in Landscape Architecture Conference, Charlottesville, Virginia, October 17.

Sutton, R. 1977. "Circles on the Plains—Center Pivot Irrigation." *Landscape,* 22(1):3–10.

Taylor, F. 1947. *The Principles of Scientific Management.* New York. Harper & Row.

Thayer, R. 1976. "Visual Ecology: Revitalizing the Aesthetics of Landscape Architecture." *Landscape,* 20(2):37–43.

Thayer, R. 1980. "Conspicuous Non-Consumption." In *EDRA Proceedings 11.* Environmental Design Research Association, pp. 176–182.

Thayer, R. 1989. "Redesigning the Community Watershed." *Landscape Architecture,* 79(8):160.

Thayer, R. 1989. "The Experience of Sustainable Landscapes." *Landscape Journal,* 8(2):101–110.

Thayer, R. 1990. "Dimensions and Dynamic Meanings of Technology in the American Landscape." *International Synergy Journal,* 5(2):19–39.

Thayer, R. 1990. "Personal Dreams and Pagan Rituals." In *The Meaning of Gardens: Idea, Place and Action,* M. Francis and R. Hester, Eds. Cambridge. MIT Press, pp. 194–197.

Thayer, R. 1990. "Pragmatism in Paradise: Technology and the American Landscape." *Landscape,* 30(3):1–11.

Thayer, R. 1990. "Technophobia and Topophilia: The Dynamic Meanings of Technology in the Landscape." In *A Delicate Balance: Technics, Culture and Consequences,* Proceedings of the Society for Social Implications of Technology Conference, Institute of Electrical and Electronic Engineers, Los Angeles, pp. 18–28.

Thayer, R. 1991. "Water Drives a Sustainable New Town." *Landscape Architecture,* 81(10):168.

Thayer, R. 1992. "Philosophical Opposition?" Letter to the editor. *Landscape Architecture* 82(6):18–20.

Thayer, R. and C. Freeman. 1987. "Altamont: Public Perceptions of a Wind Energy Landscape." *Landscape and Urban Planning,* 14:379–398.

Thayer, R. and H. Hansen. 1988. "Wind on the Land—Renewable Energy and Pastoral Scenery Vie for Dominance in the siting of Wind Energy Developments." *Landscape Architecture,* 88(2):68–75.

Thayer, R. and H. Hansen. 1989. *Consumer Attitude and Choice in Local Energy Development.* Center for Design Research, University of California, Davis.

Thayer, R. and H. Hansen. 1991. *Wind Energy Siting Conflicts in California: Implications for Energy Policy.* Center for Design Research, University of California, Davis.

Thompson, D. 1917. *On Growth and Form.* Cambridge, England. Cambridge University Press.

Thompson, J. W. 1990. "Suburbia: Ready for Foot & Rail?" *Landscape Architecture,* 80(7):58–60.

Thompson, W. I. 1989. *Imaginary Landscape—Making World of Myth and Science.* New York. St. Martin's Press.

Thompson, W. I. 1991. *The American Replacement of Nature.* New York. Doubleday.

Tilley, R. 1991. "Blueprint for Survival." *Architecture,* May, pp. 64–71.

Tocqueville, Alexis de. 1946. *Democracy in America,* Phillips Bradley, Ed. New York (2 volumes).

Town Forum, Inc., The. 1982. *Cerro Gordo—Plans, Progress, and Processes.* Cottage Grove, Oregon.

Tuan, Y. 1974. *Topophilia: A Study of Environmental Perception, Attitudes, and Values.* Englewood Cliffs, New Jersey. Prentice-Hall.

Tuan, Y. 1989. "Surface Phenomena and Aesthetic Experience." *Annals of the Association of American Geographers.* **79**(2) pp. 233–241.

Ulrich, R. 1984. "View Through a Window May Influence Recovery From Surgery." *Science,* 224:420–421.

Ulrich, R., R. Simons, B. Losito, E. Fiorito, M. Miles, and M. Zelson. 1991. "Stress Recovery During Exposure to Natural and Urban Environments." *Journal of Environmental Psychology,* 11:201–230.

Unger, S. 1982. *Controlling Technology: Ethics and the Responsible Engineer.* New York. Holt, Rinehart and Winston.

United States Bureau of the Census. 1990. *Statistical Abstracts of the United States.* Washington, DC. Department of Commerce.

United States Department of the Interior, National Park Service. 1991. *America's Industrial Heritage—Southwestern Pennsylvania.* Southwestern Pennsylvania Heritage Preservation Commission.

United States Department of the Interior, National Park Service. 1992. *Sustainable Design: A National Park Service Initiative.* Denver. Brochure.

Van der Ryn, S. and P. Calthorpe, Eds. 1986. *Sustainable Communities.* San Francisco. Sierra Club Books.

Village of Euclid v. *Ambler Realty Company.* 272 U.S. 365, 395 (1926). United States Supreme Court Decision.

Wallace, D. 1983. *The Klamath Knot.* San Francisco. Sierra Club Books.

Wallace, D. 1992. "Is 'Eco' Tourism for Real?" *Landscape Architecture,* 82(8):34–36.

Waldrop, M. 1992. "Complexity: the Emerging Science at the Edge of Order and Chaos." New York. Simon & Schuster.

Waters, F. 1963. *The Book of the Hopi.* New York. Penguin Books.

Watkins, B. and R. Meader. *Technology and Human Values—Collision and Solution.* Ann Arbor. Ann Arbor Science Publishers.

Watson, L. 1982. *Lightning Bird—One Man's Journey Into Africa.* New York. Simon and Schuster.

White, L. 1967. "The Historical Roots of Our Ecologic Crisis." *Science,* 155(3767):1203–1207.

Whitehead, A. 1929. *The Aims of Education and Other Essays.* New York. The Free Press.

Wiener, N. 1948, 1961. *Control and Communication in the Animal and the Machine.* Cambridge, Massachusetts. MIT Press.

Williams, R. 1990. *Notes on the Underground.* Cambridge, Massachusetts. MIT Press.

Wilson, E. 1984. *Biophilia—The Human Bond with Other Species.* Cambridge, Massachusetts. Harvard University Press.

Winner, L. 1977. *Autonomous Technology.* Cambridge, Massachusetts. MIT Press.

Winner, L. 1986. *The Whale and the Reactor.* Chicago. University of Chicago Press.

Winner, L. 1991. "Fear and Loathing on the Nuclear Bandwagon." *Technology Review,* 94(6):74.

Wohlwill, J. 1983. "The Concept of Nature: A Psychologist's View." In *Behavior and the Natural Environment,* I. Altman and J. Wohlwill, Eds. New York. Plenum, pp. 1–37.

Wood, D. 1989. "Unnatural Illusions: Some Words About Visual Resource Management." *Landscape Journal,* 7(2):192–205.

World Commission on Environment and Development. 1987. *Our Common Future.* New York. Oxford University Press.

Worldwatch Institute. 1990. *State of the World.* New York. W. W. Norton & Company.

Worldwatch Institute. 1991. *State of the World.* New York. W. W. Norton & Company.

Worldwatch Institute. 1992. *State of the World.* New York. W. W. Norton & Company.

Wright, R. 1988. *Three Scientists and Their Gods.* New York. Random House.

Young, J. 1991. "Discarding the Throwaway Society." *Worldwatch Paper #101.* Washington, D.C. Worldwatch Institute.

Zanetto, J. 1985. "Total Home Competition Winners, 1985." *New Shelter.*

Zube, E., J. Sell, and G. Taylor. 1982. "Landscape Perception: Research, Application, and Theory." *Landscape Planning,* 9:1–33.

Index

343

Stormwater, 126, 244, 261–263, 281–282, 290, 294
Stourhead, 18
Strang, G., 311
Stream restoration, 282
Style, 316
Subdivision design standards, 35
Suburbia, 276–277, 279
Sumerian theology, 136
Superstrings, 173
Surface properties of landscape, 140–141, 214, 229
Sustainability:
 and behavior, 292
 as a buzzword, 232, 249
 and community, 292
 contradiction of sustainable growth, 237
 and core relationships, 194
 definition, 99
 and ecology of materials, 282–287
 emergence of, 99, 232, 235
 as an essential concept, 232–233, 294, 315
 as a future alternative, 230
 historical origins, 235–236
 limitation on time and rates of change, 99
 opposition to simulation, 218
 as a reaction to dilemma of technology and nature, 99, 100, 160, 294
 relation to carrying capacity, 99
 and responsible artifacts, 222
 and sustainable agriculture, 235–236
 sustainable economy, 237
 sustainable use, 237
 and sustained yield forestry, 235–236
 as an umbrella term, 238
Sustainable development:
 and carrying capacity, 100
 definition, 100, 237
 emergence of, 236–237
 necessity of, 296
 possibility of, 296
 and quality of life, 100
Sustainable landscapes:
 archetypes of, 228
 and carrying capacity, 100
 characteristics of, 243
 definition, 100, 235
 difficulty in making, 324
 economic base, 268
 and energy, 228, 238
 and entropy, 228
 experiential role of, 309–329
 and human communities, 100
 importance, 308–309
 and nature, 228
 relation to fantasy, 228
 as resolution of the nature/technology conflict, 161
 and resource use, 100, 238
 as a response to current conditions, 233
 surface and core relationships, 228

and time, 238, 242
transparency, 227–228
and utopian vision, 233
and visibility, 194
Sustainable technology:
 in Chaco culture, 145
 definition, 100, 242
 in landscape perception and meaning, 122, 126–127
 relation to carrying capacity, 100
 in sustainable community planning, 272
Sustainable use, definition of, 100
Sutton, R., 120
Symbolic level (of landscape meaning), 102, 109, 110, 111, 122–135
Synesthesia, 123

T
Taiwan, 267
"Taste-free" landscape, 33, 34
Technocracy, 167
Technological determinism, 31–33, 50, 63, 96, 177–179, 273
Technological drift, 177
Technological theme park, America as, 169–171
Technology:
 authoritarian, 51
 autonomous, 177
 camouflage of, 74–77
 centralized, 51
 and Christianity, 58–59
 concealment of, 74–77
 conflict with nature, 49, 287, 329
 as context for life, 31
 and cultural meaning, 108–135
 as a de facto religion, 63
 definition, *xvi*
 denial and avoidance, 67
 dimension of in the landscape, 104–135
 disappearance of, 190–193
 divided, 94
 feminist critique of history of, 166
 "good" and "bad," 81–85
 having a life of its own, 45
 and hierarchical social systems, 50
 and human nature, 307
 idealized, 95
 indigenous materials and, 143
 information, 197
 and intentional design, 36–38
 invisible, 187–193
 joint origin with art, 25
 landscape products of, 36–37
 and material abundance, 50, 51
 as means for living, 31, 45
 military, 44
 natural feeling of, 85
 origins of, 25–28, 108
 and pastoralism, 20
 personal, 83–85, 94–96